Making JFK Matter

MAKING JFK MATTER

Popular Memory and the Thirty-fifth President

Paul H. Santa Cruz

Denton, Texas

Printed in the United States of America.

10 9 8 7 6 5 4 3 2 1

Permissions:

University of North Texas Press

1155 Union Circle #311336

Denton, TX 76203-5017

The paper used in this book meets the minimum requirements of the American National Standard for Permanence of Paper for Printed Library Materials, z39.48.1984. Binding materials have been chosen for durability.

Library of Congress Cataloging-in-Publication Data

Santa Cruz, Paul H., 1983- author.

Making JFK matter : popular memory and the 35th president / Paul H. Santa Cruz. -- First edition.

pages cm

Includes bibliographical references and index.

ISBN 978-1-57441-597-1 (cloth : alk. paper) --

1. Kennedy, John F. (John Fitzgerald), 1917-1963--In mass media. 2. Presidents--United States. 3. Collective memory. 4. Johnson, Lyndon B. (Lyndon Baines), 1908-1973. 5. Kennedy, Robert F., 1925-1968. I. Title.

E842.5.S26 2015

973.922092--dc23

2014042650

978-1-57441-603-9 (ebook)

The electronic edition of this book was made possible by the support of the Vick Family Foundation.

I dedicate this book to the unsung heroes and heroines of any work of history: to the archivists and librarians —those whose knowledge, hard work, courtesy, professional conduct, good judgment, and sense of humor make them an incomparable asset to the public.

TABLE OF CONTENTS

LIST OF PHOTOS

PREFACE

I wrote this book almost by accident. When I first decided to write about President Kennedy and popular memory, it was not my intention that I would revisit the subject and examine it to the extent I have done. Whether history is more of a seductress or a tormentor, it has ultimately compelled me to stop merely considering this topic and to go a step further by writing a book. Given the absence of any systematic study or discussion of JFK and popular memory, producing a monograph on the subject seemed logical.

The idea of writing on JFK and popular memory originated in a seminar course I took at Southwestern University in Georgetown, Texas, during the fall semester of 2005. The theme of the seminar was memory, and the principle assignment was a 30-page paper on a topic of each student's choosing—provided, of course, that it dealt with memory in some way. Because of my interest in JFK, I chose to write the seminar paper on how he has been memorialized and how people have used his memory.

Not knowing exactly what areas of popular memory I would focus on at the time I selected the topic, I was pleasantly surprised to find two such areas to write about: how the city of Dallas memorialized the late president and how President Lyndon Johnson invoked the Kennedy name to pass social legislation. Both of these areas of memory seemed feasible for such an assignment. As I was to discover, both were extremely interesting. It was also helpful for the seminar paper that the idea of President Kennedy and popular memory was one that had not previously been given much examination. This struck me, as it should strike anybody interested in JFK, as unusual. Due to our continuing fascination with him, one would expect that every conceivable aspect of his life had been written about (exhaustively) already. In the research I did for that seminar paper, I encountered a few books in which the popular memory of him is mentioned either outright or appears as an unstated force in the background. But nothing, or at least nothing I was able to find, treated JFK and popular memory as a topic of discussion in its own right. There had not been any systematic study of the uses of memorialization in the context of John Kennedy.

Having written the paper and completed the course, I did not give the subject any further thought until two years later. By the summer of 2007, I was finishing the first year of a two-year Masters program in history at Southern Methodist University in Dallas; during the course of my studies there, I thought it would be both interesting and worthwhile to revisit the topic. I reviewed the notes I had compiled for the 2005 seminar paper and saw that it was indeed possible to expand it into something far more comprehensive in terms of the number of areas of popular memory I could address, the number of pages devoted to each, and the variety of sources I could use. The initial steps in restarting the project consisted of making a list of potential primary and secondary sources, as well as notes on what new ideas and points I should make, and an initial plan as to how an expanded study of JFK and popular memory would be organized. In early 2008, I began my second journey into the topic. The result was a larger (and hopefully improved) study of JFK and popular memory, completed later that year in the fall of 2008.

There, matters might have remained, but I have decided to engage the subject for a third time, so some explanation is necessary. Why write a book about President Kennedy and popular memory? What contribution do I hope to make? In light of the fact that so much has been written —and continues to be written—about our 35th president, isn't another book about him redundant by this point?

As I mentioned above, no singular examination of JFK and popular memory had been undertaken—particularly how that memory was created and used, and what it means. The invocation of his name in the wake of his sudden death provoked much emotion and therefore became a powerful force. Memory of him took on a sort of aromatic quality, lingering and perceptible, if not always immediately visible, which might explain why there has been so little effort to capture and define it. It influenced how Americans viewed the 1960s and the way Lyndon Johnson conducted the first year of his presidency. Popular memory of JFK also imbued Americans with conceptions (albeit romanticized) about the way a president should govern. Kennedy's brief presidency is certainly not the first to be used as a measuring stick by which subsequent administrations are judged. However, it is reasonable to say that his was one of the most enduring in this respect.

Yet it seems that in the midst of our endless fascination with his presidency, private life, rhetoric, health, and death, we have overlooked the impact that popular memory of this man has had. I, at least, have found this topic intriguing, both for the stories it tells about how the country tried to pull meaning and consolation from his life in the wake of his death, and for what it says about popular conceptions of our chief executive as a public figure and as a political leader. Interest in any given topic is reason enough to continue learning, thinking, and writing about it, but a book on JFK and popular memory seemed necessary as a way of filling in a gap in our understanding of him.

Those old enough to remember Kennedy's tenure in office may find it hard to believe that it has been fifty years since he was assassinated. And those not old enough to remember may find it surprising that we will soon mark the centennial of his birth—that a man born so long ago (in the midst of World War I) still seems to matter so much.

Creating a title for the book was rather difficult, both because I am not good at coining catchy phrases that would make interesting titles, and because I chose to avoid any reference to Camelot. Camelot conjures up certain images that bear little resemblance to the reality of the Kennedy presidency. Plus, after more than four decades of use, the term is rather cliché.

While it is certainly true that Kennedy's death was a national (indeed, international) tragedy, it was also very much a *personal* event for so many people. Many likened the assassination to losing a member of one's own family[1]. I believe that this sense of loss, magnified by the unprecedented media coverage that rapidly disseminated news and commentary on the tragedy, left many Americans with the belief that the assassination ultimately had to be redirected toward some larger end. Chief Justice Earl Warren, anticipating the need for—and importance of—remembering the late president, commented shortly after the president's death, "We who survive him should use this adversity to memorialize his farsightedness and humanitarianism. That memorial should be the consummation of his ideal for our nation. I feel confident that there are millions of Americans, of whom I am one, who will consider this to be their solemn duty."[2] In each of the examples I discuss in the following pages, the late president was given some larger significance that played upon and helped shape the public's memory. Popular memory was used to make him relevant. Many were not content with just remembering him as a noble and progressive figure; his supposedly great attributes had to serve some important purpose. The "martyred" president had to be martyred for something.[3] The American people needed to make President Kennedy matter; hence, the title of this work.

One final note is appropriate. I have found that the personal nature of the assassination is still readily evident among those old enough to remember it. The ever-lengthening distance in time between November

22, 1963, and today makes the memories of those who lived through it no less striking. For example, the former Catholic chaplain at Southern Methodist University recalled his brother-in-law who, as a boy, sang in a choir that performed at the breakfast President Kennedy attended in Fort Worth prior to his arrival in Dallas. That morning, the choir members had the privilege of meeting President Kennedy and Vice President Johnson. Unbeknownst to him at the time, he met two presidents that day.[4] A former coworker spoke of how she, having returned home early from school that day due to the shooting, received a phone call from her father. He reported seeing a police motorcycle escort accompanying a hearse speed down Harry Hines Boulevard in Dallas toward Parkland Hospital where Kennedy had been taken. Reasoning that the hearse could not have been meant for anybody else, he concluded that the president had already died. A friend told me of how her mother, a native of San Antonio, had stood on the sidewalk and watched President and Mrs. Kennedy as they drove by her school just one day before his death.

To these recollections, I add one from my own family. My grandfather worked at the Neiman-Marcus department store on Main Street in downtown Dallas on that infamous day. The visit of a president was much more publicized in that era, and he was one of many who filled the street to watch JFK ride past his place of work. He took a photo of the president and the First Lady, which my grandmother has kept all these years. The square, slightly blurry color photograph shows Mrs. Kennedy waving as their car went by. My grandfather later wrote home to his family in Mexico City, describing the day that turned tragic only minutes after the moment he captured on film.

Stories like these made the memory of President Kennedy such a highly potent force following his death. In the narrative that follows, I hope to make some small (but, I think, necessary) contribution to the massive body of writing on him by demonstrating how practical, effective, divisive, frustrating—and enduring—the popular memory of John F. Kennedy has been since that day half a century ago when he came to Dallas.

NOTES

[1]A woman from Michigan, for example, wrote to Mrs. Kennedy the day after the assassination that, "Never even with the loss of several of my family have I been more deeply touched than with the loss of President Kennedy." Ellen Fitzpatrick, *Letters to Jackie: Condolences from a Grieving Nation* (New York: Ecco, 2010), 41.

[2]Robert Dallek, *An Unfinished Life: John F. Kennedy, 1917-1963* (Boston: Little, Brown and Company, 2003), 695.

[3]As one college student from California put it in a letter to his parents, "We cannot make him into a martyr because that's just what he is...we ask the question 'Why?' Let's hope there is an answer. Let's hope he did not die without cause. Such a thought is unbearable." Ellen Fitzpatrick, *Letters to Jackie*, 45.

[4]Video recording. Bronson Havard Oral History Interview, 8/3/2010, by Stephen Fagin. Oral

Acknowledgments

It would be unfair, and wrong, to suggest that this work is the product of my labor alone, for many others have made contributions that must be acknowledged. Because I wrote on this subject three different times at two-year intervals, I list these people in rough chronological order. I first thank Dr. Lisa Leff, whose history courses I took at Southwestern University in Georgetown (but who now teaches at American University), for her guidance when I first explored JFK and popular memory in her history seminar in the fall of 2005. My interest in this topic originated there, and taking her classes is a highlight of any history major's course of study. Dr. Leff provided valuable advice at several points during the drafting and completion of the original seminar paper, and the final version was undoubtedly better because of it. It is the mark of a great teacher when he or she keeps a student interested in something even after the assignment is graded and the class is finished, and Dr. Leff easily earns this distinction. My advisor in the SMU history department, Dr. Tom Knock, never failed to offer ideas and suggestions for further sources to explore, when I returned to this subject—Round Two—in 2007-2008. His editing resulted in an expanded project that was clearer and more concise than it would have been if I were left to my own, sometimes rambling, writing. Likewise, I thank Drs. Benjamin Johnson and Tom Stone for their contributions.

Readers of any historical work should be aware that it is the primary sources, and the archivists who preserve them and acquire knowledge about them, that make the final product possible. The role of the archivist is important, and I say this not only because I am part of that profession and am trying to give myself a pat on the back, but because it really is true. Joan Gosnell of the DeGolyer Library at SMU was of great help with the Earle Cabell, J. Erik Jonsson, and Stanley Marcus collections, all of which were important in understanding what Dallas was confronting from the moment gunfire rang out in Dealey Plaza. I am grateful to her for all she has done, not only research-wise, but also for launching me toward my own career in the archiving world. Archivist Tim Binkley of Bridwell Library at SMU Perkins School of Theology suggested materials from Bridwell's holdings that also enhanced the chapter on Dallas. I appreciate further the research-related discussions I had with him during a work assignment at Bridwell in June 2011. Stephen Fagin, Associate Curator of the Sixth Floor Museum, assisted in locating oral histories of important Dallasites who remembered the assassination, and also those who helped bring the Museum into being.

At the Lyndon B. Johnson Presidential Library in Austin, archivist Barbara Cline kindly answered questions and advised on archival collections I should consult beyond those I was already aware of. No less fervently do I thank the research room attendants whose courtesy never flagged as they brought up one cartload after another of presidential records, only to be presented with additional pull requests. Combing through fifty-year old White House memoranda is a treat, and at LBJ, it is enlivened by the unforgettable retro red carpeting in the research room; it only reminds me of how many researchers have had the same enjoyable experience there over the years.

My research with records from the John F. Kennedy Presidential Library in Boston was a bit different. They have undertaken a records digitization project of considerable proportions in recent years. Patrons are able to conduct research in person and avail themselves of the excellent vistas of Dorchester Bay from the research room, but they can *also* view documents online, flipping from one page to another as if they had just pulled an actual folder from a box. For the most part, that is what I did for Chapter 5 where I made use of primary sources from the Kennedy Library most heavily. The work that JFK archivists have done in digitizing so much material has made their holdings more accessible to the public, and it serves as a model for other presidential libraries to follow. Recognition is especially owed to Archives Technician Michael Desmond for his great work in making available other records that were not yet digitized; I also thank AV Specialist Jim Hill for his kindness in giving me a tour of the Library in 2010. Tom Putnam, Director at JFK, was very generous in answering my questions related to his institution, and I am grateful for his contribution to my research.

In selecting photographs, I also benefitted from the work and generosity of several people to whom I am very thankful. Christopher Banks at the LBJ Library, Maryrose Grossman and Laurie Austin at the JFK Library, and Mark Davies at the Sixth Floor Museum, all helped locate photographs that have enhanced my narrative. And I thank George Lois, designer of the *Esquire* cover used in Chapter 3, and Jessie Kissinger of *Esquire*, for their kindness in allowing me to reproduce it. Jodie Steck, AV Specialist at the George W. Bush Presidential Library, contributed her considerable photographic skills in the form of the author photograph for the book; not with a photograph, but with these few inadequate words, do I convey my thanks.

I cannot more fervently express my appreciation to Ronald Chrisman, Editor at University of North Texas Press, for his constant support in orchestrating the publication of this work. Someone once told me that anyone trying to publish a book should expect to encounter some frustration along the way. That has not at all been the case with UNT Press. Ronald was always helpful and prompt in explaining what I needed to do next in the publication process. For all of this, I owe him a lot, and my debt to him is even greater for his willingness from the start to take a chance on a newcomer to the world of publishing. Professor James Giglio at Missouri State University, and Professor Benjamin Hufbauer at the University of Louisville, reviewed the manuscript during the publication process, and I am glad they did. Their suggestions resulted in a stronger final product. Many thanks are due to Aprell Feagin at UNT Press for her editing expertise; her skills are a major asset for any publisher and author.

Several people who provided insight on writing and publishing a book, great company and a place to sleep, and their editing skills for each chapter as I finished writing it must also be recognized. Sam Childers, of Friends of SMU Libraries and himself a presidential history enthusiast; Nicola Longford, Executive Director of the Sixth Floor Museum; Sean and Caitlin Kissinger; and the Seykora family were all recipients of my musings and questions on bringing the project to a successful conclusion. College friends Ben and Jennifer Lake generously opened their house to me during an LBJ Library research trip. I am in their debt, not only for their hospitality , but also for their friendship. And many thanks are due to my mother Jeanne for her editing skills. The same quality she brings to the dental journal articles she edits was applied to my work. My manuscript was sharper and cleaner due to her efforts, and she did moderate—however temporarily the effects of her editing pen may last on me—the ongoing love affair I seem to have with the comma.

This is the third time I have engaged the topic of President Kennedy and popular memory, and I hope that all those who have played a role in bringing it to completion get as much pleasure out of seeing it in print as I do. If this book represents my last, and hopefully best stab at the subject, the satisfaction of a work that is finally finished belongs to them as much as it may belong to me.

Making JFK Matter

Introduction

> For all of us, life goes on—but brightness has fallen from the air.
> The world continues in the same orbit—but it is a different world.
> His hand-picked successor has picked up the fallen torch and
> carries it proudly and ably forward—but a Golden age is over and
> it will never be again.
>
> —Kennedy speechwriter Theodore Sorensen, 1964[1]

Oliver Stone's 1995 film *Nixon* may appear an odd place to begin a discussion about the public's memory of John F. Kennedy, but the movie suggests one of the reasons why Kennedy remains fondly remembered by so many. In the film, President Nixon, played by Anthony Hopkins, wanders through the darkened first floor of the White House one night. It is late in his presidency. Because of the Watergate scandal, his ability to govern is steadily disappearing. Upon approaching the portrait of JFK, and ever mindful of the way the fallen president could excite people and seemingly bring out their best, the fictional President Nixon sadly comments, "When they look at you, they see what they want to be. When they look at me, they see what they are."[2]

The actual President Nixon, wandering through the actual White House, probably did not say this. Regardless, this fictional comment succinctly points to part of the reason why, half a century after President Kennedy's assassination in Dallas in November 1963 and despite new information about him that has abundantly revealed his human frailties, many Americans continue to hold him in high regard. The loss of the youth, idealism, vigor, glamour, and inspiration many remember him for marked the transition of the country into the divided and cynical times of the 1960s and 70s. The emotional ties formed with the American people, especially following his sudden death, have remained very strong. Judging from the media coverage he continues to receive, Kennedy is still remembered largely the same way, and for the same things he was remembered for in the aftermath of his death.[3] When Americans look at John Kennedy, even with his presidency now almost half a century in the past, they not only see what they want to be, but they also continue to see JFK the way they think he was.

Few leaders have been able to form such a strong emotional link with the people, especially after having governed for so short a time. Perhaps the most evident example of the American people's continuing love and fascination with President Kennedy has been the unending trove of information on him and anything related to him, from the time he became president until today. Everything about him, from the most profound and important to the most trivial—from his presidency to his enjoyment of golf—has been written about. In addition, movies, documentaries, photograph anthologies, commemorative coins, stamps, schools, streets, and a space center, have all been produced or named in his honor.[4] Certainly one major area of continuing interest and investigation is his death. The press covered his assassination from the moment it happened, and since the results of the official government investigation into his murder were released in the fall of 1964, countless publications have appeared proposing one conspiracy theory or another. Others have argued instead that there actually was no wider plot at all and that the accused assassin—Lee Harvey Oswald—was indeed the lone gunman.[5]

Photo 1. President John F. Kennedy greets the crowd outside his hotel in Fort Worth, November 22, 1963, roughly four hours before his assassination.

Photo courtesy of the John F. Kennedy Presidential Library (Cecil Stoughton); ST-525-8-63.

President Kennedy came to Texas in late November 1963 to raise money and begin rounding up support for the following year's presidential election. Attempting to restore peace within the Democratic Party was also on the president's agenda. Disputes between the liberal and conservative wings of the party in Texas, especially over JFK's support for civil rights legislation, threatened to undermine party unity for the 1964 election. Kennedy planned to visit San Antonio, Houston, Fort Worth, Dallas, and Austin. In each place they visited, the Kennedys received enthusiastic welcomes, especially in Dallas, despite the city's reputation as a rather extremist-friendly city. The president, riding in an open limousine from Dallas Love Field through the downtown area, was to deliver a luncheon address at the Trade Mart before flying to Austin for a fundraiser.[6] Riding through Dealey Plaza on the edge of downtown, Kennedy and Texas

Governor John Connally were shot at 12:30—the president in the neck and head, and the Governor in the back. They were rushed to Parkland Hospital a few miles away; although Connally survived his wounds, doctors were unable to save Kennedy. He was pronounced dead at 1 PM, and Vice President Lyndon Johnson was sworn in as president later that afternoon on Air Force One before returning to Washington.[7]

Kennedy's memorialization began at the very moment of his assassination. Countless home movies and photographs were taken that day by spectators. Newspapers and magazines covered the story widely. Television played an invaluable role that day and in the days following. The assassination was one of the first major events to be broadcast on television, and millions learned of Kennedy's death firsthand from news flashes that appeared only minutes after the shooting.[8] One historian commented, "When the shots were fired in Dallas, the importance of TV news changed virtually overnight...this was the quintessential exciting moment. The *New York Times* got word of the shooting at 12:40 PM and had thirty-two reporters assigned to the story within hours."[9] It did not take long for people around the nation and around the world to learn what had happened, and over the next few days, huge numbers of people everywhere watched the events in Washington and Dallas. Public consumption of documentaries, movies, books, and articles on JFK has remained steady ever since.

And yet, in spite of this widespread interest in all things Kennedy, surprisingly little systematic attention has been paid to JFK and popular memory: what he is remembered for, how popular memory of him has been used, what are the benefits and risks of invoking that memory (for there are both), and why that memory matters in the context of American politics today. There can be little doubt that he is frequently identified with youth, vigor, leadership, idealism, and the belief that Americans had the responsibility to promote the cause of world freedom, a cause which, as he said in his inaugural address, "will truly light the world."[10] This absence of a discussion of President Kennedy and popular memory seems especially odd in view of the fact that our conceptions of him are replayed constantly, often without our knowledge that they are being reinforced. One does not have to search very far for these conceptions, as books and articles on him are still being produced at a steady rate. And what we see in so many of those books and articles truly is a reinforcement of those high ideals and comforting images he supposedly embodied, and which, for many, have yet to be seen again in a public figure.

The cover story of the November 2007 issue of *Vanity Fair*, for example, featured a collection of previously unpublished photographs of JFK and his family. Who can forget the heavily documented style and elegance of Jacqueline Kennedy, or the playful activities of their small children? So much of the popular memory of the First Family was shaped by the media, which captured on film what many considered to be the American version of royalty: "John F. Kennedy was a prince...in [Richard] Avedon's photos there are no gilded crowns or ermine robes, but there is a palpable sense of his subjects as a natural aristocracy, and of Jack and Jackie as deeply human but also above and apart." Photographers such as Richard Avedon, Jacques Lowe, and James Spada portrayed what Robert Frost said at Kennedy's inauguration was "the glory of a next Augustan age."[11] A recent anthology of photos by Kennedy White House photographer Cecil W. Stoughton further exemplifies the power of film to tell a story. If they don't detail much in the way of substance (i.e., governance), the photos do reinforce the images that so often come to mind when one thinks of the Kennedy years.[12]

Photo 2. President Kennedy signs the naval quarantine proclamation during the Cuban Missile Crisis, October 23, 1962. The Crisis has been widely regarded as Kennedy's greatest moment as President.

Photo courtesy of the John F. Kennedy Presidential Library (Abbie Rowe); AR7558-A.

Or consider an issue of *Time* from earlier in 2007, which featured a series of articles and essays on the Kennedy administration under the cover headline "What We Can Learn From JFK." The leader depicted in those pages was one who, while standing up to the Soviet Union, was still actively involved in the pursuit of peace between the superpowers. We are told that the speech Kennedy was about to deliver in Dallas was a logical follow-up to his famous "Peace Speech" given at American University in June 1963. The contrast is between the extremist, anti-Kennedy atmosphere Dallas was known for prior to the president's trip, and his supposedly "courageous" speech that was to call for the United States to adopt a less militaristic approach to the world, and instead emphasize social justice and equal rights.[13]

The memory of Kennedy is not only media-driven. Politicians in the past four decades have discovered that to successfully associate themselves with him is to gain a type of legitimacy, to be given the right to carry on in his name. In the 2008 presidential campaign, for example, Democratic candidate Barack Obama was frequently the subject of admiring comparisons with the late president. When JFK's younger brother Edward Kennedy and his daughter Caroline Kennedy gave Senator Obama their endorsements, they did so by making him one with the purposes and ideals for which President Kennedy himself had supposedly fought.[14] Popular memory of him has been unfailingly positive, and many political figures have striven to align themselves in the Kennedy tradition to become the "next" JFK.[15]

The purpose of this book, thus, is not to examine what the popular memory of Kennedy is: what is being remembered, or whether those things for which he is remembered are an accurate reflection of his tenure as president. The historiography on his administration tends to argue they are not. Rather, I intend to examine how he has been memorialized and why. Put another way, this study will demonstrate an important characteristic of memory: its *practical* quality, often used for political ends. As I hope to make clear, it did not take long for that memorializing to begin, but the main point of interest is the significance that those who memorialized JFK attached to him, what their purposes were in doing so, and why popular memory of him matters today. Along the way, they helped build onto the public's memory of him, crafting a popular memory that probably would have surprised even Kennedy himself. Memorializing President Kennedy, as I will argue, is not just about commemorating someone who established strong emotional ties with the nation he served. Nor is it intended only as an expression of support for the agenda he supposedly promoted. Rather, memorializing JFK has had an eminently functional, utilitarian purpose. Although I hope to show what a few of those purposes have been, the central point is that Americans' memorialization of him has served definite ends—to accomplish particular objectives—as much as it has expressed sorrow at the untimely death of a man many believed was a truly great president.

What, then, have been those objectives? They ultimately depend on who is doing the memorializing and what part of JFK's memory is emphasized. It is true that we have attached many qualities and attributes to him that we are convinced he personified. But it is, nevertheless, equally true that different people have chosen to play up different parts of his life, depending on their purpose in using popular memory. In this study, I am primarily interested in how the city of Dallas, Lyndon Johnson, and Robert Kennedy chose to use popular memory of the fallen president. In each case, a different facet of the Kennedy memory was highlighted. Each offers an example of how popular memory was mobilized to accomplish a particular goal, and how one could benefit from successfully creating a link between that memory and one's own purposes.

President Kennedy's place in history is certainly relevant as far as this study is concerned, but a distinction should be drawn at the outset between memory and legacy. The difference between the two prohibits the terms from being used interchangeably. How does memory differ from legacy? A person's legacy is not limited to what is remembered about him or her. Strictly defined, legacy refers to whatever someone from the past has left behind to those who have followed, such as physical items like money or a family heirloom. It could also mean ideas, like democracy or religious freedom. Historians examine these things that have been left behind and try to make sense out of them. They look at what Kennedy left behind—his ideas and beliefs, his achievements, his failures, his style, what the United States was like during the time he governed, his motivations and reasoning (to the extent they can be determined), his unfinished business—and draw conclusions on his presidency. Legacy, in other words, forms historiography. The sum of what he left us enables historians to judge how he should rank as a leader, the impact of his presidency on American and world history—in short, what history's verdict on him should be.

Although this study only briefly touches upon the historiography on the Kennedy presidency, many would be surprised at the wide chasm between the historical community's collective verdict on his legacy and what the public still chooses to believe. Americans generally still consider him one of our greatest presidents; in some cases, he has surpassed even Franklin Roosevelt. The consensus from the historical community has hardly been as generous. While scholars indeed credit Kennedy with having some good qualities and high ideals, he ultimately failed to meet the high expectations he set. What he left us, many scholars would argue, was a presidency heavy on the *style* of governing, but generally light on the positive *results* of it.[16]

Photo 3. JFK and "court historian" Arthur Schlesinger, Jr. in the Oval Office, July 26, 1962. Schlesinger remained one of Kennedy's most vocal advocates in the decades after his death.

Photo courtesy of the John F. Kennedy Presidential Library (Cecil Stoughton); ST-322-1-62.

The early historiography on his presidency was dominated by former Kennedy advisers and close observers, and they treated their fallen leader very well. Early works, such as Arthur Schlesinger's *A Thousand Days: John F. Kennedy in the White House*, and Theodore Sorensen's *Kennedy*,[17] were eagerly consumed by an American public still emotionally traumatized by the president's death. Both were published in 1965 and became two of the ten best-selling books for that year.[18] Schlesinger's book reflects the way many Americans view the Kennedy presidency today. Acknowledging the painfully brief time that JFK had been president, he nonetheless suggested that the late president should still be recognized for the things he supposedly had accomplished: the treaty banning atmospheric nuclear testing, new policies toward Latin America, "the emancipation of the American Negro," and the greater hope and possibility of world peace that his presidency had fostered.[19]

By the last few months of the president's life, according to his court historian, he was optimistic about his prospects for reelection and what the years beyond 1964 promised. That year was expected to be a period of great achievement, with the advancement of his legislative agenda and reelection at home. Abroad, Schlesinger mentioned the possibility of a summit in the Soviet Union and further steps to advance the détente that had begun with the Test Ban Treaty.[20] Kennedy, Schlesinger seemed to be suggesting, needed to be judged not only on what he did during his presidency—with the brief duration of his administration kept in mind—but also on what he wanted to do beyond 1964. History's verdict on JFK had to take into account the supposed fact that he was in the process of learning and changing by November 1963. This process could only hint at the great things he would have done had he lived to win another term.[21]

More recent research and writing on JFK has brought him much more down to earth and has shown that the images that he and his administration worked so hard to cultivate, both before and after his death, were quite removed from the truth. Within the last quarter century, historians such as Herbert Parmet, Nick Bryant, Thomas Paterson, and journalists like Seymour Hersh have redrawn the shape of the Kennedy presidency. They have noted, for example, his administration's repeated efforts to assassinate Fidel Castro, continued up until the very day Kennedy died. It was those efforts that are now thought to have motivated Soviet Premier Nikita Khrushchev to send Soviet missiles and military personnel to Cuba to stave off a feared American invasion—the genesis of the Cuban Missile Crisis in the fall of 1962.[22]

These historians have further noted JFK's lack of achievement in his domestic proposals. Although his years in office were not entirely devoid of legislative accomplishments, by the time of his death, his biggest and most important legislative initiatives on medical care, education, civil rights, and taxes had gotten nowhere.[23] Kennedy took a cautious and even timid approach in turning his proposals into law. As one political scientist commented during the Kennedy years, "President Kennedy has been bold in word and cautious in deed. In terms of accomplishment, the New Frontier is no New Deal. The one falls thirty years later than the other, and thirty Acts behind it."[24] Although the New Frontier may connote forceful and dramatic executive leadership, it cannot possibly compare with either the New Deal preceding it or the Great Society that followed it.[25]

In what was arguably the biggest domestic problem the United States confronted in the early 1960s—civil rights—Kennedy had initially appeared to be sympathetic to the problems of black Americans and willing to spur greater executive and legislative action to address those problems. Yet, at the time of his death, his civil rights bill had not cleared Congress. His administration failed to get much done regarding black voter registration, greater access to housing, greater access to government jobs, and school desegregation.[26] Nor has Kennedy's personal life been immune from criticism. The well-known stories of womanizing, the connections with organized crime that likely helped JFK win the 1960 election, and the persistent health problems that were covered up during his life for fear they would call into question his ability to govern have likewise resulted in a much different-looking Kennedy presidency than the one the American people have been sold for so long.[27]

Legacy, then, should not be confused with popular memory. Popular memory can be defined as the general, or prevailing, conceptions the American people have of President Kennedy. It is what those who were old enough at the time remembered about him—all of those individual memories put together. At the risk of generalizing , most people have a certain set of memories or beliefs about President Kennedy that were greatly influenced by his sudden death. Many remember him as a great leader who challenged people and inspired them to be better. His assassination seemed to remove from the American scene one of the few political leaders of recent history who was considered a truly monumental figure. Memory itself may not be a tangible thing, but it can be captured in various tangible forms: memorials, speeches and eulogies, oral histories, and the identification of oneself or one's cause with whatever or whoever is being remembered.

Why focus on Dallas, Lyndon Johnson, and Robert Kennedy in considering the impact of JFK's popular memory? These are certainly not the only cases in which popular memory of President Kennedy has been used, whether successfully or not. I have chosen these examples because these were three of the earliest attempts to define what memory of President Kennedy was and why it needed to be used to move various efforts forward after the assassination. I also think that the three cases examined in this study clearly demonstrate the practical ends which memory serves: the rebuilding of a city's image and the political benefits of successfully using that memory. But other ways in which popular memory of JFK has been used—and created—also should be mentioned and discussed, and I also spend time examining those.

Jacqueline Kennedy's depiction of her husband's presidency as "Camelot," Oliver Stone's recreation (some would say, "invention") of events in his film *JFK*, and countless books and articles purporting to explain the assassination have likewise interacted with popular memory of JFK by either helping to shape it or by being influenced by it. Mrs. Kennedy arguably had a greater hand in conceptualizing the public's memory of her husband than anybody else when she described his tenure as "Camelot" to journalist Theodore White shortly after her husband's death. And our fond memories of President Kennedy have enabled conspiracy theorists (including Stone) over the years to ply their trade by arguing that a truly great president could only have been eliminated by powerful forces that were opposed to his good work—forces that have yet to be brought to justice.[28]

In three primary areas of memory, I hope to demonstrate not only the practical uses of memory, but also its two-sided nature. Simply put, using memory can backfire. If successfully done, linking oneself with the memory of a cherished fallen leader can instill in others the belief that you are worthy of carrying on in that leader's name—that you represent the same things he or she did. In each of the three cases I discuss in this work, those who used popular memory of President Kennedy were successful, but only to a limited extent. The paradox of popular memory here is that by aligning so closely with the late president and building him up to mythical stature, anybody trying to use memory of him is rendered permanently inadequate by comparison.

Popular memory of JFK has, I think, also had a marked impact on American national politics, and in particular, the development of the institution of the presidency in the last several decades. More than simply a way for aspiring politicians to appeal to the public, that memory has also advanced certain ideas as to what the president is supposed to do as a leader. The rise of the modern presidency with both its positive and negative implications for the country did not begin with Kennedy's election. However, he furthered the belief that the president is supposed to inspire as well as support grand national goals. Americans have long believed that they are a people set apart, a people meant to do grand things. This seemed to be especially true while he was in office. The act of governing through inspiration and the cultivation of an air of celebrity as

Kennedy did could certainly be used to constructive ends, but it also led to the rise of politics as little more than theater. If a president was now expected to inspire, he was also expected to entertain. JFK is remembered as a leader who could ably do both, but in doing so, he may have set a precedent for future presidents to appeal more to people's emotions than to their intellects—resulting in a weakening of the overall quality of political discourse in the country. So the effect of popular memory of President Kennedy on politics in our time is also worthy of examination.

One caveat I would like to offer before going any further is that I am not suggesting that the desire to memorialize President Kennedy stems only from a cynical desire to exploit popular memory for our benefit. It is not my intention to argue that those I discuss here cared only to manipulate the public's memory of the late president because they understood the legitimizing power contained in that popular memory. No doubt the vast majority of Americans were shocked by his death and paid tribute to him because they loved and admired him. Lyndon Johnson, for example, although never close to his boss, should still be taken at his word when he wrote of his sadness and grief at his death.[29] It is also fair to say that his and others' efforts to memorialize JFK arose from the belief that he deserved to be remembered. But what I argue is that the reasons for memorializing go beyond this. The power of that popular memory and the legitimacy it conveys, especially if an entire range of meanings and values can be attached to the person or thing being remembered, means that popular memory can be used as much to promote, let's say, a legislative agenda, as it is done to pay tribute.

One way this practicality and legitimizing power of popular memory has been demonstrated elsewhere is the concept of what French historian Pierre Nora called a "site of memory," or a *lieu de mémoire*. The series of works Nora edited in the 1980s and early 1990s examined how memory interacted with major historical figures, institutions, and national symbols throughout French history: Joan of Arc, Rene Descartes, Bastille Day, the Louvre, the monarchy, and the *Marseillaise*.[30] Nora identified these *lieux de mémoire* as shared points, which may not necessarily have the same meaning for everyone, but they nonetheless serve as a point of reference. They are places at which something happened that changed the world as we had known it. There is, in other words, a sort of break, producing a sense of discontinuity. Paradoxically, these are points that everyone can relate to in one way or another, even though we all may end up forming our own interpretations and drawing different lessons from them. Each point of origin is a common experience, but our understanding of it is not.[31]

In his writing, Nora referred to Bastille Day in France as one such *lieu de mémoire*, but this concept can be applied to far more than one particular event or the history of a particular nation. It can potentially be used for any situation in which people feel the need to memorialize a person or event. As Nora said, "These *lieux* have washed up from a sea of memory in which we no longer dwell: they are potentially official and institutional, partly affective and sentimental. We all recognize them without feeling any sense of unanimity about them."[32]

In one Nora-edited essay about French national identity and memory , Joan of Arc was cited as an example of somebody who, like President Kennedy, embodied a variety of meanings, depending on who claimed to represent and portray her. Like Kennedy, she has been depicted in every conceivable way in French culture: books, movies, poems, advertising, statues, and buildings.[33] She was widely remembered, but depending on the group commemorating her, memory of her was molded and remolded in a seemingly infinite number of ways. During the French Revolution she became the great defender of the people, who no doubt would have been at the vanguard of the movement against the corrupt French ruling classes. Napoleon Bonaparte emphasized her role as a symbol of French independence. During the 19th century, Joan became a standard-bearer for other groups. She became, coincidentally, a heroine of French Catholics, as well as a venerable figure of French secular nationalists and republicans who played up her credentials as an early defender of French liberty, and as a victim of the excesses of the Roman Catholic Church. The remolding of Joan's memory continued into the 20th century, with even the Nazi-backed Vichy government using her during World War II as an exemplar of French nationalism and resistance against supposedly harmful foreign influences (meaning, for the regime, Jews and the British).[34]

What the American people have done with John F. Kennedy in the last four decades is exactly what has been done with Joan of Arc. Americans all remember him, but there, the similarity stops. We remember him "without feeling any sense of unanimity." The three cases examined in this book demonstrate exactly that. In Dallas, some wanted to memorialize the late president as a way of absolving the city from any perception of guilt in the assassination. Others thought a memorial would forever link the city with his death and therefore should not be built at all. And, as nationalists and republicans did with Joan of Arc, the memory of JFK took on a very political character for Lyndon Johnson and Robert Kennedy. For Johnson, it was an opportunity to enact the late president's legislative agenda, as he claimed it was being done in Kennedy's name and with his posthumous blessing.[35] In the case of RFK, many interpreted the late president's memory as a sort of unfulfilled promise and potential that only he could rightfully represent and bring to fruition. Robert Kennedy himself encouraged this belief, proclaiming after he was elected to the Senate in 1964 that he had been given a mandate to continue his brother's policies.[36] Different ends, as well as the different interests to which they each identified themselves, thus dictated the aspects of the public's memory of JFK they chose to emphasize: his life (those who wanted the memorial), his death (those who didn't), and his unfinished presidency (LBJ and RFK, who both strove to position themselves as the one who would "finish" it).

Assessing the role of memory may, at first glance, appear rather elusive because it seems intangible, and therefore, difficult to grasp. What is popular memory in a concrete sense, or rather, in what way is popular memory "contained" in tangible things that can be themselves examined?

In the case of the Kennedy assassination, a written recollection of someone old enough to remember is one physical example of memory, but it is not the only type of remembrance . A memorial is another example. Chapter One examines the Kennedy memorial in Dallas. I look at some of the documents from those involved firsthand in the efforts to build it: Mayor Earle Cabell, J. Erik Jonsson of the Dallas Citizens Council, and Dallas retailer Stanley Marcus. What was the nature of the public's response to the assassination, and to the proposal for a memorial? What did city leaders think a memorial would accomplish in terms of the city's image? What influenced the memorial's design? Why did some not want a memorial at all? And what was the memorial actually remembering? Other primary source materials used here include publications from the Sixth Floor Museum on the creation of the memorial, the recollections of civic leaders as to what Dallas was like in the period before and after JFK's death, and news stories on how Dallas' image fared in later years.

The challenge in looking at Lyndon Johnson and Robert Kennedy (Chapters Two and Three, respectively) is locating those places and things they used to invoke the memory of JFK. In what ways did they infuse that memory, and what symbols did they use to connect themselves with him? The late president's policies and legislative proposals, the explicit or implicit references to him that populated their rhetoric, JFK's manner of speaking, and physical places associated with him all became highly contested territory over which they fought, and through which the public compared them with Kennedy.

By the early 1960s, Dallas had acquired a reputation as not only a conservative city, but as one in which an open embrace of right-wing extremism was accepted. Billboards advocating the impeachment of Supreme Court Chief Justice Earl Warren were common and, by 1963, the city was not the friendliest of places for members of the Kennedy administration. Vice President Johnson, a native Texan, as well as Adlai Stevenson, JFK's ambassador to the United Nations, had both encountered hostile crowds during their respective visits to Dallas. Johnson and his wife had been spat upon during their 1960 campaign visit to the city, and Stevenson was actually struck with a picketer's sign three years later.[37] But Kennedy's murder was the event that finally forced city leaders to examine the zealotry that had been tolerated for so long, with many across the nation and the world blaming Dallas itself for the tragedy. Although few tried to depict Lee Harvey Oswald as a right-wing extremist, many certainly charged that an "atmosphere of hatred" had been allowed to fester within the city—an atmosphere that had resulted in the most infamous crime in Dallas history.[38] City leaders were thus charged with acting quickly to repair Dallas' image, and a memorial to Kennedy was one way to go about it.

Plans for a memorial of some sort were suggested not too long after the assassination, and with the completion of the memorial in June 1970, the city attempted to distance itself from the tragedy. The memorial served as a reminder that the people of Dallas, no less than citizens elsewhere, loved and admired President Kennedy.[39] Popular memory of the late president in this case served to argue the city's innocence, and although the memorial design was intentionally ambiguous about what exactly was being remembered, it nevertheless utilized popular memory of JFK to honor him and resurrect the city's image.[40] But because the memorial deliberately did not convey any central message about JFK to visitors, it was largely forgotten. Its influence as a site of memory in the years since its dedication has been negligible.

President Lyndon Johnson emphasized the images of John Kennedy as a visionary and committed legislative leader and civil rights advocate to ensure passage of the Kennedy legislative program, setting the stage for his own Great Society. Johnson had been on the Texas trip, riding only two cars behind Kennedy when he was assassinated; he took the oath of office later that afternoon on Air Force One. From the beginning, LBJ sought to establish continuity between his administration and that of his predecessor, arguing that the unfinished Kennedy agenda must be fully adopted. First and foremost, that included the Kennedy civil rights legislation, as well as his tax cut intended to inject money into the economy.[41] In identifying so closely with JFK, Johnson saw himself as the holder and interpreter of the Kennedy legacy. It became his job to translate the public's shock over the assassination and the public's love of Kennedy into accomplishments that would not only launch JFK into the ranks of presidential greatness, but LBJ himself as well.[42] Writing in his memoirs years later, Johnson commented that, "Everything I had ever learned in the history books taught me that martyrs have to die for causes. John Kennedy had died. But his 'cause' was not really clear. That was my job. I had to take the dead man's program and turn it into a martyr's cause."[43]

Johnson successfully mobilized the public's memory and love of John Kennedy to secure the much-needed legislation that he had proposed, but positioning himself as the rightful heir to the Kennedy legend ended up cutting both ways. While Johnson was a very effective president domestically—passing the bills that JFK could not—the fact that he tried to identify himself so much with Kennedy led many to see Johnson as merely a wheeling-and-dealing politician, and not at all like the statesman that Kennedy had been. Even LBJ's own domestic reforms, impressive though they may have been, could not engender for him the love and devotion that many felt for JFK. Popular memory was thus turned against Johnson, as many did compare him with his predecessor and found Johnson considerably lacking.[44]

Following his brother's death, Robert F. Kennedy became perhaps the prime beneficiary of the Kennedy "dream." With his older brother dead, he became not only the leader of the Kennedy family, but for many, the custodian of the Kennedy legacy—and the one many expected to return the Kennedys to the White House. RFK saw himself, not LBJ, as the true heir to his brother, and this conviction extended even to how his brother's assassination was written about.[45] With the turmoil and national division over civil rights, the Vietnam War, and poverty that marked the 1960s, many Americans saw Robert Kennedy as the only one who could solve the nation's problems and turn the clock back to the glorious days before November 22, 1963.[46] Others charged that RFK's presidential bid was grounded in the Kennedy's overwhelming drive for power, instead of his desire to end the war in Vietnam and foster peace at home.[47]

After JFK's death, the public's love of him was transferred to his brother, and Robert Kennedy benefited from a popular memory of the Kennedy years that he had helped to create, and later used, to further his own presidential ambitions. As one author said, RFK "knew that the cheering crowds saw him as a stand-in for his brother. At one rally, as the crowd stomped and whistled its allegiance, he turned to an aide and said mournfully, 'They're cheering him.' And of course they were, but in the process, part of that emotion was being transferred to him."[48] The result was a building up and a glorification of Robert Kennedy that positioned him as the one who could have made the United States what his brother would have made it, had he not been killed. This placed him in direct opposition to President Johnson, and the well-publicized feud between the two, although brought about by differences in background and a clash of ambitions, can also be seen as a fight over who had the right to benefit from the public's memory of Kennedy—who was worthy of finishing what JFK had begun.

One journalist, reflecting on the need to give some kind of meaning to John Kennedy's life a year after his death, commented that, "The four harrowing days that began on November 22, 1963, brought us face to face with the future. What happens next is up to us...We relive that time of tragedy less to commemorate a departed president than to dedicate ourselves."[49] But it is what they dedicated themselves to, by commemorating President Kennedy, that will be examined in the pages that follow. Dallas city leaders, Lyndon Johnson, and Robert Kennedy each created a link between themselves and him. In doing so, they simultaneously drew support from, and helped reinforce, the popular memory of him that is still so readily evident half a century later.

NOTES

1. Theodore C. Sorensen, "Foreword," in Pierre Salinger and Sander Vanocur, eds., *A Tribute to John F. Kennedy* (New York: Dell Publishing Co., 1964), 14-15.
2. *Nixon.* Oliver Stone, Stephen J. Rivele, and Christopher Wilkinson. Videocassette. Walt Disney Video, 1995. Time index: 2:58:26.
3. The *New York Times,* for example, in marking the 40th anniversary of the assassination, admitted that we will never be able to reach definitive conclusions about his place in history. Still, the *Times* editorialized, JFK should be given credit on a range of issues from defending American interests against the Soviets to actively promoting civil rights—and perhaps most enduringly, giving the country a new dose of idealism and re-instilling the belief that public service truly was noble. "Remembering John F. Kennedy," *New York Times,* November 22, 2003, A14.
4. Worldwide, Kennedy continues to be well-regarded. U.S. Ambassador to Argentina Edwin Martin recalled receiving monthly invitations to dedicate new buildings and roads named in honor of the late president. James N. Giglio, *The Presidency of John F. Kennedy* (Lawrence: University of Kansas Press, 1991), 282; and Stephen G. Rabe, *The Most Dangerous Area in the World: John F. Kennedy Confronts Communist Revolution in Latin America* (Chapel Hill: The University Press of North Carolina, 1999), 1.
5. Herbert S. Parmet, *JFK: The Presidency of John F. Kennedy* (New York: Penguin Books, 1984), 346-347; and Michael L. Kurtz, *The JFK Assassination Debates: Lone Gunman versus Conspiracy* (Lawrence: University of Kansas Press, 2006), vii-xi.
6. Herbert S. Parmet, *JFK*, 341-345.
7. Ibid., 346.
8. United Press International reporter Merriman Smith, riding in the Dallas motorcade, radioed news of the shooting to New York; his bulletin hit teletype machines around the country and the world at 12:34 PM, a scant four minutes after the shots were fired. Five minutes later came word that the President's wounds were possibly fatal. Bruce Catton (ed.), *Four Days: The Historical Record of the Death of President Kennedy compiled by United Press International and American Heritage Magazine* (New York: American Heritage Publishing Co., Inc., 1964), 22-23.

9. Conover Hunt, *JFK for a New Generation* (Dallas: The Sixth Floor Museum and Southern Methodist University Press, 1996), 102-103.

10. James M. McPherson (ed.), *To the Best of My Ability: The American Presidents* (New York: Dorling Kindersley, 2000), 432.

11. Robert Dallek, "As Camelot Began: The Unseen Portraits of the Kennedys, by Richard Avedon," *Vanity Fair*, November 2007, 292.

12. Richard Reeves, *Portrait of Camelot: A Thousand Days in the Kennedy White House* (New York: Abrams, 2010), 6-10.

13. This is, however, a distorted picture of what Kennedy was to say in Dallas. The majority of the speech was on national defense. The President intended to highlight the steps he had taken during his presidency to beef up the nation's military capabilities. The speech specifically cited modernization of American nuclear capabilities, the more rapid deployment of tactical nuclear forces to allies in Europe, improvements in American conventional forces and Special Forces, and the importance of continuing military assistance to anti-Communist governments in the Third World, including South Vietnam. In only one paragraph of the speech, coming almost at the end, are social justice and equal rights mentioned. Even then, they appear only in the context of how they can work to the advantage of the United States in the worldwide struggle against communism. David Talbot, "A Warrior For Peace," *Time*, July 2, 2007, 50; and Public Papers of the Presidents/American Presidency Project, "John F. Kennedy: Prepared Remarks for Delivery at the Trade Mart in Dallas, November 22, 1963," available from http://www.presidency. ucsb.edu/ws/index.php?pid=9539&st=&st1=#axzz1N0GuGfRh; accessed from Internet May 18, 2011.

14. Mike Dorning, "Obama Endorsed by Two Generations of Kennedys," *Dallas Morning News*, January 29, 2008, 6A; and Vincent Bzdek, *The Kennedy Legacy: Jack, Bobby and Ted and a Family Dream Fulfilled* (New York: Palgrave Macmillan, 2009), 248-250.

15. Arguably, the politician who could most seriously claim this position has been Obama. Campaign manager David Plouffe, in recalling the important endorsement Obama received in early 2008 from the Kennedys, noted that Caroline Kennedy campaigned more actively for him than she had for anybody outside her family. Further, Plouffe stated that Edward Kennedy's endorsement was the only time since JFK's death that his brother had so definitively anointed another political candidate as the true heir to the late president. David Plouffe, *The Audacity to Win: The*

Inside Story and Lessons of Barack Obama's Historic Victory (New York: Viking, 2009), 165-166.

16. Robert Dallek, *Hail to the Chief: The Making and Unmaking of American Presidents* (Oxford: Oxford University Press, 1996), 25; and Sidney Milkis and Michael Nelson, *The American Presidency: Origins and Development, 1776-2002* (Washington, D.C.: CQ Press, 2003), 310-317.

17. Theodore C. Sorensen, *Kennedy* (New York: Harper & Row, 1965), 1-7.

18. Paul R. Henggeler, *In His Steps: Lyndon Johnson and the Kennedy Mystique* (Chicago: Ivan R. Dee, 1991), 100.

19. Arthur M. Schlesinger, Jr., *A Thousand Days: John F. Kennedy in the White House* (Boston: Houghton Mifflin Company, 1965), 1030.

20. Ibid., 1016-1017.

21. Kennedy's former advisers remained loyal to their boss in spite of the passage of time and the more critical interpretations of his presidency from recent historians. Both Schlesinger and Sorensen remained undeterred in their belief that JFK had been a great president who would have spared the nation much turmoil had he not been killed. On the 20th anniversary of Kennedy's death, Schlesinger wrote in his diary, "Nothing is more exasperating than the revisionist idea that JFK was a reckless, risk-taking, macho cold warrior. On the contrary, he was cautious, circumspect, and conciliatory. There can be no doubt about this whatsoever." Likewise for Sorensen; while he demurred from calling the Kennedy administration "Camelot," he still insisted decades later that "John Kennedy's administration was a golden era." Arthur Schlesinger, Jr., *Journals: 1952-2000* (New York: The Penguin Press, 2007), 558; and Ted Sorensen, *Counselor: A Life at the Edge of History* (New York: Harper-Collins, 2008), 523-525.

22. Thomas G. Paterson, "Fixation with Cuba: The Bay of Pigs, Missile Crisis, and Covert War Against Castro," in Thomas G. Paterson (ed.), *Kennedy's Quest for Victory: American Foreign Policy, 1961-1963* (New York: Oxford University Press, 1989), 140-141.

23. James Giglio, *The Presidency of John F. Kennedy*, 120-121.

24. William E. Leuchtenberg, *In the Shadow of FDR: From Harry Truman to George W. Bush* (Ithaca: Cornell University Press, 2001), 114.

25. Kennedy's political position seemed increasingly precarious in the summer and fall of 1963. *Time* cited a Gallup poll that placed Kennedy's public approval at its lowest point (still in the high 50s, however) during his presidency, mostly due to his stance on civil rights. Some predicted that in a Kennedy-Barry Goldwater contest in 1964, a Goldwater vic-

tory was not out of the question. Moreover, the President faced ongoing difficulties in getting his legislative agenda passed. *U.S. News & World Report* noted an increasing reluctance on the part of the White House—owing primarily to the upcoming election—to pressure Congress to act. The post-assassination praise Kennedy received for his legislative vision notwithstanding, the *Report* observed in early November 1963 that there was "no rush to the New Frontier." "Box Score for '64: Can Anybody Beat Kennedy?" *Time*, October 4, 1963, 34-35; and "The Nation," *Time*, October 18, 1963, 28; and "Where Kennedy is Changing Course," *U.S. News & World Report*, November 4, 1963, 31-32.

26. Nick Bryant, *The Bystander: John F. Kennedy and the Struggle for Black Equality*, (New York: Basic Books, 2006), 463, 468.

27. I refrain from a more extensive examination of the allegations, both old and new, of JFK's sexual indiscretions. I consider this to be more related to Kennedy's legacy as opposed to popular memory. To be sure, his personal failings are important in how we rank him as a leader and as a person. Still, it is not really an aspect of Kennedy that bears much relevance to how we have remembered him, except to say that the "behind the scenes" goings-on of the Kennedy White House have not had much detrimental effect upon our conceptions of him. For further discussion on this, see Seymour M. Hersh, *The Dark Side of Camelot* (Boston: Little, Brown and Company, 1997), 1-12.

28. As an editorial in the *New York Times* noted in 2003, "It is more frightening, not less, to think that a figure like Kennedy can be murdered by a 24-year-old warehouse clerk, as opposed to, say, the CIA." Especially when one compares the tumult of the years following JFK's death with the supposed glamour and tranquility of the Kennedy years, many Americans take it as an article of faith that Lee Harvey Oswald could not possibly have been the sole assassin—that such an explanation is too simple, too mindless, and an insult to Kennedy's memory. Thomas Mallon, "Freed from Conspiracy," *New York Times*, November 21, 2003, A-31; and Michael L. Kurtz, *The JFK Assassination Debates*, x-xi.

29. Lyndon B. Johnson, *The Vantage Point: Perspectives on the Presidency, 1963-1969* (New York: Holt, Rinehart and Winston, 1971), 10.

30. Lawrence D. Kritzman, "In Remembrance of Things French," in Pierre Nora, ed., *Realms of Memory: Rethinking the French Past*, trans. Arthur Goldhammer (New York: Columbia University Press, 1996) I: ix-x.

31. Pierre Nora, "General Introduction: Between Memory and History," in Pierre Nora, ed., *Realms of Memory*, I: 1.

32. Ibid., 7.
33. Michel Winock, "Joan of Arc," in Pierre Nora, ed., *Realms of Memory: Rethinking the French Past,* trans. Arthur Goldhammer (New York: Columbia University Press, 1996), II: 433-436.
34. Ibid, 440, 449, 455-457, 470-471.
35. Robert Dallek, *Flawed Giant: Lyndon Johnson and His Times* (New York: Oxford University Press, 1998), 59-60; and Michael R. Beschloss (ed.), *Taking Charge: The Johnson White House Tapes, 1963-1964* (New York: Simon & Schuster, 1997), 25.
36. Thurston Clarke, "The Last Good Campaign," *Vanity Fair,* June 2008, 118.
37. Steve Blow and Sam Attlesey, "The Tenor of the Times: Far-right-wingers and Democratic discords set the stage for Kennedy's visit," in Blow, et al., *November 22: The Day Remembered as Reported by The Dallas Morning News* (Dallas: Taylor Publishing Company, 1990), 1-3.
38. A resident of Garland, Texas wrote the Dallas mayor, "Now that Dallas has established itself in the headlines, you people at the top in the city can come out from under cover and wear your Ku Klux Klan robes at the council meetings and civic functions and not feel self-conscious about them anymore." An Ohio writer exclaimed, "You Texans like to brag a lot, well now you can boast that in your narrow-minded, hate-ridden, prejudice (sic) town our President John F. Kennedy was murdered!!!!" Letters to Mayor Cabell (Box 11, Folder 4, "Earle Cabell Mayoral Correspondence, Kennedy Assassination, November 26, 1963") in Earle Cabell Papers, DeGolyer Special Collections Library, Southern Methodist University, Dallas, Texas.
39. Lacie Ballinger, *The Rededication of the John Fitzgerald Kennedy Memorial: June 24, 2000* (Dallas: The Sixth Floor Museum, 2000), 2.
40. Tom Johnson, "JFK Honored Today," *Dallas Morning News* June 24, 1970, A1; and Jim Featherston, "Kennedy Memorial Dedicated in Plaza," *Dallas Times Herald,* June 24, 1970, 1, 10.
41. Jim F. Heath, *Decade of Disillusionment: The Kennedy-Johnson Years* (Bloomington: Indiana University Press, 1975), 166-169.
42. Paul R. Henggeler, *In His Steps,* 251.
43. Robert Dallek, *Flawed Giant,* 63.
44. Paul R. Henggeler, *In His Steps,* 119-121.
45. I refer here to the 1966 controversy over the publication—and the attempts by the Kennedys to stop publication—of William Manchester's book on the assassination. Manchester had been hired by RFK and Jacqueline Kennedy; upon his refusal to make changes to the manuscript

they requested, they took legal action against the publisher. LBJ was portrayed very negatively, and probably inaccurately, in the book. In the end, it was the Kennedys, not Johnson, who wound up getting hit by the fallout over the book, as their lawsuit against the publisher looked like an attempt to control how the assassination was written about, as if they owned all interpretive rights over the event. Jeff Shesol, *Mutual Contempt: Lyndon Johnson, Robert Kennedy, and the Feud that Defined a Decade* (New York: W.W. Norton & Company, 1997), 143, 353-356; and Evan Thomas, *Robert Kennedy: His Life* (New York: Simon & Schuster, 2000), 290.

46. Ronald Steel, *In Love with Night: The American Romance with Robert Kennedy* (New York: Touchstone, 2000), 101-103.

47. This was certainly the view of Senator Eugene McCarthy and his supporters. It was McCarthy, and not RFK, who had initially been willing to challenge LBJ for the Democratic presidential nomination in 1968. Kennedy had first decided not to run in 1968 because he feared he would destroy his chances of ever becoming president by engaging in a losing fight with Johnson. But the charge that Kennedy was driven primarily by a lust to retake the presidency was not made only by his detractors. Washington journalist Joseph Alsop, a longtime friend of the Kennedy family, commented several years after the 1968 campaign that, "I couldn't help but be even a little shocked by the sense of prerogative that they all had, actually. It was as though a ruling family had been displaced by unjust fortune. In America we don't have ruling families, and I hope we never do." Charles Kaiser, *1968 in America: Music, Politics, Chaos, Counterculture, and the Shaping of a Generation* (New York: Grove Press, 1988), 106-111; and Transcript. Joseph W. Alsop Oral History Interview, 6/10/1971, by Roberta W. Greene. Robert F. Kennedy Oral History Collection, John F. Kennedy Presidential Library, Boston, Massachusetts.

48. Ronald Steel, *In Love with Night*, 118.

49. Bruce Catton (ed.), "Introduction," in *Four Days*, 5.

CHAPTER ONE

THE CASE OF DALLAS

CONSTRUCTING A MEMORIAL
AND CREATING A NEW CITY

> There is no use beating around the bush. Dallas is a sick city. There are powerful leaders who have encouraged or condoned or at best remained silent while the preachment of hate helped condition a citizenry to support the most reactionary sort of political philosophy...I feel that it will take years for Dallas to recover.
>
> —Allan Maley, secretary-treasurer for the Dallas chapter of the AFL-CIO, commenting shortly after the Kennedy assassination[1]

Because Dallas today is regarded as a conservative city and is known for things besides the fateful Kennedy visit, it is easy to overlook the political atmosphere that existed in the city in the late 1950s and early 1960s. Easier still is to overlook the furor that erupted in the days after President Kennedy's assassination. In memorializing him in the weeks, months, and years after his death, Dallas helped to reinforce the public's admiration of the fallen leader, but also emphasized those parts of his popular memory that would help the city deflect the national shock and anger directed toward it. Memorializing JFK by focusing on his life and what he had supposedly dedicated his presidency to, rather than his sudden death, illustrates how popular memory of JFK not only could be used for very practical ends, but also could be worked and reworked in any number of ways, depending on what those ends are.

Dallas in 1963 was a conservative city with a very pronounced right-wing element that did not hesitate either to express extremist opinions or to provoke embarrassing incidents. Economically, the city had grown and prospered in the years after World War II, making a name for itself in the fashion, aerospace, and electronics industries. This prosperity manifested itself in a distinct pride, even a swagger, which seemed to blend a southern and western setting with a cultured and cosmopolitan feel. Politically, the city was still aligned with the Democratic Party, but that alignment had weakened in the years following World War II. Conservatism in the country was making a comeback, and Dallas was very much a part of this trend; one result was that the area was becoming a progressively friendlier place for Republicans. In the 1948 presidential election, the city had supported Democratic President Harry Truman.[2] The next decade marked a shift in the city's political loyalties, as Dallas twice voted for Republican Dwight Eisenhower and, in 1960, voted overwhelmingly for Richard Nixon. Nixon's margin of victory over John Kennedy was greater in Dallas than in any other city.[3]

The problem, however, was not so much its newfound Republican allegiance as it was the small, but prominent, group of extremists who resided there and who, by the fall of 1963, had become something of an embarrassment for city leaders. Among those spokesmen for the far-right was General Edwin A. Walker. Walker had left the Army in 1961 after accusations that he was inappropriately promoting and distributing far-right propaganda from the John Birch Society to troops under his command. The general seemed to be most interested in denouncing various political figures for supposedly selling the nation out to commu-nism. He was known to fly the American flag in front of his home upside down in protest against what he feared was an impending communist takeover.[4] Walker was certainly not alone in his outlook. Well-known oil millionaire H.L. Hunt was a noted contributor to a right-wing Dallas organization, Facts Forum, as well as a radio program sponsor; he had also authored several works, including one entitled *Hitler Was a Liberal*. R.A. Criswell, head of the First Baptist Church of Dallas, was also a critic of the Kennedy administration and had argued in 1960 that electing a Roman Catholic as president would lead to the undermining of the constitutional guarantee of freedom of religion.[5] Former FBI agent Dan Smoot broadcast a radio show of his own from Dallas, denouncing Kennedy for supposedly leading the nation toward socialism through his advocacy of civil rights and due to the administration's ties with the Council on Foreign Relations. Moreover, a number of new ultraconservative organizations, some headquartered in Dallas, could boast of very active and vocal chapters. The John Birch Society, the Dallas Committee of American Freedom Rallies, the Committee for the Retention of the Poll Tax, the Committee for the Monroe Doctrine, Women for Constitutional Government, the Dallas Committee to Impeach Earl Warren, and the National Indignation Convention were several such organizations in which many influential Dallasites held membership.[6]

Despite the presence of several outspoken representatives of the far-right, it would be unfair to say that the rest of the city marched in lockstep with the ideas those individuals promoted. It was not, in fact, until after Kennedy's assassination that Dallas became branded as the foremost ultraconservative city in the nation. The problem seemed to be, however, that those few who considered themselves ultraconservative were both assertive in expressing their opinions and well-publicized, counting one of the two major daily newspapers as an ally. The *Dallas Morning News* had consistently adopted conservative viewpoints for years, condemning the New Deal, and more recently, JFK's proposed civil rights legislation.[7] It is not surprising that, even while Dallas' city government was not itself extremist, those who served at city hall attacked figures such as General Walker and H.L Hunt only at their own risk.[8] Nor is it surprising that some did not relish the prospect of the president coming to Dallas. Some feared that Kennedy would be subjected to nasty propaganda or some embarrassing incident,[9] especially after visits to the city by two well-known members of the Kennedy Administration—visits that seemed to show Dallas as incapable of hosting prominent figures disliked by the extreme right.

Those who, by the fall of 1963, were wary of bringing President Kennedy to Dallas recalled two ugly incidents showing the hostility of ultraconservatives toward anyone in the administration. The episodes involved then-vice presidential candidate Lyndon Johnson and his wife, and JFK's ambassador to the United Nations, Adlai Stevenson. Johnson and Lady Bird, campaigning for the JFK-LBJ ticket during the last few days of the 1960 campaign, had stopped in Dallas for a luncheon at the downtown Adolphus Hotel. There, they were subjected to jeering from an angry crowd in the street outside the hotel and in the lobby. They were spat upon while trying to cross the street, and although nobody was injured, it took at least half an hour just to get inside the hotel.[10] Adding to what was already an unfortunate situation for the city was the presence of Dallas Republican Congressman Bruce Alger who actually joined the protest by wielding a sign declaring, "LBJ Sold Out to the Yankee Socialists."[11]

Three years later in October 1963, just a month before the president's trip to Dallas, UN Ambassador Adlai Stevenson came to the city to deliver a speech commemorating United Nations Day at the city's Memorial Auditorium. Stevenson was able to give the speech, but not without heckling and shouting from several members of the audience. The crowd who had heard his speech was generally friendly, but those who had shown up to protest also tried to prevent him from leaving. Upon leaving the building, Stevenson was actually struck by a protestor's sign and spat upon as he was trying to enter his car.[12] Some began rocking his car, and Stevenson had to make a quick departure to escape them.[13]

The president would visit Dallas only weeks later, and prominent Dallasites seemed divided over whether a presidential visit was a good idea in view of the city's political climate. As would happen to a much greater degree after the assassination, the Stevenson incident caused some to advocate a self-examination of whether the city was fostering a tolerant and moderate image. Even the conservative *Dallas Morning News* observed after the ambassador's visit, "If the time has come when a distinguished gentleman in his position cannot express his beliefs without abuse, then this city should examine itself."[14] Although administration spokesmen made it clear that, even after Stevenson's visit, the president still planned on coming, some were convinced he would be better off avoiding the city. Dallas retailer Stanley Marcus, of Neiman-Marcus fame, tried to talk Vice President Johnson into dissuading the president from coming, pleading "I sure wish to hell you'd persuade Kennedy not to come. It is a grave mistake to come to Dallas."[15] Likewise, Byron Skelton, an official with the Democratic Party in Texas, sent a letter to Attorney General Robert Kennedy advising JFK to avoid Dallas. He argued that, due to the Stevenson incident and the presence of General Walker, the president could be exposing himself to more than just an embarrassing incident if he chose to come.[16]

In what would later turn out to be the cruelest of ironies, others in Dallas saw President Kennedy's visit as an opportunity to burnish the image of the city in light of the Johnson and Stevenson incidents. Shortly after the Stevenson visit, Mayor Earle Cabell commented, "We have the opportunity to redeem ourselves when the president pays us a visit next month."[17] Dallas' ability to pull off a presidential visit without a hitch would go a long way toward reestablishing its reputation as a tolerant and hospitable city, not one that habitually demeaned prominent national visitors. An editorial appearing in the *Dallas Morning News* on the day the president arrived began hopefully, "Dallas sheds its sharp cleavages of partisanship at noon today in extending the hand of fellowship to the President and his attractive wife...The *News*, along with thousands in this area, has disagreed sharply with many of [Kennedy's] policies but the opposition is not personal."[18] Such may have been the hope of the editorial staff, but others had a more critical opinion of the Kennedy visit. The president, in Fort Worth that morning for a Chamber of Commerce breakfast, may or may not have seen that editorial, but he certainly saw at least one of the two hostile full-page ads taken out in the Dallas newspapers for his visit. A black-bordered ad in the *Dallas Morning News*, curiously titled "Welcome Mr. Kennedy to Dallas," accused him of failing to defend the nation and its allies against communism by directing a series of questions to him, such as, "Why have you scrapped the Monroe Doctrine in favor of the 'Spirit of Moscow?'"[19]

A similar, though more obnoxious ad, placed in the *Dallas Times Herald* featured frontal and profile photos of the president with the heading "Wanted for Treason."[20] That ad included similar soft-on-communism charges, and also accused the president of covering up a secret marriage and divorce before his later marriage to the First Lady. Looking over the ads in his Fort Worth hotel suite just hours before his death, Kennedy commented to his wife, "We're heading into nut country today. But, Jackie, if somebody wants to shoot me from a window with a rifle, nobody can stop it, so why worry about it?"[21] The anticipated hostility in Dallas produced gallows observations from Vice President Johnson as well. His introductory remarks at that evening's fundraiser in Austin were to include the wisecrack, "And thank God, Mr. President, that you came out of Dallas alive."[22]

The president was shot at 12:30 PM, and it did not take Dallas city leaders long to realize both the depth of the hostility being directed at them and the entire city, and the need to do something to rebuild Dallas' image.[23] Within only a couple of weeks, that realization led to the establishment of a committee of prominent citizens charged with determining how Kennedy should be memorialized. This process of memorialization became a sort of cleansing ritual. Dallas city leaders would remind people what Kennedy had stood for during his lifetime, and those qualities would become the keys to relegating the city's newly acquired position as the nation's foremost ultraconservative metropolis to the past. Dallas would remember Kennedy's life and commemorate what he represented, while distancing itself from the fact that he had died there.

National grief in the days after the assassination was accompanied by national anger at Dallas and the suspected climate of hatred that had now resulted in the death of a president. Many of the letters received by Mayor Cabell left no doubt as to who was considered responsible for the act in the eyes of so many.[24] Moreover, after the killing of the suspected assassin, the city was further accused of careless and unprofessional police work that would preclude the American people from ever knowing what had really happened.[25]

The reaction of many Americans toward Dallas was fierce. One letter from Oakland, California, asserted, "The people of the City of Dallas and you, as the civic leaders of the City of Dallas, should all hang your heads in shame at the terrible crime that was allowed to happen...People of Dallas, hang your heads in shame and pray to God for forgiveness."[26] Another from St. Louis: "Your city has become a blemish on the complexion of human civilization. Congratulations...you and your city will live forever in infamy." One writer from Houston wrote, "The country damns you and your town."[27] Another from Pennsylvania blamed Texas as a whole, wondering whether Mexico could be persuaded to take Texas back.[28] One anonymous note from a man in Great Britain was addressed "To Barbarians of Dallas," and compared its citizens to Nazis.[29] Telegrams received by Dallas City Hall included one from California hoping that the city would secede from the country, and one from Detroit addressed to the mayor stated simply, "You stink."[30] Lamenting Kennedy's murder and disgusted with the shooting of Lee Harvey Oswald on national television, the *New Republic* editorialized two weeks later, "This is a hapless situation, set off by a senseless horror in Dallas, where they breed such things."[31] Mayor Cabell was subjected to death threats that weekend after he accepted an invitation from San Antonio Mayor Walter McAllister to join him and a delegation of other Texas mayors at the funeral in Washington. A bomb threat against Cabell's airplane delayed his departure. Due to other threats against him, he was only one of two dignitaries attending the funeral who received police protection.[32] In another sign of the public's anger, the Dallas Cowboys were referred to as "assassins" when they played in New York against the Giants two weeks later.[33]

Of course, not every letter sent to the city's leadership blamed Dallas for the assassination, and many people wrote to express their support and sympathy. In these letters, the most common observation was that the tragedy could have happened anywhere. Still, this support could hardly have comforted Mayor Cabell and other civic leaders as they had to contend with what their official response should be. The atmosphere within the city in the days immediately following the assassination was one of shock, but there also seemed to be excessive preoccupation with how Dallas' image would be affected and too little readiness to assess how much blame the city should bear.[34] The *New York Times* reported two days after the president's death, "The defensiveness [by Dallasites] was massive. It verged sometimes on combativeness. It came out often without prompting...Dallas appeared self-conscious and defensive, as if a mass conscience had been aroused." And although the *Times* was careful to mention that many were primarily saddened and concerned for the slain president's family, it also noted that the priority for others was to simply deny that anything was wrong with Dallas at all.[35]

The combination of citywide shock and nationwide outrage at Dallas meant that a more contrite response than simply a denial that the city had done anything wrong would have to come from city leaders. J. Erik Jonsson, president of the influential Dallas Citizens' Council and later mayor of Dallas, recalled years afterward the descent upon Dallas of the national and international press who, he says, portrayed the city in very negative and distorted terms. Dallas both "looked dead and behaved dead," and was quickly found guilty in the eyes of the media.[36] The chief goal of the city for the period ahead was to prove to everyone that Dallasites were not the bigoted, hateful people of the popular conceptions at the time. A memorial would not be the only way to change things, but it would certainly be a start. Jonsson said years later he was not worried that the assassination would cause irreparable harm to Dallas. Nonetheless, it was true that, "We should be taking some active part in the kind of missions that would make it clear what kind of people the citizens of Dallas were. We were hardworking...we were decent, hardworking people that could get along without using unfriendly descriptives about us."[37]

Calls for a memorial of some sort began coming in only hours after the assassination and continued for the next several days and weeks.[38] Equally rapid were the comparisons made between John Kennedy and other great American historical figures. The association between Kennedy and all of the ideals for which he is still remembered began being drawn only days after his death.[39] The public's high regard for him belied the difficulties he had in advancing his domestic policies, and his unpopularity in some regions of the country toward the end of his presidency. . Although by November 1963 he was confronting the lowest public approval numbers of his presidency (still above 50 percent, however),[40] national reaction to his assassination suggested that the nation had suddenly lost a man who was truly a great statesman, even a Second Emancipator. One example of this attitude was that expressed by the *Detroit Free Press* on November 23, 1963. The newspaper's editors solemnly noted, "President Kennedy was not the first martyr to human rights and human justice. He was not the first President to be assassinated for this cause."[41]

J. Erik Jonsson was approached the day after the assassination by Stanley Marcus regarding the possibility of constructing a memorial,[42] and Dallas County Judge Lew Sterrett likewise proposed a memorial that would remind people of the love and support Dallas had for Kennedy.[43] Sterrett's idea was for the memorial to be placed at the site of the assassination. Mayor Cabell was in agreement by the next week that an effort to build a memorial, located in Washington DC, if not in Dallas, should be undertaken.[44] Creation of a committee to develop a memorial plan, however, would have to wait, as the most pressing problem the city faced was its immediate response to the assassination. Initially, the reaction by the mayor was to deny that the city was culpable in any way for what had happened, but he acknowledged that the events and people that had given Dallas the reputation as a far-right city may have contributed to the event.[45]

By the following Tuesday, November 26, Cabell and others were realizing that such a reaction was unacceptable. While it may have been true that Dallas had not killed the president, many inside and outside the city had already concluded that Dallasites were not exactly innocent bystanders either. Dallas was indeed guilty of killing President Kennedy in the eyes of many; the assassination was only the most recent and tragic event that took place in a city that tolerated and perhaps even encouraged extremism. Dallas would define its memorialization of JFK in a civic virtue/citizenship context. President Kennedy had supposedly been a model citizen and a dedicated public servant. He was moderate, progressive, tolerant, not carried away by ideology—all of the things Dallas appeared not to be at the end of 1963. The city would have to become what it believed President Kennedy was.[46] These concerns did not first appear after his death, but the tragedy revealed deeper problems within Dallas that had not received adequate attention. If Kennedy's murder was the agent of exposing what was wrong in Dallas, Kennedy's memorialization would be at least part of the solution. In a resolution unanimously approved that day by the Dallas City Council, Mayor Cabell asserted, "It would be quite fitting to erect a visible monument. But today I want to speak to the people of Dallas about a great memorial which we can construct...to exemplify the fundamental principles of the nation which we love and which he was serving when he died." He continued, "For it will not be sufficient for us to say we are sorry. It is also required of us that we combine all of the talents of our city to renew the vital spirit of our people."[47]

Reaction elsewhere seemed to reflect this idea that one step in creating a "new" Dallas would be to enshrine JFK in both thought and deed. A statement released by the faculty of Perkins Theological Seminary at Southern Methodist University urged, "We pray that Dallas will be remembered not simply as the scene of President Kennedy's death, but that his death will be recalled as the event in which this city began a new and more authentic life."[48] At a memorial service held in Austin three days after the assassination, Judge W.A. Morrison saw the entire state of Texas, not just Dallas, as responsible for honoring Kennedy with a change in attitude and approach to society. Morrison implied, as did many others, that the public's memorials coincided perfectly with Kennedy's own beliefs and attributes. If the late president had worked so hard for human rights and greater understanding between the races, the public should do likewise: "We must rid ourselves, each of us, of all racial bigotry. We must school ourselves to look at and treat every man with complete equality...From this day forward, Texans must be known as progressive thinkers, just as was President Kennedy. We must abandon the ways of the old South."[49]

Perhaps the most clearly expressed argument that a memorial to JFK could help resurrect the city's image was made in a *Look* magazine article in the spring of 1964. Entitled "Memo from a Dallas Citizen," the article was written by Dallas oil executive J.M. Shea, Jr. Shea forthrightly acknowledged that at least some of the negative perceptions of Dallas were unfortunately justified; as he indicated, not even the assassination had resulted in a respite from the hatred by some. Citing a priest at his parish being criticized for holding a Requiem Mass in honor of the late president, the oilman wrote, "If assassination was the only way to get rid of Kennedy, the protesting Christian informed the priest, then the event should be celebrated."[50] Shea also remembered that "a prominent businessman, a leading Baptist layman, said in my presence, 'I'm glad the son of a bitch is dead.'"[51] Observing hesitation from other Dallasites to acknowledge what had happened in their city, and reluctance to do anything about it, he argued that Dallas owed to Kennedy, and to itself, some constructive effort to come to terms with November 22, 1963. The city could no longer afford to indulge itself in the extremist type of politics that—rightly or wrongly—the people of Dallas were now accused of encouraging and approving. It may have been true that a memorial would not erase all the hostility or repair what seemed to be the general conception people now had of Dallas. But a memorial, as an act of citywide humility, would greatly help to show that the "lessons" of the assassination—whatever those lessons turned out to be—were not lost on Dallas. As Shea stated, "Many people here are ashamed to have been caught acting like fools...his death, more than his life, shocked people out of the hysterics they had worked themselves into. Big D's penance for its silly years should lead to a meaningful memorial to its dead teacher. Or his death will be, for Dallas, in vain."[52]

Shea was not the only citizen to argue that something had indeed gone wrong with the city, nor was he alone in facing condemnation and threats for so vocally condemning the atmosphere that Dallas had tolerated. In a story that made national news, William Holmes, a Methodist minister in north Dallas, attacked that atmosphere and the city's response to the president's death in a sermon delivered two days afterward. Holmes decried the extremism that flourished in the city, noting "The spirit of assassination has been with us for some time...In the name of God, what kind of city have we become?" Referring to the false hope that Kennedy's visit would restore the city's reputation after the Johnson and Stevenson incidents, Holmes declared, "We cannot, month after month, and year after year, sow seeds of intolerance and hate and then upon learning of the president's visit, just throw a switch and hope all rancor will disappear." Holmes' diagnosis of the problem was the same as that of both Shea and Rabbi Olan: denial that Kennedy's death was anything other than an accidental tragedy for the city. Rather, Dallas would have to take a hard look at itself and encourage a new spirit of moderation and tolerance for political pluralism. As Holmes told his congregation, any true memorialization of JFK had to focus on not merely the image of the city but also its character.[53]

In spite of all the attention given to what Dallas should do, or possibly because of it, there were those who argued in the days and weeks after the assassination that a memorial or any other act of penance would be inappropriate. The problem for them was that a memorial would do exactly what its advocates said it would—forever link President Kennedy (and inevitably, his assassination) to the city of Dallas—and so it should *not* be built. A return to normalcy, or as much of a return as possible, was the best course for the city. Former Dallas Mayor R.L. Thornton urged, "We'll be back at work Monday. We'll be lined up and at it in just a day or so. We'll go ahead and build Dallas as we have in the past... Dallas hasn't done anything. Dallas is a great city and we have nothing to be ashamed of. Forget it and go about your business."[54] Although others may have disagreed with Thornton as to the need for citywide humility, some certainly would have concurred that the city's priorities were misplaced. Two weeks after the assassination, one letter writer to Mayor Cabell from Waco criticized the city for supposedly being more concerned with its tarnished image and remaking that image, than with acknowledging at least some fault in Kennedy's death.[55]

But rehabilitating Dallas did assume priority for city leaders, and it was therefore unrealistic to adopt Thornton's advice and continue as if nothing had happened. In a letter dated December 2, 1963, Cabell, along with Dallas County Judge Lew Sterrett, established the Citizens Memorial to John F. Kennedy Committee. A memorial of some sort would be built, and the committee was entrusted with determining its location, what form it would take, and how funds would be raised for its construction. Members of the committee included prominent citizens such as Joe Dealey of the *Dallas Morning News*; Dr. Willis Tate, President of Southern Methodist University; Stanley Marcus; and Robert Cullum of the Dallas Chamber of Commerce.[56] As the committee began discussing what type of memorial Dallas should build, it was certainly not lacking in ideas from the general public. Minutes from the committee's meetings indicate that within a few weeks, several hundred responses suggesting all kinds of memorial concepts had been received. Part of the challenge the committee faced was not only what type of memorial should be built (assuming the committee chose a physical memorial, as opposed to establishing some type of "living" memorial), but where it should be located. Out of 570 suggestions the committee received as of mid-January 1964, 234 argued that the assassination site at Dealey Plaza should be the location.[57]

Photo 4. Dealey Plaza and the former Texas School Book Depository, today the location of the Sixth Floor Museum.

Photo courtesy of the author.

At first glance, this location may have been the most logical and obvious memorial site, but many thought that placing the memorial there would be too evocative of the president's murder. San Antonio Mayor McAllister, for example, wrote Cabell strongly supporting the idea of a memorial, but also advising that it be built elsewhere.[58] A memorial situated in Dealey Plaza—whatever it looked like and regardless of the idea it was designed to convey—would inevitably be overshadowed by its location in "an internationally recognized murder site."[59] The prospect of a Dealey Plaza memorial reminding visitors of where the murder happened, instead of telling them what Kennedy had stood for, was no doubt on Cabell's mind. At a city council meeting three days after the assassination, he opined that whatever memorial was decided upon should not be in Dallas at all but rather in Washington.[60] Although the committee initially planned for the memorial to consist of a wall located in Dealey Plaza, the site was later rejected. A later pamphlet explaining the creation of the memorial noted only that the idea of using the plaza "evaporated under scrutiny."[61]

Ideas for what sort of memorial to create varied from the abstract to the inspirational to the bizarre. What is perhaps most notable about the proposals was that, only a few weeks after the assassination, people already knew what they were memorializing. The process by which a collective memory of President Kennedy was created took a remarkably short period of time. While years and decades would need to pass before his legacy as president could emerge, formation of popular memory required only days and weeks. It was as if, through these memorial ideas, the public already knew what he represented and that they apparently thought he deserved a place in the hearts of the American people next to Washington and Lincoln. Those who wrote to the memorial committee asked themselves how the memorial should reflect what they thought about Kennedy. Out of their letters came their conceptions of him as a friend and supporter of young people, an aficionado of the arts, a dedicated public servant who believed that politics was the noblest profession, a committed proponent of racial equality, and a man ahead of his time in all things. In this sense, nobody needed to shape, or be responsible for shaping, the popular memory of JFK; the public had quickly made up its mind as to what John Kennedy meant, and therefore how he should be memorialized.

This brings up an important question: how did such fond memories of Kennedy arise? When the national media spoke so lovingly of the attributes and accomplishments they were certain the late president embodied, were they promoting their own conceptions of what his memory consisted of, or were they simply reiterating what the public already believed? The power of the press to influence how people thought about JFK in the context of memorial creation is of no small importance. The assassination was the first national event to be experienced primarily via television. The ability of the networks to saturate the public with the latest updates, eyewitness accounts, and recaps of the late president's career all lessened the distance between the events taking place that weekend in Dallas and Washington and people tuning in. That weekend, one historian noted, Americans watched an average of eight hours each day of assassination coverage on television, and the effect of this viewer participation was that the assassination per se was not the only event the entire nation experienced. Absorbing all of the media coverage of the assassination became a national event in itself. It bound "the nation to a common experience—the televised assassination—to create acute emotional intensity and to present a chaotic, inchoate event as holistic and, therefore, capable of being cathartic and therapeutic."[62] This reasoning helps explain, if only in part, how so many were able to define the Kennedy presidency with such certainty so quickly: "Because television made Kennedy's death into a unifying event, his presidency gained a coherence in public memory that had been lacking in his lifetime."[63]

The initial observations and conclusions made that weekend about JFK and his presidency should rightfully be judged cautiously, keeping in mind the grief and shock everyone was experiencing. Kennedy, like any other president, had admirers and detractors during his presidency. One should not forget the suspicion, if not outright hatred, many in the South had for him due to his supposed advocacy of civil rights. But death has a way of erasing, or at least diminishing, a person's flaws and magnifying the nobler aspects of his or her character. An untimely death lends itself to myth-making. In the absence of proof to the contrary, people are more willing to believe that the deceased would have accomplished great things—that their place in history would have been assured had they lived. JFK's sudden death prompted many to see him as a symbol, a martyr, and an image. Many Americans were already familiar with his life's story, and even if they weren't, they were reminded of it (or at least, the glamorized version) in the days and weeks following: his large family, his PT-109 heroism, his attractive wife and children, his wit and humor, on display at press conferences, his eloquence. The paradox of saturating the public with images and information about JFK during that weekend is that it was traumatic yet strangely comforting and even reassuring. The tragic beauty and emotion of the state funeral left many convinced that a great president had just passed, however sanitized the interpretations of his life may have been. This belief appeared repeatedly in the letters coming into Dallas City Hall, conveying what President Kennedy had meant—and therefore, how he should be remembered.

Many of the suggestions received by the committee proposed a "living" memorial: scholarships, for example, or—in view of Kennedy's perceived love and support of the arts—some sort of arts-related memorial such as a John F. Kennedy arts center. One writer even suggested the creation of a musical production in his honor. JFK's interest in young people was one reason given in favor of the establishment of an educational center or a faculty chair; one idea was the creation of a JFK school of government, possibly at SMU.[64] Texas Congressman Henry Gonzalez proposed renaming the Cotton Bowl in Dallas after Kennedy, in recognition of his support for youth and physical fitness.[65] Some thought a medically related memorial was best: funding or institution of a center for care of the mentally retarded. The Texas Retarded Children's Foundation advocated construction of a JFK Memorial Community Center for the Retarded; another writer suggested locating an educational center for retarded children in the Texas School Book Depository.[66]

Other writers supported a living memorial consisting of a citywide (or even nationwide) commitment to ideals President Kennedy supposedly believed in. One thought a fitting memorial would be for people to dedicate themselves to promoting racial equality. The "restoration of justice and order within the nation and throughout the world" would ensure that the late president had at least died for a cause he believed in.

Among those who favored a physical memorial in Dealey Plaza, several suggested an eternal flame like the one placed at Kennedy's grave in Arlington National Cemetery. A statue or bust of the president, a "modern free-form sculpture" representing freedom, and a carillon bell tower were also proposed. Among the more unusual ideas were life-size statues of the Kennedy family walking hand-in-hand in Dealey Plaza, statues of Lincoln and Kennedy with Lincoln's hand on Kennedy's shoulder welcoming him, a statue of JFK in his famous rocking chair, and even a grand arch bigger than France's Arc de Triomphe.[67] Some called for the demolition of the Texas School Book Depository, to be replaced with a chapel or other type of monument; one citizen suggested relocating the book depository, sealing up the building, and painting it black.[68]

Those who thought a memorial should be constructed elsewhere proposed a park along the Trinity River, or renaming the state fairgrounds or Parkland Hospital in Kennedy's honor. Several wrote to the committee urging that Main Street, or even Dealey Plaza, be renamed. One citizen promoted renaming the three streets that ran through Dealey Plaza after those whom Lee Harvey Oswald had targeted (Elm Street renamed after Kennedy, Main after Connally, and Commerce after Dallas Policeman J.D. Tippit). In addition, some thought that the Boeing 707 that had brought the president to Dallas and that had borne his body back to Washington should be returned to Dallas as a memorial once it was retired. Still others advocated renaming Love Field or replacing the Texas Ranger statue in the airport terminal with a statue of the late president.[69]

Having decided against a Dealey Plaza memorial, the committee instead selected a small piece of land one block off the plaza, next to the Old Red Courthouse; fundraising efforts were also undertaken in 1964. The committee raised $200,000 by the end of the year, but no funding was provided by City Hall. At first glance, there appeared to be widespread interest in a memorial, but a substantial portion of the money raised was given in small increments. Many among the city's elite apparently preferred to simply forget rather than donate money for a project that would forever recall the tragedy that had occurred. Commenting on the difficulty in securing enough funding for the project, Stanley Marcus later recalled, "There weren't many rich Democrats to approach."[70]

It was not until 1965 that the committee selected a design and an architect for the project. The committee, acting on the suggestion of Marcus, chose New York architect Philip Johnson, a fitting choice. He was an acquaintance of the Kennedy family and was noted for his design work nationwide, especially in Texas. By 1963, he had designed Houston's St. Thomas University campus, as well as the Amon Carter Museum in Fort Worth. In the years after the Kennedy memorial was built, he also designed the Fort Worth Water Gardens, Dallas' Thanksgiving Square, and the Crescent Hotel, also in Dallas.[71]

Photo 5. John F. Kennedy Memorial in Dallas, designed by Philip Johnson and dedicated in 1970.

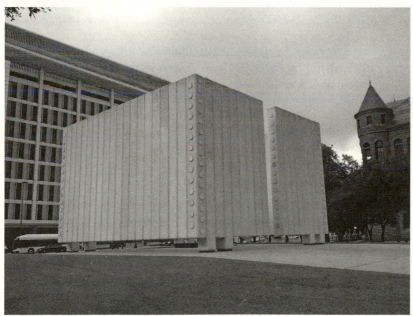

Photo courtesy of the author.

The design that Johnson submitted for the memorial called for a cenotaph—an open tomb—to be placed at the center, surrounded by four square walls with no roof. The only words in the entire memorial, on the cenotaph, would be simply, "John Fitzgerald Kennedy."[72] The corners of the walls have concrete circles, an apparent reflection of the log ends of the nearby cabin belonging to Dallas founder John Neely Bryan. There is no representation of Kennedy, no plaque explaining the memorial—only walls and a low slab of dark granite. There is almost a sense of being alone, but also an expectation on the viewer's part that some representation of JFK should be there. It is a spot for quiet reflection, even in the midst of the surrounding downtown noise. The high white walls are barely supported and seem to float in midair.[73] A pamphlet about the history and development of the memorial describes it thus:

> The Kennedy Memorial's walls are not really walls at all. They are, instead, made of seventy-two white pre-cast concrete columns, sixty-four of which float with no visible support two feet above the earth. Eight touch the ground, acting as legs that seem inadequate to their task—too far apart and too small actually to hold up the other sixty-four. The floating columns are, thus, not columns at all, as they support nothing...Philip Johnson's roofless room is full of potential—for reflection, for memory, even for an occasional flash of recognition that might not occur elsewhere. Yet its emptiness is radical and, thus, disturbing to most viewers...It is, oddly and appropriately enough, a place as much about the "forgetting" as about the "remembering."[74]

Construction of the memorial was delayed, as city leaders argued over the building of a parking lot directly underneath the memorial site. Existing buildings were demolished, and work on the parking garage (which had to be built before work on the memorial could begin) was started. By December 1969, the first wall of the memorial had been finished. The John Fitzgerald Kennedy Memorial was finally dedicated on June 24, 1970. No member of the Kennedy family was in attendance, but several Dallas civic and religious leaders were present: architect

Philip Johnson, Dallas Chamber of Commerce President Robert Cullum, Dallas Judge Lew Sterrett, and Bishop Thomas Tschoepe of the Catholic Diocese of Dallas.[75]

Photo 6. The cenotaph, or empty tomb, of the Kennedy Memorial, with the inscription "John Fitzgerald Kennedy"—the only wording on the structure.

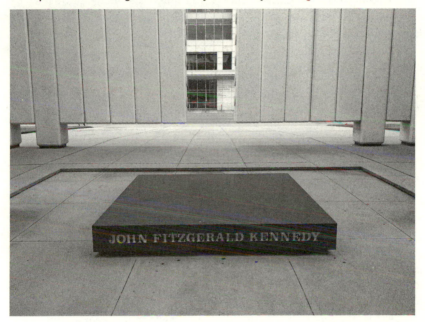

Photo courtesy of the author.

Johnson's creation was intended to provoke multiple responses by visitors; just as each person experienced the assassination in his own way, everyone could interpret the memorial in his own way. Each person takes their own meaning from it. The simplicity of the design precludes having one aspect of JFK being the only thing, or the primary thing, remembered.[76] However, it is difficult to ascertain anything about him that the memorial evokes. Kennedy the man? His death, as the cenotaph seems to imply? The memorial doesn't specifically suggest tragedy or sadness, so could it be that viewers are called upon to remember the ideals he promoted? Or does the memorial serve simply as an historical marker? The fact that the memorial is in Dallas and that its design reflects the log cabin of the city's founder could merely denote that a significant event took place there.[77]

If Dallas constructed the memorial to remake the image of the city by reminding viewers not of the assassination, but of President Kennedy in some abstract or idealized sense, the first question to consider is, did it work? To some extent, the answer is yes. The years following the assassination did mark a turn away from the divisive politics of the past, at least insofar as the vocal right-wing minority was concerned. Those who made up that minority were still there, to be sure, but if anything, their ability to make headlines in the city was lessened. Dallas contended with some of the same problems other major urban areas in the United States faced in the 1960s: integration and other racially related issues, poverty, and decay of city centers. However, it was a source of relief to many that there were no more embarrassing incidents set off by the far-right. Several ultraconservative officeholders lost their bids for reelection in the years after Kennedy's assassination, and although they had never dominated Dallas' municipal government, their respective defeats gave the leadership and representation of the city a decisively moderate character.[78] Mayor Earle Cabell, for example, resigned his office in 1964 to challenge Bruce Alger for his congressional seat and defeated the incumbent comfortably. Divisions within the city certainly persisted, but the emphasis became "a return to political moderation and consensus building," with "refocused attention on the city rather than on political or ideological issues."[79] Even some who were critics of the "oligarchic" character of the Dallas governing establishment favorably noted the new citywide agenda. Dallas addressed the challenges of desegregation, voting rights and city representation, and more open governance—all of which helped to at least partially cleanse the stain left by the assassination and the political atmosphere of the city which then prevailed.[80]

In the years after the assassination, some local observers did argue that there was a greater degree of tolerance and concern for problem-solving within the city.[81] Reverend Holmes, the Methodist minister who had spoken out against the city on the Sunday after the assassination and who had been threatened because of his harsh sermon, later recalled that he thought the atmosphere in the city did change for the better. The extreme right-wing, as he remembered, was greatly discredited and did not enjoy as much notoriety in later years, and "the Dallas majority seized the city and took responsibility for creating a new climate in the city. My impression is that, not long thereafter, a lot of good things happened in Dallas...my impression was that in the years that followed, Dallas reclaimed a far more moderate point of view and image for the city."[82] The *Dallas Times Herald*, which had previously lamented the mixture of hatred and violence that had infected the city, casting it through "the dark night of the soul,"[83] later praised Dallas for having come so far in shaking off its maladies, and for dedicating itself to civic improvement. In an article in the *Times Herald* appearing on January 3, 1971, looking back on the events of 1970 (the year the Kennedy memorial was completed), the newspaper mentioned several ways the city was vibrant and compassionate, with no trace of the discord that had been apparent just a few years earlier. With the war in Vietnam still the greatest ongoing national problem at the end of the year, the *Times Herald* observed, "Many things were wrong in the world in 1970...But in Dallas, in 1970, many things were right. Although many cities slumbered in apathy last year, Dallas proved its concern for the world, for human misery and suffering, time and again in 1970."[84] The article detailed the city's many contributions to charitable organizations and fundraising drives. Even the Dallas Police Department, so reviled after the Kennedy and Oswald slayings, received praise, as the newspaper suggested a new motto for the department reflective of the mood of the city: "We care."[85]

The memorial was only one step Dallas took to refocus itself on civic issues. A civic improvement campaign was established in the years after the assassination under the direction of Mayor J. Erik Jonsson.

The impetus for this initiative, as Jonsson acknowledged, was indeed the negative image of Dallas that dominated post-1963. The project's objective, later published in book form as *Goals for Dallas*, was to identify the city's problems and propose solutions by engaging ordinary citizens along the way. The process was as important as the results; by taking stock of itself in a democratic and more bottom-up manner, Dallas could begin to push itself away from JFK's death and dilute the concentration of political and economic power by the city "oligarchy." Goals for Dallas, Mayor Jonsson said, "would get the people of the city involved and keep them busy thinking about what they were trying to build here in the way of a city...that could certainly demonstrate that we were anything but a City of Hate."[86]

Jonsson saw the assassination as an opportunity to unite the city through community-oriented action, as opposed to city leaders deciding from above what Dallas' priorities would be. Far from simply addressing infrastructure needs, the initiative examined citywide quality of life problems.[87] Many saw the Goals for Dallas initiative as a major impetus behind the period of improvement and expansion that Dallas experienced in the decade after the assassination. Some of the more notable accomplishments included the successful planning and construction with Fort Worth of the Dallas/Fort Worth International Airport, the establishment of a local branch of the University of Texas,[88] improvement of public libraries, and the construction of a strikingly original new City Hall.[89] The Goals for Dallas program led to a greater citywide concern with the welfare of Dallas, and, as one author wrote, it "was credited with helping the city recover emotionally from the assassination." It is fair to say that the political atmosphere of Dallas did shift in favor of a more moderate type of governance; that same author also argued that, "the Kennedy assassination brought the city together in the midst of outside criticism and gave a rebirth—albeit a temporary one—to the 'city as a whole' approach to local government."[90]

If in fact the city had successfully remade itself, it would be an overreach to attribute the new era of good feelings solely to its efforts to memorialize JFK. Beyond the memorialization Dallas undertook, the simple persistence of memory precluded any quick relegation of the assassination to the past. For many years afterward, people around the nation and around the world remembered Dallas as the place where John Kennedy had met his untimely death.[91] This stigma persisted, even as everyone moved on and came to terms with what had happened. One history professor at Southern Methodist University, who did not begin teaching there until several years after 1963 , still recalled people's responses upon telling them he was from Dallas. People remarked, "That's where they killed... Dallas? Oh, you're from Dallas? That's where they kill presidents."[92] Dallas moved on, but for a long time, the event was something many residents preferred not to talk about. Although the city later became known for other, more positive things, such as the 1980s-era soap opera *Dallas* and the Dallas Cowboys of the 1990s, the fact that JFK died there still lingered long after his fateful visit.

Dallas' goal, in the decades after Kennedy, was to portray its dedication to moderation and progress. Still, changes in the city's character in later years tended to be judged in terms of how they helped Dallas cope with the ever-present albatross of the assassination. And although the event was not exactly the most popular topic of conversation around town, it was still very much on the minds of many, both inside and outside Dallas.[93] Perhaps the best proof of these lingering thoughts was the repeated references to the assassination made in the context of citywide development and efforts to present an image of Dallas as a truly national and international center of commerce and culture. In 1978, a *New York Times* article on the completion of the well-known Reunion Tower, and the ongoing work to advertise the region as a cosmopolitan, business-friendly locale, still employed the events of 1963 as the measuring stick of the city's progress. New architectural landmarks remaking the city skyline, the *Times* said, represented the new Dallas, but the nearby Texas School Book Depository still represented the past that many preferred to forget.[94]

That same year, another article noted that the assassination stigma might have eased somewhat with the passage of time, but it had not been totally erased. Certainly the political leadership in the city desired to turn away from 1963. City Councilman (and later Mayor) Steve Bartlett commented hopefully, "I think the majority of people just wish it would go away. Dallas has changed and evolved into a different kind of city. I think that most people hope that after the Assassination Committee [the House Select Committee on Assassinations] finishes its work they won't have to learn about it except in the history books."[95] And several years later, the election of A. Starke Taylor, Jr. as mayor brought the spotlight again on the assassination and how the event had influenced the city's history and politics. Twenty years after President Kennedy had come to town, "the city seems determined to purge itself of whatever residue of civic shame that might remain," and Taylor was more than ready to consign the event to the past.[96]

But the assassination surfaced again shortly thereafter as the city prepared to host the 1984 Republican National Convention. The successful completion of such a high-profile event would spread the new vision of Dallas that its civic leadership strove for. Nevertheless, it seemed as if the city still had something to prove—that it was a changed city and that the assassination was no longer an active force in Dallas' psyche. In that sense, things had not changed much from 1963. Dallas still felt the need to "exorcise the specter of the assassination."[97] Whatever else the city might achieve, events and symbols alone could not delete the association between Dallas and JFK's death from the public's memory. That unpleasant fact would seemingly be strengthened with the approach of each major anniversary of the assassination, even while those solemn milestones moved observers to remark that Dallas had indeed changed for the better in the interregnum. But noting how far the city had come only served to resurrect, yet again, the fact that the assassination remained an ever-present facet of the city's makeup.[98]

The Kennedy memorial, therefore, did not cause people to forget what had happened a mere block away. But it was part of an effort to rework the image of the city, an effort that was (and continues to be) aided by time and the resulting cooling of passions. Giving the city a much cleaner bill of health, as the *Dallas Times Herald* did at the beginning of 1971, may have been premature, but it did anticipate a time in which Dallasites would not have President Kennedy's death constantly overhead—a time when the public's memory of him would not automatically dredge up hatred toward Dallas. On the 25th anniversary of the assassination in 1988, the *New York Times* noted at least one effect of the passage of time: "Few people here or elsewhere blame Dallas anymore for the assassination," and cited a recent national survey showing that only 11 percent of those polled associated the city first and foremost with JFK. Only 4 percent thought that the city's atmosphere had led to the president's death.[99]

Such may have been the state of things in 1988. But in the years immediately following JFK's death, many in Dallas saw some sort of public atonement for the event as necessary if the city were ever to shake off the stigma directed toward it. Pairing the ideals he believed in with the goals of the city enabled Dallas to make amends by invoking the public's memory of the late president. In this manner, Dallas could argue that it did what he would have done. City leaders recognized the power contained in the popular memory of JFK and used it accordingly. The process of building a memorial coincided with an improvement in the city's perception of itself, and if observers such as J.M. Shea were correct to link the future of the city with how it paid tribute to Kennedy, building a physical memorial and making the entire city a "memorial" to his beliefs did give Dallas' stock a much-needed boost.

Curiously, one factor working in the city's favor was the national dissension and violence that were so painfully apparent during the remainder of the decade. Some speculated in the days after Kennedy's death that Dallas would forever be vilified in a way that the two other American cities where presidents were assassinated were not, that it would assume a place in history alongside Auschwitz, Sarajevo, and Munich.[100] But if many thought Dallas had been solely responsible for what happened, later events of the 1960s may have changed their minds. The rifts within American society, exemplified by the later deaths of Malcolm X, Martin Luther King, Jr., and Robert F. Kennedy, suggested that JFK truly could have been assassinated anywhere.[101] Dallas could hardly be blamed for an act of violence that turned out to be only the first in a series of such events marking a divided and troubled era.

But if the memorial was intended to direct people's attention and memory away from the assassination, it was unsuccessful. Before and after the completion of the Kennedy memorial, the center of gravity of the public's memory and interest in him continued to be Dealey Plaza. With the establishment of the Sixth Floor Museum in the late 1980s, the official Dallas memorial to President Kennedy was largely forgotten. Visitors to Dallas seeking to pay tribute to him went instead to the assassination site.[102] The original intention of the memorial committee may have been to place it in the plaza, but moving the memorial elsewhere resulted in eliminating it entirely from the process of remembering. Despite the successful effort by city leaders to relocate the memorial, visitors through the years have consistently gone to the museum and the plaza instead, considering them to be the most meaningful places for reflection and remembering.[103]

The Sixth Floor Museum, like the official Kennedy memorial, was born out of the polar opposites in Dallas set in motion by the assassination: the need to remember and the desire to forget. The school book company housed in the building in 1963 vacated it several years later, and some advocated razing the depository—if not to forget, then at least to preclude it becoming an unseemly tourist curiosity.[104] City and county officials legitimately feared that it might become a cash cow for an unscrupulous developer, but public interest in the building never abated. Dallas County acquired the structure in 1977 and established offices there. The seemingly surreal atmosphere, with everyday county business inside juxtaposed with the ever-present visitors exploring the plaza outside as if it were still November 1963, led to calls for a JFK exhibit to satisfy the public's fascination. A museum charged with forthrightly explaining the death of the president, instead of submersing the event in abstraction as the Johnson memorial had done, seemed both necessary and appropriate with the approach of the 25th anniversary of the assassination in 1988.[105]

The creation of the Sixth Floor Museum at Dealey Plaza—on the very floor and around the very window from which Lee Harvey Oswald shot President Kennedy—satisfied visitors' need for narrative about the assassination, historical context, and commemoration. The focal point of the exhibit is the corner window; it has been sealed off and boxes placed around it in the same way that it was found by police on November 22, 1963. From adjacent windows, visitors can see what Oswald was looking at as he was shooting. Museum visitors go from the first directly to the sixth (or seventh) floor of the building. Whatever is housed on the intermediate floors is not available, as if the rest of the building doesn't matter. Those two floors are now directed to one purpose: that of recreating the setting for what has been called by so many people the "darkest day in Dallas' history."

But if the Sixth Floor Museum has become the public's unofficial memorial, those who created the museum intended for the exhibits to discuss more than just the assassination itself. The corner window may be the principal object of interest when people visit, but museum designers refrained from over-dramatizing the act of assassination.[106] There is no gun protruding from the window, and the items visitors see before getting there are boards with photos and information on John Kennedy's life, family, and campaign for president. What is memorialized here, in other words, is not simply the president's violent death but his entire life as well. The purpose of the exhibit as a whole is to leave visitors with more than just physical reminders of what happened in that building on the day Kennedy came to Dallas.[107] In this sense, the museum fulfills the same purpose as the memorial—there is not just one aspect of Kennedy that is being remembered. The museum, however, is far more explicit about what it is remembering, which is part of what makes it the more attractive locale for visitors. Perhaps more than the memorial, it is the museum situated at the assassination site that gave the city the ability to move on. This sentiment appears repeatedly in the memory books placed at the end of the tour for visitors to record their thoughts. Many of those who viewed the exhibit when it opened in 1989 believed it was long overdue, not only for its examination of the assassination, but also for enabling the city to remember, honor, and give people a chance to reflect. As two visitors expressed, "This museum puts a final chapter to this tragic event for Dallas," and "You have given Dallas something not to be ashamed of –let us now look forward!"[108] By discussing the assassination directly instead of trying to downplay it—in a manner that still truthfully presented it as an historical event and that gave visitors a place to remember—Dallas may have come closer to coping with the tragedy with the museum than through the actual memorial.[109] Establishing the exhibit took courage, with November 1963 still a tender subject for some even two decades later. As Lindalyn Adams, one of the exhibit's creators, stated in a *Dallas Times Herald* article shortly before the opening of the Sixth Floor Museum, "How remarkable it is, then, that we have been able to put our own sensitivities aside and fulfill our historic responsibility."[110]

The irony here is that the chief instrument the city created to aid people in remembering has been itself largely forgotten. Why is this? It is due in part to the fact that the memorial is physically separated from the assassination site. People come to Dealey Plaza, visit the museum, and walk around the grassy knoll, but the official memorial is nowhere in sight. Many who walk a block east from the plaza to see it are confused as to its meaning, and to what they are supposed to take away from it. The architect intended his design to commemorate Kennedy's life, but intentionally made it ambiguous as to what the memorial was meant to say. Viewers aren't sure what to think of it—they don't know its meaning or significance.[111]

This confusion indicates the influence of the popular memory of Kennedy. Part of the reason why the public prefers Dealey Plaza over the memorial is because of the absence of any central message in Philip Johnson's creation—because popular memory of President Kennedy acts to dictate what sort of memorial people expect to see. Visitors expect to encounter a statue or some sort of likeness of the late president, or perhaps an eternal flame, or a plaque with words from his inaugural address—something that will indicate the point of the memorial. But with its "enforced neutrality," the memorial fails to reinforce the American people's popular perceptions of JFK, so they go elsewhere to reflect.[112]

This lack of interest raises the question, why bother studying the memorial at all? Since it seems to have been generally ignored from its completion until today, what is the relevance of the memorial as far as the subject matter of this study is concerned? While it is true that the Kennedy memorial has been forgotten to a great extent, it is still worthy of study for at least two reasons. First, the memorial formed a major part of Dallas' response to the assassination. It was an answer to the national and international condemnation so apparent in the correspondence flooding city hall in the days and weeks after the tragic event. The memorial, however much it might seem out of place today, was nevertheless the city's way of coming to terms with the events of November 22, 1963. As an act of penance, it sheds light on what Dallas was like before, and in the period immediately after, President Kennedy visited. The fact that it exists at all should lead to questions as to why it was built, why Dallas city leaders thought such a memorial was necessary, how it proved to be relevant (or not) in the overall process of memorialization, and what that process meant to a city trying to recover from what was arguably the greatest crime in its history. Such are the questions this chapter has tried to address.

There is a second reason why the memorial should not be ignored by historians, even if it has been more or less forgotten by the general public. The memorial is relevant because, quite simply, it is part of the process of memorialization. It is no less important than the role played by the museum, Lyndon Johnson, or Robert Kennedy. In the end, the value of the memorial may be the process by which it came to be, if not the actual structure itself. The importance of it may lie in the story of why it was created, as opposed to what was created. As part of that process, the Kennedy memorial was one of the first attempts by anyone to ascertain how JFK should be remembered and for what purpose. City leaders gave the popular memory of JFK an importance that, arguably, other cities did not. Dallas was not the only city that expressed sorrow and union with Kennedy through the building of a memorial. But what makes the case of Dallas different is that it alone was reviled because people thought that it had somehow facilitated his death. The process of memorialization taking place there in the years afterward reflected the collective sorrow of Dallasites, but there had to be something else at work. So the significance that the public's memory of JFK was given in Dallas was different from what occurred elsewhere, for the task that the city faced was different. It was important to recognize Kennedy for all of his accomplishments (or for those things Americans consistently argued were his accomplishments), but of equal importance was the opportunity Dallas had to employ him in the effort to create a "new" city. Taking advantage of the emotion expended by the assassination and the state funeral reminiscent of Lincoln's, Dallas found a way to tacitly acknowledge what had happened and honor John F. Kennedy without making it seem as if the city was also admitting guilt.

Nor did the city fail in the years ahead to publicly express its continuing fidelity to the Kennedy ideals. Dallas had learned from the assassination and had rejected the politics of extremism that many thought had taken over by 1963. In a speech given on the four-year anniversary of the event in 1967, Mayor Jonsson reconnected the link between JFK and the city where he died, the city that had now adopted JFK as the standard by which citizens' commitments to unity and civic responsibility were measured. Speaking in Dealey Plaza, Jonsson declared, "We meet to renew in prayer our commitment to the principles upon which this nation was founded and for which he stood and labored...We are caused to remember: A man is truly free only as he is likewise responsible. John F. Kennedy lived in this way and thus he lives on."[113] President Kennedy, the implication was, would have been pleased if he could have seen how far Dallas had come. "Thus it is that in recent months, thousands of citizens of Dallas—representatives of all walks of life, backgrounds, creeds, races, viewpoints, interests, occupations, age—have worked with diligence and dedication for continuing renewal consistent with the highest ideals... and with the highest order of unity."[114]

In memorializing JFK, Dallas demonstrated not only the practical uses of popular memory, but also its malleability. While it is true that the public's memory of him remains dominated by his glamour, wit, inspiring rhetoric, youth, exhortations to Americans to sacrifice in the name of the country and the world, and his tragic death, Dallas chose to emphasize those parts of the popular memory that served its purpose: the president's moderation, tolerance, and civic-mindedness. Dallas leadership feared that the city would never be able to shake off the acrimony aroused by its perceived guilt if the sole or dominant memory of JFK it reinforced through a memorial was associated with violence or tragedy.[115] Moving on would be impossible if the message Dallas conveyed was that, at the risk of employing a cliché, the dream had died there. The clearest proof of this sensitivity is how many handled the task of creating the memorial. Former Dallas mayor R.L. Thornton, it is fair to say, probably expressed quite accurately the private opinion of many when he commented two weeks after the assassination, "For my part, I don't want anything to remind me that a president was killed in the streets of Dallas. I want to forget."[116]

The decisions made by the city as to how JFK would be remembered were guided by this concern. The memorial was not situated in Dealey Plaza so that the city could use it to commemorate something about Kennedy other than his death—as many people who wrote to city hall and the memorial committee advised. The Kennedy memorial's message or lesson, although ambiguous, also enabled many to claim (and, owing to the design, not untruthfully) that its purpose was to remember JFK's life and the way he lived. A special book printed to commemorate the memorial's completion argued, "It is not a memorial to the pain and sorrow of death, but stands as a permanent tribute to the joy and excitement of one man's cause. The life of John Fitzgerald Kennedy."[117] More than building only a physical memorial, Dallas tried to create a "living" memorial as well through a renewed commitment to civic responsibility, equality, and tolerance. In celebrating Kennedy's life, Dallasites could argue that, in their city, the Kennedy "dream" had not died at all, but lived on.

Dallas city leaders were not the only ones who sought to harness the power of the popular memory of John Kennedy to accomplish their objectives. As was true with Joan of Arc in the Pierre Nora anthology, memory of JFK was both well-suited to practical ends and multifaceted, enabling its use by practically any individual or group. This memorialization was certainly the case with Dallas, and it was also true with Lyndon B. Johnson. The fact that the public was so overwhelmed by images of President Kennedy meant that the ability to link oneself or one's cause with him could give legitimacy to act in his name. This phenomenon was perhaps nowhere more evident than on the national level with LBJ. Johnson quickly saw the advantages of not only associating himself with Kennedy, but with invoking the memory of the slain leader to advance the legislative agenda he had been unable to pass during his brief tenure. In working to pass social welfare legislation, especially the civil rights legislation of the mid-1960s, Lyndon Johnson argued that only by picking up where JFK had left off could the American people properly, and fully, do him homage.

Notes

1. H.D. Quigg, "Town in Torment," in Bruce Catton (ed.), *Four Days: The Historical Record of the Death of President Kennedy compiled by United Press International and American Heritage Magazine* (New York: American Heritage Publishing Co., Inc., 1964), 61.
2. Ibid., 60; and Richard Austin Smith, "How Business Failed Dallas," *Fortune 500* July 1964 (Vol. LXX, No. 1), 159.
3. Darwin Payne, *Big D: Triumphs and Troubles of an American Supercity in the 20th Century* (Dallas: Three Forks Press, 1994), 307; and Steve Blow and Sam Attlesey, "The Tenor of the Times," in Blow, et al., *November 22*, 2.
4. Transcript. Rev. William A. Holmes Oral History Interview, 3/2/2007, by Stephen Fagin. Oral History Collection, The Sixth Floor Museum at Dealey Plaza, Dallas, Texas.
5. Texas voted for the JFK-LBJ ticket in 1960, but the administration was viewed with suspicion by the extreme right. In his examination of the political character of Dallas in the early 1960s, Warren Leslie noted that the city had "a seemingly inexhaustible supply of young and middle-aged people, most of them college-educated, who see black and white and nothing else. Almost without exception, these are people who feel that their greatest enemy is not the Soviet Union or Communist China, but the government of the United States." Leslie continued, "During the Kennedy Administration, an expressed admiration for the President could literally ruin a dinner party." Darwin Payne, *Big D*, 308-309; and Warren Leslie, *Dallas Public and Private: Aspects of an American City* (New York: Grossman Publishers, 1964), 89-90.
6. Bill Minutaglio and Steven L. Davis, *Dallas 1963* (New York: Twelve, 2013), 97, 221-222.
7. Steve Blow and Sam Attlesey, "The Tenor of the Times," in Blow, et al., *November 22*, 4-5.
8. Darwin Payne, *Big D*, 312-313.
9. KRLD reporter Bill Mercer, who helped cover the events of the assassination weekend, later commented, "I wasn't worried about [President Kennedy's] physical safety, but like my colleagues, I feared that some of the strongest anti-Kennedy groups would somehow embarrass him and his entourage...I could not imagine what might happen—maybe huge

signs, people throwing things. A gut feeling was churning around that Kennedy would be insulted by one of the highly charged groups in Dallas." Bill Mercer, "Gunman, Mob, and Mourners," in Bob Huffaker, et al., *When the News Went Live: Dallas 1963* (Lanham: Taylor Trade Publishing, 2004), 93.

10. Darwin Payne, *Big D*, 305-306; and Allen Duckworth, "Senator Jeered at Dallas Hotel," *Dallas Morning News* November 5, 1960, 1.
11. Steve Blow and Sam Attlesey, "The Tenor of the Times," in Blow, et al., *November 22*, 2.
12. Conover Hunt, *JFK for a New Generation*, 3.
13. Steve Blow and Sam Attlesey, "The Tenor of the Times," in Blow, et al., *November 22*, 3; and Mike Quinn, "Stevenson Struck with Sign, Booed," *Dallas Morning News* October 25, 1963, 1.
14. Darwin Payne, *Big D*, 313.
15. Ibid., 313-314.
16. Skelton had sent several letters to the administration expressing concern that a presidential visit to the city was not a good idea. In his November 4, 1963 letter to RFK, Skelton had cited a comment from General Walker that, "Kennedy is a liability to the free world." In a letter sent two days later to LBJ aide Walter Jenkins, Skelton said, "We are looking forward to the visit of the President and Vice President to Texas, although I have some misgivings about their visiting Dallas. I would prefer that they not do so." Letters to Robert F. Kennedy and Walter Jenkins (Box 1), in Byron Skelton papers, Lyndon B. Johnson Presidential Library, Austin, Texas.
17. Steve Blow and Sam Attlesey, "The Tenor of the Times," in Blow, et al., *November 22*, 5; and Richard Austin Smith, "How Business Failed Dallas," in *Fortune 500*, 157-158.
18. *Dallas Morning News* editorial, November 22, 1963 (Box 91, Folder 11, "Kennedy-Related, 1963-1967"), in J. Erik Jonsson papers, DeGolyer Special Collections Library, Southern Methodist University, Dallas, Texas, A1998.2191.
19. *Dallas Morning News* advertisement, November 22, 1963 ("Unprocessed Marcus Home Letters, 1964-1967 Kennedy Assassination"), in Stanley Marcus papers, DeGolyer Special Collections Library, Southern Methodist University, Dallas, Texas, A1993.1869.
20. Leaflets with the same charges against the President had also been distributed during Ambassador Stevenson's visit. Ibid.; and Warren Leslie, *Dallas Public and Private*, 198-199.
21. Robert Dallek, *An Unfinished Life*, 693.

22. Bill Minutaglio and Steven L. Davis, *Dallas 1963*, 290.

23. Darwin Payne, "JFK Death Left Deep City Imprint," *Dallas Times Herald,* November 22, 1964, 1A, 26A; and Fred Powledge, "Kennedy Epilogue: A Shocked Dallas Changing Its Ways," *New York Times,* November 22, 1964, 1, 74.

24. Dallas' reputation certainly did not benefit from a rumor that emerged in the hours after the assassination that an elementary school class had begun cheering upon hearing news of the tragedy. Although KRLD newsman Bill Mercer recalled years later that the story had been reported by an anonymous citizen, and its truthfulness doubted by KRLD, it was later aired via CBS on national television—only adding to the stigma the city was confronting. The exact location of this incident—and for that matter, the very credibility of the report—has apparently never been verified. One elementary school in University Park (near Southern Methodist University) was suspected to have been the site of the schoolchildren cheering, but the school's administration later asserted that such a rumor was untrue. They claimed that any cheering may have resulted from children learning that school was cancelled, apart from news of the assassination. Dallas schools superintendent W.T. White took the rumor seriously enough to investigate whether the cheering had come from his district. White later released a statement affirming that no fourth-grade class (as the rumor claimed) in the Dallas schools had cheered. He also said he contacted the original source of the story (a minister), but that source refused to talk to him about the matter. Bob Huffaker, "Epicenter of Grief," and Bill Mercer, "Gunman, Mob, and Mourners," in Bob Huffaker, et al., *When the News Went Live,* 68, 102; and Letters to Mayor Cabell (Box 11, Folder 8, "Earle Cabell Mayoral Correspondence, December 1-5, 1963") in Earle Cabell papers, DeGolyer Special Collections Library, Southern Methodist University, Dallas, Texas, Mss 0016.

25. Michel Kurtz details the failure of the Dallas Police to conduct a careful investigation. In the interest of accuracy, however, the work done by federal authorities in their own inquiries into the President's death was hardly any better. Michael L. Kurtz, *The JFK Assassination Debates,* 23-26; and Darwin Payne, "J. Erik Jonsson: Center Stage at a National Tragedy," *Legacies* Fall 2006 (Vol. 18, No. 2), 8.

26. Letters to Mayor Cabell (Box 11, Folder 1, "Earle Cabell Mayoral Correspondence, Kennedy Assassination, November 24, 1963") in Earle Cabell papers.

27. Ibid.

28. Telegrams to Mayor Cabell (Box 11, Folder 13, "Kennedy Assassination Telegrams") in Earle Cabell papers.

29. Letters to Mayor Cabell (Box 11, Folder 12, "Earle Cabell Mayoral Correspondence, Kennedy Assassination") in Earle Cabell papers.

30. Telegrams to Mayor Earle (Box 11, Folder 13, "Kennedy Assassination Telegrams") in Earle Cabell papers.

31. "The Johnson Style," *The New Republic* December 7, 1963 (Vol. 149, No. 23, Issue 2557), 29.

32. Michael V. Hazel, "Earle Cabell: Calm Leadership in a Time of Crisis," *Legacies* Fall 2006 (Vol. 18, No. 2), 51.

33. In a momentous decision, National Football League Commissioner Pete Rozelle had decided that the games scheduled for the weekend after the assassination would not be cancelled. John Rosenfield, "Our Geographical 'Guilt,'" *Dallas Morning News* December 5, 1963, 4-2; and David Maraniss, *When Pride Still Mattered: A Life of Vince Lombardi* (New York: Touchstone, 1999), 351.

34. Rabbi Levi Olan of Dallas' Temple Emanu-El was one of the more prominent observers of the sensitivity of some in Dallas to any suggestion that something was wrong with the city. He noted this lingering state of denial in a radio sermon in January 1964, but even a year after the assassination, he believed that the city was still primarily concerned with improving its image. Few were interested, according to him, in probing the true extent of Dallas' problems that the assassination had highlighted. "What Should Dallas Do Now?" January 19, 1964; and "The First Anniversary of a Tragedy" November 22, 1964 (Box 780, Folder 28, "Speeches—Temple Emanu-El Radio Program Scripts, 1964") in the Collection on Levi Olan, Bridwell Library, Perkins School of Theology, Southern Methodist University.

35. Mayor Cabell himself was not immune from this accusation, his later statement in tribute to Kennedy notwithstanding. In a religious journal article one month after the assassination, one author recalled, "I watched the Mayor speak on television. It was clear that his concern was not to find out, at whatever cost, the whole truth. It was rather to establish, in whatever haste, the innocence of Dallas. The Mayor was the town's high priest, and its Pilate." "Dallas Asks Why It Happened; Worry Over 'Image' is Voiced," *New York Times,* November 24, 1963, 2; and Tom F. Driver, "Thoughts on the Day of the Funeral," *Christianity and Crisis,* December 23, 1963 (Vol. 23, No. 22), 239.

36. Transcript. J. Erik Jonsson Oral History Interview, 6/30/1992, by Wes Wise with Bob Porter. Oral History Collection, The Sixth Floor Museum at Dealey Plaza, Dallas, Texas.

37. In an extensive examination of Dallas' state of development and leadership shortly after the assassination, *Fortune 500* noted the domination of civic affairs by the "oligarchic" Dallas Citizens Council that made the city a hobgoblin of contradictions. While there was a genuine spirit of civic mindedness, city leaders were also reluctant to address problems such as poverty. An overriding attitude of conformity and complacency prevailed. As Richard Austin Smith stated, "This lack of running dissent has robbed Dallas of the tension it needs to become a truly great city... The leadership obviously can't go on building new fifty-story skyscrapers; it will have to build a well-rounded city and invite, even court, dissent." Ibid.; and Richard Austin Smith, "How Business Failed Dallas," in *Fortune 500*, 158-163, 216.

38. "Group Asks Suggestions on Memorial," *Dallas Morning News*, December 5, 1963, 1-20.

39. In eulogies to Kennedy delivered by congressional leaders, Senator Mike Mansfield praised the late president for combating prejudice and hatred; House Speaker John McCormack asserted, "President John F. Kennedy possessed all the qualities of greatness." Congressman Spark Matsunaga of Hawaii compared JFK with Abraham Lincoln, as did Paul Findley of Illinois. Both believed Kennedy, like Lincoln, had been martyred in the pursuit of equal rights for all. *Congressional Record*, November 26, 1963 (Vol. 109, Pt. 17, F. 3/4), 22695, 22818.

40. Jim F. Heath, *Decade of Disillusionment*, 153.

41. *Detroit Free Press* editorial, November 23, 1963 (Box 90, Folder 39, "Kennedy Assassination 1967) in Earle Cabell papers.

42. Darwin Payne, "J. Erik Jonsson," in *Legacies*, 8.

43. Lacie Ballinger, *The Rededication of the John Fitzgerald Kennedy Memorial: June 24, 2000* (Dallas: The Sixth Floor Museum, 2000), 2.

44. Michael V. Hazel, "Earle Cabell," in *Legacies*, 51-52.

45. Ibid.

46. Warren Leslie lent his support to the image of Kennedy as the paragon of civic mindedness when he advised that a focus on "excellence" in the spirit of the late president would be most appropriate: "The people of Dallas might well recall President Kennedy's quest for excellence. When something was to be written, he wanted it written well...when a man said something, he wanted it to make sense and to shed new light...If he

could have his choice, I think he would wish his memorial in Dallas to be the pursuit of excellence in the city in which he died." Warren Leslie, *Dallas Public and Private*, 227-228.

47. Press release (Box 11, Folder 15, "Press Release—Cabell's Statement on Death of JFK") in Earle Cabell papers.

48. Letters to Mayor Cabell (Box 11, Folder 5, "Earle Cabell Mayoral Correspondence, November 27, 1963") in Earle Cabell papers.

49. H.D. Quigg, "Town in Torment," in Bruce Catton, ed., *Four Days*, 61.

50. Magazine article, "Memo from a Dallas Citizen," in *Look*, March 24, 1964, 88 ("Unprocessed Home Letters, 1964-1967 Kennedy Assassination Newsclips") in Stanley Marcus papers.

51. Ibid., 94.

52. Shea's comments notwithstanding, completion of any memorial at all was hardly assured. Direction of a memorial project, while technically in the hands of a private committee, was still influenced by the city and county. No memorial would be built at Dealey Plaza, and even after the final site was selected, some city and county officials apparently still thought the land could be put to better use. Ibid., 88; and David Dillon, "Making of a Memorial: Seeking the Appropriate," *Dallas Morning News*, November 20, 1983, 67.

53. Transcript, Rev. William A. Holmes Oral History Interview; and "One Thing Worse Than This," William A. Holmes, Subject Files: Holmes, William A. Bridwell Library, Perkins School of Theology, Southern Methodist University.

54. Or, as Lone Star Gas President Lester T. Potter put it, "It was not Dallas, and Dallas should not purge itself." Craig Flournoy, "Dallas on Trial: Accusations and Self-Doubts Torment the City," in Blow, et al., *November 22*, 144; and Richard Austin Smith, "How Business Failed Dallas," in *Fortune 500*, 159.

55. This opinion was shared by many. *Life* reported that the initial feelings of shame by city leaders were never followed up with concrete actions to examine the amount of culpability Dallas had in creating an inhospitable atmosphere at the time of President Kennedy's visit. An attitude of defensiveness, only two months after JFK's death, seemed to prevail. Letters to Mayor Cabell (Box 11, Folder 8, "Earle Cabell Mayoral Correspondence, December 1-5, 1963") in Earle Cabell papers; and Robert Wallace, "What Kind of Place is Dallas?" *Life* January 31, 1964 (Vol. 56, No. 5), 70.

56. JFK memorial committee records (Box 11, Folder 16, "Citizen's Memorial to JFK"), in Earle Cabell papers.

57. Ibid.

58. Letters to Mayor Cabell (Box 11, Folder 9, "Earle Cabell Mayoral Correspondence, December 6-31, 1963") in Earle Cabell papers.

59. Arlinda Abbot, *Dealey Plaza: The Front Door of Dallas* (Dallas: The Sixth Floor Museum, 2003), 14.

60. Lacie Ballinger, *The Rededication of the John Fitzgerald Kennedy Memorial*, 5.

61. Ibid., 2-3.

62. W.J. Rorabaugh, *Kennedy and the Promise of the Sixties* (Cambridge: Cambridge University Press, 2002), 225.

63. Ibid., 227.

64. JFK memorial committee records (Box 11, Folder 16, "Citizen's Memorial to JFK"), in Earle Cabell papers.

65. Letters to Mayor Cabell (Box 11, Folder 9, "Earle Cabell Mayoral Correspondence, December 6-31, 1963") in Earle Cabell papers.

66. JFK memorial committee records (Box 11, Folder 16, "Citizen's Memorial to JFK"), in Earle Cabell papers.

67. Ibid.

68. Ibid

69. Ibid.

70. For the sake of comparison, Dallas' memorialization efforts were ultimately more successful than those of the state of Texas. A state memorial committee was created, but had similar problems generating enough money and public interest. The committee folded in 1970, and no state memorial to Kennedy was built. Frank D. Welch, *Philip Johnson & Texas* (Austin: University of Texas Press, 2000), 123-125; and David Dillon, "Making of a Memorial," in *Dallas Morning News*, 67.

71. Lacie Ballinger, *The Rededication of the John Fitzgerald Kennedy Memorial*, 2-3, 12-13, 30.

72. Johnson's original intention was to have depicted excerpts from Kennedy's speeches on the memorial. Dallas city leaders were apparently not keen on that idea, and no inscription other than "John Fitzgerald Kennedy" appears on the structure. Frank D. Welch, *Philip Johnson*, 123-125.

73. Lacie Ballinger, *The Rededication of the John Fitzgerald Kennedy Memorial*, 27-29.

74. Ibid., 26-29.

75. Lacie Ballinger, *The Rededication of the John Fitzgerald Kennedy Memorial,* 18-19.

76. Frank D. Welch, *Philip Johnson,* 123-125.

77. In his history of Dallas, Harvey Graff argues that the city may have wanted to remember JFK, but this effort was largely overridden by the desire to simply forget the assassination and move on; this, more than anything else, led to a memorial design that was uninspiring and largely devoid of meaning. Even civic leaders such as J. Erik Jonsson and Stanley Marcus, according to Graff, were ultimately more interested in refocusing attention away from the assassination instead of making a genuine effort to understand the meaning of the event and what Dallas' role in it was. The entire process of memorial construction, as well the fact that it was forgotten and allowed to fall into disrepair in the following decades, suggested that the city's attempt to honor the late president was largely superficial. Harvey Graff, *The Dallas Myth: The Making and Unmaking of an American City* (Minneapolis: University of Minnesota Press, 2008), 21-24.

78. Dick Hitt, "Dallas Stunned as World Turns Anger on the City," *Dallas Times Herald,* November 21, 1973, C1, C5.

79. Robert B. Fairbanks, "The Assassination and Dallas Politics: Changes to Continuity," *Legacies* Fall 1998 (Vol. 10, No. 2), 19.

80. Video recording. Jerry Bartos Oral History Interview, 3/8/2004, by Stephen Fagin. Oral History Collection, The Sixth Floor Museum at Dealey Plaza, Dallas, Texas; and Video recording. Bronson Havard Oral History Interview.

81. "The Legacy of Kennedy," *Dallas Times Herald,* November 22, 1973, 2D.

82. Transcript. Rev. William A. Holmes Oral History Interview.

83. H.D. Quigg, "Town in Torment," in Bruce Catton, ed., *Four Days,* 60.

84. *Dallas Times Herald* article, January 3, 1971 (Box 106, Folder 3, "Clippings—City of Dallas Image and Reputation, 1965-1971") in J. Erik Jonsson papers.

85. Ibid.

86. Transcript. J. Erik Jonsson Oral History Interview, 8/17/1992, by Wes Wise with Bob Porter. Oral History Collection, The Sixth Floor Museum at Dealey Plaza, Dallas, Texas.

87. Robert Fairbanks, *For the City as a Whole: Planning, Politics, and the Public Interest in Dallas, Texas, 1900-1965* (Columbus: Ohio State University Press, 1998), 241-243.

88. Robert Fairbanks, "The Assassination and Dallas Politics," in *Legacies,* 21.

89. Transcript. J. Erik Jonsson Oral History Interview, 11/10/1992, by Wes Wise with Bob Porter. Oral History Collection, The Sixth Floor Museum at Dealey Plaza, Dallas, Texas.

90. Robert Fairbanks, "The Assassination and Dallas Politics," in *Legacies*, 21-22; and Richard Aguirre, "'City of Hate' Still Fighting its Reputation: JFK Anniversary Revives Memories," *Dallas Times Herald*, November 22, 1988, A1, A4.

91. At the 1973 meeting of the U.S. Conference of Mayors, for example, Dallas Mayor Wes Wise was asked by another conference participant, half in jest, "How does it feel to be the mayor of the city that killed the president?" Transcript. Wes Wise Oral History Interview, 1/25/1993, by Bob Porter. Oral History Collection, The Sixth Floor Museum at Dealey Plaza, Dallas, Texas.

92. Transcript. Dr. Glenn Linden Oral History Interview, 5/24/2006, by Bob Porter with Ray Langston. Oral history Collection, The Sixth Floor Museum at Dealey Plaza, Dallas, Texas.

93. Wayne King, "Dallas Still Wondering: Did It Help Pull the Trigger?" *New York Times*, November 22, 1978, A24.

94. Paul Goldberger, "Reunion Complex in Dallas—Centerpiece for the City," *New York Times*, June 18, 1978, 58.

95. "The Assassination Lives on in Dallas," *New York Times*, December 31, 1978, 8.

96. "Dallas Mayor-Elect Says He Will Chart an International Course for His City," *New York Times*, May 1, 1983, A26.

97. Peter Applebome, "Dallas Fighting '63 Specter As Convention Approaches," *New York Times*, November 7, 1983, A18.

98. Richard Aguirre, "'City of Hate' Still Fighting its Reputation," *Dallas Times Herald*, A1, A4.

99. Peter Applebome, "25 Years After the Death of Kennedy, Dallas Looks at its Changed Image," *New York Times*, November 21, 1988, A14.

100. Darwin Payne, "J. Erik Jonsson," in *Legacies*, 11.

101. Craig Flournoy, "Dallas on Trial," in Blow, et al., *November 22*, 149.

102. Arlinda Abbot, *Dealey Plaza*, 45.

103. Lacie Ballinger, *The Rededication of the John Fitzgerald Kennedy Memorial*, 3-4.

104. Conover Hunt, *JFK for a New Generation*, 122-124.

105. Video recording, Lee Jackson Oral History Interview, 1/12/2001, by Bob Porter and Stephen Fagin. Oral History Collection, The Sixth Floor Museum at Dealey Plaza, Dallas, Texas; and Jeff Collins, "'The Sixth

Floor' Provides a Window to the Past," *Dallas Times Herald*, November 22, 1988, 6E.

106. Or as Dallas County Judge Lee Jackson recalled, "It's far more than a ballistics exhibit." The exhibit creators faced the difficult task of designing a space that would forthrightly acknowledge the assassination, but that was also tastefully done and that put JFK's death in some sort of a larger perspective—something that, arguably, the official Kennedy memorial had failed to do. Ibid.

107. Video, Robert Staples and Barbara Charles Oral History Interview, 8/30/1994, by Stephen Fagin, Oral History Collection, The Sixth Floor Museum at Dealey Plaza, Dallas, Texas.

108. Visitor Memory Books, 1989 (digitized), The Sixth Floor Museum at Dealey Plaza, Dallas, Texas.

109. Transcript, Dr. Glenn Linden Oral History Interview.

110. Lindalyn Adams, "Opening of Sixth Floor to Fulfill a Historic Responsibility," *Dallas Times Herald*, November 22, 1988, A9.

111. Johnson's memorial design has received mixed reviews from art and architecture critics. Some thought that if the memorial was intended to mark JFK's death, its starkness was appropriate. The memorial's unadorned, even severe, appearance fit with the sorrow so many experienced at the tragedy that took place only a few blocks away. Others, however, derided not only the lack of a central memorial "message," but also the design itself. One critic compared the memorial with a *urinoir*—the public toilets found in the streets of Paris. Frank D. Welch, *Philip Johnson*, 129.

112. Lacie Ballinger, *The Rededication of the John Fitzgerald Kennedy Memorial*, 25-26.

113. "In Memoriam to President John F. Kennedy: Address by Mayor J. Erik Jonsson, November 22, 1967" (Box 3, Folder 25, "JFK Memorial, November 22, 1967") in J. Erik Jonsson papers.

114. Ibid.

115. As the assassination became more a historical event and less of a raw personal memory a quarter century later, the desire to simply move on was ever present. It did not go unnoticed that, even at the official Kennedy memorial, the city held no events to mark the 25th anniversary of JFK's death. "Hundreds Gather at JFK Memorial," *Houston Post*, November 22, 1988, A3.

116. Lacie Ballinger, *The Rededication of the John Fitzgerald Kennedy Memorial*, 24.

117. (no author given), *The John Fitzgerald Kennedy Memorial, Dallas, Texas* (no publishing info given), 1, in Stanley Marcus Collection, F394.D2 J6

CHAPTER TWO

THE CASE OF LYNDON B. JOHNSON

TAKING CARE OF HIS OWN PRESIDENCY BY TAKING CARE OF JOHN KENNEDY'S

Everything I had ever learned in the history books taught me that martyrs have to die for causes. John Kennedy had died. But his "cause" was not really clear. That was my job. I had to take the dead man's program and turn it into a martyr's cause. That way Kennedy would live on forever and so would I.

—Lyndon B. Johnson.[1]

Lyndon B. Johnson's presidential ambition was well-known to anyone with a basic understanding of the American political scene in the late 1950s. He opposed John Kennedy for the 1960 Democratic presidential nomination and had to settle instead for the vice presidential slot on the party's ticket. Johnson's three years as vice president were uncomfortable and, by the fall of 1963, there was speculation that his political career would conclude with his tenure as vice president.[2] Some predicted that Johnson would end up one of many men who came within reach of the presidency, only to be denied. However, his ambition was fulfilled with

Kennedy's death. Two hours after the assassination, he took the oath of office on Air Force One before returning to Washington.

Johnson, although now president, could hardly have been thrilled with the way in which he had assumed office, nor could he have been excited about the task confronting him. With the nation shocked and grieving after the assassination, it was now LBJ's responsibility to bring the nation out of that shock.[3] He would also take upon himself the role of interpreter of the Kennedy presidency; he would give it meaning and use the late president's unfinished agenda as a prelude to his own designs for the country.[4] And no less important for Johnson was the 1964 presidential election, now less than a year away. Johnson would use popular memory of President Kennedy as a means of providing meaning to his presidency—and his death—and of creating a new sense of national purpose after the complacency and inaction of the previous decade. Kennedy, while inspiring to many, had enjoyed little success in getting his legislative agenda through Congress. At the time of his death, his proposals for a tax cut, civil rights, and his initial plans for antipoverty legislation had yet to become law.[5]

How did Johnson use popular memory of John Kennedy and why? As did so many others, LBJ quickly recognized that the public's memory of JFK could benefit him in a number of ways. Along with the belief that the nation had lost a great president, many also observed a sense of expectation, a feeling that there was unfinished national business.[6] Just as city leaders recognized that Dallas could not simply go back to business as usual, Johnson argued that the nation, even in the midst of its grief, could not continue to ignore its formidable domestic challenges. In pointing out those problems and unfinished business, LBJ asserted that the country could never be true to the memory and ideals of Kennedy if it did *not* reject its past apathy and adopt a proactive attitude. Johnson's public comments and speeches during this period, as well as his later memoirs, and his Oval Office conversations (which he recorded and are now publicly available) all make clear his belief that he was not only

Kennedy's successor by law, but the rightful inheritor of the Kennedy vision .[7]

The presidential memory that Johnson helped sustain was of JFK as a legislative leader and of his unfinished presidency. Johnson intended to memorialize his unfinished agenda and his supposed dedication to social justice. Kennedy was not a great legislator, either during his time in Congress or in the White House. Engaging in the work necessary to get bills passed generally bored him.[8] But Johnson reminded Americans that John Kennedy had had the vision to propose tax reform, civil rights, and anti-poverty legislation. Now, it was up to the rest of the country to do what JFK was prevented from doing.

But much more was at stake here than simply honoring the late president by fulfilling his legislative wishes. What motivated Lyndon Johnson to identify himself so closely with his predecessor during the first several months after the assassination were three principal objectives. First and foremost, he had to maintain continuity between himself and Kennedy to reassure the nation that there was strong leadership at the top, and reassure everyone that he would not initiate any sudden departures from JFK's policies.[9] Second, he saw Kennedy's memory as a useful way of passing legislation that was indisputably long overdue. This, in turn, would establish a record of achievement that Johnson could use in winning his own four-year term. Building upon Kennedy's policies could help him amass a strong domestic legacy similar to that of his hero, Franklin Roosevelt. The opportunity in 1963-1964 to change national angst into national achievement marked a period when good policy and smart politics fused.[10] Third, LBJ used JFK to solidify his credentials as a liberal Democrat by committing himself ideologically to the liberal goals Kennedy had championed late in his presidency. In his first few days and weeks as president, Johnson suspected, not incorrectly, that some within his party were already intending to stop him from receiving the 1964 presidential nomination. By making his loyalty to JFK and his own liberal beliefs beyond question, by promising to fulfill, and even go beyond, what Kennedy had intended to do, Johnson would insulate himself from any intra-party threats to his candidacy.[11] Writing in his memoirs years later, Johnson claimed that throughout his presidency, he tried to protect his predecessor's legacy, and honor the public's memory of him, by governing in the way he thought John Kennedy would have been proud of. LBJ certainly must have been struck by the irony that he, who had played a minor role in JFK's administration and had privately ridiculed his lack of legislative accomplishments,[12] was now pledging to dedicate himself to the perpetuation of the late president's memory. Johnson always believed that he was "the caretaker of both his people and his policies...I did what I believed he would have wanted me to do. I never wavered from that sense of responsibility, even after I was elected in my own right...I never lost sight of the fact that I was the trustee and custodian of the Kennedy administration."[13] But whether Johnson really could be considered the rightful user of the public's memory of John Kennedy can be debated (and during his presidency, it was), but what is certain is that the new president had found an excellent way to accomplish almost whatever he wanted. By invoking the public's love of Kennedy and declaring a piece of legislation to have been the desire of his predecessor, Johnson greatly increased the chances of that legislation clearing Congress.. By arguing that Kennedy's death now required "renewed dedication and renewed vigor,"[14] Johnson shrewdly made the proposed tax cut and civil rights legislation essential parts of the country's memorialization of JFK; it was a clever way to guarantee passage of those items. The potential power contained in the popular memory of Kennedy, with an estimated 93 percent of all televisions in the country tuned in to the state funeral and 175,000,000 people watching,[15] was sure to be recognized by a skilled politician. Johnson, who could have written a textbook on power politics, surely knew the effect he would have on the public by asserting that Kennedy's agenda—now his own agenda—acted as a memorial to the late president.

Although Kennedy had pledged during his 1960 campaign to "get the country moving again," the country as a whole seemed generally satisfied with the status quo, and this did not change much with his election. There was little sense of urgency—few thought the federal government should address those problems, and this general lack of activism extended itself from the Eisenhower into the Kennedy years.[16] At one point during the Kennedy presidency, a miniscule 4 percent of the American people thought that civil rights was the biggest issue the country faced.[17] Even after the president made his case for comprehensive civil rights legislation in the summer of 1963, half the country thought the bill would force integration too quickly.[18]

On the national level, the assassination seemed to bluntly expose the domestic problems—civil rights and poverty foremost among them—that the United States faced. With the country about evenly split in the summer of 1963 on whether the Kennedy bill was a good idea, Johnson's portrayal of Kennedy as a civil rights president surely changed a few minds. It should have been relatively clear how Johnson would win passage of the Kennedy proposals. If LBJ declared that civil rights legislation was what President Kennedy had wanted, who would be willing to risk the anger of the public by contradicting that declaration? One political science text written in 1964 predicted that, by keeping the memory of the late president fresh in the minds of both the public and lawmakers, Johnson would accomplish a lot in the scant period of time he had until the 1964 election. To be sure, he benefited from the public support generated by his sudden accession to the White House—the so-called "honeymoon" normally given to incoming presidents. That, combined with "a possible wish by the captains of Congress to pay their respects to the fallen President by acceding, posthumously for him, to a large portion of his program, seem[s] likely to allow President Johnson to reap a larger harvest of the legislative program sown by Kennedy than the latter could reasonably have expected to harvest himself."[19]

Along with the power encompassed within the popular memory of JFK came a feeling of expectation as to where the country needed to go. President Johnson was not the only one to sense that action had to be taken. If anything, the assassination was reason enough for the nation to ponder its future, and whether the American people would make Kennedy's memory mean anything was now the big question. As the Senior Editor of *American Heritage* observed: "The four harrowing days that began on November 22, 1963, brought us face to face with the future. What happens next is up to us...We relive that time of tragedy less to commemorate a departed president than to dedicate ourselves."[20] Commenting on the mood of the nation in the days after the assassination, Johnson said, "This act of violence shocked the nation deeply and created the impetus to send the country surging forward. His death touched all our hearts and made us, for a while at least, a more compassionate people...the people were ready for action."[21]

But surging forward to do what? To what were the American people supposed to dedicate themselves? In two of his first major speeches as president, both to Joint Sessions of Congress, Johnson invoked the memory and accomplishments of John Kennedy repeatedly. He asserted that the country would be unfaithful to the late president if it did not demand—and Congress would be unfaithful if it did not enact—the Kennedy tax cut and civil rights bills at the earliest possible moment.[22] The new president, as well as Dallas city leaders, seemed to attribute the death of JFK to a simple, but all too prevalent, hatred coursing through American society. The remedy for that hatred, as Johnson and an increasing number of people believed, was the passage of those two pieces of legislation. Berl Bernhard, Director of the U.S. Commission on Civil Rights, noted that, while civil rights legislation had advanced slowly under Kennedy, he should still be remembered as a civil rights president. Comparing JFK with civil rights leader Medgar Evers, assassinated only five months before the president, Bernhard stated "Both were cut down by the hatred they sought to end."[23] In a November 24, 1963, phone call with civil rights leader Whitney Young of the National Urban League, during which Johnson discussed with him the upcoming Joint Session of Congress speech, Young himself opined that Johnson would do well to turn the hatred that had claimed the life of JFK into positive legislative achievements. Young argued, "It's good to point out that...for the good of the civil rights thing, that the death of President Kennedy points out, that hate anywhere...goes unchecked." Johnson replied, "I dictated a whole page on hate. Hate internationally, hate domestically...and just say that this hate that produces inequality, this hate produces poverty—that's why we've got to have a tax bill...the hate that produces injustice—that's why we got to have [a] civil rights bill."[24]

His first opportunity to link himself publicly with JFK and, as Johnson would later recall, to "turn the dead man's program into a martyr's cause," came five days after the assassination when he appeared before Congress. Declaring Kennedy to be "the greatest leader of our time," the new president reassured the nation that he did not intend to strike out on his own, away from the Kennedy domestic program, and that he would honor the nation's international commitments "from South Viet-Nam to West Berlin." But Johnson also sounded a note of impatience. The speech was notable not only for the two major legislative items that Johnson demanded, but also for the urgency he tried to impart. The national grief was strong, but it would fade in time, and Johnson feared the ability to make progress would lessen. The grief of the nation had to be channeled to constructive ends. He was now the steward of the Kennedy presidency, and he asked those assembled—even those who still opposed the Kennedy legislation—to pass it for the good of the country and as the best memorial to JFK the country could construct. LBJ declared, "And now, the ideas and the ideals which he so nobly represented must and will be translated into effective action...this is no time for delay. It is a time for action—strong, forward-looking action. The need is here. The need is now. I ask your help."[25]

Photo 7. President Lyndon B. Johnson addresses a Joint Session of Congress five days after Dallas, November 27, 1963.

Photo courtesy of the Lyndon B. Johnson Presidential Library (Cecil Stoughton); CA-11-3-WH63.

Johnson paid homage again to Kennedy in January 1964 in his first State of the Union address. Lest anyone had forgotten since his previous appearance, Johnson renewed the sense of urgency, and even appeared to up the ante. The stakes confronting the Congress, he argued, were not just whether John Kennedy would be properly honored, but whether a democratic system of government could work effectively in the aftermath of crisis. Johnson seemed to imply that President Kennedy was not the only one watching them. They were in the presence of history, as well: "We have in 1964 a unique opportunity and obligation—to prove the success of our system...If we fail, if we fritter and fumble away our opportunity in needless, senseless quarrels...then history will rightfully judge us harshly."[26] The president also resolved that, in the diplomatic arena, the United States would honor JFK by continuing his prudent use of the threat of force while still working to attain peace: "We must continue to use that strength as John Kennedy used it in the Cuban crisis and for the test ban treaty—to demonstrate both the futility of nuclear war and the possibilities of lasting peace."[27] He concluded this speech the same way he had finished the prior one, with an exhortation to memorialize JFK through concrete action and achievements and to not prolong the divisions that—Johnson purported—Kennedy had spent his presidency trying to remove:

> In these last 7 sorrowful weeks, we have learned anew that nothing is so enduring as faith, and nothing is so degrading as hate. John Kennedy was a victim of hate, but he was also a great builder of faith—faith in our fellow Americans, whatever their creed or their color or their station in life; faith in the future of man, whatever his divisions or his differences.[28]

Out of these two speeches emerged the two unfinished Kennedy legislative items that Johnson intended to tackle first. He began with JFK's tax cut proposal. The tax cut was part of a larger legislative package concerning general tax reform, and Johnson saw this as a logical precursor to the initiatives on poverty that he was interested in proposing later. To make his ambitious agenda fiscally possible, he would need a strong economy yielding ever-greater amounts of tax revenue to Washington, D.C. Kennedy had managed to win approval for his tax reform bill in the House of Representatives where the measure had passed in September 1963. The bill had then gone into the Senate Finance Committee, where it remained at the time Johnson became president. The problem seemed to be with the budget Kennedy had originally given Congress; he had called for expenditures that were greater than the expected government revenue, which would have created a deficit of about $9 billion. Coupled with a proposed tax cut of $11 billion, the bill was not likely to pass without some sort of modification easing the fiscal strain between money collected and money spent.[29]

The Kennedy tax cut was a good place for Johnson to begin, as it tested his ability to maneuver Congress into passing something it had been reluctant to pass prior to Kennedy's death. It also demonstrated the depth of LBJ's own commitment to working for legislation he was initially hesitant about. Originally, Johnson had not seemed to favor the idea of a tax cut. While the liberal argument was that any deficit could be closed by the revenue generated by a tax cut (an argument Ronald Reagan would make 20 years later), Johnson himself preferred a balanced budget instead of even short-term deficits. The fact that the original tax reform bill also eliminated several preferences and loopholes, such as the oil depletion allowance (the elimination of which was opposed by the oil industry), also suggested that his support for the bill would be based more on his publicly professed commitment to John Kennedy than on his belief in the bill's merits.[30]

However, recognizing the need to identify himself with Kennedy's program, Johnson set his own opinion of the legislation aside and decided to support it, with modifications. That the tax cut would more than make up for itself in later tax revenue—funds that could be used for social programs—was no doubt important.[31] Publicly, LBJ wanted passage of the bill as only the first of many such steps in honoring JFK. In his speech to Congress on November 27, 1963, he declared, "No act of ours could more fittingly continue the work of President Kennedy than the early passage of the tax bill for which he fought all this long year."[32] Privately, Johnson made a much clearer, and a more politically based, connection between the tax bill, the late president, and the anticipated benefits to be derived from the use of popular memory. In a phone conversation with Florida Senator George Smathers only 24 hours after becoming president, Johnson disagreed with Smathers' advice that he might consider withdrawing, or at least putting off for the foreseeable future, the tax cut from Senate consideration. Johnson argued:

> That would destroy the [Democratic] party and destroy the election and destroy everything. We've got to carry on. We can't abandon this fellow's program, because he is a national hero and there are going to be those people [who] want his program passed and we've got to keep this Kennedy aura around us through the election.[33]

Meanwhile, the Johnson administration quickly secured passage of an unresolved Kennedy initiative that, while minor on its face, became a critical early round in the new president's drive to force congressional action in the wake of the assassination. Kennedy had proposed the sale of American wheat to the Soviet Union through the U.S. Export-Import Bank. By November 1963, the deal had stalled in Congress and was still in jeopardy when JFK traveled to Texas.[34] Upon taking office, Johnson attempted to get the measure passed by characterizing it as a vote of confidence in his new administration. Congress was set to vote on the wheat deal on November 26, the Monday after the assassination. Johnson understood how critical the vote was, for if the legislation met defeat, progress on far greater issues such as civil rights would be extremely unlikely. LBJ and his team went to work to defeat the proposed amendment to the bill by South Dakota Senator Karl Mundt, who opposed the deal; the Mundt amendment would have blocked completion of the sale by the Export-Import Bank. Killing the amendment would enable passage of the Kennedy bill. Johnson was not shy in playing upon legislators' emotions toward JFK only days after his death, telling them that in voting against the bill, they would be undermining a new president and dishonoring the late one. Washington journalistic duo Rowland Evans and Robert Novak characterized the president's appeal to senators as, "Do you want the first action of the United States Senate to be a posthumous repudiation of John F. Kennedy and a slap in the face of Lyndon Johnson?"[35] His private conversations indicate that, in his mind, approval of the wheat sale was a means of memorializing the late president. In a phone call with JFK's legislative liaison, Larry O'Brien (who had pledged to work for the new president), Johnson was pleased that he was able to get the deal approved. The president observed, "I think it would be a terrible thing to Kennedy's memory to have this wheat sale thing repudiated...I did tell [Senate Majority Leader Mike] Mansfield that I thought it would be...a hell of a way to launch a new administration."[36] Even on what seemed a rather mundane matter, at least compared to a massive tax cut and later civil rights and antipoverty legislation, Johnson still proved ready to link the fate of legislation with the memory of his predecessor—and, as Johnson's comments to O'Brien indicate, to his own political well-being.[37]

Passage of JFK's tax bill, however, was still in doubt. Even with Johnson's reminder that the bill was originally John Kennedy's request, the Senate was nevertheless unwilling to approve the tax cut unless the entire federal budget could be cut below $100 billion.[38] In his State of the Union message, Johnson indicated that his proposed budget would come in at slightly under $98 billion,[39] although he had originally feared he would not be able to cut spending below $102 billion. In any event, the president, making a deal with Senate Finance Committee chairman Harry Byrd, was able to achieve the necessary cut in spending, and the bill was moved to the full Senate where it was approved by a comfortable margin at the end of February 1964.[40] The final bill included a total of $11.5 billion in cuts to both individual and corporate tax rates, the largest tax cut in American history up to that time. Even though the legislation passed by an impressive 74-19 Senate vote, many of the tax code reforms originally proposed by JFK were shelved. Nonetheless, Johnson was able to mark his first major legislative triumph in signing what the *New York Times* called the "keystone of the economic policy of both the Kennedy and Johnson administrations."[41] In a televised East Room speech celebrating the bill's passage, the president noted its inception by JFK and went immediately after the ceremony to Jacqueline Kennedy's Washington, D.C. home to present her with pens used to sign it.[42] Having made good on his pledge to memorialize his predecessor by working for his tax bill (or, in LBJ's parlance, "nailing the coonskin to the wall"), the president next turned to the far more momentous and divisive unfinished business of civil rights.

Far more than cutting taxes, pushing civil rights legislation through Congress would go a long way toward satisfying the sudden national urge for swift action in the wake of Kennedy's death. The desire that something be done to get the nation back on track created momentum for "finishing" the Kennedy presidency, and passage of civil rights legislation would be the centerpiece of that effort. Civil rights became almost a form of national atonement for the hatred that President Johnson had argued was behind JFK's death. *The Nation*, as did many others, dubbed Kennedy a "martyred" civil rights leader for whom a robust civil rights law must be passed; it was now "more or less obligatory as a memorial to President Kennedy."[43] A *Life* magazine commemorative reprint issue (on the 40th anniversary of the assassination) suggested that people at the time thought that here indeed was an opportunity to get something meaningful accomplished. In one essay, the magazine explained, "The area of Kennedy's greatest problem—the deadlock over domestic policy —is the area of Johnson's greatest strength," and later,

> President Johnson is now in a strong position to carry forward 'the vigil of justice'...The long stalemate over civil rights was becoming an ugly stain on our democratic system at the time of Kennedy's death. Cannot this stain be removed by positive action now? Let President Johnson lead Congress and the nation on a new adventure in our old tradition of equality. More than any statue such action would be a fitting memorial to John F. Kennedy.[44]

Of all the social issues that the nation confronted during the 1960s, arguably the most important was civil rights. The demonstrations and unrest that broke out later in the decade were already beginning to appear during Kennedy's presidency. He had been reluctant to introduce a civil rights bill prior to June 1963. The justifications he consistently gave for not acting forcefully on the issue was that a civil rights bill would have stalled the progression through Congress of his other initiatives, and that a bill would probably not pass anyway.[45] However, after two black students were blocked from entering the University of Alabama, forcing Kennedy to mobilize the National Guard to ensure their admission peacefully, he finally resolved to act.[46] Speaking eloquently to the American people in June of 1963, he argued that the cause of civil rights was more than simply a legal or social issue. The nation, he said, was "confronted primarily with a moral issue. It is as old as the scriptures and is as clear as the American constitution. The heart of the question is whether all Americans are to be afforded equal rights and equal opportunities...Now the time has come for the nation to fulfill its promise."[47] Kennedy announced that he would soon be submitting comprehensive civil rights legislation "giving all Americans the right to be served in facilities which are open to the public—hotels, restaurants, theaters, retail stores, and similar establishments," and that, "We cannot say to 10 percent of the population that you can't have that right...I think we owe them, and we owe ourselves, a better country than that."[48] The Kennedy civil rights legislation, like his tax reform bill, had not cleared Congress before his death. A fight on this issue was all but assured, as southern lawmakers made it clear that they intended to prevent the passage of a civil rights bill through their customary use of the filibuster in the Senate.[49] Civil rights legislation had been passed during the Eisenhower administration, but the scope of those bills was small compared with the ambitiousness of the Kennedy-sponsored legislation. His original bill provided for job training, steps to end segregation in educational institutions, and prohibition of discrimination in public facilities, among other things.[50] Johnson, as vice president, had not been involved in the creation of the bill, even though his legislative experience would have come in handy, and he was critical of the way it was presented to Congress. As vice president, he advised Kennedy staff members that the bill's makeup, and the strategy employed to gain approval, would both have to be changed if it was to have any chance of passing.[51] Now that he was president, it was up to him to somehow get it through Congress.

Civil rights was the other legislative item he exhorted Congress to pass in the late president's memory in his speech of November 27. "No memorial oration or eulogy could more eloquently honor President Kennedy's memory," Johnson said, " than the earliest possible passage of the civil rights bill for which he fought so long. We have talked long enough in this country about equal rights. We have talked for one hundred years or more."[52] The growing strength of the civil rights movement, and JFK's appeal to the nation to ignore the problem of racial inequality no longer, had already imbued the bill before Congress with great moral power. The tax cut looked rather prosaic by comparison. But the effect of Johnson's associating the late president with civil rights, as if JFK's final request had been that this bill become law, was to make a refusal to pass it tantamount to a denial of what Kennedy represented and what he had given his life for.[53] And, as LBJ well knew, the American people—and therefore, the Congress—would not stand for that.

When he became president, Johnson recognized that he would have a difficult time convincing others that he actually favored a civil rights bill. Although he felt it was the right thing to do, his own record on civil rights, and the fact that he was a southerner, did not ease concerns among civil rights leaders that Kennedy's assassination considerably imperiled the bill's chances of passing.[54] But the president's death actually had the opposite effect by quickly changing the nation's mind as to both the desirability and the necessity of civil rights. Polls indicated a considerable shift in public opinion in favor of the proposed bill. Not long after Kennedy had introduced his bill, 50 percent of the country thought it would force integration too quickly. This perception shifted decisively following the assassination: in February 1964, only 30 percent opposed action on civil rights and, by the end of April, a solid majority favored Johnson's efforts on the issue.[55]

LBJ surely must have been aware of this shift, a shift that was due primarily to the death of JFK, and proceeded to gain as much mileage as possible by reminding the public who had originally proposed the legislation. To a great extent, Johnson contributed to the belief that Kennedy had been a civil rights president, and that defeat of the bill would be not only a denial of justice to black Americans, but also repudiation of what the slain president had worked for. Johnson was careful to link civil rights with the memory of JFK but not excessively. Many were already remembering Kennedy as a civil rights advocate, and recognizing that strong action on the issue was a key part of memorializing him.[56] In a telephone conversation on November 25, 1963, with Dr. Martin Luther King, Jr. (two days *before* LBJ first argued publicly before Congress that memorializing his predecessor had to include passage of civil rights), King himself suggested that Kennedy be remembered primarily through civil rights. Johnson had commented that, "We know what a difficult period this is...We've got a budget coming up that's...practically already made and we've got a civil rights bill...We've just got to not let up on any of 'em and keep going." King replied, "Well, this is mighty fine...I think one of the great tributes that we can pay to the memory of President Kennedy is to try to enact some of the great progressive policies that he sought to initiate." The president declared, "I'm going to support 'em all and you can count on that."[57]

Passage in the House of Representatives came fairly early, as Republican support proved to be crucial;[58] the bill passed by a very comfortable margin in February 1964. The trip through the Senate proved more difficult, as southern legislators, most notably LBJ's friend and mentor, Richard Russell of Georgia, attempted to filibuster. A combination of pressure from Johnson, northern Democratic support, and support from Republicans under the prodding of minority leader Everett Dirksen, yielded enough votes to end the filibuster and bring the legislation to a vote.[59] The bill was approved by the Senate and sent to LBJ for his signature. Upon signing it at the White House in early July 1964, the president argued that the new civil rights legislation was the culmination of the struggle for liberty that had begun with the American Revolution and the direct result of efforts began a year earlier when "our late and beloved President John F. Kennedy," first called for its passage.[60]

Photo 8. President Johnson signs the Kennedy-conceived Civil Rights Act of 1964, July 2, 1964.

Photo courtesy of the Lyndon B. Johnson Presidential Library (Cecil Stoughton); 276-10-WH64.

Thus were the benefits apparent of using the popular memory of President Kennedy to pass national legislation. However, President Johnson's reasons for tying himself to his predecessor went further than just a resolution to finish Kennedy's agenda. Through repeated references to JFK and assertions that he was acting with his posthumous blessing, the president found an effective way of making himself more appealing to the Democratic Party. This was especially important with respect to party liberals who had consistently doubted Johnson's commitment to their causes.[61] The paramount objective in his first weeks in office was to provide strong and steady leadership and bring the nation out of the shock over his predecessor's assassination. But, ever the politician, what could not have been far from his mind was securing control over the Democratic Party and establishing enough of a record to win his own presidential term. Forty years of hindsight may call into question the importance of the president's efforts in this respect, as today it seems obvious that LBJ would have gotten the 1964 nomination. Who else could or would have run at the top of the Democratic ticket if not him? Who else would have been a stronger or a more obvious candidate?

Was Lyndon Johnson worthy and capable of nurturing Kennedy's agenda? That became the question following the latter's death, and there were certainly those within the Democratic Party who were afraid that Johnson would prove to be nothing more than a retrograde Southern politician with no intention at all of furthering civil rights or any other liberal initiative. Johnson was afraid that some in the party were surreptitiously working to stop him from being nominated,[62] and this fear drove him to identify himself as the true heir of JFK. Kennedy, Johnson argued, had devoted his presidency to liberal causes, and so would he. As he commented to an aide not too long after his predecessor's death, "If you look at my record, you would know that I am a Roosevelt New Dealer. As a matter of fact, John F. Kennedy was a little too conservative to suit my taste."[63] In light of the results of the 1964 election, and the subsequent onslaught of social legislation that flowed from the Johnson White House, it seems hard to believe that anyone questioned whether the new president was either electable or a liberal in the tradition of Franklin Roosevelt or JFK (although JFK confronted the same doubts in 1960). But many did doubt his qualifications as a liberal. In surveying his political career in late 1963, the *New Republic* worriedly noted LBJ's swings between the liberal and conservative wings of the Democratic Party. He had been both an ardent New Dealer, but also a defender of the conservative Texas oil barons. He worked to get civil rights legislation passed during the Eisenhower years, but his overall record on the issue was erratic. Skeptical about the new president's chances of winning his own presidential term, the *New Republic* asserted that he would soon have to make a definitive choice as to which of the two camps he would belong. "A civil rights bill would be an absolute 'must'" if LBJ opted for the liberal camp. Was Johnson, in this time of national crisis, capable of upholding liberal principles the way JFK was thought to have done? Could the new president overcome the perception that his political vision went no farther than simply cutting whatever deal he could, no matter what the issue?[64]

As later events would demonstrate, the magazine underestimated considerably the president's ability to walk a liberal path the way the "martyred" JFK supposedly had. Still, was the public's memory of Kennedy —or rather, Johnson's use of that memory—really necessary to ensure that LBJ would not go down in history as simply an accidental president? Considering what the new president was dealing with following the assassination, his concern over whether he would be seen as the true ideological, not just constitutional, heir to JFK seemed justified, and not only because of genuine doubts as to his dedication to a liberal agenda. Reflecting on his first few days and weeks as president years later, Johnson said, "I became President. But for millions of Americans I was still illegitimate, a naked man with no presidential covering, a pretender to the throne...there were the bigots and the dividers and the Eastern intellectuals who were waiting to knock me down before I could even begin to stand up."[65] Even allowing for the fact that Johnson could occasionally get carried away with his own hyperbole, the transition was no doubt difficult, and he was correct in suspecting some of trying to stop him from becoming the Democratic Party's standard bearer.[66]

The rapidity with which some began talking of Johnson's political demise, and their unwillingness to give the new president any sympathy or benefit of the doubt, is striking. Barely 24 hours after the assassination, historian and Kennedy adviser Arthur Schlesinger, Jr., was already conferring with other members of the Kennedy administration, including Secretary of Defense Robert McNamara, about whether the Democrats could deny Johnson the presidential nomination for 1964.[67] As Kennedy ambassador to India John Kenneth Galbraith recorded, Schlesinger suggested that they work to get Robert Kennedy nominated, with Hubert Humphrey as his running mate. Galbraith, although never a close friend or advisor to Johnson, thought such a plan was simply unrealistic, given LBJ's formidable political skills and the wide support he commanded from the public.[68] The episode does suggest, however, that Johnson's doubts about the readiness of some within his own party to accept him—doubts which led to his use of the Kennedy memory—were not without some basis in truth.

Arthur Schlesinger's diary seems to confirm the new president's suspicions. He repeatedly mentioned the Kennedy family's efforts to solidify their own political base in preparation for an eventual attempt to retake power, whether or not it meant a direct challenge to Johnson in 1964. With LBJ's presidency only a couple of months old, Schlesinger and RFK apparently believed that the new president was dependent upon them—that the only way he could govern was if he appeased them. One month after the assassination, Schlesinger thought RFK could possibly get a cabinet appointment; if not, "the alternative would be to entrench the Kennedys in the executive branch and give them the great powers of being the heir-apparent." Robert Kennedy, who had attempted to block Johnson's nomination as vice president in 1960, now thought Johnson "will have to consult the Kennedys about the vice presidency [for 1964], and that the Kennedys will be able to exert some influence about the choice of Secretary of State in the next cabinet."[69] With the Kennedy clan so abruptly thrown out of power, talk about maneuvering RFK onto the 1964 ticket as Johnson's vice president began just two weeks after the assassination—with the ultimate objective of the younger Kennedy succeeding LBJ. Johnson's suspicions of an eventual power grab by the Kennedys were hardly wide of the mark. Schlesinger confided in his diary that the younger Kennedy "obviously wants to be President himself," and therefore thought it essential for their supporters within the government to remain unified behind him, and not the new president, for the future restoration.[70] Kenneth O'Donnell, the late president's political advisor, had begun thinking along the same lines even earlier than this. With a combination of bitterness and arrogant certainty, as if the Kennedy family owned the presidency, O'Donnell voiced his determination to exact political retribution upon Johnson, as if Kennedy's death had been his fault. Seated in the back of Air Force One just a few hours after the assassination as the plane flew back to Washington, O'Donnell is said to have pointed at Johnson's back and told press secretary Malcolm Kilduff (who had made the official announcement of JFK's death), "He's got what he wants now. We'll take it back in '68."[71]

It should come as no surprise, therefore, that the biggest threat to Johnson's plans for 1964—in his mind—was Robert Kennedy. Johnson convinced himself that he faced a genuine threat from RFK for the nomination.[72] A month before the Democratic Party's national convention in late July 1964, Johnson thought a last-minute attempt by Kennedy to steal the nomination was still very possible. In a phone conversation with Chicago Mayor Richard Daley, the president had predicted, "My people think they're [RFK supporters] relying primarily on emotionalism. They think that most of these delegates that go...will be delegates that were there in '60 and will be people that like the name [Kennedy]... and they'll say...he's got a lot of friends, and we need this name, and we just ought to go ahead and give him [RFK] a vote."[73] Nor was the idea of Kennedy as vice president a notion being considered only by a few teary-eyed party members who had backed JFK four years earlier. As 1964 began, polls indicated that the Attorney General was ahead of Senator Hubert Humphrey (the eventual vice presidential nominee) and Adlai Stevenson (two-time Democratic party standard bearer). The RFK threat, for Johnson, was serious. From the start of his presidency, LBJ did what he could to outflank any real or potential efforts to nominate somebody else. He insisted that all of JFK's advisors continue to work for him, which was done not only for continuity's sake, but also to give him the benefit of their proximity to the late president.[74]

Thanks to his professed commitment to the late president, culminating in his signature on the 1964 Civil Rights Act, Johnson could credibly position himself in the liberal wing of his party by the time the August 1964 Democratic convention opened. By demonstrating that he was as close as possible to his predecessor, Johnson could present himself as both a committed liberal, and as *the indispensable* heir to JFK. He would reassure all within his party about what sort of presidency he would pursue by demonstrating that he intended to pass everything JFK had ever dreamed about—not only out of a sense of loyalty, but also out of ideological solidarity. By hinting that he could, to paraphrase a friend, "out-Kennedy" even Kennedy himself through the promise of broader social legislation, any credible intra-party threats to his nomination would cease.[75] To some extent, Johnson's strategy of making his liberal alignment beyond reproach worked, as some supporters and Kennedy administration aides were pleased with the new president's efforts to promote liberal legislation. However, as journalist Theodore White noted, others chose to see his efforts as little more than a cheap attempt to play off the public's affection of John Kennedy for personal political gain. Johnson's ostensible commitment to liberalism may have either been nothing more than a strategy to win favor from both sides of his party, to "please *The New York Times* and get a pat on the back from Dick Russell —both at the same time," as one critic suggested.[76] What is clear, in any event, is that Johnson's apparent conclusion that the memory of Kennedy had its benefits in the political arena was certainly not a point lost on those who, privately or publicly, accused him of using the memory of his predecessor for strictly political gain.

On the night he gave his acceptance speech at the convention, he once again placed himself as Kennedy's successor, arguing that he was the one with both the ideological commitment and the political skills to accomplish further liberal reforms. Standing on a platform underneath large portraits of Franklin Roosevelt and Harry Truman on either side, with one of John Kennedy in the middle and a banner that read "Let Us Continue" (and flanked by even larger portraits of himself),[77] he declared that the program of the late president was not yet finished. In a speech that many thought was not among Johnson's most notable or eloquent,[78] but which was still important for its references to JFK, he reminded his audience of the sadness still lingering after the assassination and once again implored people to make something good come from it: "Let none of us stop to rest until we have written into the law of the land all the suggestions that made up the John Fitzgerald Kennedy program. And then let us continue to supplement that program with the kind of laws that he would have us write."[79] The president's message was clear: I have been faithful to my predecessor's program. I intend to follow through with my own liberal program, and John Kennedy, if he were here, would indeed approve of what I intend to do.[80]

During 1964, Johnson was looking ahead to his own four-year term, and his own liberal agenda. The war on poverty, as part of his Great Society, became a sort of transitional issue between Kennedy and him. JFK had grown ever more aware of the problem of poverty near the end of his presidency. Michael Harrington's well-known study of poverty, *The Other America*, had argued that poverty in the United States, although invisible to most Americans partaking in the country's general prosperity, was still a major problem. Harrington's book made a significant impression on Kennedy, and he began floating the idea of an antipoverty legislative package for 1964 or sometime in his second term.[81] In the months prior to his death, Kennedy had proposed a few such measures, but did not articulate an overall vision or commitment to fighting poverty as Johnson did in the years to come.[82]

Johnson, within the first few days of his accession to the presidency, signaled his interest in an antipoverty agenda of some sort, but what is interesting about his treatment of the issue from his first public pronouncements on it is the absence of any link between a "war on poverty" and his predecessor. While it is true that, unlike the Kennedy tax and civil rights bills, there was no grand antipoverty plan being considered at the time of Kennedy's death for which LBJ could use the public's memory, it is fair to argue that Johnson did not want his poverty agenda to appear as simply an addendum to that of his predecessor. A war on poverty, in other words, would be sold as a Johnson, and not as a Kennedy, initiative.[83] LBJ wanted his presidency as a whole to be seen as *his own*, and not a Kennedy administration, part two. Speaking to his friend Horace Busby about the draft of his Joint Session speech the day before he was to go to the Congress for the first time as president, LBJ appeared not to want to overdo his commitment to the Kennedy agenda. He commented, "I don't believe I want to say that the old program is *my* program. I want to say on foreign policy that we're going to have a continuity and not confusion...But I don't want everything—every time they want to see what Johnson's program is, to go look and see what Kennedy *said*"[84] (original italics of the transcript). If he could help it, Johnson did not want to unintentionally create the impression, now that he had achieved his lifetime ambition of becoming president, that his administration would be concerned only with doing John Kennedy's posthumous bidding. [85]

While the memory of the late president is invoked a few times in Johnson's 1964 State of the Union message, his name does not appear anywhere in Johnson's plans for battling poverty. The speech is notable for being the first time that Johnson publicly declared an "unconditional war on poverty in America," but in the entire section of the address dealing with the issue, John Kennedy is nowhere mentioned directly or implied in any way. Further, as if to clarify exactly where the idea for such a war was coming from, Johnson stated, "*This administration*, here and now, declares unconditional war on poverty in America," (italics mine) instead of something like "This administration, in accordance with the wishes of our beloved President Kennedy..."[86] The new president took up the Kennedy antipoverty proposals—stimulating economic development in the Appalachian region, youth employment, a domestic peace corps, and hospital care for the elderly—but they would largely be remembered as Johnson ideas. Walter Lippmann noted after the State of the Union speech that the antipoverty program developed thus far was largely JFK's program, but still argued that Johnson's sincerity in completing that program was genuine.[87] But whatever the scope of Kennedy's intent with regard to fighting poverty may have been, this issue marked the starting point for Johnson's own designs for the country.

Part of the reason for this could be the fact that whatever conception JFK had for what a "war on poverty" type of program would be like, it was not as ambitious or as comprehensive as what Johnson wanted. LBJ pointed out in his memoirs that Kennedy had not given Council of Economic Advisers Chairman Walter Heller specifics when he instructed him to begin planning an antipoverty program in late 1963.[88] Seemingly a minor observation, it nevertheless had major implications for Johnson's legacy. The new president may have followed JFK's lead in advancing his tax cut and civil rights bills, but the absence of any already-existing vision on how to fight poverty from his predecessor meant that LBJ could enumerate an antipoverty agenda however he wanted—and that it would be remembered differently. Lyndon Johnson would be remembered as the president who fought poverty. Left largely with a blank slate on poverty, which was not the case with the tax cut, civil rights, and, most ominously, with Vietnam, Johnson could make this issue truly his own.[89] This he did in his "Special Message to the Congress Proposing a Nationwide War on the Sources of Poverty," submitted in March 1964. The president asked for programs to help students pay for college, job training, a domestic version of the Peace Corps, incentives to alleviate chronic unemployment, and the creation of an Office of Economic Opportunity to ensure a coordinated federal approach to fighting poverty.[90]

The message did refer to proposals made over "the past three years" (without mentioning JFK) that targeted specific aspects of the national poverty problem, but repeatedly billed the Johnson administration's vision as a break with the past. It was "an entirely new course of hope for our people," and "a beginning." To whatever extent the late president deserved credit for making poverty a matter of federal concern, the message did not pay even passing tribute.[91]

In examining Johnson's definitive ideas for his Great Society, explained in full during his famous commencement address at the University of Michigan in May 1964, there is likewise no reference to President Kennedy. In contrast to the several major speeches cited previously,

Johnson does not invoke his predecessor when asking his audience for a commitment to improve the quality of life in the United States. The speech called for government activism in the areas of urban renewal and development, environmental protection, and greater federal concern with the state of American education.[92] But Johnson did not want a Great Society—his Great Society—to appear simply as one more Kennedy program that he was promoting. No doubt his plans were in keeping with the aspirations of his three Democratic predecessors,[93] but the scale of what he was calling for justified a break away from Kennedy. Johnson, it seems, was in the process of making JFK a civil rights president. He did not intend to give Kennedy posthumous credit for what he himself had spent decades in Washington trying to do.[94]

This reluctance to associate JFK with fighting poverty was not only limited to the period leading up to the 1964 election when Johnson would have been especially concerned with building his own record of accomplishment. In later years as well, the administration repeatedly reminded itself and the public that it was Johnson who truly took on the poverty problem in a systematic way, Johnson whom the public should remember as the poverty president—with JFK left in the background. Former Kennedy advisers insisted that even on poverty, LBJ did little more than act as a follower of the late president. Johnson would have countered that he could make poverty truly his issue because there had not been anything for him to follow in the first place, other than bare outlines of what the Kennedy administration *might* have been thinking of doing. In a February 17, 1965 letter to Congress in which the president requested additional antipoverty measures, the White House wrote as if attacking poverty had been wholly a Johnson idea, an idea that had never been given attention until he became president. "We knew, and said then," the letter read, in prose ironically evocative of JFK, "that this [antipoverty] battle would not be easily or swiftly won. But we began." A draft of the letter dated February 9 read: "We have, however, just begun. What the last Congress [the 88th Congress] initiated, this Congress and this administration must continue."[95] Johnson had repeatedly mentioned

President Kennedy a year before, both publicly and privately, in the battles over taxes and civil rights. So it is notable that LBJ—very much the practitioner of presidency-centered leadership—would omit even the mention of the previous president while still paying tribute to the previous Congress. It was as if any progress made on poverty up until that point had been strictly due to Capitol Hill and not the Kennedy administration.

The Johnson Presidential Library contains other evidence of the ongoing concern the White House had with how LBJ would be compared with JFK with regard to poverty. A November 1966 memo from administration pollster Fred Panzer to presidential aide Jake Jacobsen accounted for each instance when Kennedy had talked about poverty or related issues such as job training, as well as the success he had in passing antipoverty measures. The memo reads like a scorecard of JFK's commitment to fighting poverty by using his own words and actions, compared to those of Johnson. It noted that LBJ, in the first month of his presidency, talked more about poverty than JFK had in the nearly three years of his administration. "It is significant that there is no reference to 'poverty,' 'antipoverty,' 'war on poverty,' or 'economic opportunity' in the three volumes of his [JFK's] Public Papers covering 1961, 1962, and 1963." Almost as if the arguments of the memo were meant somehow as talking points for the public, Panzer acknowledged that, while Kennedy had mentioned poverty sporadically, he never addressed the issue in terms of the underlying causes of poverty, or as something requiring sustained action from the federal government.[96]

Interestingly, the basic point that Johnson wanted to convey—that even the venerated John Kennedy fell short in comparison to Johnson when it came to fighting economic inequality—was momentarily lost on the president's speechwriters in early 1967. In preparing a speech on poverty that LBJ later delivered at a White House event in May of that year, they initially included a reference to JFK that neither Johnson nor most historians today would have thought was sustained by the respective legislative records of the two men. The draft of the speech claimed that President Kennedy had declared a "total war on poverty" in his 1961 Inaugural Address, and credited him with "strong leadership" on the issue.[97] It is not clear whether Johnson ever saw that particular speech draft. If he did, it is reasonable to say that he would hardly have been pleased not only that his predecessor was receiving unjustified accolades for his supposed leadership on poverty, but that it was being done by employing language—"war on poverty"—that was very much a Johnsonian term. The version of the speech delivered by the president contained neither this nor any other mention of JFK.[98]

How did Johnson weigh the impact, and the benefits and disadvantages, of using the public's memory of John Kennedy? Reflecting years later on the accomplishments of his first year in office, he seemed satisfied with the changes that had taken place, in terms of congressional willingness to honor Kennedy, and with what he thought was a more proactive stance on the part of the legislative branch:

> We had finally begun to break up the stubborn legislative barriers behind which so much serious and vital legislation had languished. The major battles lay ahead, but we had won our first big test with the Congress. We had pruned the budget far below the level that anyone believed possible, and we had put the power and the prestige of the Presidency solidly behind the most sweeping civil rights bill since Reconstruction...Looking back, I believe that John Kennedy would have approved of the way his successor brought the nation together and mobilized its energies in the wake of tragedy, uncertainty, and doubt. That remains one of the great satisfactions of my Presidency.[99]

But interestingly, while LBJ was willing to use the public's memory of his predecessor, his legislative plans after the 1964 election suggest that that willingness had very definite limits. Johnson saw popular memory of Kennedy as a useful tool, and he used it accordingly. Certainly Johnson's success in breaking the legislative logjam and implementing long overdue changes was at least as much due to his own legislative skills as it was to people's fond memories of John Kennedy and their desire to fulfill some of the unfinished work of his presidency. But the public's love and memories of the late president also frustrated Johnson. He was never quite able to figure out exactly how Kennedy could create such an image about himself. Unfairly for LBJ, it was Kennedy—not him—who would be given much of the credit for civil rights. Over time, the popular conception became one of Kennedy as the inspiring, progressive leader, and of Johnson as simply the politician who got things done.[100]

No matter how much he tried, he was never able to capture the public's love and attention and articulate a vision the way Kennedy had been able to do. One starkly clear example of this was on a Johnson trip to Appalachia to spotlight the poverty of the region and the necessity for programs to alleviate it. After meeting with an impoverished family in their home, Johnson turned to leave, when he noticed two pictures the family had tacked on the wall, one of Jesus Christ and one of President Kennedy. "I felt," Johnson lamented, "as if I'd been slapped in the face."[101] Popular memory of John Kennedy is proof enough that in politics, image matters—perhaps even more than substance. While Johnson was the more skilled and experienced politician, he couldn't inspire and excite people the way Kennedy could. Any vice president who succeeds to the presidency must be able to show that he can govern in his own right. Johnson was no exception to this, but he *also* had to contend with the simple fact that he was not John Kennedy. And while Johnson was distressed by his predecessor's death, and genuinely wanted to honor his memory, he was also trying to move away from him and establish that *he* was now president, pursuing *his* agenda.[102]

As time went on, however, especially regarding civil rights and the "long hot summers" that were imminent, LBJ would come to be viewed, not as the man who fulfilled the Kennedy presidency, but as the man who interrupted it. What if Kennedy had lived? Would things have become as turbulent as they did during the remainder of the decade? As one historian noted, "Some people argued that if Kennedy were still president, blacks

would not have felt the disenchantment that pushed them to violence...
it fixed John Kennedy's image as a moral leader of the movement and
underscored Lyndon Johnson's role as a mere political operator."[103] For
all of Johnson's efforts to secure legislation on civil rights, voting rights,
and poverty, Kennedy was the hero and the one whom history would
remember, not LBJ. In this sense, popular memory of Kennedy served as
a double-edged sword—it acted to strengthen Johnson's hand in passing
legislation, but also denied him the legacy he felt was rightfully his. At
times, Johnson ridiculed the (for him) unfounded adoration the public
gave to Kennedy, a man who came into office generally inexperienced and
without much of a legislative record. Referring to Kennedy's legislative
skills (or lack thereof), Johnson commented, "Kennedy couldn't even get
the Ten Commandments past Congress," and, "They say Jack Kennedy
had style, but I'm the one who's got the bills passed."[104]

Talking about the practical uses of popular memory of John Kennedy
as far as Lyndon Johnson was concerned raises an important question:
was that popular memory the determining factor in the passage of the
Kennedy legislation? Was it really the necessary ingredient that made
the difference between legislative failure (JFK) and success (LBJ)? Earlier,
the question at hand was whether the use of Kennedy's memory by
Dallas city leaders actually worked in directing people's attention away
from the fact that he had been killed there. The answer in the case of
LBJ seems to likewise defy a complete yes or no. Popular memory of JFK
was certainly crucial in altering the course of public opinion, especially
on civil rights. It may well have taken a traumatic event like the sudden
death of a president in broad daylight to shock the American people out
of the general indifference shown toward the nation's social problems. So
if the assassination caused more people to think about those problems—
and question what sort of society could have allowed JFK's murder to
happen—then it is reasonable to say that they interpreted the event as a
national call to action, making Lyndon Johnson's job easier.

One could argue, however, that using Kennedy's memory was not instrumental to Johnson's success—either in pushing his predecessor's legislation or his own during 1965 and thereafter. To credit the public's love of Kennedy as the only, or even the main, reason why Johnson could boast of impressive legislative achievements during his early years as president (until Vietnam reduced his ability to pursue further social reforms), is to ignore Johnson's own leadership skills and his known reputation as a very formidable politician. In the legislative fight over civil rights, for example, his former mentor and chief opponent on the issue —Georgia Senator Richard Russell—ruefully acknowledged Johnson's ability to make his will felt on Congress. Some observers debate whether President Kennedy could have eventually gotten civil rights passed (his brother argued that he would have), but Russell thought otherwise: "We could have beaten Kennedy on civil rights, but we can't beat Lyndon. The way that fellow operates, he'll probably get the whole bill, every last bit of it."[105] The clearest proof of Lyndon Johnson's success in domestic affairs is the astounding volume of legislation secured during his presidency. One has only to take out a copy of his memoirs and open the front cover to see a listing of the major items passed: Voting Rights, Medicare, Aid to Education, Aid to Appalachia, Urban Mass Transit, Model Cities, Highway Safety, Air Pollution Control, the Arts and Humanities Foundation, and Fair Housing, to name but a few examples.[106]

This being said, we are still left with the question why Johnson chose to identify himself, with his predecessor. Why did he bother referring to him so often and essentially giving JFK credit for bills that Johnson was responsible for passing? The new president's professed fidelity to his predecessor was more than just short-term legislative and political strategy. We should also understand the use of popular memory here as a reaction to the conditions in which he entered the White House, and the state of Kennedy's own administration at the time he was killed. Johnson's rise to the presidency was born out of tragedy, to be sure, but in one sense, the circumstances he faced were not overly unusual. He was not the first vice president to become president following the death of the chief executive; November 22, 1963, marked the fourth time in the twentieth century that this had happened. At the time of Kennedy's assassination, the most recent presidential succession had been in 1945 when Harry Truman became president upon the passing of Franklin Roosevelt. What made the use of popular memory all the more necessary (and useful) was the unfinished state of John Kennedy's presidency by November 1963. Johnson's situation was considerably different from that of Truman, as far as popular memory of their respective predecessors is concerned, because people already knew FDR's accomplishments and what he stood for. Roosevelt, people could argue, was the one who had rescued the country from economic collapse, and perhaps even revolution, during the Great Depression. He then devoted the rest of his presidency (and his life) to combating the threat of German and Japanese totalitarianism during World War II. Although he died a month before V-E Day, Roosevelt won the war for the United States. FDR decisively changed the nature of the presidency through these two crises, as his tenure led to a considerable growth of the federal government's power and a more active, visible chief executive. The New Deal institutionalized the belief that government should play a role in the economic activities of the nation and provide some relief and protection for those who could not make their own way within the system.

But what did Kennedy stand for? What were his definite accomplishments by the time he died? What did his presidency mean? The assassination created a much greater sense of shock than did Roosevelt's death.[107] FDR had been ill for some time, and many thought he might not live long enough to complete his fourth term. In Kennedy's case, these questions had no clear answers in the aftermath of November 22, 1963, so the prevalent feeling was one of unfinished business. Someone had to decide what John Kennedy's presidency and death meant; that someone, according to Lyndon Johnson, was him. He took it upon himself to channel the popular memory of JFK and define what his presidency meant; this had to be done if JFK was to mean anything. It would have to be done if Johnson himself was to mean anything. Johnson felt he owed it to JFK to ensure that his premature death did not infringe upon his presidential legacy.[108]

LBJ's detractors would be correct, up to a point, to argue that it was little more than political opportunism to latch onto the popular memory of his predecessor to complete his unfinished agenda—the genuine justifications of that agenda notwithstanding. Certainly it was opportunism bordering on the unseemly for Johnson to glorify Kennedy in order to solidify his own political position going into the 1964 election, given the mistrust of him by the Kennedy camp that seemed only to intensify after the assassination. A political greenhorn Lyndon Johnson was not; he understood that the route to the esteemed presidential legacy he wanted ran through John Kennedy, at least through the end of 1964. But if Johnson effectively exploited the public's memory of the late president, such proved to be no less true of the Kennedy family and their partisans. In both camps, there was opportunism and cynicism as to how President Kennedy could be used to maximum political benefit.[109] The tug of war that ensued for nearly the rest of the decade saw both attempt to claim the public's affection for JFK as their property, and dismiss the other side as, in Johnson's phrase, the "illegal usurper."

As we have seen, aides to the fallen president began plotting their re-conquest of the presidency within weeks after Dallas. More than just mapping RFK's political future, however, some later suggested that Johnson had no political legitimacy at all—either as president or vice-president. Evelyn Lincoln, JFK's personal secretary, charged in a 1968 memoir that her boss not only planned to replace LBJ on the 1964 Democratic ticket, but that he had never intended to name him as his running mate in 1960 in the first place. Lincoln argued that the placement of Johnson on the 1960 ticket was due to Johnson's allies at the Democratic convention leaking false reports that he was a contender. The choice of Johnson as the vice presidential candidate—and indirectly, as president three and a half years later—was due more to his own unscrupulous machinations than JFK's interest in nominating him.[110]

Kennedy, according to his devoted secretary, was little more inclined to keeping Johnson as his running mate as the 1964 election approached. Mrs. Lincoln recalled a conversation with JFK in the fall of 1963 in which he supposedly confided that he would likely drop Johnson; the president mentioned North Carolina Governor Terry Sanford as one possible replacement. While he had not decided definitively by the time he left for Texas, Mrs. Lincoln recalled the president telling her, "It will not be Lyndon."[111]

The implications of such anecdotes are clear: Lyndon Johnson should never have been vice-president, let alone president. That he was able to sit in what was John Kennedy's Oval Office was the result of intrigue and tragic circumstance. Lincoln's version of events does strain credulity,[112] but it also suggests how unwilling the Kennedy camp was to give Johnson any room to claim he was JFK's true successor. For them, Johnson became president according to nothing more than the strictest letter of the law. How could he possibly declare he was the guardian and interpreter of Camelot when the slain King Arthur himself had never intended to place him in his court? With public expectations of an RFK bid for the presidency, and with private maneuvering within the Kennedy circle to set that process in motion as early as 1964, how could LBJ be anything more than a placeholder for a Kennedy restoration? The new president, far from being the faithful Kennedy disciple he claimed to be, was simply using the late president's agenda as his ticket to a 1964 election victory that should have been John Kennedy's.

The Johnson White House, on the other hand, saw the same opportunism congealing within the Kennedy family. The effect of JFK's popular memory upon his younger brother will be explored further in the next chapter, but suffice it to say here that Johnson loyalists regarded the Kennedys as the usurpers, attempting to snatch away what the new president had inherited by virtue of presidential succession. LBJ aide Marvin Watson, charged with planning the 1964 Democratic convention, discovered what he believed to be a plot by Kennedy loyalists within the party to pack the convention with their own supporters who would try to deliver to RFK the *presidential* nomination. Confronting JFK-appointed DNC chairman John Bailey, Watson recalled years later that Bailey supposedly admitted that plans were afoot to make it a Kennedy convention. With the delegates still emotionally traumatized over the assassination, a film tribute to JFK and a convention speech by his younger brother could have induced a stampede to nominate RFK.[113] According to his memoir, Watson candidly told Chairman Bailey where the magic of JFK should rightfully rub off. Emotions from the assassination were still raw, and as Watson explained, "it remained politically important for continuity to remain between the slain president and his successor who thus far had not won the office in his own right."[114] His recollections, like those of Evelyn Lincoln, should be taken rather skeptically. Fears of a convention setup that would result in RFK receiving the presidential nomination may have been overblown. The more plausible scenario is that Kennedy was trying to get the nod as Johnson's running mate. Nevertheless, as evidenced by LBJ's telephone conversation with Mayor Daley, the president took seriously any threat by the Kennedys to convert emotion into votes. And Watson's conversation with Bailey is telling. Few others may have been willing to argue so bluntly that the emotion over the "martyred" President Kennedy could be converted into votes, or that Lyndon Johnson was the one who owned the rights to that conversion. Johnson recognized the power contained in popular memory of his predecessor. It is naïve to suggest that his invocation of Kennedy stemmed solely from idealistic intentions. But it would, however, be unfair to omit from consideration that the Kennedy family was just as determined as he was to fulfill their dreams of a "restoration" by way of the late president. Neither camp failed to understand how beneficial JFK could be to their respective ambitions.

Looking at the popular memory of John Kennedy in terms of how Lyndon Johnson used and was affected by it is instructive in pointing out the drawbacks of using memory to promote oneself. Johnson may have wanted Americans to see him as the legitimate heir to "Camelot," but many ended up giving Kennedy the credit for the accomplishments and promise of the 1960s, while reserving the blame for what went wrong for LBJ. Domestic unrest over race relations and divisions over Vietnam— although beginning to appear during Kennedy's watch—exploded during Johnson's tenure. Many Americans became convinced that Johnson had taken the country down a completely different path than the one JFK would have chosen. Although President Reagan would be dubbed the "Teflon President" twenty years later, perhaps this appellation applies just as much to John Kennedy. He remained undefiled, untouched by what happened in the years after his murder. Perhaps his shocking death, and the accompanying belief that he simply hadn't had a fair chance, contributed to people's willingness to see Kennedy in overwhelmingly positive terms. But whatever the reason, the popular memory of Kennedy worked to LBJ's detriment.[115]

Johnson himself confronted an opportunity in the popular memory of the late president, but the balancing act he was never able to master was to benefit from that memory without becoming a victim of it. This balancing act preoccupied him during the entire length of his presidency; former advisor Joseph Califano later wrote that LBJ was "haunted" by the Kennedys. The president was, according to Califano, "caught between the glorious memories of an assassinated President and the evident ambition of the brother who considered himself the heir apparent."[116] How to draw close enough to that memory to achieve great things, without remaining so close to it that the American people would perpetually judge him as being less than the great JFK, regardless of what he did, was the ever-present challenge Lyndon Johnson confronted throughout his five years in the White House. Indeed, the president expressed his concern that everything he did during his first year in office would be ascribed to his predecessor. Johnson began thinking of his own program as the successor to the New Deal, not the New Frontier. In a strange way, casting himself as a new Franklin Roosevelt was easier than becoming a new John Kennedy.[117] Johnson's phone transcripts indicate his reluctance to continue acting as the servant of JFK's vision and agenda. In a conversation with Whitney Young in early January 1964, LBJ expressed interest in appointing two black attorneys to vacant judicial posts. He complained, however, that he himself would not receive any credit for it because the suggestion for appointing them came from someone in the Kennedy administration. Although Young tried to reassure Johnson that he would in fact be recognized for the appointments, the president nonetheless replied, "Now, the President [Kennedy] wanted it, and he would have done it. I feel like I've got an obligation to it. But I don't want to do it unless the whole Negro community knows that I'm doing it, and the Democrats are doing it."[118]

Johnson quickly grew frustrated with people's constant expectations that his actions as president would, and should, conform to what they thought Kennedy would have done. In one example of his irritation that he was expected to play the role of John Kennedy, barely two weeks after the assassination, the new president discussed with advisors an upcoming Medal of Freedom ceremony. But when Johnson was told that the late president had planned on making the event 45 minutes long and that he should do the same, the president expressed his anger at the fine line he had to walk in honoring Kennedy while still trying to govern in his own right. As Theodore White described LBJ's reaction, "Johnson burst out that he was tired of people telling him he had to do this or that or another thing because it had been the most important thing in the world to John F. Kennedy—it would take him fifteen years to do it all. He wouldn't give the ceremony more than ten minutes for television."[119] For some, not much changed even after the 1964 election. Having won one of the most impressive electoral victories of the 20th century, and with Democratic majorities in both houses of Congress offering the prospect of truly historic legislative achievement in the years to come, the president was still expected to keep John Kennedy's agenda at the forefront. LBJ could not have been pleased with what the editors of the *New Republic* decided the 1964 election meant. Incongruously, they asserted that the election gave him the type of mandate and power that Kennedy (and most presidents) had never had. Yet, it was a mandate more about Kennedy than about himself: "The President can self-confidently get to work on unfinished business of the Kennedy administration—Medicare, an expanded poverty program, aid to education...He is now President in his own right—and with real power."[120]

Simply put, the popular memory of JFK was unfair to his successor. If Kennedy was able to wryly quip, "Oh, well, just think of what we'll pass on to the poor fellow who comes after me,"[121] it was indeed the poor fellow who came after him who appreciated the truth, in so many respects, of that comment. What Kennedy unintentionally left behind were the various problems that would so trouble Johnson later, but the most important intangible thing he passed on was a popular vision and expectation of presidential leadership that neither Johnson, nor probably anybody else, could ever fulfill. Lyndon Johnson may have been right to constantly remind people that his accomplishments in office were considerably more impressive than what Kennedy could have boasted of, but he still missed the point. Looking at the amount and scope of the legislation either president secured, LBJ clearly was the more accomplished leader, even allowing for the fact that he spent more time as president than did JFK. Regardless, how could actual accomplishments compete with the popular memory of a young, inspiring leader who was cut down in the prime of life before he could see his agenda become reality? Although we tend to assume that a fictional second Kennedy term would have been successful, and that the 1960s could have been a far different era, the tantalizing *possibilities* of Kennedy's interrupted presidency outshone anything Johnson could have achieved.

Photo 9. LBJ listens to a tape recording made by his son-in-law serving in Vietnam, July 31, 1968. As the Johnson presidency wore on, JFK, always an unstated force in the background, became a burden instead of a benefit.

Photo courtesy of the Lyndon B. Johnson Presidential Library (Jack Kightlinger); B1274-16.

Popular memory—the images of John Kennedy that the public persisted in holding—proved stronger than actual achievements in this case. It was Kennedy, not Johnson, who was considered the truly great president, the civil rights president, the one who would have made the United States immeasurably better had he lived. Kennedy, not Johnson, would be memorialized in popular culture in such ways as Dion's song "Abraham, Martin, and John." The trick of memorializing somebody in this case was not in how to do it, or whether to do it, or what a memorial to that person should look like. The difficulty lay, rather, in trying to use the public's memory, but at the same time, not get used by it. Perhaps *Newsweek* magazine said it best in this regard when, in commenting on the public's different perceptions of Johnson and Kennedy, stated, "One clear pattern, even Mr. Johnson's supporters are less taken with him personally than they are impressed by his record of getting things done." Johnson's legislative success simply couldn't match the public's enduring memory of Kennedy; Johnson's "impact on the electorate is dominated by voters' reaction to what he has done as opposed to what he is or seems to be."[122]

NOTES

1. Doris Kearns Goodwin, *Lyndon Johnson and the American Dream* (New York: Harper & Row, 1976), 178.
2. Paul R. Henggeler, *In His Steps*, 61-64.
3. Maurice Isserman and Michael Kazin, *America Divided: The Civil War of the 1960s* (New York: Oxford University Press, 2000), 103-104.
4. Many of the letters the new president received in the days and weeks after the assassination fully supported the completion of JFK's program; many expressed confidence that, as one writer from Chicago said, "You will carry on the ideals that President Kennedy died for." Several contained specific references to civil rights, although it is important to note that some of these letters were written after LBJ had declared before Congress that he would indeed pursue the Kennedy civil rights bill. Letters from the Public, Support after Death of President Kennedy (Box 28), in White House Central Files, Public Relations, Lyndon B. Johnson Presidential Library, Austin, Texas.
5. Theodore H. White, *The Making of the President 1964* (New York: Atheneum Publishers, 1964), 48.
6. Doris Kearns Goodwin, *Lyndon Johnson and the American Dream*, 171-173.
7. Both Kennedy and Johnson aides confirm this belief. LBJ advisor Joseph Califano recalled a 1968 meeting between the President and Robert Kennedy in which Johnson asserted, "I've never thought of my administration as just the Johnson administration, but as a continuation of the Kennedy-Johnson administration." Ted Sorensen, present at the same meeting, remembered him saying, "I still regard myself as carrying out the Kennedy-Johnson partnership," and that JFK, "looking down" upon him, would have felt that his agenda had been faithfully followed. Joseph A. Califano, Jr., *The Triumph and Tragedy of Lyndon Johnson: The White House Years* (College Station: Texas A&M University Press, 2000), 295; and Theodore Sorensen, *Counselor: A Life at the Edge of History* (New York: HarperCollins, 2008), 462.
8. James N. Giglio, *The Presidency of John F. Kennedy*, 38-39.
9. Lyndon B. Johnson, *The Vantage Point*, 22-23, 42.

10. Chalmers M. Roberts, "Tax, Rights Moves Key to Johnson's Intentions" *Washington Post*, November 27, 1963, A2; and Robert Dallek, *Flawed Giant*, 60-61.
11. Maurice Isserman and Michael Kazin, *America Divided*, 103-104.
12. Paul R. Henggeler, *In His Steps*, 122.
13. Lyndon B. Johnson, *The Vantage Point*, 19.
14. Lyndon B. Johnson Library and Museum, "President Johnson's Address before a Joint Session of the Congress: November 27, 1963," available from http://www.lbjlib.utexas.edu/johnson/archives.hom/speeches.hom/631127.asp; accessed from Internet March 25, 2008.
15. Melville Bell Grosvenor, "The Last Full Measure: The World Pays Tribute to President Kennedy," *National Geographic Magazine* 125, no. 3 (March 1964), 312.
16. Tom Wicker, *JFK and LBJ: The Influence of Personality upon Politics* (New York: Penguin, 1968), 85-86; and Jim F. Heath, *Decade of Disillusionment*, 7-8.
17. Maurice Isserman and Michael Kazin, *America Divided*, 84.
18. Robert Dallek, *Flawed Giant*, 114.
19. Francis M. Carney and H. Frank Way, Jr. (eds.), *Politics 1964* (Belmont, California: Wadsworth Publishing Company, Inc., 1964), Postscript.
20. Bruce Catton, "Introduction," in *Four Days*, 5.
21. Lyndon B. Johnson, *The Vantage Point*, 71.
22. As the *Washington Post* editorialized the day after Johnson's Joint Session address, "Action upon the whole broad program before [Congress] is what they owe the President who appealed to them for help and the President who is beyond all human help." Understandably, comments such as those are indicative of the emotional atmosphere after JFK's death—but they still highlight the rapid transition the nation apparently made within only a few days from a feeling of complacency to concern that the fork in the road the country faced be negotiated wisely. "A Time for Action," *Washington Post*, November 28, 1963, A20.
23. "Kennedy Praised on Civil Rights," *New York Times*, November 27, 1963, 24.
24. Max Holland (ed.), *The Presidential Recordings of Lyndon B. Johnson: The Kennedy Assassination and the Transfer of Power, November 1963-January 1964, Volume One* (New York: W.W. Norton & Company, 2005), 140.
25. LBJ Library and Museum, "President Lyndon B. Johnson's Address Before a Joint Session of Congress."

26. Lyndon B. Johnson Library and Museum, "President Lyndon B. Johnson's Annual Message to the Congress on the State of the Union: January 8, 1964," available from http://www.lbjlib.utexas.edu/johnson/archives. hom/speeches.hom/640108.asp; accessed from Internet March 25, 2008.

27. Ibid.

28. Ibid.

29. John D. Morris, "Leaders Press for Legislation," *New York Times,* November 26, 1963, 1; and Paul R. Henggeler, *In His Steps,* 118.

30. Interestingly, LBJ appeared to claim later that he had always agreed wholeheartedly on the idea of lowering taxes. In his remarks upon signing the tax cut (as a part of the Revenue Act of 1964), he noted, "President Kennedy—who first requested this legislation early last year—was convinced that it constituted the single most important measure we could take to strengthen our economy. *I have fully shared that conviction.*" (italics mine) Statement by the President, P.L. 88-272, Revenue Act of 1964, H.R. 8363 (Box 4), in Reports of Enrolled Legislation, December 31, 1963-February 26, 1964, Lyndon B. Johnson Presidential Library, Austin, Texas; and Robert Dallek, *Flawed Giant,* 71.

31. Ibid.

32. LBJ Library and Museum, "President Lyndon B. Johnson's Annual Message to the Congress on the State of the Union."

33. Michael R. Beschloss (ed.), *Taking Charge: The Johnson White House Tapes, 1963-1964* (New York: Simon & Schuster, 1997), 25.

34. The Kennedy administration found benefits and costs to the proposed wheat sale. While it was not expected to measurably diminish the American wheat surplus, it would benefit Midwest farmers; yet, it could arouse opposition from Polish, Irish, and German Americans as an election year approached. A Gallup poll recorded public support for the sale at 60 percent. JFK was in the process of working out a deal with Congress that would allow the sale to be completed as long as all produce was transported by American shipping, but the deal had not yet been finalized. Michael R. Beschloss, *The Crisis Years: Kennedy and Khrushchev, 1960-1963* (New York: HarperCollins, 1991), 644-645; and Lyndon B. Johnson, *The Vantage Point,* 39-40.

35. Robert A. Caro, *The Years of Lyndon Johnson: The Passage of Power* (New York: Alfred A. Knopf, 2012), 398-399, 424-425.

36. Michael R. Beschloss (ed.), *Taking Charge,* 37.

37. Johnson acknowledged the influence of Kennedy's memory upon his young presidency both privately and in more formal settings. In his first

cabinet meeting held within days of JFK's murder, Secretary of Agriculture Orville Freeman recalled the new President asserting, "I do not want to get into a fight with the [Kennedy] family, and the aura of Kennedy is important to all of us." Randall Woods, *LBJ: Architect of American Ambition* (New York: Free Press, 2006), 425.

38. JFK had had to figure out how to address Byrd's objection that the tax cut would lead to federal deficits and was therefore fiscally unsound. The administration also had to contend with Tennessee Senator Albert Gore Sr.'s charge that the cut would primarily benefit the wealthy; as of early November 1963, it was thought that the strongest objections to the bill would come from these two senators. Memo from Lawrence O'Brien to Frazar B. Wilde, November 2, 1963 (Box 9), in White House Aides, Office Files of Mike Manatos, Tax Bill 1963-1965 (1 of 2), Lyndon B. Johnson Presidential Library, Austin, Texas; and Maurice Isserman and Michael Kazin, *America Divided*, 106.

39. LBJ Library and Museum, "President Lyndon B. Johnson's Annual Message to the Congress on the State of the Union."

40. Robert Dallek, *Flawed Giant*, 72-74.

41. Richard Lyons, "Income Tax Slash Is Signed into Law," *Washington Post,* February 27, 1964, A1, A6; and John D. Morris, "President Signs Tax Bill with $11.5 Billion in Cuts; Sees a Stronger Nation," *New York Times,* February 27, 1964, 1, 18.

42. Tom Wicker, "Johnson Goes Directly from Talk to Give Pens to Mrs. Kennedy," *New York Times,* February 27, 1964, 18.

43. "The New President," in *The Nation,* December 14, 1963 (Vol. 197, No. 20), 405.

44. George P. Hunt, "An Intelligent Courageous Presidency," *Life* Magazine 40th Anniversary Reprint Edition, Fall 2003, 44.

45. Robert Dallek, *An Unfinished Life,* 640-642.

46. James N. Giglio, *The Presidency of John F. Kennedy,* 179-181.

47. John F. Kennedy Library and Museum, "Radio and Television Report to the American People on Civil Rights," available from http://www. jfklibrary.org/j061163.htm; accessed from Internet March 28, 2008.

48. Ibid.

49. In fact, shortly after Kennedy's civil rights address, a memo from Mike Mansfield to Larry O'Brien cited a recent congressional poll that showed it to be "virtually impossible" for the JFK bill to pass the Senate. Chances for the approval of the Kennedy tax bill in the Senate Finance Committee were also not good. Memo from Robert Baker to Senator Mike Mans-

field (and passed along to Larry O'Brien), June 27, 1963 (Box 6), in White House Aides, Office Files of Mike Manatos, Civil Rights 1963-1965 (1 of 2), LBJ Library.

50. Conover Hunt, *JFK for a New Generation*, 49.

51. LBJ believed that introducing the civil rights bill while the tax legislation was still pending was a mistake; Southern lawmakers would filibuster civil rights and thereby also prevent the tax bill from being voted upon in the Senate. Knowing all too well how the southern bloc operated, Johnson had urged President Kennedy in the summer of 1963 not to introduce his civil rights legislation at that time, predicting that the administration's other legislative initiatives would be held up as "hostages" until civil rights was effectively defeated. His advice was ignored, but the vice president proved to be correct. Not only Kennedy's tax cut, but also his bills on health care, education, and foreign aid were all frozen in their paths through Congress by November. Paul R. Henggeler, *In His Steps*, 112-113; and Robert A. Caro, *The Years of Lyndon Johnson: The Passage of Power*, 345-346, 462.

52. LBJ Library and Museum, "President Lyndon B. Johnson's Address Before a Joint Session of Congress."

53. Jim F. Heath, *Decade of Disillusionment*, 168.

54. Johnson had taken a far more hesitant stance on civil rights in his earlier political career. In his 1954 remarks to the Senate following the Supreme Court's Brown v. Board of Education ruling, for example, he stated that the decision must be obeyed, but absent was any assertion on his part that "separate but equal" was wrong, or that the nation was morally compelled to ensure equal rights to all of its citizens. In fact, he seemed to defend "separate but equal," lamenting that that system had not been allowed to bring about social change in a more gradual manner. "The decision is an accomplished fact," Johnson said. "However we may question the judgment of the men who made this ruling, it has been made...on the basis of the 'separate but equal' doctrine, we [Texans] have made enormous strides over the years." May 18, 1954 speech, Senate floor concerning Supreme Court ruling on segregation (Box 15), in Statements of LBJ, March 16, 1954-June 1954, Lyndon B. Johnson Presidential Library, Austin, Texas; and Maurice Isserman and Michael Kazin, *America Divided*, 106.

55. Robert Dallek, *Flawed Giant*, 114.

56. Max Holland (ed.), *The Presidential Recordings of Lyndon B. Johnson*, 117.

57. Michael R. Beschloss, *Taking Charge*, 37.

58. In a December 2, 1963 memo to Larry O'Brien, LBJ aide Henry Wilson predicted that of the 95 Democratic House members from the former Confederate states, almost none would vote for the civil rights bill. With several other congressmen also predicted to vote against it, Wilson estimated that between 90-100 Democrats in the House would not support the bill; Republican support was therefore essential, as 60-70 Republicans would be needed just to achieve a slight majority. Memo from Henry H. Wilson, Jr. to Lawrence O'Brien, December 2, 1963 (Box 2), White House Aides, Office Files of Henry Hall Wilson, "Civil Rights," LBJ Library.

59. Robert Kennedy suggested that memory of JFK played a role in securing Dirksen's support. "Everett Dirksen liked President Kennedy a great deal and much, much, much more than he liked Lyndon Johnson. And I think that he made an effort—at least, part of his motivation, in the last analysis, was because of President Kennedy." Edwin O. Guthman and Jeffrey Schulman (eds.), *Robert F. Kennedy in His Own Words: The Unpublished Recollections of the Kennedy Years* (New York: Bantam Press, 1988), 212; and Jim F. Heath, *Decade of Disillusionment*, 175-176.

60. References to the late president, in terms of popular memory, within the Johnson administration's internal correspondence are surprisingly few. LBJ publicly linked his predecessor to civil rights in his first few major addresses, and so it would have been unnecessary for his aides to remind him to do so to ensure success on his legislative program. In any event, one place where there is such a reminder is in a page of notes written by aide Lee White, apparently when reviewing a draft of the statement the President would make upon signing the Civil Rights Act. The first of his suggestions was, "I would urge some reference to President Kennedy." By this point, with passage of the bill presumably assured, LBJ would have referred to the late president as a way of further strengthening his position in the eyes of the public as the true successor to JFK. Johnson followed White's advice, as his remarks at the bill's signing did invoke Kennedy. Lee White's notes on LBJ civil rights speech (Box 1), in White House Aides, Office Files of Lee White, LBJ Library; and Lyndon B. Johnson Library and Museum, "President Lyndon B. Johnson's Radio and Television Remarks Upon Signing the Civil Rights Bill: July 2, 1864," available from http://www.lbjlib.utexas.edu/johnson/archives. hom/speeches.hom/640702.asp; accessed from Internet April 7, 2008.

61. Godfrey Hodgson, *America in Our Time: From World War II to Nixon— What Happened and Why* (Princeton: Princeton University Press, 2005), 171-172; and Paul R. Henggeler, *In His Steps*, 67.

62. Gary Donaldson, *Liberalism's Last Hurrah: The Presidential Campaign of 1964* (Armonk, New York: M.E. Sharpe, 2003), 107-108.

63. Robert Dallek, *Flawed Giant*, 61.

64. "What About 1964" and "The Johnson Style" in the *New Republic* December 7, 1963 (Vol. 149, No. 23, Issue 2557), 3, 29; and Leonard Baker, *The Johnson Eclipse: A President's Vice Presidency* (New York: The Macmillan Company, 1966), 188-197.

65. Doris Kearns Goodwin, *Lyndon Johnson and the American Dream*, 170.

66. Theodore Sorensen acknowledged the hostility amongst former Kennedy aides toward the new president: "It was becoming increasingly difficult to remain in the White House...The antipathy among some White House staffers toward Johnson—almost as if he were an undeserving, unworthy usurper...rose to the point that it threatened to divide our previously close-knit team into open factions." Theodore Sorensen, *Counselor*, 385.

67. Paul R. Henggeler, *In His Steps*, 96-97.

68. Gary Donaldson, *Liberalism's Last Hurrah*, 105-106; and Robert A. Caro, *The Years of Lyndon Johnson: The Passage of Power*, 409-410.

69. Arthur Schlesinger, Jr., *Journals*, 217-218.

70. Ibid., 211-212, 214.

71. Washington political journalist Stewart Alsop noted that this disdainful attitude toward Johnson, owing to the circumstances in which he became president, was shared not only by Kennedy staffers, but by many in the press. His effusive praise of Kennedy notwithstanding, LBJ confronted an "instinctive and subconscious" air of hostility from the day he took office. Transcript. Stewart Alsop Oral History Interview, 07/15/1969, by Paige E. Mulhollan. Oral History Collection, Lyndon B. Johnson Presidential Library, Austin, Texas; and Jim Bishop, *The Day Kennedy Was Shot* (New York: Gramercy Books, 1968), 617-618.

72. Maurice Isserman and Michael Kazin, *America Divided*, 104.

73. Michael R. Beschloss, *Taking Charge*, 463.

74. On this, however, the President was trying to move in two directions at once. As aide George Reedy recalled, LBJ considered 1964 as still being Kennedy's term. While Johnson thought keeping the Kennedy staffers around him was a good idea, he was also trying to establish his own "completely and absolutely independent" presidency—hence part of the reason why he blocked RFK from being nominated as vice president. Transcript. George Reedy Oral History Interview, 11/16/1990, by Michael L. Gillette. Oral History Collection, Lyndon B. Johnson Presi-

dential Library, Austin, Texas; and Doris Kearns Goodwin, *Lyndon Johnson and the American Dream*, 175, 177-178; and Robert David Johnson, *All the Way with LBJ: The 1964 Presidential Election Campaign* (Cambridge: Cambridge University Press, 2009), 56.

75. *LBJ: The American Experience*, videocassette, narrated by David McCullough (PBS Home Video, 1997).

76. Theodore H. White, *The Making of the President*, 48-49.

77. Douglas E. Schoen (ed.), *On the Campaign Trail: The Long Road of Presidential Politics, 1860-2004* (New York: ReganBooks, 2004), 187.

78. Robert Dallek, *Flawed Giant*, 166.

79. Lyndon B. Johnson Library and Museum, "President Lyndon B. Johnson's Remarks before the National Convention upon Accepting the Nomination: August 27, 1964," available from http://www.lbjlib.utexas.edu/johnson/archives.hom/speeches.hom/640827.asp; accessed from Internet April 7, 2008.

80. Many thought the late president was indeed present in spirit at the convention, and although LBJ emerged with the wholehearted endorsement of the Democratic party, many surely did make comparisons between the man who could have (or should have) received the nomination, and the man who was nominated instead. As William F. Buckley, Jr. sardonically commented, "The Kennedy crowd, though they are for Johnson, miss greatly their fallen hero, who gave them a sense of style, which Uncle Cornpone simply cannot duplicate." Recalling what he felt had been expectations by some JFK supporters in 1960 that he was "a man who would transubstantiate politics," Buckley continued, "Myths die hard, and [Lee Harvey] Oswald saw to it that this one would never die. LBJ is said to be disturbed about this myth which moves always ahead of him." William F. Buckley, Jr., "Atlantic City without the Girls," in *National Review* Vol. XVI, No. 36 (September 8, 1964), 763.

81. James N. Giglio, *The Presidency of John F. Kennedy*, 25; Robert Dallek, *An Unfinished Life*, 640; and Godfrey Hodgson, *America in Our Time*, 172-173.

82. Kennedy's chairman of the Council of Economic Advisers, Walter Heller, had been soliciting ideas on what to include in such a package at least as early as June 1963. In a November 5, 1963 memorandum, Heller requested policy recommendations from cabinet secretaries and agency heads to be submitted to Theodore Sorensen by Thanksgiving. At that point, it seems that only the very broadest of parameters for a JFK poverty agenda had been sketched out. In what may have been the only

issue on which the Kennedy administration failed to leave posterity with a memorable turn of phrase, possible slogans for the poverty initiative included "Human Conservation and Development," "Access to Opportunity," and "Attack on Poverty." The rather roundabout "Widening Participation in Prosperity" was at that time the working slogan, but Heller candidly admitted that they were looking for something better. Walter Heller memo to Robert J. Lampman, June 3, 1963; and Heller memo to cabinet secretaries and agency heads, November 6, 1963 (Box 1), in Legislative Background: Economic Opportunity Act of 1964, War on Poverty, "CEA Draft History of the War on Poverty [1 of 3]," Lyndon B. Johnson Library, Austin, Texas.

83. While it is true that federal efforts to fight poverty during the 1960s would be associated more with Johnson than with Kennedy, some historians would argue that it was still JFK who asked his advisors for antipoverty legislative proposals, and that even on this issue, Johnson was to some extent following what his predecessor had already set in motion. Even the term "war on poverty," written for LBJ's 1964 State of the Union address, was conjured up by a JFK speechwriter. On this issue, as with civil rights, it may ultimately be most accurate and fair to conclude that what Kennedy started, Johnson finished and used to go even further in the way of social legislation. Godfrey Hodgson, *America in Our Time*, 174.

84. Max Holland (ed.), *The Presidential Recordings of Lyndon B. Johnson*, 179.

85. Even had this been his intention, it is unlikely Johnson would have won over his predecessor's supporters. Arthur Schlesinger seemed unwilling to give him any credit for accomplishing what JFK had been unable to, and thought that Johnson's presidency would be little more than a second Kennedy administration. Following the 1964 Democratic Convention, Schlesinger recorded, "On issues and programs, I have no doubt that LBJ will continue to carry forward the Kennedy policies...The test will come when he runs out of ideas. Up to this point he has been living intellectually off the Kennedy years." Unwilling to acknowledge Johnson's own formidable skills as a politician and ability to amass his own record as president, Schlesinger even commented months later that "the irony is that he [LBJ] has been so dependent thus far on the man whose memory he is trying to erase...LBJ has no idea of his own but consensus." Arthur Schlesinger, Jr., *Journals*, 232, 236.

86. LBJ Library and Museum, "President Lyndon B. Johnson's Annual Message to the Congress on the State of the Union."

87. Robert C. Albright, "Congress Asked to Pass Tax-Cut Measure by Feb. 1," *Washington Post,* January 8, 1964, A1, A5; and Walter Lippmann, "Johnson's First Message," *Washington Post,* January 9, 1964, A19.
88. Lyndon B. Johnson, *The Vantage Point,* 69.
89. John A. Andrew III, *Lyndon B. Johnson and the Great Society* (Chicago: Ivan R. Dee, 1998), 56.
90. Public Papers of the Presidents/American Presidency Project, "Lyndon B. Johnson: Special Message to the Congress Proposing a Nationwide War on the Sources of Poverty, March 16, 1964," available from http://www.presidency.ucsb.edu/ws/index.php?pid=26109#axzz1nVl0rGFc; accessed from Internet February 12, 2012.
91. Ibid.
92. Lyndon B. Johnson Library and Museum, "President Lyndon B. Johnson's Remarks at the University of Michigan: May 22, 1964," available from http://www.lbjlib.utexas.edu/johnson/archives.hom/speeches.hom/6405 22.asp; accessed from Internet April 8, 2008.
93. Bruce J. Schulman, *Lyndon B. Johnson and American Liberalism: A Brief Biography with Documents* (Boston: Bedford/St. Martin's, 1995), 84.
94. LBJ later argued that the solution to solving the problem of poverty required three elements: the need for action, the willingness to act (strengthened by JFK's death), and "the disposition to lead," which he attributed to himself. "When I looked inside myself," he said, "I believed that I could provide the third ingredient." Almost as if he intended to make a contrast between his approach to poverty and Kennedy's late and vague support for antipoverty measures, he continued, "My entire life, from boyhood on, had helped me recognize the work that needed to be done in America...The poverty program [Walter] Heller described was my kind of undertaking. 'I'm interested,' I responded. 'I'm sympathetic. Go ahead. Give it the highest priority. Push ahead full tilt.'" This Heller did, and a month into Johnson's presidency, he recommended a 10-year antipoverty program, to be unveiled as a major component of the President's 1964 legislative agenda, which would focus on the prevention of poverty among the young and on measures aimed at helping older Americans escape economic deprivation. Lyndon B. Johnson, *The Vantage Point,* 71; and Rowland Evans and Robert Novak, *Lyndon B. Johnson: The Exercise of Power* (New York: The New American Library, Inc., 1966), 427, 431; and Walter Heller memo to Theodore Sorensen on poverty program (Box 1), in Legislative Background: Economic Oppor-

tunity Act of 1964, War on Poverty, "Bureau of the Budget Papers on Poverty," LBJ Library.

95. Letter to Congress, February 17, 1965; and Draft of Letter to Congress, February 9, 1965 (Box 32) in White House Aides, Office Files of Richard N. Goodwin, "Poverty Message," Lyndon B. Johnson Presidential Library, Austin, Texas.

96. Memorandum from Fred Panzer to Jake Jacobsen, November 26, 1966 (Box 371) in White House Aides, Office Files of Fred Panzer, "Kennedy Poverty Quotes," Lyndon B. Johnson Presidential Library, Austin, Texas.

97. Draft of Poverty Speech (Box 12) in White House Aides, Office Files of Ben Wattenberg, "Poverty Speech & Memorandum to the President," Lyndon B. Johnson Presidential Library, Austin, Texas.

98. The initial JFK reference in the draft may have been removed due to Johnson's political sensitivities, but it might also have been deleted because as a matter of fact, Kennedy did not at all declare a war on poverty in his Inaugural Address. That speech was almost entirely a foreign affairs-related speech, and historians have noted how little attention JFK devoted in his address to domestic issues. Kennedy may have intended to focus on poverty had he not been assassinated, but crediting him with showing "strong leadership" on poverty—whether by LBJ or anybody else —would have been an unjustified stretch. Public Papers of the Presidents/ American Presidency Project, "Lyndon B. Johnson: Remarks at a Reception for Participants in the Conference on Women in the War on Poverty," available from http://www.presidency.ucsb.edu/ws/index.php?pid=2824 1&st=&st1=#axzz1tcpmaul3 ; accessed from Internet May 6, 2012.

99. Lyndon B. Johnson, *The Vantage* Point, 41.

100. Joseph Califano recalled Johnson making the comparison "what we recommended to Congress and what we got," with "what Kennedy recommended to Congress and what he got." It was a valid point, but one that LBJ felt was lost on too many people, even perhaps himself. Califano observed that Johnson "was possessed by an internal class struggle with an icon, and tortured by an envy he could not exorcise." Joseph A. Califano, Jr., *The Triumph & Tragedy of Lyndon Johnson*, 294-295.

101. Paul R. Henggeler, *In His Steps*, 121.

102. LBJ's desire that his presidency would be considered his own by right of election was at least part of the reason why he kept RFK off the 1964 Democratic ticket. Kenneth O'Donnell claimed that Johnson once commented, "I don't want history to say I was elected to this office because I had Bobby on the ticket with me." Ever the pragmatist, Johnson then

reportedly added, "But I'll take him if I need him." Jules Witcover, *Party of the People: A History of the Democrats* (New York: Random House, 2003), 521; and Paul R. Henggeler, *In His Steps*, 110.

103. Ibid., 115.

104. Ibid., 122.

105. Jeff Shesol, *Mutual Contempt*, 164, 114; and Bruce J. Schulman, *Lyndon B. Johnson and American Liberalism*, 74.

106. Lyndon B. Johnson, *The Vantage Point*, inside front cover.

107. William E. Leuchtenberg, *In the Shadow of FDR*, 116.

108. Even if no offense against Johnson was intended, there were many who believed this should be his primary concern as president; no short-age of reminders about how he became president and where so much of the political momentum he enjoyed in 1964 came from. Consider *Newsweek*'s observation in August 1964: "Of all the top-priority items on Lyndon Johnson's legislative shopping list, only the $947.5 mil-lion anti-poverty bill was his very own—and not, like the Presidency itself, the legacy of John F. Kennedy." "Congress: The Brand of LBJ," *Newsweek* Vol. LXIV, No. 7 (August 17, 1964), 32.

109. Johnson biographer Randall Woods suggests that there was indeed exploitation of the assassination by the Kennedy family, taking the form of monument-building and naming in the immediate aftermath. One example was Jacqueline Kennedy requesting, at RFK's urging, that President Johnson name the space center at Cape Canaveral after her husband—thus forever linking JFK and space exploration. According to Woods, the family tried to "get all [they] could while the getting was good," while simultaneously taking a disdainful and mocking attitude toward LBJ. Randall Woods, *LBJ: Architect of American Ambition*, 424.

110. Evelyn Lincoln, *Kennedy & Johnson* (New York: Holt, Rinehart and Winston, 1968), 91.

111. Ibid., 205.

112. JFK biographer Robert Dallek attributed Johnson's selection by Kennedy in 1960 to the simple fact that it was the politically wise thing to do. Despite the chaotic series of events by which LBJ was offered and accepted the vice-presidential spot (which produced considerable bitterness between Johnson and RFK), and the fact that the two candi-dates had little in common, Kennedy thought Johnson's presence on the ticket would improve the chances of a November electoral victory. The choice of LBJ can be explained as simple political pragmatism, not Kennedy being railroaded by Johnson supporters into picking their

man as his running mate. Lincoln's contention that President Kennedy was ready to dump Johnson for 1964 is contradicted by Arthur Schlesinger, Jr., who noted that rumors of LBJ's political demise at the hands of JFK were "wholly fanciful." According to Schlesinger's narrative, at an election planning meeting among the President's political circle less than two weeks before the Texas trip, the idea of finding a new vice president was never considered. Robert Dallek, *An Unfinished Life*, 269-274; and Arthur Schlesinger, Jr., *A Thousand Days*, 1018.

113. W. Marvin Watson and Sherwin Markman, *Chief of Staff: Lyndon Johnson and His Presidency* (New York: Thomas Dunne Books-St. Martin's Press, 2004), 58-60.

114. Ibid., 60.

115. It could not have helped matters that Johnson had poured what can only be described as exuberant praise upon Kennedy in the first few months after the assassination. It is ironic to think that LBJ's frustration over appearing small in comparison to JFK was caused in part by his own gushing tributes. In a January 1964 ceremony at the Lincoln Memorial in which he concluded the official period of mourning, Johnson effectively compared Kennedy with Abraham Lincoln in a speech evocative of the Gettysburg Address: "The world will not forget what [JFK] did here," he said, adding, "Let us here determine that John Kennedy did not live or die in vain, that this Nation under God shall have a new birth of freedom." "President Says Goodbye to John Kennedy," *Life* January 3, 1964 (Vol. 56, No. 1), 22.

116. Joseph A. Califano, Jr., *The Triumph & Tragedy of Lyndon Johnson*, 11-12.

117. William E. Leuchtenberg, *In the Shadow of FDR*, 137-138.

118. Kent B. Germany and Robert David Johnson (eds.), *The Presidential Recordings of Lyndon B. Johnson: The Kennedy Assassination and the Transfer of Power, November 1963-January 1964, Volume Three* (New York: W.W. Norton & Company, 2005), 181, 183.

119. Theodore H. White, *The Making of the President*, 59.

120. "Back to Work," in *The New Republic* November 14, 1964 (Vol. 151, No. 20), 3.

121. Warren Bass, *Support Any Friend: Kennedy's Middle East and the Making of the U.S.-Israel Alliance* (New York: Oxford University Press, 2003), 14.

122. "The LBJ Image," *Newsweek*, August 31, 1964 (Vol. XLIV, No. 9), 27.

CHAPTER THREE

THE CASE OF ROBERT F. KENNEDY

THE ONCE AND FUTURE KING AND THE GREAT EXPECTATIONS OF A KENNEDY RESTORATION

> There is such a thing as evocation of the great dead, and there is also such a thing as the exploitation of corpses. Senator Kennedy seems appallingly far from recognizing the difference.
> —Journalist Murray Kempton, on Senator Robert F. Kennedy's announcement on his candidacy in the 1968 presidential election.[1]

It is ironic that the chief source of grief for Robert F. Kennedy during the 1960s also proved to be perhaps his greatest asset when he decided to run for president in March 1968. His brother's assassination left him in charge of not only the Kennedy family, but also the Kennedy legend: the unfulfilled "promise of greatness" that John Kennedy had left behind.[2] Like Lyndon Johnson, RFK tried to capture for himself the benefits of the public's memory of the late president. As one historian on the two Kennedy brothers has written, "He could convert the adoration of JFK, Robert came quickly to realize, into a power base sufficient to challenge Johnson and ultimately regain what he felt was rightfully his...Kennedy turned to the task of preserving JFK's memory and fashioning a JFK mystique and legacy." His central objective was "to see that legacy transmitted into the political culture, embraced by political survivors (beginning with himself) and kept alive for future progeny."[3]

Robert Kennedy however, hardly needed to remind people of his proximity to Camelot. With the nation seemingly at war with itself by 1968, many Americans—although, not as many as is commonly assumed today—responded to him with great enthusiasm and emotion during his three-month quest for the presidency.[4] RFK's supporters saw in him the tantalizing possibility of returning the country to a more tranquil, pre-Vietnam, pre-assassination setting.[5] The flip side to this was, as this chapter's opening quote suggests, that other Americans leveled the same accusations of cynicism and opportunism at Robert Kennedy that President Johnson had faced. Kennedy's campaign, many asserted, was based on a sentiment-laden yearning for a supposedly more glorious past that his brother embodied, which the younger Kennedy thought he could somehow restore.[6] And because the Vietnam War was at center stage in American politics in 1968, some used JFK against him, arguing that Robert Kennedy could not credibly identify himself as an anti-war candidate when he had been an advocate of American involvement in South Vietnam during the Kennedy administration.[7] This uncomfortable fact led to candidate Kennedy's attempts to decouple his brother from the war by claiming that the late president had actually decided, by the end of his life, to withdraw from Vietnam. RFK wanted people to remember Lyndon Johnson, and not John Kennedy, as the one responsible for getting the country hopelessly involved in a war that was becoming more unpopular by the month.[8]

Robert Kennedy would find, as did Dallas city leaders and Lyndon Johnson, that popular memory of President Kennedy was very much a mixed blessing. JFK's assassination was not the origin of the distrust and hatred between the late president's brother and vice president, but it intensified their bitterness toward each other. Both believed that the other was bent on hijacking his rights to leadership in the aftermath of

JFK's death. The story of the LBJ-RFK "feud" has been well told by others, and so this chapter will not explore it in detail.[9] But we can understand this feud after 1963 as being driven to a large extent by popular memory: which of the two could most effectively associate himself in the public's mind with President Kennedy and therefore lead the country in his stead?

But the terms by which RFK could capture the country's love of John Kennedy were considerably different than those for either Dallas or President Johnson for one obvious, though crucial, reason. As the president's brother and most trusted advisor, he was the person most able (aside from Jacqueline Kennedy) to authoritatively define what JFK meant and therefore how he should be remembered. He, unlike Dallas city leaders and LBJ, did not have to establish his fealty to President Kennedy. He did not need the sort of methodical, step-by-step process over time that Lyndon Johnson followed in order to establish trust with the public. Indeed, the idea that Robert Kennedy would have found it necessary to build a memorial or pass a tax cut to prove to everyone his loyalty to JFK would have been regarded as ridiculous. The younger Kennedy had both a greater right to speak for his brother and a lesser need to remind the public of it, but all of this may have created impossibly grandiose expectations for what he could have accomplished had he ever actually become president.

Rather than taking a chronological approach to discussing popular memory of JFK in relation to Robert Kennedy—examining his contributions to and uses of it one by one—it is more practical to adopt a thematic approach. Because of his proximity to President Kennedy, we can group his interaction with the public's memory around two broad themes: how and where RFK influenced the memory of JFK, and the ways in which the spectral presence of the late president influenced his own political career as a senator and presidential candidate. The latter built upon the former to some extent. Bobby Kennedy, by helping keep his brother relevant in American politics, also kept himself in a prime position to win the White House. One cannot understand the widespread belief among both admirers and detractors alike that he would run for president sooner or later, without assessing the vital role that popular memory of JFK played. Former Kennedy aide Ted Sorensen very candidly commented that memory was a primary factor in why he and others hoped so much that Bobby Kennedy would run: "The majority of us ultimately rallied around the banner of RFK as a means of fulfilling the Kennedy dream. We sought not the restoration of Camelot but a continuation of our effort to build a better society."[10]

One could reasonably argue that "Camelot" and the "Kennedy dream" were effectively the same thing, thus making Sorensen's disclaimer of not being interested in "Camelot" a bit misleading. It was essentially the same conundrum President Johnson faced when the *New Republic* declared that he was now president in his own right—meaning he was empowered to finish the JFK agenda. Sorensen's recollections suggest the RFK campaign was also trying to figure out how close to the late president was too close; like LBJ, their attempts to move toward and away from the memory of JFK both succeeded and failed.

The year 1964 proved to be just as important for Robert Kennedy as it was for Lyndon Johnson in terms of popular memory of John Kennedy. The new president repeatedly referred to his predecessor both publicly and privately in pushing for his legislation. During that year, the late president's younger brother began making his own pronouncements on JFK's importance to the nation. With the shock of Dallas still fresh, people wanted to hear about what he stood for and what he meant—and Robert Kennedy told them. One of his first opportunities was in a book foreword he authored for a memorial edition of *Profiles in Courage*. In his essay, he argued that the courage demonstrated by the men portrayed in the book was the same courage that President Kennedy had exemplified throughout his life. Moreover, RFK identified the signal moments in the Kennedy administration as unqualified examples of courageous leadership. He asserted, "When [JFK] took the blame completely on himself for the failure at the Bay of Pigs, when he fought the steel companies...when he forced the withdrawal of the Soviet missiles from Cuba, when he spoke and fought for the equal rights for all our citizens...he was reflecting what is the best in the human being."[11] It was not enough, RFK was suggesting, to simply recognize President Kennedy for the courage that had been a hallmark of his life. His sudden death had left the work of his presidency unfinished. Kennedy echoed his brother's 1960 challenge to the country to embrace a greater sense of activism in the face of all that remained to be done: "If there is a lesson from his life and from his death, it is that in this world of ours none of us can afford to be lookers-on, the critics standing on the sidelines...What happens to the country, to the world, depends on what we do with what others have left us."[12]

Although it would have been inappropriate in this context to promote himself politically, the younger Kennedy called for a renewed effort to solve the nation's problems. He did not mention himself specifically as the one who could solve those problems, but if people were already beginning to see him as his brother's true successor, he would not have needed to. In what sounded very similar to the rhetoric of his 1968 campaign, he argued, "There will be future Cubas. There will be future crises. We have the problems of the hungry, the neglected, the poor and the downtrodden. They must receive more help. And just as solutions had to be found in October 1962, answers must be found for these other problems that still face us."[13]

The slain president's younger brother also promoted the image of John Kennedy as an advocate of young people, and this portrayal fit well with his message of unfinished business and the responsibility of others to carry on in his name. This linkage of JFK with youth would be readily evident later in the 1968 campaign. Polls showed younger Americans supporting Kennedy and Eugene McCarthy as well, in considerably higher numbers than they did Hubert Humphrey.[14] If both Dallas and Lyndon Johnson had demonstrated that the assassination should lead to a national dedication to tolerance and an end to hatred, Robert Kennedy argued that the tragedy—and a genuine effort at honoring the memory of the late president—must result in activism on the part of young people everywhere to solve the problems of the world.[15] During one 1964 overseas trip, RFK asserted that President Kennedy "was not only President of one nation, he was president of young people all over the world. If President Kennedy's life and death are to mean anything, *we* young people must work harder for a better life for all the people of the world"[16] (italics mine). At the 1965 dedication of a library in Brazil named for JFK, Senator Kennedy reminded his audience of his brother's lifelong fondness for reading and learning. He directed his comments at the young people of the community, calling upon them to dedicate themselves to the ideals of freedom and social progress that JFK had strongly believed in: "free institutions...the importance of the individual and [of] the State serving the individual," thereby connecting the late president with the struggle for freedom and social progress in the Third World.[17]

RFK played up his older brother's appeal to young people repeatedly and tried to direct the same type of loyalty toward himself that they'd had for JFK. In several of his speeches, both before and after his election to the Senate, he blended this recognition of the importance of young people, and his own identification as one of them, with his belief that they could honor President Kennedy by working on behalf of less fortunate people both in the United States and internationally. In a commencement address at Marquette University in June 1964, RFK concluded his remarks by reminding his audience of the late president's visit to Milwaukee two years before, when he defined the choice facing the nation as one of either progress or complacency.[18] It was now the responsibility of the nation's youth to accept the challenge that JFK had laid before them. The idealistic conception of public service with which the Attorney General associated his brother later became a recurring topic in subsequent years. In a commencement speech a year later at Queens College in New York City, RFK declared, "We must remember our revolutionary heritage. We must dare to remember what President Kennedy said we could not dare to forget—that we are the heirs of a revolution that lit the imagination of all those who seek a better life...that we must stand, not for the status quo, but for progress."[19] And in an address given two years later in South Africa, again at a university, he made his self-identification as part of the youth of the world even clearer when he said:

> We are—if a man of forty can claim that privilege—fellow members of the world's largest younger generation. Each of us have our own work to do...President Kennedy was speaking to the young people of America, but beyond them to young people everywhere, when he said that "the energy, the faith, the devotion, which we bring to this endeavor will light our country and all who serve it —and the glow from that fire can truly light the world."[20]

Kennedy memorialized his brother on a truly national stage in a tribute he presented at the Democratic national convention in the fall of 1964. President Johnson, as already discussed, rightly feared a sudden grassroots movement resulting in the placement of RFK on the party ticket, even perhaps replacing him as the presidential nominee. While that did not happen, the months leading up to the convention did feature at least one major attempt, during the New Hampshire primary, to make Kennedy LBJ's running mate.[21] RFK's memorialization of his brother, and Johnson's realization of the power and emotion behind the memory of the late president, converged at the Atlantic City convention, despite Johnson's earlier assertions (as if there was any doubt about the matter) that he would not tap Kennedy for vice president.[22]

Johnson, who had expended so much effort to appear as a Kennedy-style liberal, was frightened at the prospect of the convention getting carried away with memories of John Kennedy and possibly nominating his brother by acclamation instead of himself.[23] Many Americans were already beginning to see RFK as the more logical heir to the throne and even as the one who should be nominated for president that year. In the New Hampshire primary, Kennedy had actually received about 26,000 votes to LBJ's 30,000.[24] At the convention, the president arranged the schedule of events to ensure that Robert Kennedy would pay tribute to the slain president only *after* LBJ and vice presidential nominee Hubert

Humphrey had the nomination safely in hand. Even then, the attorney general was originally supposed to speak for a brief two minutes to introduce a film tribute to his brother.[25] Johnson expected that the convention would wholeheartedly shower the accolades of the party upon him, but Atlantic City instead became a celebration of two presidents— or three, if the reaction of attendees to RFK's appearance was a sign of things to come. The convention demonstrated that LBJ may have captured for himself the party's loyalty, but the late President Kennedy still commanded its love. As *Time* magazine reported, "Throughout Atlantic City, memory or mention of Jack Kennedy, that man of electric personality, evoked the most emotional, truly spontaneous reaction of the week." In a rare post-assassination public appearance, Jacqueline Kennedy attended one of the convention receptions. Her presence, no less than that of Robert Kennedy, heightened the grief of many convention attendees who had, less than a year ago, expected to be celebrating the re-nomination of JFK. "Many in the crowd shouted 'Hi, Jackie.' Others, just seeing her, sobbed."[26] The political ramifications of this for RFK did not go unnoticed.[27]

The crowd that gathered to hear Kennedy's remarks honoring JFK and to watch the film was still very emotionally charged over the assassination, breaking into cheering at the mere mention of the late president's name.[28] Not even Kennedy himself could have been prepared for the response the convention gave him before he could begin to speak. When he appeared onstage, the delegates erupted in a frenzy.[29] RFK biographer and friend Arthur Schlesinger, Jr., who was in the hall at the time, described the almost frightening scene:

> I stood on the floor in the midst of the thunderous ovation. I had never seen anything like it...the demonstration roared on, reaching a new intensity every time that Robert Kennedy, standing with a wistful half-smile on his face, tried to bring it to an end...he repressed his tears. Many in the crowd did not. He seemed slight,

almost frail, as the crowd screamed itself hoarse. It went on for twenty-two minutes.[30]

The ovation that Robert Kennedy received that night should not obscure what he said in his speech. Thanking the party for its work in electing his brother four years earlier, he then went beyond the idea of courage in his *Profiles in Courage* essay. He cast the late president as the latest in a long line of illustrious Democratic presidents, wholly committed to the party's domestic policy proposals: extension of Social Security benefits and the minimum wage, improvement of housing, medical care for the elderly, and civil rights. "To all this he *dedicated* himself," RFK declared (italics mine), again giving President Kennedy unqualified credit for achievements on domestic issues, when he had been criticized during his presidency for his lack of sufficient interest in and accomplishment on precisely those concerns. In foreign relations he praised JFK for both maintaining American military superiority and seeking peace with the Soviet Union. Not surprisingly, he paid tribute to his brother for prevailing over the Soviets in the Cuban Missile Crisis; "the Soviets withdrew their missiles and bombers from Cuba," according to RFK, due to President Kennedy's efforts to keep the United States strong militarily. Effectively endorsing Lyndon Johnson as John Kennedy's heir, in words he must have regretted four years later as he himself ran for president, RFK declared, "I join with you in realizing that what started four years ago...that that's to be continued. The same efforts and the same energy and the same dedication that was given to President John F. Kennedy must be given to President Lyndon Johnson and Hubert Humphrey."[31]

The film tribute, no less than Kennedy's speech, left delegates not only with a sense of tragic heroism in their fallen standard bearer, but also with the feeling that both the past and the future of the party converged in his younger brother. Today, national party conventions produce little in the way of unexpected drama or memorable moments, but the 1964 Democratic convention became second only to the state funeral in terms of the creation of JFK mythology, as well as the number of Americans who took part in it. The "A Thousand Days" film showed JFK with his children, delivering his stirring inaugural address, hard at work resolving the Cuban Missile Crisis, and signing the Nuclear Test Ban Treaty. Footage of Kennedy advocating for the Alliance for Progress in Latin America, creating pandemonium in Berlin with his famous "Ich bin ein Berliner" speech, and wryly introducing himself abroad as "the man who accompanied Jacqueline Kennedy to Paris," emphasized the force for good in the world that the Kennedy presidency represented. Convention attendees and viewers watching the tribute on national television heard the late president delivering his trademark witticisms at news conferences, and they heard Richard Burton's recital of King Arthur's lines from "Camelot."[32] Given the scant nine months that had elapsed since the assassination and the renewed wave of emotion set off by the JFK tribute, *Newsweek* later took a surprisingly skeptical attitude, observing that "the Kennedy film surpassed common political puffery." The homage paid to President Kennedy, while perhaps excessive, nevertheless reinforced the image of greatness many were associating with him: "At Atlantic City—and in countless living rooms across the land—it was plain that many had come to believe it."[33]

What was it that the convention crowd responded to? Partly it was the presence of the late president's younger brother, now almost a tragic figure in his grief, but it was also the images of John Kennedy conveyed to them. One has only to listen to a recording of the speech to understand that Robert Kennedy possessed little of JFK's oratorical skill. His delivery was rather monotone, and he seemed hesitant, unsure of himself.[34] But the reaction of the audience was ample proof, "if nothing else," as *Time* put it, "of the magic of the Kennedy name and memory."[35] There was potential power in that memory; it was not simply an emotional demonstration of a gloried era that was forever gone, relegated to the history books as a period seemingly so long past that nobody could remember it. It was not just the memory of a president's supposedly noble deeds and character that had no real use except as inspirational speech material for reminding people of what *had been* done. Robert Kennedy made that memory relevant for the future. He, more than anyone else, could turn the potential power of that memory into actual power. His proximity to the late president, and his words themselves, gave him authority to define what JFK had meant to the nation. It surely must have crossed a few minds in the convention hall that evening that RFK, as his brother's closest adviser, and a participant in many of his important decisions, enabled him to define—and even embody—what JFK believed and what he meant.[36]

Robert Kennedy's two books published during this period, *Thirteen Days* and *To Seek a Newer World*, are additional proof of his hand in sculpting and reinforcing the public's memory of his brother's presidency. In his well-known memoir of the 1962 Cuban Missile Crisis, *Thirteen Days*, the younger Kennedy gave his brother and key administration members a distinctly flattering portrayal in retelling what many at the time (and even today) thought was JFK's finest hour as president. The book presented then-Attorney General Kennedy as heavily involved in the decision-making and in the final, supposedly victorious, resolution.[37] The management of the crisis, *Thirteen Days* suggested, featured President Kennedy's restraint and prudence that made the difference between peace and war. The administration's ultimate willingness to employ a diplomatic instead of strictly military strategy was intended to contrast starkly with the recklessness and flawed decision-making of President Kennedy's successor in his handling of the Vietnam War.[38] Recalling the unattractive military options of either destroying the Soviet missiles through a surgical air strike or invading Cuba outright, RFK argued, "President Kennedy was disturbed by this inability to look beyond the limited military field."[39] Later, he recalled JFK's reference to Barbara Tuchman's *The Guns of August* one night during the crisis as a guide for what he would not get drawn into. Tuchman's book examined the flawed assumptions and military strategies of the western European powers in the years prior to World War I that initially resulted in widespread enthusiasm at the prospect of continent-wide hostilities. Reflecting on the slaughter that resulted, and the sadly misplaced confidence of both sides that victory would come easily, RFK wrote that his brother resolved during the crisis, "I am not going to follow a course that will allow anyone to write a comparable book about this time...If anybody is around to write after this, they are going to understand that we made every effort to find peace and every effort to give our adversary room to move."[40]

As if to make clear the message of the Cuban Missile Crisis—in light of the strife Vietnam was causing—Kennedy argued that it showed "how important it was to be respected around the world, how vital it was to have allies and friends...I discern a feeling of isolationism...a resentment of the fact that we do not have greater support in Vietnam...I think it would be well to think back to those days in October 1962."[41] We can, therefore, characterize RFK's *Thirteen Days* as not simply his recollections from the most dangerous point in the Cold War, but also as a piece of campaign literature. It was a means of enhancing his own leadership as the driving force in favor of a blockade and his negotiations with Soviet officials in bringing the matter to a peaceful end. That same ability was desperately needed again in Vietnam, or so the implication seemed to be.[42] President Kennedy, his brother was arguing, had successfully avoided engulfing the country in a nuclear war with the Soviets, but it seemed that his forbearance in spite of American military power had died with him. Although the book was written in 1967, before Kennedy had definitely committed himself to running for president the following year, there was still politics—and memory—at work here.[43] Recalling JFK's greatest victory as president and placing himself at the center of the action allowed the Senator to claim the same qualities his brother had. The country, he suggested, was very much in need of those qualities.

Historians, however, have generally not upheld RFK's version of the missile crisis as accurate, even though his account of President Kennedy's heroic management of the crisis has endured with the public. In a 2000 motion picture, perhaps not un-coincidentally bearing the same name as RFK's memoir, no mention exists of Operation Mongoose—the ongoing Kennedy administration efforts to overthrow Fidel Castro, a major factor in the Soviets' decision to install nuclear missiles in Cuba. Robert Kennedy, an early supporter of a military solution to the crisis, was instead portrayed consistently in favor of a political/diplomatic course of action. Viewers of the movie—and readers of RFK's *Thirteen Days*—were left with the impression that President Kennedy (and Senator Kennedy) had come to a greater understanding of the limits of military force, as well as the need for flexibility in foreign relations. The film does not have the backdrop of Vietnam unlike the book. It culminates with President Kennedy delivering his uplifting 1963 American University commencement address, conveying a sense of leadership and the promise of world peace irrevocably lost after 1963.[44]

Senator Kennedy further sold the idea that progress begun by the late president had stalled in the years following the assassination in his campaign book *To Seek a Newer World*. The book, much of it written by his political advisor John Seigenthaler,[45] had more of an overt political tone than *Thirteen Days*, for it was a sort of campaign manifesto—setting out Kennedy's perspectives and proposed solutions for several areas of national concern. JFK was cited multiple times, although not excessively so. But *To Seek a Newer World* brought him into focus in several ways. JFK was often directly quoted. Three of the six chapters began with a quote by him in the opening paragraphs. Perhaps deliberately, those three chapters covered issues with which he was strongly identified: the Alliance for Progress and Latin America, nuclear control, and Vietnam. As if to anticipate the critics' argument that the proposals outlined were unrealistic, RFK took the same idealistic approach as had his brother. The Senator tried to craft an agenda that reminded Americans of JFK. He was responding to the nation's problems, but doing so by recalling President Kennedy's belief that "idealism, high aspirations, and deep convictions are not incompatible with the most practical and efficient of programs—that there is no basic inconsistency between ideals and realistic possibilities, no separation between the deepest desires of heart and mind and the rational application of human effort to human problems."[46] In effect, Kennedy gave his own White House bid and policy pronouncements the posthumous endorsement of JFK. RFK wanted his audience to believe that, had the late president read *To Seek a Newer World*, he would not have dismissed it as idealistic folly, but instead would have thoroughly approved of what his brother intended to do.

RFK built his own agenda for the White House on that of President Kennedy. The book promoted the image of John Kennedy embarking on bold new initiatives that had languished or been mishandled in the years since his death. RFK wanted those initiatives to be pursued anew —not simply as a way of memorializing the late president, but also on their own merit as components of a restructured American foreign policy. For example, the chapter on the Alliance for Progress began with a reminder that the Alliance was conceived by President Kennedy as "a vast cooperative effort, unparalleled in magnitude and nobility of purpose, to satisfy the basic needs of the American people...[and] a plan to transform the 1960s into an historic decade of democratic progress."[47] Such was President Kennedy's conception, although RFK did not mention that the idea for the program had originally come from the Eisenhower administration.[48] According to the Senator, progress in achieving the goals of the Alliance had been minimal because American political leadership (meaning, of course, LBJ) had neglected to develop the program after 1963. The Alliance's failure, according to Kennedy, was due to inaction by both the U.S. and Latin American governments; it was time to restore President Kennedy's vision and commitment to the hemisphere.[49]

The book's chapter on Latin America and the Alliance for Progress was not the first place where RFK recognized his brother for a supposedly new approach to hemispheric relations. The completion of a housing project in Mexico City in November 1964 featured an RFK speech extolling JFK for his presumed commitment to political and economic progress in Mexico and the entire region—a commitment that was nothing less than revolutionary.[50] But Kennedy's extensive discussion in *To Seek a Newer World* of what remained to be done to achieve President Kennedy's plan for the hemisphere implied that he would pick up where his brother had left off. Although RFK cautioned readers on the difficulty of bringing dramatic change to the region,[51] one gets the impression that his own commitment to hemispheric political and economic development ran just as deep as his brother's—and more broadly than his earlier obsession with overthrowing Fidel Castro. RFK purported that in a second Kennedy presidency, the Alliance for Progress would regain the importance it had supposedly enjoyed in the first.

Another example of RFK establishing continuity between his brother's administration, and what he himself would do as president, are his observations on the Vietnam War in *To Seek a Newer World*. It might seem odd that he would mention JFK and the war in the context of a political tract, for the Kennedy administration had deployed thousands of American military personnel to South Vietnam—a much greater commitment than Eisenhower had made.[52] Based on the version of events in the Vietnam chapter, one would think that the late president had irrevocably decided to conclude American involvement before the U.S. became even more deeply committed. Kennedy quoted from his brother's September 1963 interview with Walter Cronkite on the boundaries the president envisioned for the American commitment to South Vietnam: "It is their war. They are the ones who have to win it or lose it. We can help them, we can give them equipment, we can send our men out there as advisers, but they have to win it, the people of Vietnam, against the Communists."[53] The fact that the president then indicated his unwillingness to leave South Vietnam to its fate was not included in the book. The president's subsequent comment "I don't agree with those who say we should withdraw. That would be a great mistake. That would be a great mistake,"[54] was omitted from *To Seek a Newer World*. This omission meant, of course, that readers were left with the mistaken impression that JFK had decided in the last months of his presidency to withdraw from Vietnam.[55] But RFK did more here than express his conviction that his brother would not have involved the country in an unwinnable war. He cited the Cuban Missile Crisis, again, as the model for how the war could be resolved. The Senator had advocated a negotiated settlement in Vietnam and was critical of the Johnson administration for failing to take advantage of opportunities to negotiate.[56] Had the United States attempted to do what was, according to RFK, done in October 1962—exploiting whatever area of the enemy's diplomatic position that had the best chance of leading to a solution—a similar resolution to the Vietnam conflict could be found. As he said, "We moved toward peace by accepting, as we wished to interpret it, that position of our adversaries which contained the greatest hopes of swift settlement. The crisis thus was resolved without open conflict. Such a technique might have yielded fruitful results in the winter of 1967...Certainly it was worth trying."[57]

Of course, whether the circumstances of the Cuban Missile Crisis in 1962 were similar enough to those of the Vietnam War by 1968 that such a strategy could have ended the war is debatable. Senator Kennedy's description of the ordeal's resolution, moreover, was simplified and misleading; the crisis did not end simply because the administration hoodwinked the Soviets into a deal that was wholly favorable to the United States. Moreover, the fact that the world came within an inch of annihilation during the Cuban episode was no small consideration in hoping that the type of diplomacy necessary to pull the world back from potential nuclear war never needed to be used again. So Kennedy's apparent belief that the diplomatic maneuvering that ended the Cuban crisis was applicable to future world conflicts was a bit misplaced. In any event, such was his attempt to burnish his qualifications for the presidency by identifying his crisis resolution experience and the lessons he had supposedly learned in October 1962, as well as by harkening back to the Kennedy administration in arguing that the country had lost its way in the years since.[58] More than this, however, was the juxtaposition RFK created between Cuba and Vietnam in promoting both himself and his brother. Vietnam was more important to the American public by 1968 than was Cuba, but Cuba became a useful way for the Senator to deflect the finger-pointing over who was responsible for American entry into the war. President Kennedy, according to RFK, deserved to be remembered for the Cuban Missile Crisis, not Vietnam. He accepted a modicum of blame for his own past assertions that the United States could win the war, but his comparison of the Cuban crisis with that of Vietnam (post-1963, of course) was his way of protecting his brother's memory while giving himself greater legitimacy as a war critic—or so he hoped.[59] Cuba became a shining example of President Kennedy *and* RFK's leadership and crisis management skills. The latter claimed credit for suggesting the so-called "Trollope ploy," in which the administration accepted Khrushchev's initial offer to withdraw the missiles in return for a no-invasion pledge, instead of his follow-up demand for mutual withdrawal of Soviet missiles in Cuba for American missiles in Turkey. This was not true, as the idea likely came instead from Kennedy National Security Adviser McGeorge Bundy. Bundy did not challenge RFK as he embellished his role in the affair before and during his presidential campaign, even after JFK's Secretary of Defense, Robert McNamara echoed Kennedy's rather spurious recollection of events. Kenneth O'Donnell, however, was not as reticent. RFK was hardly less cynical than Lyndon Johnson when it came to riding popular memory of the late president and distorting events for his own benefit. Historian Michael Beschloss wrote that O'Donnell reminded the Senator that the successful resolution of the crisis was due first and foremost to President Kennedy, not him. RFK sharply retorted, "Well, *he's* not running for President this year, and *I am*." (original italics)[60]

In any case, by reminding the public of the problem-solving of the Cuban Missile Crisis and applying it to the problem of Vietnam, Senator Kennedy was saying, in effect: this is what President Kennedy would have done. This is how he would have resolved the issue, and I intend to do what he intended to do. In the text of a speech given in Chicago the month before he announced his bid for the presidency, Kennedy admitted that he had been among those predicting victory for the U.S. in Vietnam.[61] But in acknowledging his mistake, he still did not link that tragically mistaken forecast to JFK. Other Kennedy partisans argued in a similar vein, expressing their conviction that the late president was intent on removing American military personnel in his second term. However inconclusive the evidence for this theory is, it still finds support in the American press fifty years later. *Time* argued in July 2007 that Kennedy's policies on Vietnam, albeit ambiguous and not fully disclosed to the public during his presidency, never envisioned a wider military role for the United States beyond the 17,000 advisers he sent. Supposedly, he had also told a few advisors in his administration that he had decided all of those advisers would be out after the 1964 election.[62]

Robert Kennedy's efforts to establish a clean break between JFK's and LBJ's respective decisions on Vietnam, thereby making Johnson responsible for the later debacle, were met with skepticism by others. Not everyone during the late 1960s (and certainly not today) accepted the idea that President Kennedy should avoid responsibility for the war. The *National Review* charged that RFK and former Kennedy advisers Arthur Schlesinger, Jr., Theodore Sorensen, and John Kenneth Galbraith were recasting their slain leader as an advocate for *ending* the war rather than pursuing it. Their efforts to adjust the history of the Kennedy administration to keep JFK and his brother safe from Vietnam critics, the *Review* commented, "have subtly redefined his view of the Vietnam conflict so that it seems less like Johnson's and more like Dr. [Benjamin] Spock's. Right under our noses, John Kennedy is being appropriated for the peace marchers."[63]

President Johnson's prosecution of Vietnam was in part the result of his predecessor's policies, and if the war made the Kennedy administration look a bit less bright and shining, it also posed political problems for his brother as he ran for president on a peace agenda. "If President Johnson's war policy is to be thought of as the logical extension of President Kennedy's, Robert Kennedy's role as critic of the present Administration's policy is seriously compromised."[64] RFK could hardly campaign as an opponent of the war when he had been such a strong supporter of American involvement when both Kennedy brothers had advocated a continued commitment to South Vietnam. The myth of JFK's private determination to quit Vietnam became a part of his brother's memorialization of him. Camelot would not get soiled by the war, and Robert Kennedy could offer himself as an antiwar candidate.

Courage, idealism, public service, youth, a willingness to seek peace, Latin American concerns— observers then and now could hardly be surprised that Bobby Kennedy associated these things with the late president. They are, justifiably or not, many of the qualities and issues for which President Kennedy has been remembered for decades. But in the midst of influencing the public's memory of JFK, Senator Kennedy was also conveying through his writings and speeches a recurring theme: a sense of *unfinished business*—the conviction that the death of JFK left a leadership vacuum in the nation that needed to be filled. Lyndon Johnson had made the same point, but of necessity his use of the public's memory of JFK had to have a shorter time frame: he needed to establish his legitimacy in the eyes of the public until he won his own term. RFK likewise characterized the Kennedy presidency as an unfinished project, but his attempt at a "restoration" would have to wait. LBJ benefited from the shock of the assassination; Robert Kennedy benefited from the increasing national strife of the late 1960s. Johnson had not been a central figure in the Kennedy presidency, but RFK was, and could consequently argue that the nation had deviated from the course President Kennedy would have taken.[65]

Small wonder, then, that many saw Robert F. Kennedy as the obvious ideological successor to his brother—the person most capable of solving the problems that JFK's constitutional successor had supposedly created. At the same time, however, others thought that candidate Kennedy was essentially milking the public's affection for the slain president. He was, Kennedy detractors argued, not only trying to define the public's memory of his brother, but then using that memory he created as the central justification for why he deserved to be president.[66] Considering the central role popular memory of JFK played in his brother's political fortunes requires a hard look at RFK's attributes and accomplishments as a politician by 1968. He spent only three years in the Senate and had no experience in an elected office prior to that.[67] And although he was a formidable campaign manager and political operator during his older brother's political career, he did not really have the charm and oratorical skills that came so readily to JFK. Personality-wise, he and his brother were opposites in several respects.[68] Although it would be inaccurate to argue that memory of the late president was the only card RFK could play in trying to get elected, it could be that memory mattered more than any other single factor: his experience, his ideas, or his own skills as a politician. Determining the role of popular memory in his campaign helps us understand why he ran and how he was able to do so.

The idea of brother Bobby as the successor to JFK did not first appear in the weeks and months after the assassination. Speculation that he and perhaps Edward Kennedy would follow their older brother into the White House, even if that speculation was half in jest, began prior to the 1961 inauguration. Kennedy insiders would later recall the president-elect giving RFK a cigarette case inscribed with, "When I'm through, how about you?"[69] JFK's appointment of his brother to head the Department of Justice, plus Edward Kennedy's election to the United States Senate in 1962 moved some to argue that nothing less than the establishment of a Kennedy dynasty was afoot. Confronted in 1962 with a reporter's question about whether RFK had any plans to run for president someday, the Attorney General rejected the idea as "foolish."[70] Certainly, any such talk about a dynasty in the making could not be taken seriously. Hopes for a succession of three Kennedy presidents should be understood as mostly wishful thinking. It was reflective of the optimism, which drifted into arrogance, among the Kennedy inner circle after the 1960 election. They were convinced that they could utilize the presidency far more effectively than the outgoing administration. They acted as if they knew where they were going, what they wanted to do, and how to go about doing it.[71] Such may have been the overall attitude in 1960 or 1961.

Photo 10. April 1967 cover of *Esquire*. The return of the Kennedys to the White House, or at least an attempted "restoration," was widely expected.

Photo courtesy of George Lois and *Esquire*.

Many could hypothesize about more Kennedy presidents to come without taking the idea too seriously. However, more and more people began to take that idea *very* seriously following the assassination. With President Kennedy gone, Camelot became his brother's inheritance.[72] The memorializing was evident not only in RFK's various public references to the late president, but also in his own personal habits and characteristics. Simply put, he seemed to be trying to become JFK. His efforts must have convinced at least some Kennedy partisans that he, in fact, was his brother—or at least, the next best thing. As one author described this post-1963 process of RFK becoming JFK, "He started employing his brother's characteristic gestures—one hand thrust in his suit pocket, the other jabbing the air...He began smoking the small cigars his brother favored...He let his hair grow longer. He filled his office with memorabilia of his brother."[73] When he spoke, either in tribute to JFK or on political matters, he quoted him to make the late president directly relevant to the matter at hand. RFK also began citing historical or literary figures, a speech device his brother had employed, to give his own remarks a more intellectual gloss, evocative of the late president.[74]

The younger Kennedy's ongoing work in memorializing his brother and the belief among many JFK admirers that he eventually would and *should* run for the presidency, collided with Lyndon Johnson's own efforts to gather up the public's esteem for the late president and make it work for his benefit. His concern over a last-minute, emotion-laden attempt at putting RFK on the 1964 Democratic ticket, resulting in the postponement of the JFK tribute until after the nominating process was concluded, was only one example of what many, then and now, have referred to as the "feud" between the president and RFK. One of the major areas of contention that made up the well-publicized hostility between the two men was a struggle over who could really claim the right to act in John Kennedy's name[75]—or, to use the metaphor widely employed at the time, who had the better claim to the "throne." Part of the feud, in other words, was motivated by memory of JFK. Johnson was convinced that, as Kennedy's constitutionally mandated successor and a self-proclaimed liberal Democrat, he should be the one to use that memory.[76] In contrast, Kennedy partisans believed that it was the Attorney General who was the true successor and that LBJ was unfit to appropriate the late president's program as his own.[77]

In all probability, considering the ridicule that Johnson had been subjected to as vice president, it is likely that regardless of what he did in the aftermath of the assassination, those close to John Kennedy would have looked upon the new president as merely a caretaker who had snatched away what was rightfully theirs. For his part, RFK quickly grew convinced that Johnson was intent not on furthering his brother's memory but on removing all vestiges of him from sight. The day after his brother was killed, Kennedy walked into the West Wing of the White House, only to find JFK's personal effects (including the famous rocking chair) already being removed from the Oval Office, and his personal secretary claiming that the new president had already instructed her to have her desk cleaned out that morning.[78] Kennedy could barely conceive of Johnson as the successor to his brother and was always reluctant to give him credit for anything he accomplished that had been left over from the previous administration. On multiple legislative issues during 1964, the younger Kennedy insisted that it was his brother who deserved credit, and privately complained that LBJ was taking credit for what John Kennedy had originally proposed.[79]

As we have already seen, Lyndon Johnson believed the exact opposite, arguing that it was RFK who was trying to steal what was rightfully his "inheritance." The president was certain, from the day he took office until the day Senator Kennedy died, that RFK would try to parlay the public's memory of JFK into political power of his own. As Johnson commented years later to historian Doris Kearns Goodwin, "I'd given three years of loyal service to Jack Kennedy. During all that time I'd willingly stayed in the background...Then Kennedy was killed and I became the custodian of his will...but none of this seemed to register with Bobby, who acted like *he* was the custodian of the Kennedy dream, some kind of rightful heir to the throne."[80] (original italics) Johnson was convinced not only that he would never be considered the true successor to JFK, but even that many Kennedy partisans thought he had somehow stolen the presidency from them. On one occasion Johnson remarked, "They still don't believe that President Kennedy is dead. Those touch football boys who used to make these decisions aren't making them anymore."[81] And yet, they nevertheless were convinced (recall Ken O'Donnell's November 22, 1963, comments on Air Force One) that their proximity to JFK and the public's affection for him entitled them to a continuing hold on power.

When Kennedy announced that he would run for the United States Senate from New York, challenging incumbent Republican Kenneth Keating, supporters and opponents alike understood the race as a harbinger of a second Kennedy presidency. Skepticism abounded, as critics charged RFK with "carpet-bagging," asking why New Yorkers should support a man who did not even officially take up residence in the state until his Senate bid. Never having served in elected office, Kennedy found his qualifications repeatedly questioned, even whether he was really interested in being a senator to begin with. For many, his sole motivation for running was to use the Senate as a launching pad for a presidential campaign.[82] It did not go unnoticed that Kennedy, who opened his campaign in August 1964, had stated only two months previously—when the possibility of being nominated as LBJ's running mate was as real as it may have ever been—that he was in fact *not* interested in the Senate.[83] Striking examples of cynicism toward Kennedy, in spite of the ongoing sorrow over his brother's death, were not limited to Keating supporters. *U.S. News & World Report* described a feeling of "bitterness" directed at RFK from other Democrats for blatantly using New York as a vehicle toward a future presidential bid. The challenge for the Attorney General lay in whether he could effectively sell himself and his own ideas, and convince voters that he was not simply treating New York as the most direct route available to the White House.[84] In language he would hear again in 1968, RFK was labeled "ruthless," and a "Bobby-come-lately." "Bobby Kennedy," according to one unnamed New York

Democrat, "is a ruthless and ambitious young man who aims to use the New York Democratic Party to beat a path to the White House." Whatever advantage he had due to the "magic" of his name may have been cancelled out by the public's wariness over his intentions. Shortly after entering the race, polls showed him and Keating in a dead heat.[85] And while by this point JFK was being praised as a high priest of American liberalism, his younger brother had to contend with the same suspicions aroused by President Johnson among liberals that his fidelity to the liberal cause was lacking. Some were never convinced. Notable American liberals Gore Vidal, Paul Newman, and James Baldwin threw their support to Keating, so wary they were of both the strength of RFK's liberal convictions, and the self-interested reasons for his sudden desire to be a Senator.[86]

Photo 11. President Johnson and Senate candidate Robert F. Kennedy campaign in New York, October 15, 1964.

Photo courtesy of the Lyndon B. Johnson Presidential Library (Cecil Stoughton); 415-139-WH64

John F. Kennedy was never too far away as his younger brother made his case for why he deserved to sit in the Senate. The Keating forces argued that RFK's campaign was based on little more than emotion, with the younger Kennedy seemingly arguing that electing him was tantamount to electing the late president. Even one Kennedy staffer reportedly remarked, "He's running as an incumbent of the New Frontier."[87] To be sure, he attracted large crowds as he campaigned throughout the state, and the contest garnered a considerable amount of local and national interest, both because a Kennedy was one of the candidates and because the Johnson-Goldwater race was effectively over by this point. Still, for a man who only a few years later would be revered second only to JFK himself, Bobby Kennedy had trouble convincing people that his campaign rested on real qualifications. *Newsweek* thought it was Keating who was truly able to connect with individual voters, which was not a big surprise given his considerably longer career in politics. RFK's campaign, however, was "so essentially formless that it leaves many voters with the impression that he is riding the coattails of his brother's memory." Even with so much interest in President Kennedy, and despite the response he received at the Democratic convention, some who attended candidate Kennedy's rallies grew weary of his repeated references to the late president, as if his family connection was reason enough to elect him, as if he didn't need to run on his own merit.[88] He did have some policy positions and experience he could offer, such as his work on behalf of civil rights, but it could not outweigh what even Kennedy's supporters publicly stated was perhaps his biggest political asset: his connection to President Kennedy.[89] Keating found it difficult to keep the race centered on state issues as RFK tried to tie him to Barry Goldwater and to remind voters, however subtly, of his own ties to the late president. Unlike Keating, he could not command the loyalty of New Yorkers due to a long record of service on behalf of their state. Whatever affection or motivation Kennedy elicited from those he hoped would soon be his constituents had to be borne of something else. "Keating has been a good senator," one voter remarked, "but it bothers me to vote against Kennedy," and this same dilemma must have surely confronted others as well.[90]

Proximity to President Kennedy he may have had, but to some extent it was used against RFK. *Because* he was now the keeper of the Kennedy Dream, all seemed to be fair and justified in his pursuit of elected office. JFK was one of the principal talking points in RFK's senate campaign, but few were under any illusions that the Senate, not the White House, was his intended destination. It was hardly any surprise that conservatives thought so. Referring to the suspected behind-the-scenes efforts to make Kennedy the vice-presidential nominee, William F. Buckley, Jr. argued, "It is not a part of the homage we owe to a stricken hero to nominate his brother to a position from which he stands a good chance of becoming the President of the United States."[91] But the left-leaning *The Nation* was little more impressed with the prospect of John F. Kennedy's brother as a Senator, practically calling for his defeat: "What should defeat him is his patent attempt to *use* the Senate seat, to *use* the New York electorate to further his grandiose ambitions," (original italics). *The Nation*'s position was that if RFK was truly serious about memorializing the late president, he could better serve the cause by challenging Virginia's Senator Harry Byrd, Sr., who had frequently opposed JFK's domestic agenda.[92] The *New York Times* lamented the absence of other, better-qualified Democratic Party candidates for the Senate seat, scolding Kennedy for the "imperiousness of his assumption that New York owed him a job." And *Newsweek* characterized RFK's bid as "a gamble at 38 to recapture the reins of power he once held so securely—an emotion-laden test of whether the Kennedy mystique can still win votes in 1964."[93] Kennedy, nevertheless, secured the support of enough Democrats to emerge as the front-runner in the month before the election. Keating's increasingly negative campaign tactics, such as accusing Kennedy of approving the reimbursement of funds to a German company that had done business with the Nazis during RFK's tenure at the Justice Department, contributed to shifts in the polls against him.

That, plus the support and popularity of LBJ, which played more of a role in the election than Kennedy was willing to acknowledge, led to victory.[94]

On Election Day, Kennedy beat Keating with 55 percent of the vote. It was a comfortable victory, but in the Democratic tidal wave of 1964, the overwhelming popularity of Lyndon Johnson may have counted just as much or more than the JFK factor. RFK polled 800,000 fewer votes in New York State than did the president.[95] The results of the Senate race for now Senator-elect Kennedy, like the campaign itself, were set in terms of what it meant for his future as it related to his elder brother. *The Nation* changed its tune from its earlier skepticism toward RFK in the Senate, but gave a rather contradictory assessment of why he won: "He won on his own merits as the voters saw them and, above all, by invoking the memory of his late brother." Ironically, he was now expected to fulfill the same role vis-à-vis President Kennedy as was newly elected President Johnson. After having glorified John Kennedy and trying to convince the public that he deserved elective office, he may have ended up in the late president's shadow instead. The editors left no doubt as to what Senator-elect Kennedy now had to live up to; they wished him luck and exhorted him, "as a Senator, [to] acquit himself as his brother did in the presidency."[96]

Robert Kennedy took his Senate seat in January 1965, and announced his candidacy for president just over three years later. The parlor game over when he would make his move for the White House only intensified during his brief Senate career. Kennedy confidantes were convinced that RFK was simply biding his time until a path to the presidency opened up, perhaps not in 1968 (when LBJ was expected to run again) but probably in 1972. The national press likewise plotted out his future, always keeping it in the context of the late president. When he did decide to run, it was ostensibly due to his opposition to the Vietnam War and his growing concern over the deteriorating domestic situation. But was his presidential campaign, like perhaps his Senate campaign, more about making the "Kennedy dream" come alive again than it was about responding to the nation's problems? Did he run out of principle, or were the nation's troubles simply used as pretexts for an inevitable presidential campaign?

Cynics would be correct to point out that while the turmoil the nation faced by 1968 may have been the most immediate reason why he challenged Lyndon Johnson for the Democratic nomination, Kennedy had planned on running for president sooner or later anyway. Casting himself as a noble critic of LBJ's governance was little more than thin justification after the fact for what RFK had already decided to do. It was always understood within the Kennedy circle that an attempted "restoration" would happen. Ted Sorensen recalled years later that the idea of Robert Kennedy running for president started right after President Kennedy was assassinated, and that he himself sent a memo to Senator Kennedy as early as July 1966 analyzing what would need to be done for an eventual presidential bid.[97] C. Douglas Dillon, who served as Treasury Secretary under JFK, stated in a 1970 oral history that RFK had little interest in the Senate, certainly beyond the short-term, and reasoned that his opportunity for the presidency would come in 1972.[98] Likewise, Supreme Court Justice and Kennedy family friend William O. Douglas recalled discussing a potential presidential campaign with RFK as early as 1965, with Kennedy's Senate tenure less than a year old, and before Vietnam had become a divisive national issue. It was, as Douglas described it, a sort of running joke between the two of them. A presidential bid would remain on the back burner for the foreseeable future, but Douglas would mention it from time to time, cryptically asking RFK, "How's the big plan going, Bobby?"[99]

In his memoirs, Senator Edward Kennedy recalled that his brother briefly considered contending for the vice presidential slot in 1964 but in the end did not actively pursue it. But he gave an interesting rationale for RFK's decision to run in 1968: it was due, according to him, to Vietnam, racial unrest, poverty, *and* his belief that what President Kennedy had worked for was gradually being destroyed. More than simply implying that JFK was not responsible for the national problems that exploded in the years after his death, this sort of rationale seemed to confirm what the cynics alleged—that Robert Kennedy was running in the name of his brother—but doing so less out of sheer ambition than due to an idealistic desire to serve the country in the name of the late president. As Ted Kennedy wrote, "Bobby felt that we were witnessing the deterioration of President Kennedy's legacy. And when people came to Bobby as they did, saying, 'You can change this. You can do it. It's possible. It's feasible. We're prepared to help you do it,' he felt an obligation to do something."[100] Longtime Washington journalist and Kennedy family friend Joseph Alsop seemed to think otherwise. He observed that LBJ had adhered so closely to the policies of his predecessor that the RFK camp could not really criticize the Johnson administration without indirectly criticizing the Kennedy administration as well. As Alsop said, "I think it did trouble [RFK] that in a great many cases disagreeing with Johnson meant disagreeing with his own brother whom he deeply revered...Johnson continued Kennedy's policy. And Bobby, by the end of his life was, by implication, rather violently attacking his own brother's policy."[101]

Many were not at all reluctant to speak of RFK's opportunism and use of the Camelot mythology to carry himself upward to higher office. In 1966, Senator Kennedy appeared on the covers of both *Life* and *Time* magazines, and the media stoked expectations of a restored Camelot by repeatedly talking about him in the context of President Kennedy. The articles left the reader with the sense that the use of memory of JFK in the eventual crusade of restoration was regarded even by the Kennedys as an open secret, as their electoral strategy hidden in plain sight. *Life*'s November 18 issue began with the assumption that something, even at that early date, was afoot by asking, "What is Robert Kennedy Up To?" and revealed, "In the councils of the Kennedy family they speak with easy good humor of 'the Restoration'...The President-designate, of course, is the eldest surviving son, Robert Francis."[102] What is notable about the series of articles in *Life* is the *visual* linkage between the two brothers: several of the photographs showed him either with the late president, or doing something related to his political career. And the magazine's coverage took note of the dispute between RFK and LBJ; it predicted that, in the fight that would inevitably heat up over whether the Kennedys could win the presidency again, Johnson ultimately would not prevail. The president, according to *Life*, would not be the one who fulfilled the Kennedy presidency, nor would he be able to retain the public's love for JFK at the expense of Kennedy the younger.

Without trying to diminish Johnson's accomplishments as president, *Life* instead saw him—in the context of the Kennedy family's continued presidential aspirations—as merely filling the breach between the first and second President Kennedys. As the magazine said, "Continuing national yearning for a Kennedy in the White House cannot please the President, who covets adoration above all. Johnson seems to be drifting on an island of time between Kennedys. Robert Kennedy is reaching beyond the world of his brother, and Johnson hardly fits into it."[103] The ferocious dedication "to the perpetuation of his brother's memory,"[104] *Life* said, would sooner or later culminate in RFK's own election as president. That, according to the magazine, probably would not happen in 1968 with Johnson likely to run again. But no matter, for many held great hopes for Senator Kennedy's future: "His friends and admirers fully expect him to achieve the Presidency, if not in 1972 then certainly no later than 1976. On Election Day 1976 Bobby Kennedy will be all of 50 years old. In 1984 he will be the same age as Lyndon Johnson is now."[105]

The September 16, 1966 issue of *Time* added to these expectations. Although it noted Senator Kennedy's lack of seniority and accomplishment in the Senate, and meager political clout in New York's governing circles—the types of assets typically used to gain higher office—there still appeared to be what William F. Buckley, Jr. called "the inevitability of Bobby."[106] What made a future run for the presidency so seemingly inevitable was the continuing love many Americans had for his brother, as if the younger Kennedy's political career could not be talked about apart from JFK. *Time* thought that the chief source of power for RFK—what would make him so formidable in his expected presidential campaign—

was the JFK factor. How, the magazine asked, could someone with such
an obvious lack of qualifications hope to credibly run for the nation's
highest office any time soon, and even manage to beat the incumbent
president ("the greatest vote getter of them all") in terms of their respective popularity? "The Bobby boom seems incomprehensible."[107] But in
reality, it was not. John Kennedy was very much present, and many
people were transferring their fond memories of Camelot to the Senator.
Time observed that he was reaping the benefits of "the persistence of
the legend surrounding JFK; time seems to enhance rather than diminish
the glow of his martyrdom."[108]

Considering much of the present-day scholarship on the Kennedy
presidency, the idea of him as a martyr for anything is peculiar. Nonetheless, many in the mid- to late-1960s found it easy to believe that only
the martyr's brother could authoritatively proclaim the quest for a
new Camelot. To be sure, Senator Kennedy did not make such an idea
the theme of his 1968 campaign, but he wouldn't have needed to. If it
is difficult to say with precision why so many were attracted to him
(it is probably easier to understand why others despised him),[109] it is
nevertheless true that his admirers looked at him and saw their beloved
President Kennedy. The differences between the two brothers notwithstanding, they thought that RFK represented his brother in every way,
and supported him because of it. One example can be found in Helen
O'Donnell's memoir of her father Kenneth O'Donnell, who served as
a political adviser to President Kennedy and later worked on Bobby
Kennedy's presidential campaign. O'Donnell was still very invested
emotionally in a return to the Oval Office, this time with RFK. The central
motivation for him, as it may have been for so many others, was the
possibility of a second Kennedy presidency that would evoke the glory
and fond memories of the first. As Helen O'Donnell wrote, her father
exclaimed after one RFK campaign event, "Bobby really did a beautiful
job...He was his brother! He just handled himself beautifully. He was
his brother. It was fantastic."[110] As if the central virtue in electing RFK
was that it would make things feel like the noble days of the Kennedy

administration of old, as if the only relevant consideration was how much RFK reminded people of his elder brother, O'Donnell continued,

> The women just went ga-ga over him [RFK]...all the old pros were just taken aback by how much they liked him. This was not the Bob Kennedy they had read about. This was not the ruthless, arrogant young fellow. All they kept saying was, "He's just like Jack! He's just like Jack!" I knew he could go all the way then.[111]

But if many did indeed take it for granted that Robert Kennedy was the true heir to Camelot, and would return to effect the restoration, many others saw Kennedy as simply an ambitious politician who had little to run on other than his connection to JFK. He was not immune to the accusation that he was too willing to use his brother's memory when he thought it would benefit him. Los Angeles Mayor Sam Yorty (no friend of the Kennedy family in any event) commented in 1966 that RFK's campaign would rest on little more than manipulation of the public's fond memories of his brother: "He's trying to ride on his brother's fame and his father's fortune to the presidency, and I don't think he can do it."[112] Surprising as it may be to readers forty years later accustomed to thinking of RFK in the same heroic terms as JFK, the wary attitude of some New Yorkers toward his Senate race was representative of how many across the country thought about him. The "Kennedy magic" simply did not work with everyone, even for many within the Democratic Party. Whether owing to distrust of RFK's motives, uncertainty about his qualifications, or unease as to the wisdom of him challenging an incumbent Democratic president to whom many in the party were beholden, the Senator attracted more than his share of opponents.[113] Joseph Alsop, however much he may have been favorably inclined toward Kennedy, asserted a few years after RFK's death that in all likelihood he would have been unable to win in 1968. Alsop believed that this was in no small measure due to the hostility he faced from other Democrats. As he argued, "The politicians regarded Bobby as a pretty long shot bet...I don't think he could have been elected. He started...with this terrifically big kind of an albatross composed of people who really didn't like him. It was always the Kennedy haters, many of whom were natural Democratic voters."[114] Some Democrats now saw RFK as not only reaching for power he did not deserve, but also as threatening any chances the party had of retaining the White House in 1968. In this sense, JFK himself might have been that albatross in a way he had not been during his younger brother's Senate campaign, as RFK risked shattering the party, not uniting it behind heady visions of a new Kennedy administration. Instead of a resurrected Camelot, RFK's campaign could end up completing the apotheosis of Richard Nixon's political career.

Kennedy declared his candidacy for president on March 16, 1968, making his announcement in the same room where his brother had begun his presidential campaign eight years before, and beginning his speech with the same words the late president had used on that occasion.[115] These intentional parallels between the two were certainly not lost on the reporters gathered to cover the event.[116] He again reminded the public of the accomplishments of the Kennedy administration—and implicitly, his role in it. "I am announcing today my candidacy for the presidency of the United States," Kennedy stated, later adding, "My service in the National Security Council during the Cuban Missile Crisis, the Berlin crisis of 1961 and 1962, and later the negotiations over Laos and on the Nuclear Test Ban Treaty have taught me something about both the uses and limitations of military power."[117] And although RFK's campaign was not invoking the name of the fallen president at every turn—while it did not use the memory of JFK as the answer for everything—one could detect in 1968 some of the same campaign themes and some of the same targeted audiences from 1960. JFK had campaigned by challenging the country to do better and reject the status quo, and argued that the ability of the United States to serve as both a military power and as a moral force in the world had been hindered in the preceding years.[118] The same pronouncements that he made on quality of life concerns, and the feared loss of American prestige and failure of American diplomacy, were echoed by his brother eight years later. In one campaign speech in

1960, JFK had observed, "Today the United States is living better than ever before. We have more swimming pools, freezers, boats, and air-conditioners than the world has ever seen before. A few months ago, the annual economic report painted a picture of a fat and complacent nation." Yet, "We are failing to provide for those who have too little. We are increasing our wealth, but we are failing to use that great wealth to meet the urgent needs of millions of our citizens."[119] In remarks delivered on the Senate floor in the aftermath of the failed 1960 U.S.-Soviet summit in Paris, Kennedy had criticized American leaders for relying too much on the country's military power instead of developing long-range diplomatic objectives and promoting new ideas.[120] RFK adopted a similarly critical attitude toward what he thought was a singular focus on military solutions. Reliance on American military power, he charged, had resulted in a stymied peace process in Vietnam, a curious observation given his own prior hawkish views on the war.[121]

RFK employed his brother's criticisms, both in the Senate and in his presidential campaign. In one speech delivered at the University of Kansas, Kennedy pointed out the deprivation and social dislocation experienced by many neglected groups in the country, stating repeatedly that the United States could, and must, do better. Echoing the warning that his brother had issued against being deceived by the nation's abundance, he said, "Even if we act to erase material poverty, there is another great task. It is to confront the poverty of satisfaction—a lack of purpose and dignity —that inflicts us all. Too much and too long, we seem to have surrendered community excellence and community values in the mere accumulation of things."[122] In rhetoric evocative of 1960, Kennedy's speeches were marked by repeated uses of the declaration, "I don't think we have to accept that...I think we can do better."[123] He decried the status quo with passion equal to that of JFK, even though the late president had hardly been a great social crusader, and despite the fact that the status quo the Senator attacked was presided over by a fellow Democrat. LBJ became, in this sense, what Dwight Eisenhower had been for the elder Kennedy brother: the representation of the self-satisfied, almost lifeless leadership that was costing the country its ability to lead the world and make social progress at home. If Johnson, like Eisenhower, was telling people how well things were going and noting with pleasure the abundance that seemed to be spread so broadly, RFK—like JFK—rejected these notions, charging that the Democratic party should be "the party of dissatisfaction. I say this country can do better; it must do more."[124] RFK could have been reading from one of his brother's campaign speeches.

There were many who did not buy the idea of a restored Camelot, and some even turned the memory of John Kennedy against his brother. Although Kennedy admirers would have considered it unholy to mention any failing of the Kennedy administration, critics cautioned against making assumptions that the United States would be saved by another Kennedy presidency. Several of the letters to the editor that appeared in *Time* were highly disdainful toward RFK. One correspondent lamented, "How awful to imagine that the flagrant, repeated opportunism of Robert Kennedy may be rewarded with the Democratic nomination. It is cruel and tragic that [fellow Democratic candidate Eugene] McCarthy...may be defeated by the so-called magic of the Kennedy name and the synthetic charm of young Mr. Kennedy's smile."[125] Another writer commented, "Now—having been one of the Viet Nam [sic] instigators—when it is getting really quite horribly dangerous, Bobby advocates pulling out, sans honor, sans all those lives, just like the Bay of Pigs."[126] Still another cited the inglorious moments of the Kennedy presidency by noting, "The Kennedys promised us the moon in 1960, and that particular moon consisted of the Bay of Pigs, acceleration of the war in Viet Nam [sic], the Berlin Wall...and the failure to get one New Frontier legislative program through Congress. What is Bobby going to do for an encore?"[127] Two letters written by college students displayed a marked skepticism that the Senator was anything like King Arthur's noble young brother coming to rescue the people. In one, a University of Illinois student, commenting on that issue's pop art cover portrait of Senator Kennedy, said, "Roy Lichtenstein's cover drawing of Robert Kennedy...was superb. It provided an at-a-glance character analysis: colorful, comic, callow, and caustic."[128]

Even if Robert Kennedy was seen by many as the heir to the throne, it did not mean that his bid for the presidency would have been successful, however successfully he could remind people of the late President Kennedy. In the battle for the Democratic nomination, RFK and Minnesota Senator Eugene McCarthy largely fought each other to a draw by June 1968, with McCarthy winning several states including Wisconsin and Oregon, and Kennedy prevailing in Nebraska, Indiana, and South Dakota. California became crucial; RFK had just lost the Oregon contest, and his candidacy likely would have been over if he met defeat in the California primary.[129] Many in his own campaign were considering the very real possibility that the race would be over for him if he did not win there. As one adviser recalled, "We were losing altitude, though the Kennedys today don't like to admit it."[130] And even though many compared him admiringly with President Kennedy, others did not think at all that he was like his brother. This perception was true even for some who had supported JFK in 1960. As *U.S. News & World Report* noted, "Anyone who talks with political leaders hears this again and again: 'I was for his brother, but Bobby isn't Jack.'"[131] Kennedy loyalist Ted Sorensen recalled encountering this same sentiment even from fellow Democrats.[132] From both the liberal and conservative factions of the Democratic Party came considerable reservations toward Kennedy's candidacy despite where their loyalties may have been in 1960 or in the aftermath of the assassination. The *New York Times* observed shortly after RFK's announcement of his candidacy, "There is no question that many Democrats retain some degree of identification with the campaign of John F. Kennedy in 1960 and that Senator Kennedy knows who and where they are. The extent to which he will be able to tap their loyalties...remains to be measured."[133] Establishment Democrats such as Chicago Mayor Richard Daley and New Jersey Governor Richard Hughes had reacted to RFK's announcement by reaffirming their support for LBJ. Some antiwar Democrats such as South Dakota Senator George McGovern were at first noncommittal, as were several supporters and members of the Kennedy administration for whom, one might assume, the yearning for a second

Kennedy administration would have been the strongest. Former North Carolina Governor Terry Sandford and Kennedy White House counsel Myer Feldman, for example, took a rather cautious attitude toward RFK.[134]

This uncertainty by some as to whether Senator Kennedy could accept his older brother's crown might have been due as much to the realization that the political situation of 1968 was starkly different from that of 1960, as to doubts that the younger Kennedy possessed the qualities that supposedly made John Kennedy great. The country had experienced by that point several years of Democratic rule, not Republican, as was the case when JFK ran. The two biggest issues facing the country in 1968—Vietnam and continuing racial turmoil—were seen by many as failings of the Democrats, as evidenced by the renewed strength of the Republicans since the 1966 congressional elections, and the growing backlash within the South that resulted in further erosion of Democratic control there that continued into the 1970s.[135]

The course of the 1968 presidential campaign for Robert Kennedy need not be retold in detail here. The fight over the Democratic nomination had taken an unexpected turn with President Johnson's withdrawal from the race on March 31, 1968. Senator McCarthy, campaigning as an antiwar candidate, had also proven willing to challenge LBJ for the nomination at a time, when RFK had still not decided whether to run.[136] RFK, who had praised his late brother for a supposed lifetime of courage, ironically was accused of lacking that same quality. The Senator, according to *New York Times* columnist Tom Wicker suddenly looked "like a hitchhiker on another man's work and courage" for initially deciding that he would not challenge Johnson and undermine his own future presidential prospects if he lost.[137] Despite the glorifying of him that took place after his death, even the results in California on June 4 were not the decisive win he needed. While he benefited from deep support among black and Hispanic voters, he continued to face the challenge of broadening his base to include the white blue-collar voters who usually voted Democratic. Kennedy took California narrowly, beating McCarthy by a margin of only 4 percent, failing to win at least 50 percent of the vote as he had hoped.[138] Kennedy was shot early in the morning of June 5, 1968 at the Ambassador Hotel in Los Angeles after celebrating his victory over McCarthy, and died the next day.[139] He had spent so much of his life after November 1963 ensuring that his brother would always be remembered as an American hero. Now those who had hoped for Camelot restored went to work memorializing Robert Kennedy.

Even with JFK still so fresh in people's minds, Robert Kennedy would have faced a greater struggle to win the nomination, had he not been assassinated, than his brother had in 1960. With Vice President Hubert Humphrey assured of the support of state officials and party bosses, and LBJ's control over the Democratic Party still solid, *U.S. News & World Report* predicted, shortly before Kennedy's death, that he would not stop Humphrey from being the eventual nominee. And even assuming RFK was able to win the nomination, a big assumption to make, the fact that he enjoyed considerably less support in the South than his brother had in 1960 meant that in a hypothetical race between himself and Richard Nixon, Nixon was projected to have the advantage.[140]

It is hard to say how much of a role popular memory ended up playing for Robert Kennedy, but it no doubt resided in the back of people's minds. Supporters and opponents of RFK alike commented upon the influence of popular memory of JFK. Ted Sorensen acknowledged that the late president was a factor in the 1968 Kennedy campaign, with "conscious and unconscious efforts to imitate his older brother's platform style and a strong desire to identify himself with his brother's causes."[141] Senator McCarthy thought RFK's main opponent after Johnson withdrew from the race would be his own brother; with Kennedy no longer able to benefit from the contrast between LBJ and himself, he would instead have to define himself in contrast to JFK.[142] It was a contrast that even RFK may have regarded as a burden, and it may have proven greatly troublesome for him had he ever become president. In a revealing comment made privately to Kenneth O'Donnell on the day of the California primary,

RFK confessed, "You know, Kenny, I feel now for the first time that I've shaken off the shadow of my brother. I feel I made it on my own."[143] It was an understandable sentiment from a younger brother who might have felt outdone by the glamour and accomplishments of an older brother. Nonetheless, it was odd coming from a man who seemed to be the embodiment of loyalty to his brother and family, and who had striven so hard after that brother's death to protect his memory and identify himself with him. But more than the issue of how much of his success in politics was due to JFK was the problem of how a second Kennedy administration would measure up to the first. If people were investing in Robert Kennedy all of the hopes that had been raised by President Kennedy, how could RFK have ever fulfilled those hopes if he actually won the presidency? Had he become president, he would have been expected to do the impossible. As President Johnson remarked years later to Doris Kearns Goodwin, a President Robert F. Kennedy would inevitably have fallen short. "I almost wish," the former president mused, that RFK "had become president so the country could finally see a flesh-and-blood Kennedy grappling with the daily work of the Presidency and all the inevitable disappointments, instead of their storybook image of great heroes who, because they were dead, could make anything anyone wanted happen."[144] Even the venerated president's younger brother would likely have left the believers of the nostalgic and frothy Camelot imagery disappointed.

Instead, RFK's death resulted in the same glorification conferred upon him as was done for President Kennedy. Kennedy loyalists asserted that his assassination meant that the country was denied the better future that a second Kennedy presidency promised. Arthur Schlesinger, Jr. wrote, "For the poor and the non-white, RFK represented their only stake in the political process," and later, "What kind of a President would he [RFK] have made? I think very likely a greater one than JFK...He would have re-created the excitement and exhilaration of the early sixties, and he would have restored the idealism of America."[145] The grief displayed by the American people at the time of RFK's death suggests that many felt the same way, and popular culture has remembered him very positively. *Bobby*, a recent motion picture depicting the stories of several fictional characters at the Ambassador Hotel in Los Angeles on the evening of Kennedy's assassination, mentioned none of the distrust or hostility toward him, and seemed to accept as entirely factual that he would have been elected president and that he was the only national figure at the time capable of uniting the country.[146] An essence of inevitability has been given to Robert Kennedy. Had he lived, surely he would have been elected. Surely he would have succeeded. Surely the nation would have been better for it. Bill Eppridge, a photojournalist who covered the 1968 Kennedy campaign, wrote, in a photo anthology of that campaign, "More than 22,000 American servicemen were killed in Vietnam from the time Bobby Kennedy would have been president until the U.S. withdrew their forces in 1973."[147]

But there would be no second Kennedy administration. The mythology surrounding him holds, as it did for President Kennedy, that he was in pursuit of larger, grander things when he died. RFK, like JFK, had to have died for something; he could not possibly have died *not* to become president. He could not have given his life needlessly. It is certainly debatable whether he could have been elected, let alone resolved the problems the country faced as the 1960s drew to a close. But his tragically unsuccessful three-month presidential campaign may have reserved a high place in the public's memory for both his brother and for himself far more successfully than if he had become president. However accurate it may be to label his presidential quest as quixotic more than anything else, Americans were left with a popular memory not of failure, nor of a second Kennedy administration that proved to be inadequate to their hopes, but of *potential greatness*, again forever gone. If it was ironic that RFK's chief source of grief during these years was also his biggest political asset, it could be no less so that perhaps his greatest contribution to the popular memory of JFK was also his last.

Notes

1. "The Politics of Restoration," *Time*, May 24, 1968 (Vol. 91, No. 21), 24.
2. Arthur M. Schlesinger, Jr., *Robert Kennedy and His Times* (Boston: Houghton Mifflin Company, 1978), 620; and Joseph A. Palermo, *In His Own Right: The Political Odyssey of Senator Robert F. Kennedy* (New York: Columbia University Press, 2001), 2.
3. James W. Hilty, *Robert Kennedy: Brother Protector* (Philadelphia: Temple University Press, 1997), 488-489.
4. Ronald Steel, *In Love with Night*, 28, 174.
5. Former Kennedy aide Richard Goodwin recalled years later, RFK "embodied hope of a return to the glittering promise of the prewar sixties...The very existence of Robert Kennedy, the fact of his preeminence, was evidence that the conditions of possibility still existed." "Democrats: Socking It to 'Em," *Time*, April 5, 1968 (Vol. 91, No. 14), 22; and Richard N. Goodwin, *Remembering America: A Voice from the Sixties* (Boston: Little, Brown and Company, 1988), 474.
6. William F. Buckley, Jr., "On the Right: The Unseating of Johnson," *National Review*, April 23, 1968 (Vol. 20, No. 16), 414-415; and "Democrats: The Shadow & the Substance," *Time*, September 16, 1966 (Vol. 88, No. 12), 32.
7. RFK, like his brother, believed in the "domino theory" that predicted a succession of southeast Asian nations to communism if the United States did nothing to stop it, and in early 1964, even denied that JFK was moving in the direction of American withdrawal from Vietnam. This is not to suggest, however, that the younger Kennedy did not have doubts about the war even while JFK was still alive. Historian George Herring notes that in the period leading up to the overthrow of Ngo Dinh Diem in early November 1963, RFK was concerned that American withdrawal was increasingly likely without a more effective South Vietnamese war effort. George C. Herring, *America's Longest War: The United States and Vietnam, 1950-1975* (New York: McGraw-Hill, Inc., 1996), 112; and Ronald Steel, *In Love with Night*, 129-130.
8. Ronald Steel, *In Love with Night*, 129, 154.
9. See Jeff Shesol, *Mutual Contempt: Lyndon Johnson, Robert Kennedy, and the Feud that Defined a Decade* (New York: W.W. Norton & Company, 1997).

10. Sorensen, for example, recalled years later that it was taken for granted among the Kennedy inner circle that RFK would run for president—they were convinced that a Kennedy "restoration" would take place eventually. As he stated, "Bob Kennedy and I discussed his possible candidacy for the Presidency many times after his brother's death. The question of whether he *should* run or *could* be a serious candidate was never mentioned. It was unnecessary. The question was wholly one of timing and tactics." Theodore Sorensen, *The Kennedy Legacy: A Peaceful Revolution for the Seventies* (New York: The Macmillan Company, 1969), 18-19, 116, 123.

11. John F. Kennedy, *Profiles In Courage*, Memorial Edition (New York: Harper & Row, 1964), 10.

12. Ibid., 11, 14.

13. Ibid., 13.

14. "How Young People Will Vote," *U.S. News & World Report* April 29, 1968 (Vol. 64, No. 18), 32-33.

15. Department of Justice, "Address by Attorney General Robert F. Kennedy: To the Fifth General Assembly, World Assembly of Youth, University of Massachusetts, Amherst, August 7, 1964," available from http://www.justice.gov/ag/rfkspeeches/1964/08-07-1964.pdf ; accessed from Internet July 15, 2012.

16. Joseph A. Palermo, *Robert F. Kennedy and the Death of American Idealism* (New York: Pearson Longman, 2008), 85.

17. "Transcript of Senator Kennedy's Remarks in Front of JFK Library at Santo Amaro, São Paulo," November 20, 1965 (Box 1), in Senate papers of Robert F. Kennedy, JFK Library.

18. Department of Justice, "Address by Attorney General Robert F. Kennedy: Commencement Exercises, Marquette University, June 7, 1964, Milwaukee, Wisconsin," available from http://www.justice.gov/ag/rfkspeeches/1964/06-07-1964.pdf ; accessed from Internet July 15, 2012.

19. Edwin O. Guthman and C. Richard Allen (eds.), *RFK: Collected Speeches* (New York: Viking Penguin, 1993), 133.

20. Ibid., 245.

21. Jeff Shesol, *Mutual Contempt*, 184.

22. Ibid., 208-209.

23. See, for example, from the previous chapter, Johnson's telephone conversation with Mayor Daley and aide Marvin Watson's accusation that DNC Chairman John Bailey was giving the Kennedy family too much control over convention planning.

24. Arthur M. Schlesinger, Jr., *Robert Kennedy*, 652.

25. Ibid., 662-663; and "A Thunderous Tribute to the Kennedys," *U.S. News & World Report* September 7, 1964 (Vol. LVII, No. 10), 6.

26. "The Nation: The Magic of Memory," *Time* September 4, 1964 (Vol. 84, No. 10), 29.

27. With Democratic Party delegates seemingly beside themselves with yearning for the late JFK, RFK's dramatic convention appearance, *Newsweek* observed, "vindicated Lyndon Johnson's canniness in having the documentary rescheduled," and "Had the original schedule held fast, the impact on the convention might well have posed an unbeatable challenge." *Newsweek* may have been referring to a Kennedy stampede for the vice-presidential spot as opposed to a direct challenge for the presidential nomination itself. In any case, the potential power of the memory of JFK in propelling RFK onto the ticket was accorded no small consideration by many—LBJ not least among them. "LBJ: 'I Ask For a Mandate to Begin,'" *Newsweek* September 7, 1964 (Vol. LXIV, No. 10), 27-28.

28. "Robert F. Kennedy, 1964 Democratic Convention," *The Greatest Speeches of All Time*, CD (Rolling Bay, Washington: Jerden Records, 1996), Track 6.

29. Jeff Shesol, *Mutual Contempt*, 220; and Jules Witcover, *Party of the People*, 526-528.

30. Arthur M. Schlesinger, Jr., *Robert Kennedy*, 665.

31. Edwin O. Guthman and C. Richard Allen (eds.), *RFK: Collected Speeches*, 115-117.

32. Edward T. Folliard, "They Say Farewell to John F. Kennedy," *Washington Post,* August 28, 1964, A1, A8; and "LBJ: 'I Ask For a Mandate to Begin,'" *Newsweek*, 29.

33. "LBJ: 'I Ask For a Mandate to Begin,'" *Newsweek*, 29.

34. By this, I mean that RFK was not known for the soaring rhetoric, memorable turns of phrase, and witty exchanges with audiences that his older brother excelled in. But especially in his 1968 presidential campaign, Robert Kennedy's oratory could sometimes be quite galvanizing, owing to the power of his ideas and his calming, even introspective demeanor. See, for example, his unscripted remarks in Indianapolis after the assassination of Dr. Martin Luther King, Jr. on April 4, 1968; also RFK's observations in Cleveland on national violence the following day. "Robert F. Kennedy, 1964 Democratic Convention," *The Greatest Speeches of All Time*; and Edwin O. Guthman and C. Richard Allen (eds.), *RFK: Collected Speeches*, 355-362.

35. "The Nation: The Magic of Memory," in *Time*, 29.

36. RFK was careful not to overuse the memory of his brother, and anyone combing through his books and speeches expecting to find the late president mentioned in every other paragraph will be disappointed. It is not my objective here to exhaustively examine every speech RFK gave in the years after his brother's death for whatever allusions he made to JFK. I have looked at many of the speeches contained in the anthology compiled by Edwin O. Guthman and C. Richard Allen, as well as other Kennedy speeches found on the Department of Justice website, and those in the JFK Library. The speeches I refer to in this chapter were included either because they were among his more notable speeches or because they illustrate how he influenced the popular memory of his brother. Combined with his writings from this period, we get a good sense of what he wanted the public to remember about President Kennedy. With the "Camelot" imagery accepted by many people, RFK could credibly assert years later that what JFK stood for was in jeopardy. Having defined what the late president had started, Senator Kennedy then made the case that he could finish what had been started.

37. LBJ, on the other hand, appeared only sporadically throughout the book.

38. Jeff Shesol, *Mutual Contempt*, 98. Shesol cites RFK aide Adam Walinsky in arguing that the book was partially intended to criticize LBJ about Vietnam. As he said, Walinsky "described its underlying message and intent: to contrast the cool, rational, deliberate decision-making of the Kennedy cabinet with the muddled, reactive nature of Johnson's Vietnam policy by 1967."

39. Robert F. Kennedy, *Thirteen Days: A Memoir of the Cuban Missile Crisis* (New York: W. W. Norton & Company, Inc., 1968), 91. The limitations of this book as an accurate historical source must be noted. Nowhere in his account of the crisis did RFK mention the multiple attempts to overthrow Fidel Castro—attempts that included assassination—that were a large part of the reason why the Soviet Union decided to install missiles in Cuba. Following the resolution of the crisis, RFK ensured that information about the American removal of Jupiter missiles in Turkey was not made public—to preserve the image of the Kennedys as tough negotiators who had scored a clear-cut victory over the Soviets. Later, in *Thirteen Days*, he did mention the missile swap as a way to appear rational and committed to peaceful resolution of international disputes. What also did not appear in the book was any reference to his more hawkish comments during the affair. At first, RFK had apparently thought that

a military resolution, even one initiated by American provocation, was the best course of action. Evan Thomas, *Robert Kennedy*, 232.

40. Robert F. Kennedy, *Thirteen Days*, 98.

41. Ibid., 92.

42. Evan Thomas, *Robert Kennedy*, 232.

43. *Thirteen Days* was scheduled for publication in magazine format in 1968. The book version was published in 1969, after Senator Kennedy's death. Michael R. Beschloss, *The Crisis Years*, 419n.

44. *Thirteen Days*. Roger Donaldson. DVD. New Line Home Video, 2001; and Robert F. Kennedy, *Thirteen Days*, 95-98.

45. Ronald Steel, *In Love with Night*, 124.

46. Robert F. Kennedy, *To Seek a Newer World* (New York: Bantam Books, 1968), 233-234.

47. Ibid., 61.

48. Stephen G. Rabe, *Eisenhower and Latin America: The Politics of Anti-Communism* (Chapel Hill: The University of North Carolina Press, 1988), 148-149.

49. Robert F. Kennedy, *To Seek a Newer World*, 119.

50. Remarks by Senator-Elect Robert Kennedy, Dedication of John F. Kennedy Housing Project, Mexico City," November 17, 1964, in RFK Senate papers, JFK Library.

51. Robert F. Kennedy, *To Seek a Newer World*, 121.

52. Lawrence J. Bassett and Stephen E. Pelz, "The Failed Search for Victory: Vietnam and the Politics of War," in Thomas G. Paterson (ed.), *Kennedy's Quest for Victory*, 250.

53. Robert Kennedy's assertions by 1967-68 that JFK had decided to withdraw from Vietnam were not consistent with his public comments years earlier before the war became such a divisive issue. Talking about Vietnam with the press at Columbia University during his 1964 Senate race, RFK gave no indication at all that his brother's intention during a second term or at any other point was to pull out. At that time, he repeated the late president's rather contradictory position on American support: the South Vietnamese government needed to work harder to secure the loyalty of the people, and political/social support must accompany military aid. Still, according to RFK, "I think we should continue the effort." Robert F. Kennedy, *To Seek a Newer World*, 185; and Edwin O. Guthman and C. Richard Allen (eds.), *RFK: Collected Speeches*, 126-127.

54. Howard Jones, *Death of a Generation: How the Assassination of Diem and JFK Prolonged the Vietnam War* (New York: Oxford University Press, 2003), 348.

55. It is not at all certain that JFK had decided to do this. President Kennedy's public and private comments regarding the proper role of the U.S. in Vietnam were contradictory. A compelling argument can be made that —due to his stated belief in the domino theory, his credentials as a cold warrior, and his repeated public assertions that South Vietnam would be defended—he would not have allowed the struggling nation to fall, even if that meant the deployment of American combat troops. Historian Howard Jones, a proponent of the theory that JFK would have withdrawn, argued that throughout his presidency, he remained the only consistent opponent of sending in American troops. Jones posits that Kennedy's ultimate intention was to reduce the number of American personnel to its 1961 level. Vietnam journalist David Halberstam, on the other hand, noted that the Kennedy policy toward Vietnam was highly ambiguous. Whatever his private doubts may have been, he still increased the number of advisers to nearly 17,000 by the time of his death and never publicly questioned the wisdom of keeping the U.S. involved. While it was true, Halberstam noted, that Kennedy had lost confidence in the leadership of South Vietnamese President Diem, it did not necessarily mean a concurrent loss of support for the war effort per se. Howard Jones, *Death of a Generation*, 1, 11-12; and David Halberstam, *The Best and the Brightest* (New York: Ballantine Books, 1969), 299-301.

56. Robert F. Kennedy, *To Seek a Newer World*, 195-198, 200-201.

57. Ibid., 204.

58. Another example RFK cited was nuclear testing. He argued, "The United States took the initiative and made the maximum effort to secure the nuclear test-ban treaty in 1963...We hailed the treaty not principally for its specific benefits...but for its value as the first of many necessary actions. But we have not yet taken the second step." In Latin America, the Alliance for Progress had not lived up to its promises: "What progress have we made in these six years? Economically, the Alliance is moving, but it is not moving fast enough. Governments are working, but they are not working hard enough. The United States is making a contribution, but in many ways not enough. The ideals of the Alliance stirred men's hearts and minds throughout the continent; not enough has been done to fulfill those hopes." RFK, like his brother, called for greater action on a number of fronts. Ibid., 119, 125.

59. The problem for RFK as far as memory of his brother was concerned—as it related to Vietnam—was not only the late president's deepening of American involvement in the war, but also RFK's rather muddled statements on where the Kennedy administration's policy was headed by November 1963. In 1964 oral history interviews for the Kennedy Library, he stated that the administration never entertained the idea of pulling out of Vietnam. At the same time, he also said that they were not committed to "all-out" American involvement similar to Korea. Asked whether JFK remained convinced that the U.S. had to remain in Vietnam, Kennedy responded in the affirmative. Queried further on whether ground troops would have been sent in to forestall a South Vietnamese defeat, he replied, "We'd face that when we came to it." Edwin O. Guthman and Jeffrey Schulman, *Robert Kennedy in His Own Words*, 394-395.

60. Michael R. Beschloss, *The Crisis Years*, 419n, 527-528.

61. Robert F. Kennedy, *To Seek a Newer World*, 227.

62. "A Warrior For Peace," in *Time*, 49

63. Jean Jeffries, "Why Vietnam Is Kennedy's War," *National Review*, April 23, 1968 (Vol. 20, No. 16), 396.

64. Ibid.

65. This was not the approach RFK initially took, at least publicly, toward Johnson. In several speeches, almost in the same breath, he spoke approvingly of both Presidents Kennedy and Johnson, as if LBJ truly was carrying on in the late president's stead. For example, in his August 1964 speech announcing his candidacy for the Senate, Bobby Kennedy stated, "All that President Kennedy stood for, and all that President Johnson is trying to accomplish, all the progress that has been made, is threatened... no one associated with President Kennedy and President Johnson—no one committed to participating in public life—can sit on the sidelines with so much at stake." Department of Justice, "Statement by Attorney General Robert F. Kennedy: Gracie Mansion, New York City, August 25, 1964," available from http://www.justice.gov/ag/rfkspeeches/1964/08-25-1964.pdf ; accessed from Internet July 15, 2012. The same can be found in speeches less politically driven; see also Kennedy's March 17, 1964 remarks to the Friendly Sons of St. Patrick of Lackawanna County, Scranton, Pennsylvania; also his Address to the Canadian Press, April 14, 1964; as well as his statement before a House committee on immigration legislation, July 22, 1964—all of which can be found on the Department of Justice website.

66. Ronald Steel, *In Love with Night*, 141, 147-149.

67. Ronald Steel, *In Love with Night,* 18; and "Democrats: The Shadow & the Substance," *Time,* September 16, 1966 (Vol. 18, No. 12), 32.

68. Ronald Steel, *In Love with Night,* 18, 116-117.

69. Evan Thomas, *Robert Kennedy,* 289.

70. The possibility of RFK one day winning the White House was reportedly on President Kennedy's mind. In the summer of 1963, the President pondered a cabinet reshuffle for his second term; one idea was to replace Secretary of State Dean Rusk with RFK. JFK thought that would put his brother in a prime position to win the 1968 Democratic nomination. At times, JFK seemed hesitant at the thought of the Attorney General running; Kennedy friend Charles Spalding later claimed the President complained that RFK was "overly ambitious," and did not like the prospect of his brother fighting for the 1968 nomination with LBJ. *Dangerous World: The Kennedy Years.* Videocassette. ABC, 1997; and "Democrats: The Shadow & the Substance," in *Time,* 33; and Michael R. Beschloss, *The Crisis Years,* 643.

71. Thomas G. Paterson, "John F. Kennedy's Quest for Victory and Global Crisis," in Thomas G. Paterson (ed.), *Kennedy's Quest for Victory,* 14-16, 18-19.

72. First and foremost among them was RFK himself. He and others entertained the idea of trying to secure the vice-presidential slot for Kennedy under President Johnson in the 1964 election. By 1968—or 1972 if LBJ declined to run for a second full term—the late president's brother would presumably be in a prime position to "reclaim" the presidency. Jules Witcover, *Party of the People,* 520-521. But the prediction-making reached absurd proportions with some speculating about three Kennedy presidencies. If Robert, only 42 years of age in 1968, was able to win the presidency that year, he could then be reelected four years later and leave office in 1977, thus giving the nation sixteen years of Kennedy rule in the White House. And if his brother Edward were to then run for president (and, of course, the assumption being that he likewise would serve two terms), the tri-fecta of Kennedy presidents would not conclude until January 20, 1985. However unrealistic such assumptions may have been at the time, it is no wonder LBJ feared being remembered by history as nothing more than an accidental president between the Kennedys. "With Bobby Kennedy 'Out,' a Family Dream Fades," *U.S. News & World Report* August 17, 1964 (Vol. LVII, No. 7), 63-65.

73. Jack Newfield, *Robert Kennedy: A Memoir* (New York: E. P. Dutton & Co., Inc., 1969), 31; and Robert Ajemian, "A Man's Week to Reckon," *Life* July 3, 1964 (Vol. 57, No. 1), 26.

74. "Remarks by Senator-elect Robert Kennedy, Dedication of John F. Kennedy Housing Project, Mexico City," November 17, 1964; and "Address by Senator Robert F. Kennedy, Grand Army Plaza, Brooklyn, New York," May 31, 1965 (Box 1), in Senate papers of Robert F. Kennedy, John F. Kennedy Presidential Library, Boston, Massachusetts.

75. Jeff Shesol, *Mutual Contempt*, 3.

76. As LBJ recalled, "I constantly had before me the picture that Kennedy had selected me as executor of his will." Doris Kearns Goodwin, *Lyndon Johnson and the American Dream*, 174-175.

77. Ronald Steel, *In Love with Night*, 109; and David Halberstam, *The Unfinished Odyssey of Robert Kennedy* (New York: Random House, 1968), 37.

78. Evan Thomas, *Robert Kennedy*, 278-279. Also recall Arthur Schlesinger, Jr.'s diary observation from the previous chapter that Johnson was trying to play up JFK's memory for his own benefit while also acting to "erase" that memory.

79. Jeff Shesol, *Mutual Contempt*, 172. Shesol specifically mentions the development of the A-11 plane and the destruction of fissionable nuclear materials. President Kennedy had apparently been interested in both projects, and LBJ later brought them to completion, but without—as RFK complained—giving the late president his share of the credit. But both of these projects were rather obscure compared with JFK's major policy goals (greater aid to education, a higher minimum wage, the Test Ban Treaty, civil rights, etc.), so it is quite possible that RFK was simply using these two minor issues to express his hostility towards Johnson. This, of course, was also the case with the 1964 Civil Rights Act. RFK dubiously claimed that JFK would indeed have gotten the legislation passed had he lived. Former Kennedy staffers argued likewise. Ted Sorensen wrote in his memoirs that Johnson simply repackaged Kennedy proposals as his own, and asserted that the Kennedy agenda would "have been enacted in time" anyway, as if to reduce Johnson to an inconsequential component of an inevitable, organic process. Not surprisingly, Sorensen also argued that Vietnam was wholly Johnson's problem; the wider war that developed would not have happened had JFK not been assassinated. Ted Sorensen, *Counselor*, 373; and Edwin O. Guthman and Jeffrey Schulman (eds.), *Robert F. Kennedy in His Own Words*, 407, 410.

80. Ronald Steel, *In Love with Night*, 110.

81. Hugh Sidey, "He Makes a Truce with a Man He Came Almost to Hate— LBJ," *Life* November 18, 1966 (Vol. 61, No. 21), 38.

82. Kennedy faced the carpet-bagging/ambition issue in an exchange with the press at Columbia University in New York City in October 1964, as reporters questioned whether he wanted the Senate seat simply so he could then run for president. RFK replied that the concern for voters should be selecting the candidate who could most effectively represent the state and nation's interests. He later said that his principal interest was public service: "I'd like to just be a good United States Senator." After the New York Democratic Party selected RFK as their Senate nominee, the *National Review* sarcastically remarked, ""Attorney General Kennedy appears to have the New York Senatorial nomination in the carpetbag." Edwin O. Guthman and C. Richard Allen (eds.), *RFK: Collected Speeches*, 124-127; and "The Week: Focus on November 3," *National Review* August 25, 1964 (Vol. XVI, No. 34), 711.

83. Julius Duscha, "Big Scene for Kennedy," *Washington Post,* August 24, 1964, A2.

84. Strictly in terms of political strategy, however, some observed that if RFK was intent upon eventually trying for the presidency, he would find it easier to do so by going through the Senate instead of serving in Massachusetts state government. As *U.S. News & World Report* put it—in a manner which probably did not dampen criticism of the Kennedy family's considerable ambitions—"The Kennedys seem not to aspire to Governorships." "The Kennedy Brother's Dream—A New Chapter," *U.S. News & World Report* September 14, 1964 (Vol. LVII, No. 11), 33-35.

85. "Can a Kennedy Beat the Republicans in New York?" *U.S. News & World Report,* August 31, 1964 (Vol. LVII, No. 9), 31-32.

86. Ronald Steel, *In Love with Night*, 117; and Arthur Schlesinger, Jr., *Robert Kennedy and His Times*, 669.

87. Keating vs. Kennedy: High Stakes in New York," *Newsweek*, October 12, 1964 (Vol. LXIV, No. 15), 38.

88. *Newsweek* further commented, "Wherever he went, Bobby Kennedy invoked the ghost of his brother, the martyred President...far from making an effort to dispel the inevitable identification with his brother, he invoked JFK repeatedly through quotations and examples." Ibid., 36, 43; and Joseph A. Palermo, *Robert F. Kennedy*, 87-91.

89. "Keating for Senator," *The Nation*, September 14, 1964 (Vol. 199, No. 6), 101; and "Can a Kennedy Beat the Republicans in New York?" *U.S. News & World Report*, 31-32.

90. "Keating Fights the Kennedy Magic," *Life,* October 9, 1964 (Vol. 57, No. 15), 35.

91. William F. Buckley, Jr., "Bobby for President," *National Review,* June 16, 1964 (Vol. XVI, No. 24), 481.

92. "Keating for Senator," in *The Nation,* 101.

93. "The Kennedy Blitzkrieg," *New York Times,* August 22, 1964, A-20; and "Keating vs. Kennedy," in *Newsweek,* 35; and Ronald Steel, *In Love with Night,* 118-119.

94. Arthur Schlesinger, Jr., *Robert Kennedy and His Times,* 674-675; and Joseph A. Palermo, *Robert F. Kennedy,* 90-91.

95. "Now There Are Two Senators Kennedy," *Newsweek,* November 9, 1964 (Vol. LXIV, No. 19), 35.

96. "The Brothers," *The Nation,* November 23, 1964 (Vol. 199, No. 16), 366.

97. Journalist Rowland Evans adds weight to Sorensen's candor regarding RFK's presidential hopes. Evans remembered a meeting he had with Kennedy at the Justice Department at the end of 1963 in which the Attorney General appeared noncommittal on his future—specifically what, if anything, he would do in 1964. Evans was convinced, however, that RFK had already begun contemplating a bid for president, whether or not he decided to run on the 1964 Democratic ticket as vice-president. Transcript. Rowland Evans, Jr. Oral History Interview, July 30, 1970, by Roberta W. Greene. Robert F. Kennedy Oral History Collection, John F. Kennedy Presidential Library and Museum, Boston, Massachusetts; and Theodore Sorensen, *Counselor,* 452.

98. Transcript, C. Douglas Dillon Oral History Interview, June 18, 1970, by Larry J. Hackman. Robert F. Kennedy Oral History Collection, John F. Kennedy Presidential Library and Museum, Boston, Massachusetts.

99. Transcript. William O. Douglas Oral History Interview, December 12, 1969, by Roberta W. Greene. Robert F. Kennedy Oral History Collection, John F. Kennedy Presidential Library and Museum, Boston, Massachusetts.

100. Sorensen echoed this in his own memoirs. He noted that RFK's Senate staff was urging him to challenge LBJ in the interest of ending the war, and that Kennedy believed the President had gone far beyond JFK's intentions for Vietnam (what those intentions were, it should be emphasized, is an aspect of JFK's foreign policy that has bedeviled historians for decades; in effect, Sorensen seems to be suggesting that RFK knew something everybody else did not). According to Sorensen, there was a "compelling argument" to be made that a 1968 Kennedy presi-

dential campaign may have been the only way to bring the war to an end. Thus, for Sorensen, the decision to run was due first and foremost to RFK's opposition to the war. Edward M. Kennedy, *True Compass: A Memoir* (New York: Twelve, 2009), 228, 264; and Theodore Sorensen, *Counselor*, 454, 457.

101. Transcript, Joseph W. Alsop Oral History Interview, 06/22/1971, by Roberta W. Greene. Robert F. Kennedy Oral History Collection, John F. Kennedy Presidential Library and Museum, Boston, Massachusetts.

102. "Amid Disorder in the Democratic Party, He Drives to Bring About 'The Restoration,'" *Life*, November 18, 1966 (Vol. 61, No. 21), 34-37.

103. Or as Roger Wilkins, assistant attorney general under LBJ, later phrased it, "The thing that the President really hated was...that he would be viewed as the mistake between the Kennedys." "He Makes a Truce," in *Life*, 39; and *LBJ: The American Experience*, PBS.

104. "He Uses—and Deeply Feels—the 'Legend,'" *Life* November 18, 1966 (Vol. 61, No. 21), 40.

105. Penn Kimball, "He Builds His Own Kennedy Identity and the Power Flows Freely to Him," *Life* November 18, 1966 (Vol. 61, No. 21), 129.

106. "Democrats: The Shadow and the Substance," in *Time*, 32.

107. Ibid., 31.

108. Ibid., 31-32.

109. Ronald Steel, *In Love with Night*, 28, 30; and Joseph A. Palermo, *Robert F. Kennedy*, 85.

110. Helen O'Donnell, *A Common Good: The Friendship of Robert F. Kennedy and Kenneth P. O'Donnell* (New York: William Morrow and Company, Inc., 1998), 410-411.

111. Ibid.

112. "Democrats: The Shadow and the Substance," *Time*, 32.

113. Even if some of the opposition to RFK was not because of his suspected manipulation of the memory of his brother per se, there was still the sense among some that he was more interested in his own ambitions than in maintaining party unity and playing by the rules. John J. Burns, Chairman of the New York State Democratic Party, and an RFK supporter, noted in an oral history for the JFK Presidential Library, "There were a number of Democrats...in a state of shock throughout the state that were supporting [LBJ]. You see, within a political party the old-liners feel that it's a cardinal sin to go against an incumbent President—right or wrong, the party is supposed to support him, in their opinion—and here Senator Kennedy was departing from that tradition, and

they were very upset about it." Transcript, John J. Burns Oral History Interview, 11/25/1969, by Roberta W. Greene, Robert F. Kennedy Oral History Collection, John F. Kennedy Presidential Library and Museum, Boston, Massachusetts.

114. Alsop continued, "By the same token there was another huge group of Kennedy lovers...You have forty percent of lovers, and then you have forty percent of real haters. It's a hell of a handicap to have forty percent of real haters when you're fighting for the remaining twenty percent of the electorate." Transcript, Joseph W. Alsop Oral History Interview.

115. Joseph A. Palermo, *In His Own Right*, 143.

116. "The Nation: Politics, The New Context of '68," *Time,* March 22, 1968 (Vol. 91, No. 12), 11; and John Herbers, "Scene Is the Same, But 8 Years Later," *New York Times,* March 17, 1968, 68.

117. Edwin O. Guthman and C. Richard Allen (eds.), *RFK: Collected Speeches,* 320.

118. James N. Giglio, *The Presidency of John F. Kennedy,* 16-17.

119. John F. Kennedy Library and Museum, "Remarks of Senator John F. Kennedy at Bethany College, Bethany, West Virginia: April 19, 1960," available from http://www.jfklibrary.org/Historical+Resources/Archives/Reference+Desk/Speeches/JFK/JFK+Pre-Pres/196 0/002PREPRES12SPEECHES_60APR19B.htm; accessed from Internet May 11, 2008.

120. John F. Kennedy Library and Museum, "Remarks of Senator John F. Kennedy in the Senate, June 14, 1960," available from: http://www.jfklibrary.org/Historical+Resources/Archives/Reference+Desk/Speeches/JFK/JFK+Pre-Pres/1960/002PREPRES12SPEECHES_60JUN14.htm; accessed from Internet May 11, 2008.

121. Edwin O. Guthman and C. Richard Allen (eds.), *RFK: Collected Speeches,* 313; and Robert F. Kennedy, *To Seek a Newer World,* 227-229.

122. Ibid., 328-329.

123. Ibid; and Theodore Sorensen, *The Kennedy Legacy,* 266-267.

124. "He Makes a Truce," in *Life,* 39.

125. "Letters," *Time* April 5, 1968 (Vol. 91, No. 14), 12.

126. "Letters," *Time* April 12, 1968 (Vol. 91, No. 15), 11.

127. "Letters," *Time* June 7, 1968 (Vol. 91, No. 23), 15.

128. Ibid.

129. Joseph A. Palermo, *Robert F. Kennedy,* 140-144; and Ronald Steel, *In Love with Night,* 181.

130. Evan Thomas, *Robert Kennedy*, 24.
131. "Robert Kennedy's Chances: What a Survey Shows," in *U.S. News & World Report*, 48-49.
132. In his book *The Kennedy Legacy*, Sorensen recalled that RFK was very much aware of the wariness he dealt with among groups whose loyalty to the Democratic Party was decades old. "It is easy to forget today that Bob Kennedy was not the beloved figure, even outside the South, that he seemed to be on the day of his funeral train." Kennedy himself once told him, "I'm the only candidate...who has ever united business, labor, liberals, Southerners, bosses, and intellectuals. They're all against me!" Theodore Sorensen, *The Kennedy Legacy*, 147-148, 257.
133. "Democratic Battle: Kennedy Takes on President Johnson," *New York Times*, March 17, 1968, 1E.
134. Ibid., and Richard C. Madden, "Democrats Greet Kennedy Candidacy with Caution," *New York Times*, March 17, 1968, 64.
135. Maurice Isserman and Michael Kazin, *America Divided*, 236-240.
136. George Rising, *Clean for Gene: Eugene McCarthy's 1968 Presidential Campaign* (Westport, Connecticut: Praeger, 1997), 69-70.
137. Tom Wicker, "Enter Robert Kennedy," *New York Times*, March 15, 1968, 38; and Joseph A. Palermo, *Robert F. Kennedy*, 121-123.
138. Ronald Steel, *In Love with Night*, 187.
139. Joseph A. Palermo, *Robert F. Kennedy*, 148-150.
140. In his biography of McCarthy, Dominic Sandbrook pointed out that even with his victory in California, RFK had only fought McCarthy to a draw among antiwar Democrats. Kennedy had essentially the same problem as McCarthy in that both had core groups of supporters but had trouble widening their support beyond that. Sandbrook argues that RFK would have been unable to defeat Nixon. Had he run again in 1972, he probably would have done better than Democratic nominee Senator George McGovern, but still would have lost to Nixon. Dominic Sandbrook, *Eugene McCarthy: The Rise and Fall of Postwar American Liberalism* (New York: Alfred A. Knopf, 2004), 200-202; and "If it's Nixon vs. Kennedy—The Odds," *U.S. News & World Report* April 29, 1968 (Vol. 64, No. 18), 28-30; and "Robert Kennedy's Chances: What a Survey Shows," *US News & World Report*, June 3, 1968 (Vol. 64, No. 23), 48.
141. Theodore Sorensen, *The Kennedy Legacy*, 257.
142. David Halberstam, *The Unfinished Odyssey of Robert Kennedy*, 77.
143. Evan Thomas, *Robert Kennedy*, 388-389.
144. Doris Kearns Goodwin, *Lyndon Johnson and the American Dream*, 350.

145. The same is true for Theodore Sorensen, who commented after RFK's death, "A Robert F. Kennedy administration offered the possibility of leading the country and healing it at the same time...ushering in another golden age in Washington." Arthur Schlesinger, Jr., *Journals*, 293-294; and Theodore Sorensen, *Counselor*, 466.
146. *Bobby*, Emilio Estevez, DVD, The Weinstein Company, 2007.
147. Bill Eppridge, *A Time It Was: Bobby Kennedy in the Sixties* (New York: Harry N. Abrams, Inc., 2008), 189.

CHAPTER FOUR

OTHER SITES OF MEMORY

CREATING CAMELOT AND THE
MEANING OF CONSPIRACY THEORIES

Jack Kennedy had held the most powerful office in the world, but his thirty-four-year-old widow held the power of his memory.
—Journalist and Biographer Sally Bedell Smith[1]

The objective of this work is to examine the practical value of popular memory: how the public's grief over President Kennedy's sudden death was channeled toward the accomplishment of political goals on both local and national levels. However, the construction, reinforcement, and use of JFK's memory are hardly confined to the political examples detailed in the previous three chapters. Others have similarly influenced that memory in furtherance of their own objectives, altruistic or otherwise. Repeatedly, we see that memory curiously does not always reflect reality. At times it is only partially faithful to events as they actually transpired. It is precisely for this reason that shaping memory, if done successfully, can be a potentially powerful way of selling a cause. In the case of Jacqueline Kennedy, the power and resilience of memory were based not simply on who shaped that memory, but perhaps more so upon subsequent events. Those who assume for themselves the role of sculptor of the public's memory of an individual do so in the context of surrounding circumstances. Influencing how the public chooses to remember, both at the time and decades later, is no simple task, and the manner in which one tries to define how someone should be remembered is still dependent on whether that manner of remembering validates what the public wants to believe.

When asked years after she left the White House what she believed was her most notable accomplishment, Jacqueline Kennedy replied, "I think it is that after going through a rather difficult time, I consider myself comparatively sane."[2] It was most certainly a great understatement, not simply in terms of her impact upon the nation during her brief tenure as First Lady, but more importantly in consideration of what she did and said in the days and weeks after November 22. Any discussion of how and why President Kennedy has been memorialized would be incomplete without giving attention to the person who arguably most influenced how the world has remembered him. Mrs. Kennedy was universally praised for the strength and poise she personified in the days after the assassination. In the state funeral that was largely her handiwork, she imparted images to the nation that have lost none of their power even after fifty years. The president's widow left nothing to chance as she directed the planning for JFK's burial. Historian Betty Boyd Caroli has noted that Mrs. Kennedy took a far more active role in funeral planning than did her predecessors when confronted with the deaths of their respective husbands. She was not the first presidential spouse suddenly faced with deciding the proper way of laying a president to rest but, as Caroli says, "none of them provided quite the drama Jackie Kennedy did."[3] The circumstances she confronted—the nature of her husband's death, his brief time in office, the increasing power and visibility of the presidency, and the public's interest in the Kennedy family—necessitated an active role on her part, from the earliest possible moment, in how John F. Kennedy was remembered. She was not Eleanor Roosevelt, laying to rest a husband who had served as president longer than had anyone else and who had pulled the nation through terrible economic times and world war—and whose place in history was thereby assured. And she was not Florence Harding, burying a man who had died suddenly but not violently, and who represented an era in which the president did less, said less, mattered less, and, in terms of mediocrity, could get away with more.

Photo 12. Jacqueline Kennedy leads the Kennedy family and heads of state from around the world in her husband's funeral procession, November 25, 1963.

Photo courtesy of the John F. Kennedy Presidential Library (Robert Knudsen); KN-C30746.

President Kennedy would never have the ability as a living former president to influence how the public remembered him; instead, that power now belonged to Jacqueline Kennedy. Not by accident did she model her husband's funeral upon that of Abraham Lincoln who had died almost a century earlier, and practically every aspect of the funeral proceedings was intended to symbolize a great world leader now fallen. Kennedy family friend Charles Bartlett was sent to the Library of Congress to gather details on the Lincoln funeral, and it was Mrs. Kennedy who determined the burial site. She decided to have her husband interred, not in Boston as several Kennedy aides initially wanted, but instead at Arlington National Cemetery, thus giving the burial a more national prominence. JFK became only the second president to be buried at Arlington, and Mrs. Kennedy, inspired by the Eternal Flame lit at the Arc de Triomphe in Paris, insisted on one for the grave site.[4]

The series of events during the funeral weekend—the procession to the Capitol accompanied by a rider-less horse with boots reversed in the stirrups (traditionally done in tribute to a fallen military leader), the casket on display in the Rotunda upon the same catafalque used for Lincoln and other deceased presidents, the march on foot by one of the most impressive assemblies of power ever seen (the *Washington Post* counted 13 members of royal families, 16 heads of state, and 38 foreign ministers, among others), and Jacqueline Kennedy's presence at the front and center of it all gave John Kennedy a measure of importance rarely achieved by any national or world leader even after decades of public service.[5] Kennedy's brief time in the White House and his rather thin list of accomplishments as president suddenly became irrelevant, as he was transformed that weekend into a great president. The funeral unleashed emotions that likewise could have rivaled those generated by Lincoln's funeral procession.[6] With no sense of cynicism can it be said that the Kennedy funeral was carefully planned theater—powerful theater. Lady Bird Johnson later recorded in her diary,

> I kept on comparing [the funeral] in my mind with the time Franklin Roosevelt died, but that was so different, because then everybody could be as emotional as they felt like being. The feeling persisted that I was moving, step by step, through a Greek tragedy. I remembered a definition from college days—that a Greek tragedy is concerned with a noble protagonist overtaken by an inevitable doom.[7]

Mrs. Johnson was not the only one with the conviction that what the nation was witnessing was monumental history, something on a far different scale even from the not-so-distant passing of FDR. Writing in the *Washington Post*, Alfred Friendly observed,

> For the most part, the mourners were moved in a different way from those who lined Washington's streets 18 years ago for the funeral procession of Franklin D. Roosevelt. Then, they had been seized with the paroxysms of personal grief, and lost themselves in unrestrained weeping. Yesterday, it seemed, the mourners felt themselves engaged more in a tragedy of the nation than in individual bereavement.[8]

Hardly unnoticed during those four days was the way in which Mrs. Kennedy carried herself, as if the dignified bearing she displayed before the world was one final reminder of the grace and courage that supposedly characterized the presidency now gone. JFK may have been the protagonist of the "Greek tragedy," but she served in only a slightly secondary role as director and producer. One newspaper described her as "Lady Courage;" another in the United Kingdom remarked, "Jacqueline Kennedy has given the American people from this day on one thing they have always lacked—majesty."[9] And French President Charles de Gaulle, seldom a man who was easily impressed, later paid tribute to her by commenting, "She gave an example to the whole world of how to behave."[10] Her work, however, was hardly complete. Jacqueline Kennedy imparted several enduring elements of greatness to the public in tribute to her husband: a state funeral worthy of a monumental leader, her successful efforts to have the space center at Florida's Cape Canaveral named after her husband, and the planning of his presidential library. All impacted how the public thought about President Kennedy. None, however, were as powerful as the idea of the Kennedy years as a second Camelot, as Mrs. Kennedy described it. "Camelot" became Jacqueline Kennedy's principal contribution to the perpetuation of her husband's memory.

Only two weeks after Dallas, she contacted *Life* magazine journalist Theodore White and gave him an interview—an interview marked by the first use of the imagery of King Arthur's Camelot to describe what the Kennedy era in the White House had supposedly been like. President Kennedy, she told White, had loved reading stories during his childhood about the adventures of King Arthur and his gallant knights. The Broadway musical *Camelot* had opened in December 1960, one month after Kennedy had been elected president, and Mrs. Kennedy recalled that her husband would often listen fondly to a record of the play's musical score.[11] She tried to erect a wall between the Kennedy years and everything that had happened before or after, as if to safeguard a place for him in history and in the hearts of Americans. As she told White, "There'll be wonderful Presidents again...and the Johnsons are wonderful, they've been wonderful to me—but there'll never be another Camelot again."[12] It was the image presented by the play—that of a noble group of men engaged in heroic pursuits and a glorious time that proved to be sadly transient—that, for her, most accurately represented the essence of the Kennedy administration. "She does not," wrote White, "want [people] to forget John F. Kennedy or read of him only in dusty or bigger histories. For one brief shining moment there was Camelot."[13] The interview appeared in the magazine's December 6, 1963, issue. It would be unfair to accuse the late president's widow of deviously selling the public an interpretation of JFK's presidency that she, of all people, knew was simply not accurate. Nobody's despair over the death of President Kennedy could have rivaled hers, and it is fair to say that she gave the grieving nation the Camelot myth partly as a way of easing her own sorrow. Carving out a revered place in the nation's memory for her husband was of great concern to her in the period after the assassination. The idea of Camelot provided, in the words of one recent JFK biographer, "a therapeutic shield against immobilizing grief."[14] Sublime memories of what it was like when Kennedy was president served the immediate emotional needs of not only a grieving widow, but a grieving nation and world as well.

With half a century having elapsed since 1963, how should we understand the idea of Camelot? Did its usefulness, its value in terms of the
public's memory of JFK, diminish as the shock over the assassination
faded and the nation was forced to accept what had happened and
move on? "Camelot" accomplished its immediate objective of providing
comfort, but Mrs. Kennedy's happy and glamorous rendering of her
husband's presidency did not really bring the country closer to any useful
conclusions about it. It is unfortunate that so many have bought into
the Camelot comparison in the last five decades. Any serious scholar on
JFK will maintain that the concept of his administration (or of life in the
United States during that period) as Camelot is an incredible distortion of
reality. One historian called the idea of Camelot "myth-making of maudlin
proportions,"[15] and even close Kennedy advisers thought it was excessive.
Arthur Schlesinger, Jr. opined, "JFK would have regarded [Camelot] with
derision...that was not the way we saw ourselves. Those were romantic
memories."[16] It is certainly true that Camelot has been understood by
others, including some in the Kennedy inner circle, as an accurate way of
thinking of those years. They believed that his presidency was a hopeful
time, a time when great things were possible and were achieved, an
important part of American history that they were helping to direct.[17]
Still, the comparison to Camelot was so often and unquestioningly used
by so many that it later appeared rather corny. Kennedy's Secretary of
State, Dean Rusk, agreed with Schlesinger's assessment of "Camelot" by
commenting, "JFK would have kicked the idea of Camelot right out the
window. He was a very practical...down-to-earth kind of individual who
would not have indulged in the sentiment of Camelot...In my judgment
JFK would not have played around with that idea at all."[18] Camelot should
rightly be understood as more of a postmortem glorification than a true
representation of what John Kennedy's two-year, eleven-month tenure
in the White House was really like.

But the Camelot comparison worked. It has retained a great deal of
power with the public. Why? Readers who are interested enough to find
a copy of the December 1963 issue of *Life* and read for themselves the

article where Mrs. Kennedy invoked Camelot for the first time may be surprised at the article's brevity and, from the standpoint of history, its inconclusiveness. It comprised only two pages and was just shy of eleven hundred words. Although the interview was conducted only a couple of weeks after President Kennedy was buried at Arlington, it mentioned nothing in the way of specific achievements, plans for a second term, or ideals that were important to JFK. No Cuban Missile Crisis, no civil rights, no Nuclear Test Ban Treaty, no speculation as to what Kennedy might have done on the issues of poverty in the United States or fostering better relations with the Soviet Union—all of the things for which he has subsequently (whether fairly or not) received credit. There was nothing definite Mrs. Kennedy was memorializing her husband *for*. And yet, the article would influence how Americans remembered the Kennedy White House perhaps more than anything else. Part of the reason why "Camelot" has had such staying power is straightforward: it came from no less a source than the Queen of Camelot herself. What Mrs. Kennedy said about her husband carried great credibility, and she found an incredibly appealing metaphor that succinctly captured the essence (or so many people thought) of the Kennedy years.

If the idea of Camelot is suspect from a historical sense, Jacqueline Kennedy's timing was impeccable. "Camelot" was not given to the American people years later when the grief over the assassination had diminished, and both the public and scholars had at least begun to consider how JFK should be treated by history. Mrs. Kennedy gave her husband's presidency definition at the time when the public's memory was most capable of being influenced. Indeed, as even Theodore White recalled years later, however overblown the idea of Camelot was, it was difficult for anybody—himself included—not to get caught up in the emotion of it all. Speaking about his December 1963 interview of Mrs. Kennedy, White admitted, "At that moment, she could have sold me anything from an Edsel to the Brooklyn Bridge. [Camelot] didn't seem like a hell of a lot... So I said to myself, why not? If that's all she wants, let her have it."[19]

This acquiescence did not mean that Mrs. Kennedy retained *carte blanche* over how the Kennedy administration would be remembered and written about. As former Kennedy aides moved on to other pursuits after 1963, memoirs of their time with the late president began appearing, and, in many cases, Jacqueline Kennedy was able to persuade them to revise their book manuscripts in accordance with her wishes. One has only to look at the imbroglio set off over William Manchester's book on the assassination—a work initially sanctioned by none other than Jacqueline and Robert Kennedy—to understand that even Mrs. Kennedy's ability to persuade others to accept her version of history had its limits.[20]

Clearly, the *timing* of the Camelot metaphor was every bit as crucial to its success as was its creator. The national and international strife that marked the rest of the decade, along with the personalities and considerable failings of the two men who followed John F. Kennedy in the White House only gave the Camelot idea greater credibility and luster. The United States had emerged from World War II as the most prosperous and powerful nation in the world, and many remembered Kennedy's accession to the presidency in 1961 as a time of optimism and confidence that the country was capable of solving any problem. The United States, with the government that led it, and the executive branch that led the government, seemed undoubtedly to be a force for good.[21] While the assassination by itself may not have shattered these convictions, what occurred in the years following certainly did. Vietnam, domestic unrest, Watergate, revelations of the Central Intelligence Agency's tawdry meddling in the internal affairs of other nations, and energy crises all seemed to demonstrate that the country was not quite the invincible exemplar of virtue many had previously thought it was. How different the national scene must have looked when Richard Nixon became president as the sixties closed compared with the atmosphere that prevailed when JFK took the oath of office only eight years before.

Such a comparison became even harsher when viewed in light of the considerable differences between John Kennedy and his immediate successors. It is important to understand specifically what Camelot represented to Mrs. Kennedy and countless millions of others. It was more evocative of the *way* things were done as opposed to *what* was accomplished. Camelot as applied to the Kennedy administration conjures up images of glamour; happiness; nobility of purpose; an era when all was right; an era when the president not only did the right thing, but did it with style and wit; and a time in which intellectual accomplishment and selfless dedication to public service were readily on display among the nation's leaders in a way that was never again replicated after the assassination. When compared to Lyndon Johnson and Richard Nixon, both of whom seemingly possessed only a fraction of Kennedy's qualities but seemed to compensate with so many negative attributes of their own—Johnson's crudity and narcissism, Nixon's paranoia and self-destructiveness—the Kennedy era appeared to many as a uniquely virtuous time, the "one brief shining moment" that Richard Burton sang about.

The way we evaluate and remember our chief executives depends to a surprising extent upon what happens *after* they leave office, and the case of JFK—specifically the idea of Camelot—is no exception. What if Lyndon Johnson had been successful in coping with the problems of race and poverty? What if he had not overreached so terribly and divided the country by expanding American involvement in Vietnam? What if LBJ—or Richard Nixon—had met the challenges of the time and provided the same sort of idealistic leadership that Kennedy was credited with? Had the years after 1963 turned out better, the Kennedy era might not be remembered as such an anomaly. Rather, JFK could instead be remembered as one in a series of generally successful presidents, possibly even falling a bit short by comparison in terms of his ability to get a legislative agenda passed. The idea of Camelot, in such a scenario, might never have taken hold of the public's imagination the way it did if subsequent years and the quality of American political leadership were remembered as being roughly comparable to the early 1960s.

The same process of influencing the public's memory as occurred in Dallas, and later by President Johnson and Robert Kennedy, is evident here. "Camelot" was at the same time a distortion of reality, but it still possessed a trace of the truth. Kennedy undoubtedly *did* inspire many Americans to work for the betterment of the nation and of others. He *did* effectively articulate the conviction that love of country was inextricably linked to idealism and public service. JFK presided over an era in which there was still confidence that any domestic or international problem confronting the United States could be solved through American leadership. Historian W. J. Rorabaugh argued that the JFK era, albeit brief, should be understood primarily as a transitional period in American history. It was marked by both the 1950s-era aversion to social change and general feeling of complacency resulting from the nation's material abundance, as well as by the first indications of unrest that would define the remainder of the 1960s.[22] This setting, combined with Kennedy's soaring rhetoric, style, and seeming mastery of the art of using presidential authority for good, meant that the Camelot metaphor was true to form for many who remembered these years. It helped sort out what was good from what was bad during what turned out to be a very troubling and confusing decade for so many. This metaphor was powerful because it became a neat line of demarcation (although again, not entirely an accurate one) from which point things in the country became turbulent. The rest of the 1960s only heightened the bulkheads that Jacqueline Kennedy had placed around her husband's presidency, establishing it as a glorious time in the minds of Americans.

***

One American who remembered the era this way was film director Oliver Stone. His controversial 1991 movie *JFK* was, critics charged, more pseudo-history and artful storytelling than it was a reflection of historical events. But in at least one respect, the case of *JFK* is unique among the sites of memory this work has examined. Unlike Dallas civic leaders, LBJ, RFK, and Jacqueline Kennedy, Stone did not create *JFK* in the mid-to-late 1960s when the assassination was still fresh in people's minds and a major portion of the public had firsthand recollections of it. The film appeared nearly 30 years later, thus potentially influencing, more than anyone else, younger Americans who had no memories of President Kennedy. Stone, no less than the others who influenced popular memory of the late president, was very much promoting a cause with his film. *JFK* did not contribute much in the way of a scholarly approach to the assassination, whatever its impact upon the public, but it was how Stone's cause intersected with memory that made his cinematic narrative both powerful and problematic.

The director's cause was the marketing of a high-level conspiracy theory that purported to explain not only the way the president was killed, but the larger reasons why—and the unfortunate consequences for all Americans. Stone's attempt to rationalize Kennedy's death was seen by many (certainly by many historians) as simply shining the spotlight on himself and on his own disillusionment with post-assassination America, instead of being a real search for truth. The film purported to examine the assassination by recounting the 1966 investigation initiated by New Orleans District Attorney Jim Garrison. Garrison, played by Kevin Costner, was depicted as a heroic lone crusader vainly attempting to uncover the sordid truth about the death of Kennedy and the simultaneous death of American innocence and idealism. Costner's Garrison, wandering around the sixth-floor window from which Lee Harvey Oswald fired at the motorcade (although even Stone admitted that Garrison never visited the sniper's nest), proclaims, "Let justice be done," and uncovers the truth behind Kennedy's death.[23] The late president, Stone tells us, had decided in the months leading up to his assassination, to withdraw American troops from Vietnam—thereby sparing the country the grief and national division that later resulted from the war. In perhaps the most gripping scene of the film—the meeting between Garrison and the movie's fictional character Mr. X—viewers are left with a conception of JFK as almost a radical figure. His supposed intentions to terminate American involvement in Vietnam, and to seek a permanent peace with the Soviet Union, seemingly put him in singular opposition to the wishes of the intelligence community, the military, even perhaps the majority of the U.S. government. Mr. X asserts as undisputed fact that JFK intended to end the Cold War had he lived to serve another term. "I never realized Kennedy was so dangerous to the Establishment," Costner's Garrison states, a characterization that probably better suits the fringe 1960s antiwar group the Weathermen, than it does John Kennedy. Lee Harvey Oswald is considered barely worthy of mention compared to the scale of the plot behind JFK's death. The viewer feels as if he or she has become privy to the real story as Mr. X dismisses the squabbling over how many gunmen were involved or who pulled off the shooting as simply "scenery for the public," a distraction from the larger and more disturbing question of *why* Kennedy was killed. Understanding the reasons behind the event is key to then understanding why the years following turned out so tragically. For Stone, the assassination was not simply a violent change in national leadership; it marked a clear and permanent diversion of American history from more peaceful and hopeful times to the more violent and cynical era in which we live today.[24]

Vietnam is central to Stone's narrative. It was, according to Mr. X, unquestionably JFK's intention to exit Vietnam; according to the movie character, "Vietnam started for real" only after the assassination. A potentially imminent American military draw-down was not to the military's liking, and Kennedy had barely been laid to rest before President Johnson privately told Pentagon officials that the United States would not withdraw, but would instead defend South Vietnam. "That," as Mr. X said, "was the day Vietnam started," and the movie presents images of a fictional Oval Office meeting between LBJ and top military officials, in which the president signed a National Security Council directive that led the country into the longest and most divisive war in U.S. history.[25] With the intelligence community feeling threatened, the military alienated due to defense budget cuts and a more pacifist Kennedy foreign policy, and the deliberate lack of security in Dallas on November 22, the president is compared to Julius Caesar with a massive plot against him coursing throughout Washington and his future executors all around.[26]

How did *JFK* invoke popular memory of the late president? As did other conspiracy theorists, Stone played upon people's fond memories of the late president and the period of national strife and seeming loss of purpose in the years after the assassination to argue that only a plot of huge proportions could have brought down a great president. By dismissing as ridiculous the idea that one person could have been solely responsible for what many considered the "crime of the century," Stone and other conspiracy theorists were glorifying the memory of JFK. For them, his death cheated the American people out of what surely would have been a different, and a much more hopeful, future.[27] More than simply proposing his own assassination theory, more important than the manner in which he did it (a film that even critics had to admit was very convincing, or as Rita Kempley termed it in the *Washington Post*, "compelling info-ganda"[28]) was the potential *JFK* had for altering the way the public thought about these historical events, especially as far as young people were concerned. Stone had popular memory directly in mind when he made the film, dedicating it to younger Americans who, although having no recollection of the assassination, were now (as he said) responsible for finding the truth. The movie producers even compiled a "study guide" to *JFK* for intended use in schools.[29]

Stone's intent was essentially manipulation of memory (or rather, the lack of memory) of the segment of American society who probably had never known much about John Kennedy prior to watching the movie.[30] Thus, *JFK* sought to shape popular memory, and Stone is not the only conspiracy theorist who crafted his message to influence those learning about JFK for the first time. His narrative has a tragic allure to it. From a student's vantage point, John Kennedy's presidency, death, and the Vietnam War are distant historical events encountered in textbooks or documentaries and thus, in a sense, are taken for granted as clear and inevitable from half a century looking back. The movie presents not only a seemingly plausible explanation for why his death happened, but also an alternative way things might have been. In his chain of causation, Stone tells his audience in effect that Kennedy tried to do great things, for which he was killed. Because of that, the nation suffered tremendously, but it did not have to happen that way. Had he lived, the history of the latter portion of the 20th century would have been considerably different. Younger Americans who grew up in a time of greater skepticism or outright mistrust of government might see *JFK* and conclude, not altogether incorrectly, that one of the major causes for this cynicism was the Kennedy assassination. But would the film lead them to believe that the government was responsible for the death of the president and for a subsequent cover-up? And would they be convinced of, for example, JFK's intention to end the Cold War when the historical evidence for such an idea is far less substantial than Stone suggested in the movie? The thought that if JFK had not been killed, Vietnam might never have happened and the Cold War could have ended in the late 1960s is heady stuff to consider, especially for viewers who had little or no memory or knowledge of that period before seeing *JFK*. The problem was, however, that this was little more than speculation. Although one could argue that Stone's motives were reasonable—inspiring young people to critically examine the recent course of American history—some scholars rightfully feared the potential results of selling his theory to viewers unable to discern the movie's facts from the creative liberties its director took. In the debate set off by the content of *JFK*, Stone's motives certainly received their share of scrutiny. One scholar, in a study of the media's influence on how Americans have remembered the assassination, wrote "The lack of closure surrounding the assassination tale gave rise to an ongoing contest for authorization, by which different groups attempted to promote their version of what happened in Dallas in order to promote themselves."[31]

It was exactly this sort of accusation—using the assassination for personal gain—that was leveled against Stone upon the film's release. Tom Wicker of the *New York Times*, in criticizing him for his disregard for facts and his readiness to denounce anybody who disagreed with his ideas on the assassination as either ignorant or as part of the plot themselves, commented that the film treated "matters that are highly speculative as fact and truth, in effect rewriting history."[32] Just as Stone had cast Jim Garrison as an American hero, Wicker suggested the director seemed to be claiming the same role for himself, as if the nation had fallen victim to a massive conspiracy that had finally been exposed thanks to the diligent efforts of Garrison and Stone.[33] Indeed, the director's "me-against-the world" attitude was on display in his 1992 testimony before a House committee considering legislation to review and open federal records related to the assassination. Stone criticized the "government insiders" who were responsible for the Warren Commission as well as the "official media" that, in his view, had colluded with the government "in a decision to stonewall the American people" from ever reaching the truth. He appeared to credit his film, and himself, for defying efforts by the media to denounce or silence his ideas.[34] Taking the podium at the National Press Club in Washington, D.C. around the same time, Stone questioned why his media critics were apparently uninterested in asking the hard questions about the assassination that he, by implication, had been willing to pose with his film. Although he described *JFK* as simply presenting one "hypothesis" in a "marketplace of ideas," he did not doubt it would have an impact akin to that of a documentary on the way people thought about the assassination after watching it in theaters. With release on videotape, he declared, "another 50 or so million Americans will have a little more information on their history."[35]

This, for critics, was precisely the point. As one writer on the assassination said, "One of the reasons the critics were so upset was the fear that people who did not remember the assassination would believe that *JFK* was documentary history."[36] George Lardner of the *Washington Post* assailed Stone for his desire "to take history and shape it, his way. He wants it to be our memory of the Kennedy assassination."[37] There was concern that younger movie-goers were particularly susceptible to being swayed by Stone. It was a problem, not simply because of their lack of knowledge about President Kennedy or the issues discussed in the film, but due to the manner in which younger viewers increasingly received the news or, in this case, information about historical events of which they had no firsthand memories. In 1991, with the internet not yet widely available, young people habitually relied upon television and the movies —essentially entertainment media—as their foremost sources of information and ideas. Thus, the potential of *JFK* to define the 35th president and the 1960s for an entire generation could have been great.[38] Early reaction to the movie may have been proof of this outcome. Although it received mixed reviews, with mainstream journalists tending to be more critical and movie critics overall giving it higher marks, *JFK* earned nearly $31 million after less than a month in theatres.[39]

Concerns that *JFK* would have a decisive impact upon the public, however, may have been overstated. With the Warren Commission falling into disrepute in the years after 1964, a considerable number of Americans believed in a conspiracy of some sort even before Stone contributed his motion picture to the debate. Public opinion polls taken in the two years following the movie's release did not really indicate that the public was more likely to believe in a conspiracy, despite the commercial success the movie enjoyed.[40] And some observers argued that it was hardly inevitable that younger viewers would wholeheartedly buy into what Stone was selling. The idea that those without any personal memories of JFK would unquestioningly consume the film's theories—that younger Americans as a group did not have the ability to understand more than Oliver Stone's movie—was regarded as condescending and as excessive generalization. If anything, the director's arguments, like anybody else's point of view that was so controversial, could instead produce skepticism and spur an ongoing search for answers even amongst the viewers to whom *JFK* was dedicated.[41] The film, as David Ansen suggested in *Newsweek*, was simply one opinion. As a work of art it was no different from any other movie in trying to persuade its audience of its reality. "An entire generation," Ansen acknowledged, "is hereafter going to look at [the assassination] through Stone's prism. If history is a battlefield, *JFK* has to be seen as a bold attempt to seize the turf for future debate."[42]

But perhaps Stone was not manipulating popular memory, or trying to create a certain set of memories among those too young to remember JFK, but instead *reflecting* what the public already thought. In the *American Historical Review Forum* for April 1992, Marcus Raskin (who served on the National Security Council under Kennedy) argued that focusing solely on the film's factual errors and questionable inferences about JFK missed the larger, and valid, point that Stone was trying to make. The film, according to Raskin, accurately captured the widespread belief that the truth had been covered up. If many remembered the Kennedy assassination as only the first in a series of national events that undermined the confidence of Americans in their government and other institutions, *JFK* was really an expression of those memories. Stone was acting as a spokesman for his generation in highlighting the grimier parts of American history in the 1960s and 1970s that resulted in a memory of disillusionment. With the many supposed flaws in the Warren Commission's investigation of the assassination, Raskin said, people had every right to look elsewhere for the truth, which is what Stone was doing, albeit in a highly artful way.[43]

Robert Rosenstone likewise saw the film as a genuine contribution to American history. The central message of *JFK*—that the assassination was the result of a conspiracy—was potentially still valid in spite of the film's inaccuracies. As a work of history, the primary achievement of the movie was that it deftly raised questions about American life post-1963 that an actual historian would have had a harder time conveying in a monograph or journal article. And as a work of art, *JFK* succeeded in pointing out the myriad issues and persons connected to President Kennedy and his death in a seemingly compelling way. Rosenstone opined that neither historians nor laymen should remain focused on the creative liberties that Stone took at the expense of what he was trying to say.[44] As he observed:

> Any work about the past, be it a piece of written, visual, or oral history, enters a body of preexisting knowledge and debate. To be considered 'historical,' rather than simply a costume drama that uses the past as an exotic setting for romance and adventure, a film must engage the issues, ideas, data, and arguments of that

discourse. Whatever else it does or does not do, *JFK* certainly meets these requirements as a work of history.[45]

Stone firmly believed that President Kennedy had been a sort of last hope for the United States and the world. In contrast to the war, domestic violence and unrest, loss of faith in American leadership and capabilities, and environmental degradation that dominated the years after his murder, Kennedy represented for Stone someone who could have prevented such national distress.[46] Vietnam was the most painful example of that distress, and Stone joined other Kennedy admirers (and some historians as well) in seeing his assassination as the point of entry into the war for the United States.[47] In the words of one scholar, JFK's death directly led to "the death of a generation."[48] In this sense, *JFK* was an obituary to more than just a leader, and those who believed that his presidency was a better era in America history must have found the film highly powerful.

Like many JFK partisans, Stone saw the late president's famous speech at American University in June 1963 as a first—and fleeting—moment of hope that the superpowers might have concluded the Cold War twenty-five years earlier than they did. This desire for peace on Kennedy's part, Stone argued, would surely have made the future a better place than it turned out: "Kennedy seemed to be a man far ahead of his time... and they killed him for it."[49] Stone served in Vietnam, so it is easy to understand how he could have persuaded himself that the war he fought in, and the disillusionment he and many other Americans experienced as a result of that conflict, would never have occurred had Kennedy not been killed.[50] In linking the president's death with the longest and most controversial war in American history, *JFK* highlighted the very personal nature of the tragedy. The post-assassination years represented a *personal* loss of innocence as much as a national loss, making Stone's admiration of President Kennedy so strong—and the memory of his loss all the more powerful.

There is, I think, much to be said for the Raskin and Rosenstone point of view. Stone was indisputably advocating a cause with his motion picture, but as with the other examples of popular memory this work has discussed, *JFK* did nonetheless employ traces of the truth (although very often, it amounted only to traces). It had to, if it were to have any credibility with the American people. To be sure, as a factually based examination of a historical event, it was fatally flawed. The many inaccuracies of *JFK* have been amply discussed by others, and in the interest of not recycling their arguments, I will refrain from such a listing of these inaccuracies here.[51] But the case of Oliver Stone's *JFK* is not so very different from the other ways popular memory of JFK has been used. The question of whether the director actively manipulated and distorted the memory of President Kennedy or whether he simply found, through his film, an effective way of portraying what many already believed is ultimately a chicken-and-egg proposition. It is a little of both. What is depicted in *JFK*, often as undisputed fact, is in many cases fabrication; one assumption is built upon another. But from the standpoint of popular memory, this is the wrong way to look at the issue, for *JFK* should be seen as only one part of the larger and ongoing effort to influence popular memory. Viewed in this way, the movie is not quite the egregious and sinister attempt to deceive the public as its detractors argued—even allowing for its considerable limitations as a work of history. In reality, Stone was making the same use of popular memory as did the others discussed herein. He found a very practical—some might argue crass—way of using popular memory, but his artistic creation was a blend of the real and the fake. Critics are entirely justified to argue that his movie inevitably would be consumed by millions of people with no firsthand memory of Kennedy, and Stone, therefore, as a sculptor of the public's perceptions of a historical event, should have been more responsible about what he was selling. However, was his contention that a government-orchestrated conspiracy murdered Kennedy because he was ready to exit Vietnam any more inaccurate than, for example, the contention that his presidency was like Camelot? Was Stone's argument that JFK was intent on altering the direction of American foreign policy more historically suspect than President Johnson's attempt to turn Kennedy into a civil rights martyr?

If, as Stone's critics charged, *JFK* was more about selling a movie and casting himself as a noble seeker of the truth, were Stone's motives more self-serving than LBJ or RFK identifying themselves with the late president to advance their political careers?

Examining *JFK* as a site of popular memory instead of its value as a work of pseudo-history raises the question of what is actually appropriate in how we memorialize someone. How much distortion of the truth is too much? And what about motive? In what circumstances does the use of popular memory cross the line between memorialization and simply profit-making or publicity seeking? Memory can be played upon for motives both base and sublime. Oliver Stone could be either praised for a commitment to finding the truth or condemned for trying to market a movie full of falsehoods. *JFK* thus becomes highly allegorical in more than one way. To a limited extent, the film does represent a search for answers, even if it is akin to traveling to the south Pacific in search of the *Titanic*. But the film and the controversy it set off also neatly capture the challenges involved in, and ultimately the paradoxical nature of, the construction of memory. Sometimes this construction leads to oversimplification. At times, it does produce distortion. However, in order for a particular message or perspective to become embedded in the public's memory, it still has to be within some proximity to what actually happened or what the people already believe. Stone, no less than the others, created fantasy to point out reality.

***

The proliferation of conspiracy theories has only further blurred the line between fantasy and reality. The character of these theories ranges from the measured and thoughtful (it is important to note that relatively few actual historians have written books on the assassination) to the irresponsible and incomprehensible. Moreover, the impetus for such verbiage tends to run a similar gamut—a dispassionate examination of the facts surrounding the assassination in pursuit of the truth, to a simple desire to sell books and be regarded as an assassination expert. What became a conspiracy industry began not long after the Warren Commission officially concluded, in the fall of 1964, that Lee Harvey Oswald was the lone assassin. The year 1966 saw the publication of Mark Lane's *Rush to Judgment* and Edward Jay Epstein's *Inquest*, both of which became bestsellers. Sylvia Meagher published *Accessories After the Fact* the following year, and critiques of the Warren Report also appeared from time to time in newspapers and journals with fairly small circulations such as *Ramparts* and *Liberation*. The Jim Garrison investigation, the increasing distrust of the federal government in the wake of Vietnam and Watergate, the 1975 airing of the Zapruder film on national television, and the establishment of the House Select Committee on Assassinations all demonstrated how mainstream the belief in a conspiracy of some sort had become by the late 1970s. Speculation over the existence of a conspiracy in some cases even took on a comical overtone; one satirical theatrical production titled *MacBird!* suggested a plot involving Lyndon Johnson. The equally satirical newspaper *The Onion* commented on the ever-widening possibilities of who was involved and how the shooting was carried out with a headline reading, "Kennedy Slain by CIA, Mafia, Castro, LBJ, Teamsters, Freemasons: President Shot 129 Times from 43 Different Angles."[52] If one can make any generalization about the countless books published that advocate for one conspiracy or another, it is that they have attributed Kennedy's death to much larger and powerful forces. The truth, for them, simply has to be more complex than one unhappy gunman dedicated to committing a crime that would assure himself a place in American history. Nor do conspiracy theorists on the whole buy into a plot that—in comparison to the Lincoln assassination—was greatly constricted in scope. JFK's death is more often explained as being orchestrated by much larger forces than one, two, or three individuals committing an act strictly of their own accord.[53]

Photo 13. President Johnson accepts the findings of the Warren Commission, September 24, 1964. Many Americans were unsatisfied with the Commission's lone gunman theory, and a steady market for conspiracy theories has existed ever since.

Photo courtesy of the Lyndon B. Johnson Presidential Library (Cecil Stoughton); C732-1-WH64

Kennedy was killed, as the theories go, by organized crime in the U.S., anti-Castro Cubans, Fidel Castro, Lyndon Johnson, the FBI, the CIA, the American military, or any number of other figures or organizations. JFK died because of his supposed position on civil rights, because he would not commit the U.S. to war in Vietnam, because big business was upset over his supposedly anti-business policies, because Robert Kennedy's

Justice Department was aggressively targeting the mob for prosecution, because Kennedy had apparently voiced his intention to disband the CIA, or because Kennedy stood in the way of LBJ's own presidential ambitions. Such at least are some of the more popular theories; lesser-known ideas have tended to compensate for their obscurity with sheer outlandishness.[54]

The need for the nation to learn who killed President Kennedy as a way of understanding the problems that have beset recent American history has, at least on the face of things, been the primary motivation for conspiracy theorists. The assassination was, if not the first or the last, arguably the most notorious example of what assassination writer Peter Dale Scott termed "parapolitics": a manner of effecting change in the American political system in which accountability to the public—a crucial ingredient in representative democracy—is undermined. The assassination was only one instance, along with Watergate and the Iran-Contra scandal, of irregular or extra-constitutional methods employed by persons or factions within the government that ultimately weakened the public's confidence in government. Kennedy's death is memorable in this sense because it marked a failure and even a betrayal of the principles upon which American society and government are based, but it cannot be dismissed as a tragic, highly irregular occurrence. Subsequent events have only demonstrated that the assassination was "a symptom of something wrong today, not just in 1963, in the heart of the society in which we live." Scott continues, "I have always believed, and argued, that a true understanding of the Kennedy assassination will lead, not to 'a few bad people,' but to the institutional and parapolitical arguments which constitute the way we are systematically governed."[55] Conspiracy theorists reinforce an image of the late president as perhaps the last national figure in the lifetimes of many Americans who could have decisively shaped events, as opposed to being overshadowed by them as several of his successors were. Jim Marrs, one of the more well-known theorists, wrote that his overriding purpose in looking at the death of President Kennedy was to uncover the assassin(s) of the president who could have forestalled the daunting problems and sad divisions that came in later years. "I seek," Marrs said, "the persons who killed Camelot—who killed the confidence and faith of the American people in their government and institutions." Later, in conclusion, he lamented, "Until the people of the United States confront the reality of Kennedy's death and face the power behind it, the wars, near-wars, the wasteful military buildup, foreign adventurism, death, squandered millions, trampled human rights, moral decline, and environmental pollution will continue."[56] Historians would be amused, to say the least, at the suggestion that these problematic issues were all held in check by a president who served less than three full years, and that one event—his assassination—unleashed the problems that the nation still has to cope with today.

Whatever the accuracy of Marrs' statements, they do suggest another reason why Kennedy is memorialized: the simple, nagging belief that the truth has not been told. He can never be completely put to rest until the American people learn why a "great" president and the promise of great achievements were taken from them. Remembering the late president becomes a type of national burden, almost a patriotic obligation. Continuing the fifty-year inquest into his death sheds light not only on the troubled events of the past but also enables future generations of Americans to better protect themselves against another such violation of the democratic will. In their book *High Treason* (dedicated by the authors, respectively, to young people who "must learn the truth and care about the past," and to the memory of JFK, "for his vision and compassion"), Harrison Edward Livingstone and Robert J. Groden wrote, "What we lost on November 22, 1963, cannot be measured. On that terrible day in Dallas we forfeited our innocence, idealism and confidence. We cannot begin to restore these until we have exposed the truth."[57] *Not* remembering JFK and *not* learning the lessons of his death mean the nation will be imperiled again in almost Dante-esque fashion as it was in the late 1960s and early 1970s. As they conclude,

> Whenever one powerful group thinks that the end justifies the
> means, and flagrantly breaks the law, when we turn our backs
> on the very democratic institutions and traditions we most value,
> when violence and murder become political tools, then we enter a
> nightmare world in which we are all at risk. Once descended into
> the underworld of darkness, it is impossible to emerge unscathed.
> That is the true significance of what took place in Dealey Plaza
> on the 22nd of November, 1963.[58]

We continue to debate and write about President Kennedy's death
because, according to conspiracy theorists, his memory demands it. This
seems to be a recurring motivation for their work, even when a convincing
(though not conclusive) case can be made that Lee Harvey Oswald did
indeed act alone. The fact that the evidentiary waters have become so
hopelessly muddied enables them to continue their refrain that the truth
is still unknown, information about the assassination remains withheld,
and that further belaboring of the entire issue is necessary to sort out the
mess (which partially is due to the shoddy research and outrageous ideas
from the very people who charge themselves with finding the truth).[59]
"While all these doubts remain, who can say that the case is closed?"
wrote Hugh Trevor-Roper in his introduction to Mark Lane's *Rush to
Judgment*. "In a sense it is still *sub judice*...When both sides have been
heard, and not before, posterity may judge."[60] A quarter-century later,
not much had changed. Conspiracy theorist Anthony Summers noted
that "Long after John Kennedy's death, Americans still argue the manner
of his passing. They are weary of the issue, but they do not let it drop."[61]
The public remains as obsessed with the late president's death, if not
more so, as they did with his life. Under those circumstances, even in the
absence of new documentation related to the assassination, the conspiracy
community can continue to expect brisk business in what it sells.

Gerald Posner, another researcher on the assassination, suggested that
it is the American people's glorification of President Kennedy that lies
at the heart of the continuing popularity of the conspiracy industry.

Posner, who reached very different conclusions about the event than Lane, Marrs, or the aforementioned others, argued:

> Strong psychological reasons prompted the public's early embrace of conspiracy theories. The notion that a misguided sociopath had wreaked such havoc made the crime seem senseless and devoid of political significance. By concluding that JFK was killed as the result of an elaborate plot, there is the belief he died for a purpose, that a powerful group eliminated him for some critical issue.[62]

Because many people have remembered Kennedy as a great president, a truly monumental figure in American history, *only* an elaborate and sinister plot could have been responsible for his death. People would find it inconceivable, distasteful, and even unfair to the memory of JFK, to seriously entertain the idea that he was the victim of a senseless and stupid act of violence by a lone individual.[63] And so, we have given both his life and his death larger meaning, believing that there was more to his presidency—and therefore his death—than there may in fact have been. Similarly, anti-conspiracy researcher Vincent Bugliosi wrote, "In the unconscious desire of many to make a secular saint out of the fallen president, the notion of martyrdom was inevitable. But a martyr is not one who dies at the hands of a demented non-entity. Only powerful forces who viewed Kennedy's reign as antithetical to their goals would do."[64] Choosing to believe that a conspiracy existed may not be especially comforting for those who continue to mourn the loss of JFK. But at the very least, it enables them to believe that only a deeper plot could have eliminated a great leader.

Following Posner and Bugliosi's argument, John Kennedy becomes that much greater in the eyes of the public if his death is understood as the result of a much larger and carefully designed act of violence. If we accept the idea that JFK would have, for example, ended American involvement in Vietnam, or that he was in the process of resolving the growing civil rights struggle, the scope of what we lost when he died simply doesn't seem congruent with the idea that it was due to a lone gunman, unhappy with his life and motivated by nothing other than a desire to be remembered by history. How could the course of American history be so decisively altered, for the worse, by a violent act that seemed almost spur of the moment? The Kennedy assassination, in this case, would bear much greater similarity to those of Presidents James Garfield (1881) and William McKinley (1901). Both of those crimes were far more straightforward—Garfield having been shot in a Washington, D.C. railroad station by a disappointed office seeker, McKinley killed by an anarchist at a reception in Buffalo, New York.[65] Neither of these chief executives became as powerful in death as JFK has been; neither Garfield nor McKinley figure very prominently in the public's memory today. For a man who seemed to offer so much to the country to have died due to an equally pointless shooting, after what many historians regard as a relatively unaccomplished presidency when stripped of its rhetorical and public relations veneer, seems troubling. We prefer to remember John Kennedy as a great leader who might have led the nation down a different course from the one we took during the remainder of that decade. It seems as if a conspiracy not only makes more sense —*has* to make more sense in light of the contrast between the Kennedy and post-Kennedy eras—but is also itself part of the homage we pay to him. A great man could only have been stopped by powerful forces over consequential issues.[66]

President Kennedy's assassination occupies a unique place, as it relates to conspiracies, in American history. The United States has experienced the violent removal of its chief executive from office four times in nearly two and a half centuries, a rare occurrence. But the presence or possibility of a plot behind JFK's death resulted in a still rarer interplay with popular memory. The grandiloquent comparison between Kennedy and Abraham Lincoln notwithstanding, popular memory of Kennedy was influenced by the conspiracy mill to a considerably greater extent than for Lincoln. In Lincoln's case, a conspiracy to murder him and several other of the nation's highest leaders indisputably did exist, but the president was killed *after* the conclusion of the Civil War. By the time of Lincoln's death, the great objective of his presidency—the preservation of the Union—had been achieved. To be sure, his assassination ensured his place in American history as a martyr, but the existence of a plot was not really a critical element in the deification the nation has subsequently bestowed upon him. But such is not the case with JFK. His brief time in office and the unresolved national issues that grew worse in the years after his death enable conspiracy theorists to suggest that he was in the process of accomplishing major things. He was therefore assassinated as a direct result; what happened on November 22, 1963, was at least as much about prevention as it was about revenge. The conspiracy factor proved to be far more crucial for the construction of the public's memory of Kennedy than for Lincoln.

Matthew Smith, a British conspiracy theorist, suggests that the "Establishment" in the United States is guilty essentially of two conspiracies: the president's assassination and an ongoing effort to tarnish or erase outright the public's memory of him. Smith even attributes revelations of JFK's infamous womanizing as part of this posthumous smear campaign and posits further that anti-conspiracy authors are in effect complicit in the president's death and therefore unfaithful to the perpetuation of his memory. Addressing Gerald Posner's contention that Lee Harvey Oswald acted alone, Smith acidly wrote, "I find it hard to believe [Posner's book *Case Closed*] was not part of an overall strategy on the part of the Establishment to discredit the memory of John F. Kennedy."[67] The author was convinced that Kennedy was a great national and world leader who was regarded by the Establishment as too threatening to their interests and thus had to be removed "at all costs." In Oliver Stone-esque language, Smith charged that Kennedy had been "in favour of the improvement in quality of life for all Americans and those in other lands," and thus his death was "nothing less than a coup d'etat." A leader who seemed intent upon changing national and even world history could not possibly have been eliminated due to the work of one gunman acting strictly on his own: "The murder of President Kennedy," Smith argued, "was neither a local nor a national crime. It was a crime of universal proportions."[68]

And in view of the supposed ongoing cover-up of the truth, honoring the memory of the late president should not be done simply for its own sake. In Smith's narrative, Kennedy becomes linked with the very survival of representative government in America. While the public has not forgotten him, the need for answers to his death and the crucial task of keeping the government accountable to those whom it serves makes it, according to the author, the public's responsibility to ensure that their elected representatives do not forget him, either. In making JFK such an important figure, Smith likewise assigns an important role to those who refuse to remain satisfied with the disinformation surrounding his death and instead seek the truth. They—and by implication, the author himself—become the true guardians of the memory of the late president.[69]

Ostensible claims that a search for answers and the affection for the late president are the chief motivations for conspiracy theorists' work should be taken skeptically, at least as far as the more ridiculous theories are concerned. Like any national tragedy or event that has traumatic power, there will always be those who bear no scruples about exploiting it, although this is not to suggest that all students of the Kennedy assassination are only interested in making money. Nor does it mean that anti-conspiricists are somehow giving short-shrift to the memory of JFK because they argue that a conspiracy did not actually exist, as if the depth of one's respect for him is best demonstrated by the depth of the conspiracy one is willing to construct. The point is that conspiracy theories have become an important and enduring part of the way we think about Kennedy. Their value is found in what they say collectively as opposed to the value, or lack of it, that they deserve individually. More than simply engaging in a debate over who the perpetrators of the assassination were, conspiracy theorists, through their belief that Kennedy died due to his positions on Vietnam or civil rights or the Cold War, only magnify the sense that the world changed after his passing. According to them, the president was killed, for example, because of his intention to end the Vietnam War. Before his death, the war did not appear to be a major concern, and we supposedly were close to liquidating our involvement in it. After his death, the United States became more deeply involved, and tens of thousands of young Americans died as a result. Also consider civil rights: before his death, JFK had proposed major civil rights legislation and had committed himself to the cause. In the years immediately following the assassination, the country's racial problems only got worse. Or the Cold War: those such as Oliver Stone or Matthew Smith believe Kennedy had begun taking the first steps toward permanent peace with the Soviet Union. Then he died, and the Cold War continued for another three decades. The issues that theorists identify as central to understanding why the assassination happened are all issues they credit him with solving or intending to solve. The wayward path the United States took on each of these matters makes Kennedy's murder seem like a national point of departure, as if it marked the beginning and the end of two dramatically different worlds.[70] The conspiracy community accords him a degree of influence over these problems that is incredible, given the size and complexity of them. As with anybody else who might have been elected president, JFK in all likelihood would have found it a tall order to resolve even *one* of the major challenges of his time. Yet, theorists almost religiously believe that he represented the difference between national triumph and national turmoil. If some public figures are remembered for having a consequential impact upon history, and others for the virtue of their leadership, the central message from the conspiracy community is that John Kennedy should be remembered for both.

Photo 14. A sampling of the body of literature on the Kennedy assassination.

Photo courtesy of The Sixth Floor Museum at Dealey Plaza.

The various challenges and causes with which theorists often associate President Kennedy position him as one of the most consequential world leaders of the post-World War II era. To all or some of these objectives, he had supposedly dedicated himself, and for all or some of them, he was killed. In this sense, conspiracy theorists became some of JFK's most fervent admirers. But the contention that a massive and enduring conspiracy was behind his death seems to work only if one accepts that Kennedy truly was a great president, or at least that he was killed for some significant reason. If Kennedy was not the noble and visionary leader we like to think he was, why do we find conspiracies so compelling? If he was not in fact a martyr for anything—if he instead was a generally unexceptional president more interested in maintaining the status quo, why would any of the groups most commonly cited as the culprits in his death feel at all threatened enough to eliminate him? Popular memory of JFK and the circumstances of his death reinforce each other, as if the greater we believe he was, the greater in magnitude must have been the plot behind his assassination. If, in the end, the "murder of the century" did not entail multiple gunmen overthrowing a president intent on leading the nation to a better future, but instead amounted to nothing more than one assassin shooting Kennedy as he was en route to a fundraising luncheon as part of his bid for reelection, would we still place him in the ranks of Washington, Lincoln, and Franklin Roosevelt and remember his presidency as a time of greatness?

For the conspiracy community, the memory of JFK almost seems to require an enduring absence of closure, a sense that part of him is still concealed from public view and possibly always will be. How would the public's memory of him be affected if the truth were somehow suddenly to emerge, or if the truth turned out to be much simpler than many conspiracy adherents want us to believe? Would we still consider him to be so important to 20th century American history if, in reality, there really isn't much "there" there? Conspiracy theorists continually press upon their audience their certainty of John Kennedy's greatness and continuing relevance to our times, while simultaneously giving us their rendering of the truth. The public, having consumed hundreds of books—thousands of pages explaining what "really happened" on November 22, 1963—is, if anything, left even more convinced of how elusive the truth actually is. Especially considering the more outlandish theories, those who purvey them do a disservice to the late president and the public by disseminating falsehoods and only making it more difficult to separate what is true—or at least, what is plausible—from what is ridiculous and thereby reach closure. In the ongoing debate over his death that has only prolonged the feeling that resolution to the controversy is no longer possible, President Kennedy may remain forever partially in the shadows. Absence of closure becomes, if not the primary thing we remember about him, at least one of the major components of that memory. This, in turn, only compels us to write about and discuss him even more.

***

The Sixth Floor Museum in Dallas has already been discussed for the role it played in enabling the city to finally acknowledge the assassination in a forthright manner. Opening in 1989, it was widely understood as the memorial to President Kennedy—or more specifically, the direct engagement of the tragedy and linkage of the city with it—that had led some to oppose any memorial in the 1960s. But the museum should also be understood as a site of memory on its own terms. The Sixth Floor's importance goes far beyond its function as a sort of unofficial Dallas *mea culpa*. The political considerations and raw emotions that produced the official Dallas memorial, and which then promptly cast it into oblivion due to the structure's "enforced neutrality" had receded enough by the late 1980s so that the new museum became a symbol of remembering more than forgetting. In presenting the assassination as a historical event, the Sixth Floor's objective is also to focus on and shape the public's memory, as the title of its permanent exhibit—"John F. Kennedy and the Memory of a Nation"—suggests. Far more than simply offering an interpretation of what happened in that building and on the street below, the Sixth Floor examines how popular memory of Kennedy was created, what the public's memory of him is, and why memory of him remains so powerful.

"You will be inspired!" predicts a museum pamphlet, and even those who are familiar with the less-than-inspirational aspects of the Kennedy presidency can hardly avoid feeling some of the admiration for him that the Sixth Floor tries to convey.[71] Although the permanent exhibit does not offer a comprehensive look at John Kennedy's life, the first information that visitors encounter relates to his presidential campaign, the issues of the early 1960s, and the visit to Texas, thus establishing the assassination in a larger historical context. The exhibit panels are organized to guide visitors in a certain way around the floor. As the

Sixth Floor's designers intended, the exhibit is about more than JFK's death, and patrons do not get to the sniper's window until about midway through the tour. Interspersed throughout are film clips on the Kennedy presidency and news coverage of the assassination which gives visitors, especially younger visitors, an idea of the major role television played during that weekend in influencing how and what the American people remembered. Also included are artifacts such as a teletype machine (the medium that first relayed news of the events in Dallas to the world) and home movie cameras used by spectators to film the president's visit. The infamous "sniper's nest" at the corner window has been sealed off with glass panels and cartons placed to resemble the way that police discovered the scene. The spot where Lee Harvey Oswald's rifle was found and the stairway he used after the shooting at the northwest corner of the building has likewise been preserved. The exhibit discusses the findings of the Warren Commission and House Select Committee on Assassinations and summarizes the ongoing controversy over who was responsible for the assassination, although it does not go into detail about particular conspiracy theories (certainly not the more outrageous ones; this aspect would itself require an entire museum exhibit). But it is the exhibit sections "National & World Response," and "The Legacy," both of which are accompanied by ten-minute films, which leave the most lasting impressions about President Kennedy upon visitors. The film on the funeral conveys the global scope of the grief over the president's death. The film on his legacy, narrated by former CBS news anchor Walter Cronkite, reinforces the prevalent conception among the public of JFK as a great president.[72]

Photo 15. Main exhibit of the Sixth Floor Museum, opened in 1989.

Photo courtesy of The Sixth Floor Museum at Dealey Plaza.

Cronkite's role as the film's commentator is important. As the most prominent anchorman of his era, he is readily recognized and accorded substantial credibility by older viewers. Younger viewers, who have just seen Cronkite's news coverage from the day of the assassination in one of the film clips, would regard him as an authoritative figure on the tragedy and what it has meant for the United States, due to his unique role in reporting it. We associate John Kennedy, Cronkite says, with happier times. Visitors see a montage of the best and most familiar images and ideas associated with the late president: JFK with his young children, exciting an audience with his oratorical skills, challenging the nation to reach further and try harder. Civil rights, the Peace Corps, and his 1961 entreaty for an American commitment to land on the moon by the end of the decade—with Kennedy's purely idealistic rationale: "Space is there, and we're going to climb it"—all appear as some of the key issues of his administration. The way visitors think about him is enhanced not only by what he is credited with in the film, but also by the contrast that Cronkite makes with what happened to the country after 1963. "We would never be the same again," he tells us, and later, that "things fell apart" after JFK's death. That same sentiment appears in the reflections of people in Dealey Plaza paying tribute to him in the film. One says, "He affected my life so much," while another thought that the assassination signaled "the end of my childhood." One person commented that Kennedy "was about the best president we've ever had."[73] The film and the main exhibit as a whole reaffirm how many Americans remember the years after JFK's passing as the endpoint of a better time for the nation, after which it was never as unchallenged in its ability, or as confident of its right, to lead the world as it was during and prior to his presidency.

In the early 2000s, the Sixth Floor opened up additional space on the building's seventh floor, to be used for additional exhibits and museum events. In a way, the temporary exhibits featured on the seventh floor are just as powerful in the manner they portray the assassination as the permanent exhibit below. What several of them have in common is that they examine it from the vantage point of the many ordinary individuals who suddenly became participants in a national tragedy. One exhibit detailed the experiences of medical personnel and bystanders at Parkland Memorial Hospital when President Kennedy and Governor Connally arrived. Another exhibited digitized versions of eleven home movies of President Kennedy, several of them on his Dallas visit and unseen by the public up until then, and the stories of those who took them. An exhibit shown from 2004 through 2005 examined the trial of Jack Ruby from the perspectives of people who knew him. Still another captured the story of Dallas law enforcement personnel as, within a few days, they coped with the planning of a presidential visit, the assassination, the search for the suspect(s), and finally the shooting of Lee Harvey Oswald while in police custody.[74] These exhibits represent ground-level history. Visitors come to understand the ill-fated Kennedy visit not just as history on a national scale, or as words in a textbook, or through a documentary that makes the events seem linear and far away. The value of such exhibits is the importance they place on the experiences and memories of those who were *not* the primary participants in the assassination saga. Memory of JFK acquired such power in part because so many ordinary people played a role in that saga: some as actors, some as photographers and videographers, some as responders, and some simply as witnesses. It becomes easier to understand why the concept of Camelot was so alluring, or why Lyndon Johnson thought it important to link his predecessor with civil rights, or why Robert Kennedy could be considered presidential timber after such a brief political career, when a tragedy of national or even international proportions was experienced so personally. Whether from the perspective of millions across the nation whose principal connection with the assassination was through the television coverage, or that of someone like Dr. A. Jack Jernigan, who filmed JFK waving at him as the motorcade rolled out of the Dallas airport on its way downtown, museum visitors cannot fail to come away from the Sixth Floor with a deep sense of what this event meant on an individual level. It reinforces what they have learned on the sixth floor. The entire experience demonstrates for the visitor how popular memory was so important on a national level.[75]

When considering the role it plays in both reflecting and shaping popular memory, the Sixth Floor is an example of what historian Alison Landsberg has termed "prosthetic memory."[76] Many visitors have no firsthand recollections of the assassination and so the primary function of the museum—or any other historical exhibit for that matter—is to explain what happened, to whom, and what the consequences were. The Sixth Floor does more than that; although the main exhibit is not replete with the interactive activities that are more common in museums today, the film clips of the news coverage and funeral, and especially the fact that it is all housed in the same building, on the very floor, from which the shooting occurred, all impart visitors with a feeling of immediacy with the tragedy. Younger viewers understand what happened in the plaza below and form their own judgments and memories of what John Kennedy and his time in office must have been like, based on the images and opinions they are exposed to in the longer films on the world response to the assassination and Cronkite's discussion of JFK's legacy. As Landsberg observes, prosthetic memories are "those not strictly derived from a person's lived experience. Prosthetic memories circulate publicly, and although they are not organically based, they are nevertheless experienced with a person's body as a result of an engagement with a wide range of cultural technologies," and they thus become "part of one's personal archive of experience."[77]

But the overall interpretation of President Kennedy and the assassination that the Sixth Floor delivers to its audience is decidedly more positive than negative. It is done in an informative, engaging, and tasteful manner that avoids the sort of absurd conclusions about his death that are evident in much of the assassination literature. Visitors leave the Sixth Floor with a certain set of ideas about JFK: what he sounded like, what he stood for, and what the nation lost when he was killed. It becomes hard to understand why the late president never assumed his rightful place upon Mount Rushmore in view of the many audio and visual genuflections to him that are on display. The memory of President Kennedy that younger museum patrons construct will likely bear a great deal of similarity to the way the Sixth Floor has chosen to remember him, and the artificial or "prosthetic" memory they carry with them thus becomes part of the public memory. The increasing prevalence of this type of memory as the Kennedy assassination recedes into the past is not necessarily surprising or unique to this one event. The population is increasingly comprised of those born in the years after JFK's presidency. What later generations think about him will be based to a great extent upon venues such as the Sixth Floor, as opposed to firsthand memory. Landsberg cites the Holocaust Museum in Washington, D.C. as an example of "the experiential as a mode of knowledge."[78] In giving museum patrons a sense of what the Holocaust was like, not simply as a historical event but as a *lived experience,* both through the information and artifacts on display and even in how the exhibit is constructed, the museum is in effect transferring memory. And while the Sixth Floor is not quite as oriented toward an experiential manner of presenting the assassination—good taste, for example, precludes a replica of Oswald's rifle from being placed in the corner window so visitors can look in the telescopic sight and see what he saw—it is nonetheless engaged in recreating the experience of JFK's death for its patrons.[79] The creation of popular memory thus becomes an ongoing process, not limited only to those who were "there" at the time.

The act of transferring memory by a museum exhibit attempting to place the visitor within the event carries the same risks in what the public is told about President Kennedy that apply to how the others discussed in this chapter have interpreted his death. Because there is a particular way the Sixth Floor remembers JFK—with a definite set of memories being passed along—can this type of exhibit more accurately be understood as pushing an agenda on its audience as opposed to depicting a broad span of interpretations of him and letting the public's "prosthetic" memory take shape on its own? The use of an exhibit to convey information is no less susceptible to bias or oversimplification than other ways of discussing or remembering an event, such as a fictional screenplay that at least appeared to resemble the truth to many viewers. The Sixth Floor is no *JFK*, and as Landsberg suggests, what is true for filmmakers is no less valid for any setting in which history is recreated for the general public:

> In emphasizing the potential of prosthetic memory, I do not mean to dismiss the dangers of modern, mass-mediated forms of memory... We should look skeptically at the mass media's engagement with history because of the vast possibilities for historical revision and because the media tend to simplify and streamline complicated events.[80]

The charge, I think, is not that the Sixth Floor markets a blatantly biased interpretation or that visitors will inevitably buy into whatever is placed in front of them. On the contrary, the museum, while undoubtedly leaving visitors with a pro-JFK impression, remains at least a good starting point for people interested in him. Its presentation of the controversy over who was behind the assassination is certainly more responsible than what many in the conspiracy community have to offer. If visiting the museum compels some visitors to later explore on their own the massive corpus of literature—the positive, negative, and neutral—on Kennedy's life and presidency, then the Sixth Floor has fulfilled its purpose as an educational source. In that case, the museum is contributing to a revised prosthetic memory. And it is true that visitors, even those who are not Kennedy scholars, retain a good deal of agency as to what they will believe about him and therefore what they ultimately think is worth remembering. As previously discussed, the Philip Johnson memorial failed to satisfy the public's desire to remember the late president even before there was a museum they could turn to instead. With its message being so severely neutral, its only evocation being that of President Kennedy as a modern man in terms of its architectural style, the memorial did not offer the public much to remember, and thus was never actively part of the process of memorialization.

What is arguably more interesting and relevant about the Sixth Floor as far as the creation of "prosthetic memory" is concerned is what has *not* been remembered, or more broadly, what the museum seems to be indirectly telling its patrons about the way Dallas has acknowledged the assassination. What has been remembered about the Sixth Floor is exactly opposite that of the official Dallas memorial to JFK. In the case of the latter, the intended message was lost in the competing impulses of the city to somehow both remember and forget. We remember its overall ineffectiveness in memorializing Kennedy and that is about it. This lack of effect has not been the case with the Sixth Floor; the conditions underlying its creation and *not* its subject, have been thrust into the background. The museum becomes a place of remembrance unencumbered by the controversy—the "story behind the story"—that compromised the official memorial. Although the purpose of the Sixth Floor is not to explain the history of its own existence per se, the central flaw in the memory that patrons construct is that they will not remember the difficulty Dallas had in recognizing what happened in the street below on that November day. Whether they are native to Dallas or from elsewhere, visitors today may think it natural or inevitable that an assassination museum should exist. How, after all, could that not be done for one of the most traumatic events the nation experienced during the 20th century? However, as we have seen, it was hardly that way at all. The recognition by many people at the time the museum opened that Dallas was finally confronting the assassination in a meaningful way was indicative of the fact that the city had not done so up to that point. Could such an exhibit have been created in the 1960s or even 1970s? With the high possibility that it would have only aggravated the city's ongoing sensitivity about the assassination, probably not. Now, however, the public is able to focus on and remember President Kennedy, and not the quarter century and the overlooked memorial that it took to enable the process of transferring memory to occur.

Memorials and museum exhibits are themselves historical objects to be interpreted, and it is sometimes the case that how, or whether, they are created is as important as the messages they directly give us. The Sixth Floor is only one part of the ongoing effort to remember JFK, and its status as one of the city's foremost tourist destinations demonstrates how important the late president continues to be for people of all ages, and the influence such "experiential mass cultural forms"[81] of remembering have. While it remains true that such modes of remembering are susceptible to simplification and undue glorification, the "prosthetic" memory it helps instill in its younger patrons bears much similarity to the way in which older visitors have thought about the late president over the last five decades, as the museum's memory books amply attest. The museum is therefore a faithful reflection of what we have remembered and chosen to pass along. Still, what we choose to remember and forget about a historical event is never entirely resolved, as the competing stories of Dallas' John F. Kennedy memorial and the Sixth Floor Museum suggest.

***

The John F. Kennedy Presidential Library and Museum in Boston occupies the crossroads between the interpretation of Kennedy's legacy and the perpetuation of his memory. It is, unlike the Sixth Floor Museum, a major archival institution, containing presidential textual records, photographs, tape recordings, artifacts, and oral histories related to the Kennedy administration, and to the lives of several Kennedy family members. The archives serves as the foremost source for anybody seeking to write about the Kennedy presidency. Although JFK is not buried here, visitors come to Columbia Point to learn about and remember him; in a city with historic treasures on nearly every block, the library ranks as the fifth most-visited site in Boston, attracting roughly 200,000 visitors per year.[82] But like the Sixth Floor, the Kennedy Library followed a contentious, lengthy path in how it came to be—surprisingly so, given the Kennedys' deep ties with Boston, and the especially strong emotions the citizens there had for their fallen president. And like the efforts of Dallas to memorialize him, the story behind the Kennedy Library's creation is arguably just as interesting in the context of popular memory as the story of its content. President Kennedy began thinking of his post-White House years early in his administration. In September 1961, he informed Archivist of the United States Wayne C. Grover of his intent to construct a presidential library that would preserve his White House papers; the papers would be deeded to the National Archives when Kennedy left office. JFK was interested in establishing his library, plus a school of government, at his alma mater, Harvard. Public announcement came the following month, with the expected presidential center deemed "a major cultural asset" for the scholarly community.[83] Assuming he won reelection in 1964, he would serve until early 1969. At that time, just shy of his 52nd birthday, Kennedy wanted to return to Cambridge where he would write his memoirs and perhaps teach. In 1963, the president made two visits to Harvard, where he selected a potential library site on the south side of the Charles River, near Harvard Business School and Harvard Stadium; a memorandum of understanding was drafted in September providing for the eventual use of the area for the library project.[84]

Photo 16. Aerial view of the initial JFK-selected presidential library site near Harvard Business School, Harvard Stadium at center, with Harvard Yard on the opposite side of the Charles River, April 20, 1963.

Photo courtesy of the John F. Kennedy Presidential Library (Cecil Stoughton); ST-261-1-63.

The tragedy in Dallas left his family, particularly his widow and brother Robert, with the responsibility of bringing his library into being. Judging from the widespread sympathy and tributes to JFK aroused by his death, the rapid fulfillment of practically whatever library vision the Kennedys contemplated must have looked like a foregone conclusion; a May 1964 memorandum sent to library trustees from RFK set a goal of completing and opening the building in three years. Over 800,000 letters and cards deluged Mrs. Kennedy in the weeks and months following her husband's funeral, eventually growing to 1.5 million pieces of mail.[85] Yet, nearly two decades would pass, library location would change, and library design would be modified numerous times—largely due to public outcry over both—before the institution's groundbreaking occurred in the summer of 1977 and opening in the fall of 1979.

The site selected by President Kennedy in 1963, while picturesque, was later judged too small for the intended museum, archives, and school of government. Kennedy had apparently considered a second Harvard location on land then used by the Massachusetts Bay Transportation Authority (MBTA) for its transit operations. The growth of the Harvard campus made that adjacent MBTA site very desirable for the university, and the president, in recognition of the school's interest in eventually purchasing it, decided not to try appropriating it for his presidential complex. But with the MBTA location larger and thus better able to accommodate the library project, the Kennedy family felt that Harvard should offer it to them. University President Nathan Pusey recalled Robert Kennedy telling him, in a remark that did not seem too presumptuous in the wake of the post-assassination praise being offered to JFK, "I hope you won't be offended if I say that John Kennedy's name might hold more sway than John Harvard's."[86] Planning for library construction on the MBTA site appeared to move forward, as the Massachusetts state legislature approved $7 million to purchase the land; in January 1966, Governor John Volpe signed legislation setting aside the MBTA grounds for future library construction. Difficulties then arose over relocating the company's operations. During the mid-1960s, the family was hard at work raising money, selecting an architect, and safeguarding the late president's papers. A non-profit corporation was set up to direct the project, setting a fund raising goal of $6 million and completion of the library by 1970. Appealing for donations, the corporation raised $21 million from donors small and large, with the larger contributors including the Boston Red Sox, the AFL-CIO, and the Indian and French governments. An expected $1 million was to come from Latin American nations, with fellow universities especially interested; Venezuela pledged $100,000, and Mexico was expected to offer at least a matching amount. The receipt of smaller donations was also brisk, and the *New York Times* reported in early March 1964 that 18,727 unsolicited contributions had already been received.[87] A deed of gift ceding legal ownership of JFK's White House papers to the federal government was concluded on February 25, 1965 with the National Archives and Records Service (currently the National Archives and Records Administration). These materials were temporarily housed in nearby Waltham, Massachusetts until the library's completion. The first segment of record openings was announced in October 1969, and the following year, materials from the White House Central Files collection and library oral histories were opened for research.[88]

Jacqueline Kennedy selected architect I.M. Pei in December 1964 to design the library that, at the time, was widely expected to be built at Harvard; Professor Richard Neustadt was appointed Director of the library-affiliated institute of government. The late president's Harvard idea appeared, initially, to make sense, given his status as an alumnus, his family ties to Boston, and his perceived image as an intellectual. Moreover, his interest in cooperating with Harvard to found a school of government for training future public servants made a university location even more logical. Indeed, although Kennedy was following a precedent established by Franklin Roosevelt in building a presidential library, he was creating precedent of his own by partnering his institution with a university; several of JFK's successors have done likewise.[89] But as library development proceeded, opposition to the project began growing among local residents concerned with the wisdom of situating it at Harvard and Pei's early designs. Cambridge, already a very populated college town in one of the most urbanized areas of the country, would attract potentially hundreds of thousands or millions of tourists, students, and scholars annually to a Kennedy Library built at the university. Local unease over such numbers overwhelming the campus and turning the centuries-old neighborhoods into a tourist destination hindered progression of the library project well into the 1970s, before stopping it altogether. Subjected to much local derision was a 1975 environmental impact study that reached the spurious conclusion that an estimated one million library visitors each year would have only a minor impact on the area.[90] One member of a neighborhood task force likened the library to little more than a historical "Disneyland."[91] The affection of Boston's citizens toward JFK was never in question, but, as happened with William Manchester's book on the assassination and Robert Kennedy's Senate and presidential campaigns, the use or attempted monopolization of JFK's memory by his family had definite limits, even in his own hometown and even after relatively little time had elapsed since his assassination.[92]

Put another way, the power of his memory was still there, but it seemed to count for less; or at least it ceased being a perpetual justification for whatever the Kennedy family wanted. People may have accepted RFK's comment to President Pusey in late 1963 or 1964 as simply reflective of the exalted historical station in which the American people had decided to place John F. Kennedy. By the end of the decade and the early 1970s, the suggestion that memorializing Kennedy should be of paramount importance at and near Harvard aroused increasing resistance. One writer observed, "As long as JFK's blood remained vivid in the American memory, mountains could have been moved on its behalf...the library emerged from years of political dickering only to encounter a chilly reception from [Cambridge residents] whose dread of further development overshadowed their traditional loyalty to the Kennedys."[93]

Pei's early library designs, his undeniable skills as an architect notwithstanding, did not make things any easier in selling the project to Cambridge residents. Oddly enough, his library conception may have gone *too* far in exalting the late president; if anything, his vision for what an appropriate memorial to Kennedy should look like made Harvard's neighbors even *more* likely to fight it. Pei released his first designs in May 1973. Groundbreaking was expected to take place one year later. The presidential complex consisted of a concrete, largely unadorned building of five stories that would house the archives and educational institute; the entire project totaled 300,000 square feet. Pei hoped to achieve "maximum visual interest" with the memorial and museum. The archives and institute, at 55 feet tall, would curve around an 85-foot high steel and glass pyramid (containing the museum underground) that was cut off at the top to give it an unfinished look—evocative of the unfinished Kennedy presidency.[94] The pyramid idea, which Pei later used most notably in the courtyard of the Louvre in Paris, was criticized for both the incongruity with its surroundings, and for its excessive monumentality. A modernist glass pyramid rising to the equivalent of a seven to eight-story building clashed with the old red brick, columns, and spires characteristic of the university's architecture. The stark change to the area's skyline was also regarded as excessive in terms of memory, even for a president widely perceived as one of the nation's greatest; many thought the pyramid was more a demonstration of ego than a tasteful place of remembrance. Nor was the concept of memorializing JFK with an unfinished pyramid entirely well-received in terms of design. Some argued that the use of an incomplete pyramid to honor a fallen leader lacked originality, although, in fairness to Pei, the symbolism of growth or progress suddenly and forever interrupted did appear in other Kennedy memorials.[95]

Oddly enough, the architect committed the opposite mistake with his memorial as Philip Johnson did in Dallas: Pei's glass pyramid was denounced for going too far in his glorification of Kennedy (in the president's hometown), while Johnson's concrete "empty room" was criticized for going nowhere and meaning nothing. Erecting awe-inspiring shrines to American presidents had certainly been done before, although not in the context of presidential libraries. The Roosevelt, Truman, Eisenhower, and Hoover libraries were initially small, nondescript buildings, as compared with their more recent counterparts; and, while obviously intended to memorialize their respective creators, they were architecturally restrained in doing so. The Roosevelt and Hoover institutions actually resembled private homes. That began to change with the Kennedy and Johnson libraries, with the LBJ Library in Austin especially setting a new standard for monolithic library construction. Nobody who truly knew Lyndon Johnson believed that any part of it would be unassuming. In what would today be music to Johnson's ears, his library, in all its audacity and "institutionalization of presidential ego" has probably made more of a statement architecturally, and effectively competed with its eventual Boston counterpart in many ways.[96]

Kennedy's successor got away with it, but the Kennedy Library architect was compelled to rethink his building conceptions in favor of a more toned-down approach. It would be unfair to accuse Cambridge residents of no longer being interested in remembering the late president, but if his library was to be built at Harvard, practical and aesthetic considerations would have to be accorded at least as much importance as the need for adequate commemoration. One Harvard business professor complained, "We have not quarreled with the memorial—Kennedy was a great president. But for some reason it's gotten completely out of hand."[97] And it was, after all, the simple recognition of the love that many had for JFK—manifested by visitors making their civic pilgrimages to his library over the years—that made the surrounding neighborhoods wary at what memorialization would mean on a daily basis. In a way, it very closely resembled what many citizens of Dallas were thinking around the same time, although Boston did not have something to prove as Dallas did: it was more practical, if not more politic, that the power and appeal of John Kennedy be expressed moderately. One threatening example of what was potentially to come were plans for a 19-story hotel next to the library. That would have overshadowed both the campus and the Kennedy pyramid, and thus would have been an even more visible reminder of the worsened traffic and parking problems residents continued to complain about. At the time of the design's unveiling, library advocates claimed that the influx of visitors would only result in a six or seven percent increase in area traffic; this probably mollified about as many people as the much-criticized environmental impact study did a couple of years later in 1975. Developments such as the hotel led to fears that locals over time would be forced out due to demand for library-related venues, or that potential residents would be unable to afford housing due to increased land prices. The growing conviction that Harvard was simply unsuitable for the Kennedy center united both nearby higher-end areas such as the Brattle Street neighborhood and more working class city sections like Cambridgeport.[98]

Opposition to his library concepts compelled Pei to try again, and he released a modified proposal in June 1974, now over a decade since planning had begun. His second layout provided for a smaller, shorter complex; Pei replaced his glass and steel pyramid with a brick tower to blend in with the campus. But logistically, the revised library layout presented a new problem: lack of space. The museum and records repository would be in one building, and the school of government in another, but the library's smaller overall size meant that a substantial portion of JFK's papers would have to remain at the Waltham records center.[99] Library planners finally announced in February 1975 their abandonment of a Harvard location for the museum and archives; the school of government was still established at the university. The Boston City Council proposed an alternate site at the Charlestown Navy Yard, Rhode Island expressed interest in building the library in Newport, and there was also talk of the project moving to Hyannis Port in Massachusetts near the Kennedy family residence.[100] The demise of the Harvard vision led to 175 new proposals from others interested in hosting the presidential center—proof that, even after a dozen years and numerous false starts, interest in JFK and recognition of the importance his library had remained very strong.[101] Around that time, President Robert Wood of the University of Massachusetts, also a friend of the Kennedy family, offered a 9.5-acre plot of land located at Columbia Point on Dorchester Bay that was owned by the school. The site had drawbacks, namely that it was a garbage dump, but also that it did not have the type of connection to President Kennedy that Harvard did. Still, the setting would remind visitors of Kennedy's love of learning and of the sea. The Columbia Point location was approved, and groundbreaking was finally held on June 12, 1977. Construction took just under two and a half years, and the building was dedicated on October 20, 1979.[102] In highlighting the Kennedy Library's dual role of perpetuating legacy and memory, President Jimmy Carter declared, "We will never read the books that [JFK] would have written about his own Presidency...But in this building behind me, the work of reflection and evaluation of what he did can now be very well done by others...Through our study here of his words and his deeds, the service of President Kennedy will keep its high place in the hearts of many generations of Americans to come after us."[103] An estimated 7,000 people attended the ceremony, including former members of the Kennedy administration, as well as Jacqueline Kennedy Onassis, John F. Kennedy, Jr., Caroline Kennedy, Senator Edward Kennedy, First Lady Rosalynn Carter, and Lady Bird Johnson.[104]

I.M. Pei's final design retained the dramatically modernist look, with blank surfaces, sharp lines and shapes, which he had included in his earlier renderings, with some notable changes. Gone was the controversial glass pyramid, even when the surrounding neighborhood's architecture was no longer an impediment. Because that was intended to be the dominating visual feature of the presidential center at Harvard, Pei had kept the original building housing the archives and institute long and low. In contrast, the Kennedy Library at Columbia Point was much more vertical, even soaring. The structure's characteristics appear to change depending on where the viewer is standing. From directly in front of the entrance, the plain white walls seem to slice into the sky; moving slightly to the left, the same triangular shape resembles a ship's prow approaching the viewer. The central feature (at least, from inside) is the rectangular glass atrium that stretches nearly the entire height of the library, facing out onto Dorchester Bay to capitalize on the vistas of the water. The upper floors form a triangle that, from above, appears to cut into the atrium. On the other side of the library, towards the bay, the building's high, sharp, straight lines and points are complemented by a low circular end containing theaters and portions of the permanent exhibit on the floor below. Viewed from the rear, the atrium and massive, white, concrete and windowed side of the triangle give the building a blocky appearance.

Reviews of the building praised its striking, dramatic quality, and Pei had certainly achieved his objective of garnering "visual interest." Still, for some, it almost seemed as if the architect had tried to do too much—making the building so modern and different that the various parts of it did not always work well together, and did not have the same breakthrough, startling quality that the Johnson Library had. One appraisal of the library observed, "Indeed, as a monument, the Kennedy Library makes all the right moves: soaring, gleaming, thrusting. But there is clearly something lacking. The exterior geometry is too obvious...the interior organization is too complex, leading visitors through a programmatically logical, but ultimately confusing and uninspiring maze."[105] Writing in the New York Times, architectural critic Paul Goldberger applauded Pei's creation as being highly fitting for the president it memorialized; it was "a sweeping structure [that] symbolizes years of promise," with "a quality of exhilaration to it, of confidence that strong, bold gestures will bring a better day." Goldberger thought, however, that the building's interior ultimately worked better than its exterior, as the different geometric shapes Pei employed did not fit well in the same structure. Moreover, he thought the view of the library from the waterfront was the best, but most people did not approach it that way, with the result that its front entrance felt more like a back door.[106]

There have been two main exhibits in the 35 years the Library has been open. The original exhibit, designed by Chermayeff and Geismer Associates, was in use from the building dedication until 1993. As opposed to its successor, the 1979 exhibit was a bit broader in scope and more arranged by functions of the presidency, devoting attention to the mass arrival of Irish immigrants—including President Kennedy's ancestors—to the United States in the 1840s, Robert Kennedy's 1968 presidential campaign, and the various tasks of the president. Visitors, for example, saw what the president did on a daily basis.[107] In its early years, the Library averaged nearly 300,000 visitors per year, with 1980 boasting its highest turnout of the decade at 563,571 people.[108]

Most visitors to the Kennedy Library come, not to peruse memoranda sent to the president on the 1962 steel dispute, or JFK's handwritten notes on civil rights (as enticing as such materials are), but to tour the permanent exhibit covering the 1960 campaign through his death and legacy. The current exhibit, designed by Jeff Kennedy and Associates, opened in 1993, and adopted a more experiential approach. The original exhibit of course focused on President Kennedy, but the new one was more organized around particular events and challenges of the administration—trying to place the patron at the center of major events in JFK's career.[109] News footage, campaign trinkets, and a recreation of the studio set for the Kennedy-Nixon debates greet the visitor. Reflective of the importance the media played in JFK's political career, there is a lot of television and film footage. Walter Cronkite of CBS, along with Chet Huntley and David Brinkley on NBC, announce returns from the election, Kennedy's inaugural address is screened in color, and visitors can stop by the exhibit's "briefing room" to watch film clips from the president's press conferences. The melding of glamour and presidential power that the First Couple achieved so effortlessly is seen in the recreated Cross Hall of the White House, complete with artifacts, photographs, and rooms on either side detailing various aspects of the Kennedy administration. The museum patron almost feels as if he or she is at one of the famous White House state dinners, with President or Mrs. Kennedy around the next corner. Space, the Peace Corps, the Cuban Missile Crisis, and the First Lady's accomplishments (including the Emmy she won for her televised 1962 White House tour) are all accorded attention in the exhibit. Like other presidential libraries, the Kennedy museum features a recreation of the Oval Office, with footage of JFK's famous June 1963 civil rights address, and his rocking chair on display. Arguably the sharpest moment of the visitor's experience comes when one leaves the museum displays on the Kennedy family (discussed below), and enters a small passageway bearing the date, "November 22, 1963." The contrast with the bright, open exhibits left behind is sudden, even unsettling; there is very little light, a low ceiling, and the walls are painted black, giving the visitor a feeling of loss and discomfort in such a confined space. On one side are small television screens showing news broadcasts from the assassination weekend—a small but important reminder of the role television played at the end of the Kennedy administration, as it did at so many points before and during it.[110]

There is no explanation of the assassination: why Kennedy went to Texas, photographs of the Dallas motorcade, eyewitness accounts, artifacts, or discussion of the ongoing debate over whether a conspiracy was behind the tragedy. The exhibit was not designed to overwhelm patrons with the assassination, and it does not;[111] in terms of how the museum shapes popular memory, prolonged engagement with the details of his death would be superfluous. The entire permanent exhibit, up until the dark corridor marking the end of President Kennedy's life, brings the aura of "Camelot" that Mrs. Kennedy and other JFK advocates conveyed to the public through articles and heroic biographies, into a solid, tangible form. Facts or speculation about the assassination do not matter after everything else the visitor has just seen, and the sparseness of the exhibit's assassination area in comparison with the other museum sections leaves patrons with the idealized, "Camelot" interpretation of the Kennedy presidency. Arguably the most profound impression they take with them is this before/after comparison as a conception of the Kennedy era: great issues, elegance and grace, stirring leadership—then suddenly nothing, everything gone. The exhibit's design—the subject matter, the nature and depth of the information given, and the feeling imparted to the visitor—mimics how many Americans remembered Kennedy after his death. It is, of course, a very valorous presentation on JFK and the early 1960s, and the shift in exhibit tone and content from the White House section to the assassination corridor appears to validate Walter Cronkite's lament in the Sixth Floor film that "things fell apart" after 1963 and that "we would never be the same again." Yet, like the Dallas exhibit, it is an accurate reflection of the popular memory of Kennedy for many who are old enough to remember his presidency. Given its goal of recreating the time period and enabling people to re-experience those years, the exhibit is also a prominent example of the formation of "prosthetic memory" in younger patrons. Paul Goldberger's observations on the statement the building makes architecturally are no less suitable in describing the *exhibit's* effect upon its audience, both in 1979 and today: "It is not the arrogance of this building that is striking, but the earnestness of it; how well it replicates the faith of a particular moment in history, and convinces us that it was real."[112]

No doubt the Kennedy Library succeeds in making the late president matter, but it is worth pointing out how the same site of memory produces a contradictory message. What visitors see in the exhibit differs from some of the conclusions scholars have formed on JFK thanks to the presidential records they see in the research room. To be sure, the main exhibit is not an unqualified celebration of everything he did. Historical nuance does, in some places, temper an otherwise very pro-Kennedy presentation. For example, the president's handling of civil rights is most prominently on display in the recreated Oval Office, where patrons see color footage of JFK's June 1963 civil rights address. A museum souvenir guidebook alludes to Kennedy's initial reluctance to take decisive action on civil rights by saying, "Kennedy stood in favor of integration, but at first his support of the civil rights movement was indirect, as he tried to hold onto the support of southern Democratic leaders who had helped elect him. Then events forced his hand."[113] This, at least, enters the realm of how historians judge JFK on civil rights. Thomas Reeves wrote that with both President Kennedy and his brother Robert, political pragmatism and an overall absence of concern with the problem of discrimination resulted in superficial civil rights initiatives through most of the administration. The president was upset by the Freedom Rides of 1961, not so much because of the brutality the riders faced, but because of the poor publicity they garnered as he prepared to meet with Soviet Premier Khrushchev. Even in instances where Kennedy spoke publicly on civil rights prior to June 1963, there was little acknowledgment of the issue's moral dimension. Having delayed his promised executive order prohibiting racial discrimination in public housing until late 1962, JFK finally signed a limited measure that would attract as little public attention as possible. One civil rights leader complained not long thereafter, in reference to the dearth of White House support, "We've gotten the best snow job in history," while another said, "We've got to quit begging the Kennedys for this and that. We've got to start demanding our rights."[114]

Yet, what is most obviously on display in the exhibit is the *high point* of the administration's engagement with civil rights. The use of the Oval Office, a symbol of presidential leadership and power, in conjunction with civil rights suggests that Kennedy's speech was representative of how he handled the issue throughout his presidency. It was without doubt a powerful address that put him on the record in support of civil rights legislation, but, keeping in mind the history of the previous two years that the exhibit guidebook references, it is more accurate to see the speech as a considerable change from JFK's earlier hesitancy to act; it was not demonstrative of his entire approach. Kennedy remains linked in the public's memory with civil rights, and while it is not an entirely unjustified linkage, the nature and strength of his commitment to the cause were not always as front and center as the Oval Office presentation implies. This is true for other major points of his presidency. Museum visitors run the same risk here as any of us do in drawing larger conclusions from, for example, JFK's American University address, delivered only the day before his civil rights declaration—the danger of seeing one speech as accurately summarizing the scope of Kennedy's actions and intent.

Early conceptions on the Cuban Missile Crisis held that it was a clear American victory: the Soviet Union removed its missiles in the face of American military might and President Kennedy's "grace under pressure." The main exhibit makes some effort at correcting this, with the guidebook noting that the administration had agreed to withdraw American missiles in Turkey, a not inconsiderable part of the deal that was kept secret in 1962. The Library website has interactive exhibits that, together with the main exhibit, do a nice job in not only explaining what happened, but giving viewers a taste of the documentary basis upon which the histories of the Crisis are built. Encouraging public examination of primary sources is highly commendable. Patrons can listen to JFK's private thoughts, recorded on Dictabelt, on how the United States should respond to the Soviet threat; they can also look at maps, declassified memoranda, meeting minutes, and even listen to a recording of a phone conversation between Kennedy and British Prime Minister Harold Macmillan.[115] It is a far more effective way to present the Crisis than distilling the primary sources into a few exhibit panels or website pages containing only secondary narrative and a few photographs. But, as with civil rights, there is something missing. While Operation Mongoose is mentioned, there is not an in-depth examination of administration-instigated efforts (possibly including assassination) to oust the Castro regime that contributed to the U.S.-Soviet encounter. Like the Library rendering of civil rights, we see the Crisis as one of JFK's greatest moments, but there is comparatively little on the more questionable actions preceding those moments that have, by now, been extensively researched by the historical community.[116] For example, Robert Smith Thompson noted that concern over a seemingly inevitable American invasion of Cuba and removal of Castro was one of several factors that ultimately compelled Khrushchev to try inserting nuclear warheads onto the island undetected. Owing to the provocative American actions that partly caused the confrontation, and the nuclear war we nearly came to, Thompson dismissed the idea that it was the "finest hour" of Kennedy legend. "The Cuban Missile Crisis hardly culminated in a grand victory; as a triumph for Kennedy it was, at best, ambiguous. And at worst? The Cuban Missile Crisis was the direct result, as the Soviets have reminded us repeatedly, of the American desire to overrun Cuba."[117] Exhibit treatment of other Kennedy topics that disrupt the "Camelot" aura, such as the concealment from the public of the president's numerous health problems (and his risky drug regimen used to cope with them), and his numerous extramarital affairs that may have compromised his ability to discharge his responsibilities honorably and effectively, is all slight to nonexistent. These are important issues that have provoked debate among Kennedy biographers; for instance, the medications used to remedy his back problems and Addison's disease, and whether the use of them resulted in continued ailments. That in turn leads to the very relevant question, as far as the public would be concerned, of whether such personal problems affected his performance as president.[118]

The question we confront is the same as with the sites of memory previously examined: are the conceptions of JFK that his presidential library promotes simply wrong? The messages conveyed to the public are problematic in some respects, but nonetheless illustrative of what the public's memory of JFK continues to be fifty years after his death. The ideas we see in the exhibit sometimes are at variance with the documentary record on his presidency that is located, of all places, only a few floors above. Contained within one building is the ongoing disconnect between how his presidency is graded by scholars and how it is remembered—or, in this case, how an institution is influencing memory for the vast majority of the people who visit. To some extent, this is to be expected at a presidential library. They are typically built and endowed, and the museum exhibits created, by the former president's family and supporters, and often by the former president himself.[119] This is not to say that the information presented to visitors is necessarily untruthful, but it will obviously be an interpretation that is friendly to that particular president. In that sense, a presidential library is like the former president's memoirs recreated in third-dimension—it contains both the strengths and potential drawbacks of his perspectives on his White House years. And it is worth pointing out that museum exhibits, like the literature on that administration, are never irrevocably defined. They change over time to reflect the way we think about a particular person or event, as well as the techniques used to present that information most effectively (i.e. the greater use of audiovisual and interactive components).[120] The early perspectives on a presidency can often be either highly laudatory or critical, and it is not until years or decades have elapsed before passions are tempered, archival sources become available, and the consequences of that administration's decisions are better understood—and a more clear-

minded accounting of the good and the bad can emerge. The Kennedy
Library is no exception to this. The Kennedy family remains very much
involved in how the Library presents JFK to the public; the Kennedy
Foundation has played a major role in funding and designing both the
original main exhibit and the current one that has been in use since the
early 1990s. Caroline Kennedy served as president of the Foundation until
she assumed an ambassadorial post under the Obama administration,
and her husband remains associated with it today.[121]

But the largely favorable way the Library remembers the late president is plausible, if not entirely in an historical sense, then from a
popular memory standpoint, despite national and institution-related
developments. The country does not hold the trust in its governmental
institutions that it did in the early 1960s, the Kennedy assassination is
increasingly an historical event rather than a painful lived experience, and
the feared tidal wave of visitors to the Library is instead a steady stream.
What Columbia Point has to say about the president it honors is powerful
in terms of popular memory because of the sad, and unique, pairing of
glamour and idealism with tragedy—the potent contrast patrons see as
they enter the "November 22, 1963" passageway and then arrive at the end
of the exhibit. Any commemorative structure tries to convince the viewer
that the person, place, or era being remembered was great, or worthy
of veneration or attention in some way. The other twelve presidential
libraries will each argue to varying degrees that their president did great
things, meant well, and the nation is better because of their stewardship.
The Kennedy Library is no different in this respect, but there is an ongoing
sense of loss, spoken and unspoken, that simply is not present at other
libraries and therefore does not shape how visitors judge what they see
in those institutions. Franklin Roosevelt is the only other president with
a National Archives-administered presidential library who died in office,
but he had already accomplished much by the time of his death. One
could argue that he largely achieved what he intended to, and with other
presidents since that time, we can say that they had their chance and left
the White House in the wake of the success or failure (or the mixture of

the two) of their executive decisions. This cannot be said for President Kennedy. Had he served two terms, his library would still portray his administration very positively, but the point is that the public generally accepts as valid what they see in the exhibits, as evidenced by polling on presidential ranking, and the fact that so many leave feeling inspired by their experience.[122] The nature of the Kennedy era and the tragedy that ended it still exert a lot of influence on how we remember him. And because what the exhibits show us is powerful, popular memory of JFK endures and continues to make him matter. Because we can never know how his presidency would have turned out, and because it seems that the nation has never really regained the confidence, optimism, and perhaps even arrogance that marked those years, I think those who come to the Library, young or old, are more willing to regard the exhibit messages as true to form, and as equally worthy of remembrance as the well-founded "yes, but" critiques of historians. We give JFK more benefit of the doubt in how we remember him, and this influences how we judge what the Kennedy Library tells us.

Like the Sixth Floor, the Kennedy Library preserves and transfers memory of the late president. In its educational role, it is hardly unique; it is one of thirteen such institutions across the country administered by the National Archives tasked with explaining the lives and eras of their respective presidents. But there is something else that the library does that complements its narrative on the president: it memorializes not only JFK, but the entire Kennedy family. It celebrates the idea of public service, in an apolitical sense, as practiced in a variety of ways. Looking at the library experience in its totality—its textual holdings, the scope of the exhibit, and the building addition that will house the late Senator Edward Kennedy's papers—the Kennedy presidential center can more accurately be described as a celebration not only of what one president has done, but of what an entire family has done. Just steps away from the Oval Office replica in the exhibit is the reconstructed office of Attorney General Robert Kennedy. This part of the exhibit explores RFK's work in combating organized crime and advocating for civil rights. Farther along are three areas dedicated to the Kennedys. Photographs and artifacts remind the visitor of the political offices held by family members going back to the early 20th century when John Francis Fitzgerald served as mayor of Boston; the wartime service of JFK's older brother, Joseph, and younger sister, Kathleen; and the family's Irish heritage, a connection with the Kennedys felt by many in Massachusetts and around the country. One area spotlights mental retardation and the role of JFK's sister, Eunice, in fostering greater public awareness and policy changes on behalf of Americans with special needs. Visitors see additional information on Robert and Edward Kennedy in the "Legacy" exhibit area that follows "November 22, 1963," a reminder that many saw the brothers' political careers as building upon that of JFK. In addition to President Kennedy's papers, the library also contains Joseph Kennedy, Sr.'s materials from his work in various government capacities; Robert Kennedy's Department of Justice and Senate papers; and Rose Kennedy's correspondence and speech files from decades of her own political activities.

Senator Edward Kennedy's nearly fifty-year political career, which ended with his death in 2009, has been the most recent reminder of the impact the Kennedy family has had on American politics. The anticipated 2015 opening of the Edward M. Kennedy Institute for the United States Senate at the JFK Library will only enhance the connection many Americans make between the Kennedys and public service. The Institute, which will contain storage space for the late senator's papers, replicas of the Senate and Edward Kennedy's office there, and public programming areas devoted to the history and role of that lawmaking body, complements the Library in more than one way.[123] It garnered its own share of controversy, as a considerable portion of its funding came from the federal government. While it is not a presidential library per se, it is probably the closest thing to a library that a non-president can be honored with, and the libraries administered by the National Archives have been built and endowed primarily with private contributions. Had the Kennedy name not been associated with the project, it is unlikely that federal funding would have been approved—proof again of how strong the Kennedy name continues to be, over one hundred years after John and Edward Kennedy's grandfather entered politics on the other side of Dorchester Bay.[124] And additionally, the Institute completes the Library's overall message. The permanent JFK exhibit tells patrons about the tragic, yet heroic, *brevity* of his presidency in the midst of what the Kennedy family had done up until that time. In paying tribute to a man who served in the Senate during ten presidencies, the Institute will remind visitors of the *longevity* of their influence upon American government during the twentieth and twenty-first centuries.

NOTES

1. Sally Bedell Smith, *Grace and Power: The Private World of the Kennedy White House* (New York: Random House, 2004), 458.
2. Paul F. Boller, Jr., *Presidential Wives: An Anecdotal History* (New York: Oxford University Press, 1998), 370-371.
3. Betty Boyd Caroli, *First Ladies: From Martha Washington to Michelle Obama* (New York: Oxford University Press, 2010), 273.
4. Sally Bedell Smith, *Grace and Power*, 445-446, 448, 452; and Arthur M. Schlesinger, Jr., *Robert F. Kennedy*, 611.
5. Elsie Carper, "Body to Lie in State on Lincoln Catafalque," *Washington Post,* November 24, 1963, A4; and John Maffre, "Cortege to Carry Body to Rotunda at 1 P.M.," *Washington Post,* November 24, 2963, A1, A4; and Julius Duscha, "Mighty World Rulers Pay Tribute," *Washington Post,* November 26, 1963, A1.
6. Barbara A. Perry, *Jacqueline Kennedy: First Lady of the New Frontier* (Lawrence: University Press of Kansas, 2005), 181-186; and Robert Dallek, *An Unfinished Life*, 696.
7. Lady Bird Johnson, *A White House Diary* (Austin: University of Texas Press, 2007), 9.
8. Alfred Friendly, "Hushed Throng Files Past Catafalque in Rotunda After Capitol Services," *Washington Post,* November 25, 1963, A1.
9. "'Lady Courage' Praised," *Washington Post,* November 26, 1963, D2.
10. Conover Hunt, *JFK For a New Generation*, 35.
11. James Patterson, *Grand Expectations: The United States, 1945-1974* (New York: Oxford University Press, 1996), 522-523.
12. Theodore H. White, "For President Kennedy: An Epilogue," *Life,* December 6, 1963 (Vol. 55, No. 23), 158-159.
13. Ibid.
14. Robert Dallek, *An Unfinished Life*, 697.
15. James Patterson, *Grand Expectations*, 523.
16. Gerald S. and Deborah H. Strober, *"Let Us Begin Anew:" An Oral History of the Kennedy Presidency* (New York: HarperCollins Publishers, 1993), 465-466.
17. Ibid., 467-471.
18. Ibid., 466.

19. Evan Thomas, "Grace and Iron," *Newsweek,* May 30, 1994 (Vol. CXXIII, No. 22), 36.

20. Manchester had been hired by the Kennedy family to write a history of the assassination; in return, they would have final right of approval over what he wrote. Prior to publication and appearance in abridged form in *Look* magazine in 1967, Mrs. Kennedy thought the manuscript contained too much personal information about her, as well as excessive narrative on the hostile relations between RFK and LBJ. Manchester refused to make all of the revisions Mrs. Kennedy demanded. She thereupon sued Manchester and the publisher, and the lawsuit was eventually settled out of court. Her previously high standing in public opinion polls took a considerable hit, since many thought the late president's family was trying to exert ironclad control over how JFK was written about, as if they had a sort of "copyright" on the assassination. Barbara Perry, *Jacqueline Kennedy*, 194-195; and Jeff Shesol, *Mutual Contempt*, 354, 362.

21. Godfrey Hodgson, *America in Our Time*, 5-12.

22. W.J. Rorabaugh, *Kennedy and the Promise of the Sixties*, xviii-xxi.

23. *JFK*, Oliver Stone, Barbara Kopple, and Danny Schechter, DVD-Video, Special Edition Director's Cut, Warner Home Video, 2003 (original edition 1991).

24. Ibid.

25. Ibid.

26. Ibid.

27. John Hellman, *The Kennedy Obsession: The American Myth of JFK* (New York: Columbia University Press, 1997), 160-161.

28. Rita Kempley, "*JFK*: History Through a Prism," *Washington Post,* December 20, 1991, D1.

29. "Twisted History," *Newsweek,* December 23, 1991 (Vol. CXVII, No. 26), 46-47; and John Hellman, *The Kennedy Obsession*, 160-161; and Conover Hunt, *JFK for a New Generation*, 110.

30. Such was the opinion of journalists such as Tom Wicker. Writing in the *New York Times* shortly before the film's release, Wicker worriedly commented, "Among the many Americans likely to see it...particularly those too young to remember November 22, 1963, *JFK* is all too likely to be taken as the final, unquestioned explanation." Tom Wicker, "Does *JFK* Conspire Against Reason?" *New York Times,* December 15, 1991, H-18.

31. Barbie Zelizer, *Covering the Body: The Kennedy Assassination, the Media, and the Shaping of Collective Memory* (Chicago: The University of Chicago Press, 1992), 201.

32. Ibid., 203.

33. Tom Wicker, "Does *JFK* Conspire Against Reason?" H-18.

34. C-SPAN, Oliver Stone Testimony before the House Government Operations Subcommittee, January 1992, available from http://www.youtube.com/watch?v=mq7hDywWOZI ; accessed from Internet January 19, 2013.

35. C-SPAN, Oliver Stone Remarks at the National Press Club, January 15, 1992, available from http://www.youtube.com/watch?v=Pjy6dUlF3Lk ; accessed from Internet January 20, 2013.

36. Conover Hunt, *JFK for a New Generation*, 111.

37. George Lardner, "The Way It Wasn't: In *JFK*, Stone Assassinates the Truth," *Washington Post*, December 20, 1991, D2.

38. Frank Beaver, *Oliver Stone: Wakeup America* (New York: Twayne Publishers, 1994), 178.

39. For example, Lardner condemned the movie for containing "countless buckets of manure, large measures of legitimate doubt, drippings of innuendo and pages of actual history." Movie critic Roger Ebert, however, assessing *JFK*'s value as an artistic creation, commented that it was "hypnotically watchable." It was, in his words, "a masterpiece of film assembly." Norman Kagan, *The Cinema of Oliver Stone* (New York: Continuum, 2000), 202; and Robert B. Toplin (ed.), *Oliver Stone's USA: Film, History, and Controversy* (Lawrence: University Press of Kansas, 2000), 169-170.

40. Conover Hunt, *JFK for a New Generation*, 111; and Robert Dallek, *An Unfinished Life*, 698.

41. Frank Beaver, *Oliver Stone*, 178.

42. David Ansen, "A Troublemaker for Our Times," *Newsweek*, December 23, 1991 (Vol. CXVIII, No. 26), 50.

43. Marcus Raskin, "*AHR Forum*: *JFK* and the Culture of Violence," *American Historical Review*, April 1992 (Vol. 97, No. 2), 487-490. I suspect that movie critic Roger Ebert would concur with Raskin. Ebert agreed with critics of *JFK* that it would influence the public's memory, but he did not think that the film would necessarily leave viewers with a flawed set of memories. As Ebert observed, "People go to the movies to be told a story. In the case of *JFK*, which I think is a terrific example of storytelling, what they will remember is not the countless facts and conjectures that the movie's hero spins in his lonely campaign to solve the assassination. What they will remember (or if they are young enough, they will learn) is how we all felt on November 22, 1963, and why for all the years afterward a lie

seemed to lodge in the national throat—the lie that we know the truth about who murdered Kennedy..." Norman Kagan, *The Cinema of Oliver Stone*, 202.

44. Robert A. Rosenstone, "*AHR Forum: JFK:* Historical Fact/Historical Film,' *American Historical Review* April 1992 (Vol. 97, No. 2), 506-508.

45. Ibid., 509-510.

46. *JFK*, Oliver Stone, Barbara Kopple, and Danny Schechter, 2003.

47. Stone obviously did not intend the ideas he presented in *JFK* to be regarded simply as historical fiction with no importance beyond the film. He remained committed to the belief not only that the late president was determined to withdraw from Vietnam, but that his assassination resulted from those intentions as well as his overarching foreign policy goals. In his House testimony, Stone posed the question of why Kennedy was killed and answered, "Since it has been established from other evidence that [JFK] was indeed embarked upon a course to change our foreign policy with respect to the Soviet Union, Cuba, and the nations of Southeast Asia, including a decision on paper to withdraw our advisers and send no combat troops into the military and moral quagmire of Vietnam, was this the reason?" C-SPAN, Oliver Stone Testimony before the House Government Operations Subcommittee.

48. Howard Jones, *Death of a Generation*, 1.

49. *JFK*, Oliver Stone, Barbara Kopple, and Danny Schechter, 2003.

50. Conover Hunt, *JFK For a New Generation*, 110.

51. Vincent Bugliosi devoted nearly 100 pages of his massive tome on the Kennedy assassination (arguing that Lee Harvey Oswald and Jack Ruby acted alone in their respective crimes) to what he terms the "wild fairy tales" of *JFK*. A lengthier critique of the film's errors and omissions is beyond the scope of my work; in the interests of not simply repeating everything Bugliosi says, I include these examples and direct the reader to his book for further detail. Throughout the film, District Attorney Garrison is presented as a hero, courageously attempting to bring those behind the Kennedy assassination to justice, and failing in the end to win convictions. The actual Jim Garrison was regarded by others within the New Orleans legal community as a loose cannon who habitually made irresponsible and unsustainable accusations against others. Indeed, Bugliosi notes that it has yet to be proven that Garrison had *any* credible evidence on the day he proclaimed to the press that his office had "solved the case." Those whom Garrison attempted to convict for the President's death were acquitted, not because of any per-

version of justice, but because his accusations were baseless. Bugliosi observes that Lee Harvey Oswald, despite a formidable amount of evidence connecting him to the crime, is not even a marginal figure in the film. Almost none of that evidence is discussed in *JFK*, leaving viewers with the impression—through omission—that Oswald indeed was a patsy and had no substantive part in the assassination. And on one of Stone's central charges, that President Kennedy's murder was largely caused by his supposed determination to withdraw American military advisers from Vietnam, the nature of American policy just before and right after the assassination is not presented truthfully at all. Stone's "Mr. X" scene gives viewers the mistaken idea that the National Security directive signed by President Johnson only days into his presidency was a reversal of prior Kennedy administration policy. In fact, that document, which effectively rescinded a prior Kennedy directive providing for an initial withdrawal of advisers, had been drafted while JFK was still president. LBJ, by signing what became known as NSAM (National Security Action Memorandum) 273, was not negating his predecessor's wishes, but approving them. And among the many smaller details and mysterious occurrences supposedly swirling around November 22, 1963, "Mr. X" claims the entire telephone network in Washington, D.C. went out only minutes after the shooting to hinder the exchange of information on the conspirators. This did not happen; Bugliosi writes that the phone system experienced intermittent outages due to the overwhelming volume of calls being made to Washington and Dallas, a natural occurrence after an event like the shooting of the President. Phone service around the capital city was not deliberately cut to induce confusion. Vincent Bugliosi, *Reclaiming History: The Assassination of President John F. Kennedy* (New York: W.W. Norton & Company, 2007), 1356, 1365, 1377, 1385, 1410-1411, 1428-1429.

52. Peter Knight, *The Kennedy Assassination* (Jackson: University Press of Mississippi, 2007), 79, 88-90-93.

53. That is to say, Lincoln's death was the result of a conspiracy, but it was instigated entirely by John Wilkes Booth. While his earlier plans to abduct Lincoln and transport him across enemy lines may have been revealed to a few Southern agents, so far as we know, Booth was never acting under the orders of any Confederate government official. The assassination plot never involved more than Booth and his associates. David Herbert Donald, *Lincoln* (New York: Simon & Schuster, 1995), 586-588, 596-597.

54. Other possible culprits behind Kennedy's death have included the KGB, drug smugglers, Enron, international bankers, the Corsican Mafia, and three men mistakenly thought to have been part of the assassination who were arrested in Dealey Plaza on November 22 (known as the "three hobos"). Still other people and organizations identified as the conspirators include the Illuminati, the Ku Klux Klan, the Mossad, South Vietnam, George H.W. Bush, Dallas Mayor Earle Cabell, Warren Commission member Arlen Specter, and assassination witness Abraham Zapruder. Michael L. Kurtz, *The JFK Assassination Debates*, 84; and Peter Knight, *The Kennedy Assassination*, 92-93; and Vincent Bugliosi, *Reclaiming History*, 1489-1495.

55. Peter Dale Scott, *Deep Politics and the Death of JFK* (Berkeley: University of California Press, 1993), 6-11.

56. Jim Marrs, *Crossfire: The Plot that Killed Kennedy* (New York: Carroll & Graf Publishers, Inc., 1989), Preface, Conclusions.

57. Harrison Edward Livingstone and Robert J. Groden, *High Treason: The Assassination of JFK and the Case for Conspiracy* (New York: Carroll & Graf Publishers, Inc., 1998), Dedication Page, x.

58. Ibid., 386.

59. Or, as Vincent Bugliosi described the conspiracy community in his quite lengthy assassination work that made a very convincing case that Lee Harvey Oswald acted alone, "With both feet planted firmly in the air, the conspiracy theorists created a cottage industry that thrives to this very day, and whose hallmark, with noted exceptions, has been absurdity and silliness." Vincent Bugliosi, *Reclaiming History*, xliii.

60. Mark Lane, *Rush to Judgment* (New York: Holt, Rinehart & Winston, 1966), 19.

61. Anthony Summers, *Conspiracy* (New York: Paragon House, 1989), xvii.

62. Gerald Posner, *Case Closed: Lee Harvey Oswald and the Assassination of JFK* (New York: Anchor Books, 1993), xiv.

63. As *Life* magazine observed on the one-year anniversary of the assassination, "Many Europeans have deified [JFK] posthumously, which partly explains their reluctance to accept the plain description of his murder put forth by the Warren Commission. Oswald alone, in their eyes, was an inadequate giant killer." "J.F.K.: Reflections a Year Later," *Life*, November 20, 1964 (Vol. 57, No. 21), 4.

64. The thought that the President's death might *not* have been due to any compelling national issue was clearly on the mind of Jacqueline Kennedy; Bugliosi here cites her lament, faced with the possibility that

Oswald may have been the sole assassin, that JFK "didn't even have the satisfaction of being killed for civil rights. It had to be some silly little communist. It even robs his death of meaning." Vincent Bugliosi, *Reclaiming History*, xxvii.

65. Joseph Nathan Kane, *Presidential Fact Book* (New York: Random House, Inc., 1998), 131, 156.

66. It was, according to Gerald D. McKnight, precisely the presence of such powerful forces concerned with consequential issues that explains why the federal government failed to perform a thorough inquiry into President Kennedy's death. The government did not choose to vigorously investigate "because it feared what it might uncover: the brutal truth that Kennedy was a victim of deep divisions of visceral distrust over how to solve the 'Castro problem,' and that his assassination was carried out by powerful and irrational forces within his own government." At least some of the later controversy could have been avoided, he argues, had federal authorities performed a thorough investigation. In the absence of the long sought-after "smoking gun," there will likely be no definitive resolution to the enduring questions of who committed the crime. Gerald D. McKnight, *Breach of Trust: How the Warren Commission Failed the Nation and Why* (Lawrence: University of Kansas Press, 2005), 361.

67. Matthew Smith, *Say Goodbye to America: The Sensational and Untold Story Behind the Assassination of John F. Kennedy* (Edinburgh: Mainstream Publishing, 2001), 239, 241.

68. Ibid., 12, 241-242.

69. Ibid., 242-243.

70. Even some of the less shrill conspiracy writers argue that the nation paid a massive price for the President's death. David Kaiser, one of the few historians to take up the subject of the Kennedy assassination, thought that the event did abruptly end some of the more promising administration initiatives including withdrawal from Vietnam and new diplomatic overtures to the Soviets. On the other hand, Kaiser notes, some of the divisions that opened up in American society (i.e. political and generational) after Dallas might have occurred anyway although JFK, because he probably would not have achieved what Lyndon Johnson achieved in domestic politics, would not have endured the same backlash over his policies, especially from the growing conservative movement. Still, Kaiser seems to think that the assassination was in large part the cause of some of the nation's later troubles (such as Vietnam), and a contributing factor in others (the public's weakened confidence in government).

David Kaiser, *The Road to Dallas: The Assassination of John F. Kennedy* (Cambridge: The Belknap Press, 2008), 417-419.

71. Museum pamphlet, The Sixth Floor Museum at Dealey Plaza, Dallas, Texas.
72. "John F. Kennedy and the Memory of a Nation," main exhibit, The Sixth Floor Museum at Dealey Plaza, Dallas, Texas.
73. "The Legacy" film, "John F. Kennedy and the Memory of a Nation" exhibit, The Sixth Floor Museum.
74. The Sixth Floor Museum at Dealey Plaza, "Past Exhibits," available at http://www.jfk.org/go/exhibits ; accessed from Internet February 15, 2013.
75. The Sixth Floor Museum at Dealey Plaza, "Filming Kennedy: Home Movies from Dallas—Dr. A. Jack Jernigan," available at http://www.jfk.org/go/exhibits/home-movies/dr-a-jack-jernigan ; accessed from Internet February 15, 2013.
76. Alison Landsberg, *Prosthetic Memory: The Transformation of American Remembrance in the Age of Mass Culture* (New York: Columbia University Press, 2004), 25-26.
77. Ibid., 26.
78. As Landsberg describes, "visitors are at the mercy of the museum." Once inside the exhibit, visitors must traverse its entire extent starting from the third floor and moving down. This is not history conveyed only through photographs and information boards with which visitors might only superficially interact. There are no shortcuts and few places to sit, as if some degree of physical discomfort is part of the experience. Each patron receives a card with the name and recollections of someone who endured the Holocaust to give a more personal definition to the tragedy than basic facts about it can accomplish. Visitors walk through a boxcar like the ones used to transport people to the concentration camps, and even the floor of the exhibit—cobblestones from the Warsaw ghetto—is built in such a manner that one is left with at least a bare sense of what the Holocaust felt like. Ibid., 129-133.
79. Good taste does not always prevail, however. Aside from a computer game that recreates the assassination, a company unaffiliated with the Sixth Floor Museum used to offer rides in a replica of Kennedy's limousine along the parade route he followed in Dallas. Through speakers mounted on the trunk of the car, riders could hear news coverage of the parade and shooting. I do not recall whether the sound of gunfire was also included. These rides were available from the mid 1990s through

the early 2000s, but to the best of my knowledge, they are no longer available.

80. Alison Landsberg, *Prosthetic Memory*, 113.

81. Ibid., 130.

82. Email exchanges with JFK Library Director Tom Putnam, July 13, 2014; and July 21, 2014.

83. John F. Kennedy Library and Museum, "History," available from http://www.jfklibrary.org/About-Us/About-the-JFK-Library/History. aspx; accessed from Internet July 1, 2014; and "Library in Cambridge, Mass., will House Kennedy Papers: Harvard Hails Decision," *New York Times,* November 11, 1961, 11.

84. Michael Cannell, *I.M. Pei: Mandarin of Modernism* (New York: Carol Southern Books, 1995), 166-167; and Michael Beschloss (ed.), *Jacqueline Kennedy: Historic Conversations on Life with John F. Kennedy* (New York: Hyperion, 2011), 128; and *A Keepsake Album: John F. Kennedy Presidential Library and Museum* (Lawrenceburg, IN: R.L. Ruehrwein, The Creative Company, 2009), 4; and "John Fitzgerald Kennedy Library Incorporated—Chronology" (Box 1, Folder 1, "The Beginning, 1964-1965") in Robert P. Fitzgerald Personal Papers, John F. Kennedy Presidential Library, Boston, Massachusetts.

85. Ellen Fitzpatrick, *Letters to Jackie*, xiii-xvii; and Memorandum to Kennedy Library Trustees from Robert F. Kennedy, May 1, 1964 (Box 1, Folder 1, "The Beginning, 1964-1965") in Robert P. Fitzgerald Personal Papers.

86. Michael Cannell, *I.M. Pei*, 173-174; and "Memorandum for Trustees of John Fitzgerald Kennedy Library Incorporated," from Chairman Eugene Black, December 1965 (Box 1, Folder 1, "The Beginning, 1964-1965") in Robert P. Fitzgerald Personal Papers.

87. Michael Cannell, *I.M. Pei*, 164-165, 173-175; and "Contributions are Sought for Kennedy Library," *New York Times,* December 6, 1963, 19; and Henry Raymont, "Latins will Help Kennedy Library," *New York Times,* January 2, 1964, 29; and Anthony Lewis, "Advisers on Kennedy Library Named," *New York Times,* March 5, 1964, 25; and "India Gives $100,000 to Kennedy Library," *New York Times,* July 9, 1964, 20; and "John Fitzgerald Kennedy Library Incorporated—Chronology" in Robert P. Fitzgerald Personal Papers.

88. John F. Kennedy Presidential Library and Museum, "History"; and Henry Raymont, "Kennedy Archives Illuminate Cuba Policy," *New York Times,* August 17, 1970, 1; and "Materials in the John F. Kennedy Library Avail-

able for Research Use, August 1971" (Box 2, Folder 1, "1971—Facts about the Library") in Robert P. Fitzgerald Personal Papers.

89. Benjamin Hufbauer, *Presidential Temples: How Memorials and Libraries Shape Public Memory* (Lawrence: University Press of Kansas, 2005), 71-75; and Ada Louise Huxtable, "Kennedy Family Announces the Selection of Pei to Design Library," *New York Times,* December 14, 1964, 1, 30; and "John Fitzgerald Kennedy Library Incorporated—Chronology" in Robert P. Fitzgerald Personal Papers.

90. As mentioned earlier, the Kennedy Library today attracts only about 200,000 visitors per year. Email exchange with JFK Library Director Tom Putnam, July 21, 2014.

91. Carter Wiseman, *I.M. Pei: A Profile in American Architecture* (New York: Harry N. Abrams, Inc., 1990), 103-104; and Michael Cannell, *I.M. Pei,* 175-176, 181; and Letter to City Manager John Corcoran from Robert P. Fitzgerald, March 15, 1973 (Box 3, Folder 1, "January – March 1973 – Problems with Site, City and Opposition") in Robert P. Fitzgerald Personal Papers.

92. There was even speculation that the Harvard Institute of Politics affiliated with the Kennedy Library could be used for political purposes (specifically mentioned was a Robert Kennedy presidential campaign), instead of being strictly a center for study. An article in the London *Sunday Telegraph* questioned how much separation would exist between the Kennedy-funded organizations at Harvard and the federal government. This seems to have been a minor area of objection to the library project, and was largely discounted by the university; one Harvard faculty member remarked, "It might be easier to get control of the [federal] Government than of Harvard." "Article on Kennedy Stirs Debate over Political Use of Harvard," *New York Times,* January 22, 1967, 66; and John H. Fenton, "Kennedy School Backed by Pusey," *New York Times,* January 25, 1967, 39.

93. Michael Cannell, *I.M. Pei,* 175-176.

94. Ibid., 178-180; and Carter Wiseman, *I.M. Pei,* 101-102; and Robert Reinhold, "Kennedy Library Plans Are Unveiled," *New York Times,* May 30, 1973, 44.

95. Perhaps the most prominent example of this is Yad Kennedy, the official memorial to JFK built in Israel and dedicated on July 4, 1966. The structure consists of a circular arrangement of concrete shafts directed upward, but flattened at the top, to resemble a tree cut down. Benjamin

Hufbauer, *Presidential Temples*, 72; and Warren Bass, *Support Any Friend*, 245-246; and Michael Cannell, *I.M. Pei*, 178-80.

96. Benjamin Hufbauer, *Presidential Temples*, 68-71, 98.

97. Robert Reinhold, "Kennedy Library Plans are Unveiled," *New York Times*, 44.

98. Ibid.; and Robert Reinhold, "Talks Set on Site of Hotel Near Site of Kennedy Library," *New York Times*, September 29, 1972, 28; and John Kifner, "Scaled-Down Plans for Kennedy Library Unveiled; Cost, with Glass Pyramid Gone, Put at $15 Million," *New York Times*, June 8, 1974, 62; and Letter to Stephen Smith from John H. Corcoran, January 11, 1973 (Box 3, Folder 1, "January – March 1973 – Problems with Site, City and Opposition") in Robert P. Fitzgerald Personal Papers; and Letter to Cambridge Residents from Francis H. Duehay, March 1973, Ibid.

99. Carter Wiseman, *I.M. Pei*, 103-104; and John Kifner, "Scaled-Down Plans for Kennedy Library Unveiled," *New York Times*, 62; and Paul Goldberger, "New Library Plan: A Response to the Critics," *New York Times*, June 8, 1974, 62.

100. John Kifner, "Cambridge Loses Kennedy Museum," *New York Times*, February 7, 1975, 1, 7; and John Kifner, "Kennedy Museum Blocked by Combination of Forces: Offers of Aid Pour In," *New York Times*, February 12, 1975, 40.

101. Dan H. Fenn, Jr., "Launching the John F. Kennedy Library," *The American Archivist* October 1979 (Vol. 42, No. 4), 431.

102. Michael Cannell, *I.M. Pei*, 187-188, 191; and Carter Wiseman, *I.M. Pei*, 115.

103. Public Papers of the Presidents, American Presidency Project, "Boston, Massachusetts Remarks at Dedication Ceremonies for the John F. Kennedy Library," October 20, 1979, available from http://www.presidency.ucsb.edu/ws/index.php?pid=31566&st=&st1= ; accessed from Internet July 5, 2014.

104. Terence Smith, "Carter and Kennedy Share Stage at Library Dedication," *New York Times*, October 21, 1979, 1, 31.

105. Carter Wiseman, *I.M. Pei*, 117-118.

106. Paul Goldberger, "A Sweeping Structure Symbolizes Years of Promise," *New York Times*, October 21, 1979, 30.

107. Dan H. Fenn, Jr., "Launching the John F. Kennedy Library,"438.

108. "John F. Kennedy Library: Plans, Columbia Point, 1976-1991" in David F. Powers Personal Papers, John F. Kennedy Presidential Library, Boston, Massachusetts.

109. Ibid., and Frank Rigg, "The John F. Kennedy Library," *Government Information Quarterly* 1995 (Vol. 12, No. 1), 79.

110. *A Keepsake Album: John F. Kennedy Presidential Library and Museum*, 3, 9, 24, 28-29, 36, 41; and John F. Kennedy Presidential Library and Museum pamphlet and map, Boston, Massachusetts; and Frank Rigg, "The John F. Kennedy Library," 79-81.

111. Email exchange with JFK Library Director Tom Putnam, July 13, 2014.

112. Goldberger, although not a historian, did not view the Kennedy Library's interior attributes with unqualified admiration. While he thought the building succeeded overall in symbolizing JFK, even accounting for the design's weaknesses, he wrote that the exhibit was basically accurate, and tastefully done, but it "does not fully escape from the dangers of presidential cultism to which all presidential libraries seem vulnerable." Paul Goldberger, "A Sweeping Structure Symbolizes Years of Promise," *New York Times*, 30; and Email exchange with JFK Library Director Tom Putnam, July 13, 2014.

113. *A Keepsake Album*, 36; and John F. Kennedy Presidential Library and Museum pamphlet and map.

114. Thomas C. Reeves, *A Question of Character* (New York: The Free Press, 1991), 335-348. See also Herbert S. Parmet's *JFK: The Presidency of John F. Kennedy*, full citation in bibliography. Nick Bryant examines the entirety of Kennedy's career, arguing that while JFK was not unsympathetic to the problems of black Americans, he opted not to take a strong pro-civil rights stance from the mid-1950s onward, as he increasingly needed support from southern politicians in pursuit of his political career and then of his legislative agenda as president. Bryant argues that there was some progress made during the Kennedy years in making racial discrimination less acceptable socially, but in several important respects—voter registration, the percentage of African Americans holding white collar and federal government jobs, and school desegregation—the Kennedy administration could boast of only scant advancement. Nick Bryant, *The Bystander: John F. Kennedy and the Struggle for Black Equality*, full citation in bibliography.

115. *A Keepsake Album*, 33-35; and John F. Kennedy Presidential Library and Museum pamphlet and map; and John F. Kennedy Library and Museum interactive exhibit, "World on the Brink—JFK and the Cuban Missile Crisis," available from http://microsites.jfklibrary.org/cmc/ ; accessed from Internet July 19, 2014; and John F. Kennedy Library and Museum interactive exhibit, "To the Brink," available from http://

foundationnationalarchives.org/cmc/ ; accessed from Internet July 19, 2014.

116. Michael R. Beschloss, *The Crisis Years*, 562-565; and Robert Smith Thompson, *The Missiles of October: The Declassified Story of John F. Kennedy and the Cuban Missile Crisis* (New York: Simon & Schuster, 1992), 356; see also Thomas G. Paterson's essay "Fixation with Cuba: The Bay of Pigs, Missile Crisis, and Covert War Against Castro" in the anthology *Kennedy's Quest for Victory*, full citation in bibliography.

117. Robert Smith Thompson, *The Missiles of October*, 356.

118. See, for example, the differing conclusions on JFK's medical history found in Robert Dallek's *An Unfinished Life*, and Michael O'Brien's *John F. Kennedy*; both are fairly recent works that make use of the late president's medical records found in the Kennedy Library, as well as opinions from physicians as to what they say about the true state of Kennedy's health. See full citations in bibliography.

119. Benjamin Hufbauer, *Presidential Temples*, 98-99, 182-183.

120. See Benjamin Hufbauer's chapter on the new exhibits at the Truman Library. Ibid., 139-175.

121. Email exchange with JFK Library Director Tom Putnam, July 21, 2014.

122. Ibid.

123. Email exchange with JFK Library Director Tom Putnam, July 13, 2014.

124. Karen Tumulty, "Ted Kennedy's Bricks-and-Mortar Legacy Taking Shape," *Washington Post*, June 20, 2014, http://www.washingtonpost.com/lifestyle/style/ted-kennedys-bricks-and-mortar-legacy-taking-shape/2014/06/20/fda99120-f7f6-11e3-8aa9-dad2ec039789_story.html ; accessed from Internet July 10, 2014; and Tess VandenDolder, "Ted Kennedy's Legacy Lives On with a New Interactive Institute for the Senate," *In the Capital*, June 20, 2014, http://inthecapital.streetwise.co/2014/06/20/ted-kennedys-legacy-lives-on-with-a-new-interactive-institute-for-the-senate/ ; accessed from Internet July 16, 2014.

CHAPTER FIVE

OBSERVATIONS

> How history will measure the Kennedy years cannot be foreseen, but it does seem clear that a legendary glamour, which is not dimming with time, surrounds his name and that of his family. The present generation will long be bewitched by the legend, if only because it continues to live through his widow and his two active brothers.
>
> —Journalist Richard Wilson[1]

Wilson's statement nicely encapsulates the two-track challenge we confront in understanding JFK's impact upon American history. There exists the ongoing debate among historians as to how his presidency should be judged. Much time and many hundreds or thousands of pages have been devoted to his actions and intentions related to Cuba, the Soviet Union, civil rights and the fulfillment of his domestic agenda, Vietnam, Latin America and the Alliance for Progress, his nascent interest in fighting poverty, and his interactions with the American business community and economic policies in general. Alongside this debate is the second track that has frequently clashed with the first: popular memory of Kennedy, which has remained decisively positive, influencing subsequent generations no less than that of the 1960s. A discussion of popular memory and President Kennedy would be incomplete if it did not include an assessment of not only *how* that memory has been shaped and used, but *why* it matters—what effect popular memory has had on our conception of presidential leadership. How has popular memory of JFK influenced what we expect from our chief executives? Analyzing how he has been memorialized is interesting from a historical standpoint, but does our memory of the late president offer commentary on what we want the occupant of the White House to do? I believe that it does, and some attempt must therefore be made to weigh the value of the things for which we have remembered Kennedy—to judge whether his memory has influenced us for better or worse. As is the case with his presidential legacy, the image he created for himself that has so deeply defined the public's memory has had mixed implications in terms of what presidential leadership means to us today. And it may be that the expectations we harbor about what presidents should do, and how they should do it, are the most enduring feature of both his legacy and our popular memory of him.

We rightfully remember President Kennedy for providing inspiring leadership and for challenging the nation to do big things in a way that few other presidents have been able to do. Kennedy accurately sensed the interest, especially among young Americans, in serving the country. Idealism, or what President George H.W. Bush termed "the vision thing," has made the Kennedy presidency stand out for many Americans, especially for his creation of the Peace Corps, his enthusiasm about the space program and his call for the U.S. to reach the moon by the end of the decade. He was not our first president to eloquently and memorably state what our great purposes as a nation should be, but without doubt he left his successors with a high standard to match —that the chief executive should not be simply an administrator, an executive in the literal sense who presides over the executive branch, but also a visionary leader. Owing to a considerable extent to John F. Kennedy, the ability to inspire the nation, as much as the skills necessary to persuade lawmakers behind closed doors, has become a critical element of a successful presidency. At the same time, however, much of what we remember about the Kennedy administration is not so much *what* was done as *how* things were done: the glamour, the style, and the witty press conferences. The aura of celebrity he and his family have enjoyed, then and now, simultaneously fascinate and persuade us that every president should conduct himself the way JFK did. The president's family, clothing choices, pets, personality quirks, and favorite sports have become subjects of great interest to the public. Subsequent presidents have constructed images of themselves—images that have frequently harkened back to JFK —in the hopes of influencing how the public perceives them. The role of keeping the nation amused and fascinated did not originate with President Kennedy. As historian Lewis L. Gould has noted, "The Kennedys' biggest contribution to the modern presidency was glamour and celebrity. Not since Theodore Roosevelt had a chief executive garnered such elements of matinee-idol adoration as Jack Kennedy."[2] This public focus on the celebrity aspects of the presidency often seems to supplant interest and debate over real issues of national concern; that is to say, the image-crafting at which JFK was so adept has become synonymous with the actual process of governing and leading.

This work is not intended to be an exhaustive examination of everything for which we have remembered the late president nor of whether those lingering influences have been good or bad. I do not argue, nor do I hope, that this is the final word on the subject. What I offer is some perspective on a few of those influences: why popular memory of JFK has been both positive in its effect as well as a cause for concern. Phrased differently, this study is concerned with how popular memory is inherently practical; while we have seen that practicality manifested in the *uses* of memory, it is also important to consider some of its *results.* Additionally, the purpose here is not to cast the historiography on JFK as secondary in importance, accuracy, or anything else to popular memory. The two are not mutually exclusive. The positive image President Kennedy continues to enjoy among the public does not at all negate the validity of the more critical views on him expressed by some scholars and journalists.

Historians generally have not ascribed to JFK the greatness that the public has bestowed upon him. While I think a more skeptical approach to him is appropriate, an in-depth assessment of the varying opinions as to why Kennedy was a great president (or not) would be superfluous given how much has been written in this regard already. The primary focus here is the nature of what the public thinks about Kennedy rather than the verdicts of historians. Popular memory, even if it is at odds with the overall opinion of the historical community on the Kennedy presidency, must still be a factor in how we understand him. How we have remembered him sometimes does intersect with the historiography on his presidency. For example, we credit him for his leadership on civil rights despite the fact that for most of his presidency he refrained from taking decisive action or issuing the sort of national dedication to the civil rights issue that he finally did in the summer of 1963. But because, at the risk of generalizing, scholars and the public differ in their verdicts on JFK, it is ultimately more fruitful to understand the role of popular memory on its own terms—as its own track—separate from, but equally as interesting as, the observations of historians over the past fifty years.

Appearing before Congress on May 25, 1961, President Kennedy defined the exploration and dominance of space as a new front in the ongoing Cold War with the Soviet Union—as a challenge that the United States must accept as the world's foremost free nation. "We go into space," he declared, "because whatever mankind must undertake, free men must fully share,"[3] and although he asked for action on multiple space-related initiatives, the one most remembered was his call for the United States to land on the moon by the end of the 1960s. Permeated with the imagery of an imminent crisis that had to be met, his rhetoric was almost a call to war. A moon program and other space initiatives would not be cheap, would require massive investments of manpower and technical resources, and would require sustained dedication over many years, which could not fall victim to labor disputes, squabbling among government agencies, or similar shortsighted considerations.[4] The president's vision of Americans being the first to reach the moon and return safely was remarkable, both because the country did achieve it and because such a vision was even enunciated to begin with. The October 1957 launching of Sputnik by the Soviets led to concerns bordering on panic that the United States was falling into a scientific second place in the world. President Dwight Eisenhower, very much aware of American military and technological superiority, signed legislation the following year establishing the National Aeronautics and Space Administration (NASA), but he remained skeptical about the need for a large, long-term, and costly space agenda. Some space research was undertaken, but "the bigger and more publicly galvanizing, the better," was hardly Eisenhower's criteria for which projects should be funded. He feared a permanent space program would lead to time and money being spent on initiatives, such as a moon project, geared toward publicity and bragging rights, and thus attempted to keep the newly created space agency from becoming too unwieldy in its ambitions. A prospective Eisenhower budget for 1962 had even called for a $200 million cut in NASA's funding.[5] And although candidate Kennedy had criticized the Eisenhower administration for supposedly neglecting space and allowing the USSR to jump ahead, his early months in office indicated a far more cautious attitude toward space than his campaign attacks suggested. Initially, the new president even seemed to accept the idea that the Soviets would continue to outperform the United States. It was not at all certain that JFK would place much more emphasis on space exploration than had his predecessor, let alone demand something as grandiose as a moon endeavor,.[6]

But demand it Kennedy did, associating a successful moon program with America's right to lead the free world and the nation's ability to inspire millions around the globe with American institutions, idealism, technology, and hard work. And by demanding the ambitious space agenda, not only in his May 1961 address to Congress, but repeatedly during the rest of his presidency, JFK powerfully and effectively tapped into the American belief that the nation could, and should, do big things. We have remembered him for embodying the conviction that idealism must be a motivating factor in the national priorities we set. While the space race, like most issues, involved more than an altruistic desire to inspire and benefit mankind, the challenge for Americans to reach the moon was testament to Kennedy's skills in persuading and defining a national sense of purpose—in other words, to his ability to lead. The president understood the importance of appealing to the public's imagination in arguing that there were more than simply technological or national defense-based justifications for space exploration, as important as those were. Like other presidents we have remembered for leading the country through great undertakings, Kennedy realized the value and necessity of linking the goals he advocated with national prestige. Past American challenges—westward movement across the continent, the Civil War, two world wars, and remedying the Great Depression, had been depicted in grandiose and idealistic terms (whether accurately or not). JFK did likewise in convincing the nation that space was a "new frontier" of sorts that required American leadership. There were, to be sure, a multiplicity of reasons why space took on the importance that it did: potential gains in scientific knowledge with civilian applications, military-related objectives intended to maintain U.S. superiority over the Soviets, even perhaps more immediate political objectives such as shifting attention away from the recent Bay of Pigs debacle, undertaken on Kennedy's orders, and the successful orbit of Soviet cosmonaut Yuri Gagarin.[7] But even during a period of heightened Cold War tensions in which seemingly any budget proposal could be attained if it was plausibly linked to "beating" the Russians, the president understood that an expanded space agenda, with a mission to the moon as its centerpiece, required an idealistic component. The public needed to be convinced that this effort was a high-minded pursuit intended to demonstrate the power and vitality of American society in solving a problem—even as JFK took it upon himself to depict space as a problem and then diagnose an American landing on the moon as the principal remedy.

It was the type of sales pitch—appealing to all that was good about the country—at which he excelled. Contemporary presidents, in an era of increased visibility and importance of the presidency, are always in search of the issues that define their era and the opportunities that galvanize the public to support them in order to thereby establish themselves as foresighted leaders who could see a national problem looming and lead the people to its resolution. Jimmy Carter, for example, tried to do exactly that with the energy crises that had hit the country by the late 1970s, arguing in 1977 that our character and capabilities must be devoted to what he asserted was "the moral equivalent of war." The energy crisis, Carter declared in terms John Kennedy could have employed fifteen years earlier, or that Franklin Roosevelt might have used thirty years before that, was "the greatest challenge that our country will face during our lifetime."[8] Political scientist Jeffery Tulis has observed that "Beneath the differing policies of Democrats and Republicans lies a common understanding of the essence of the modern presidency—rhetorical leadership," and further, "Today it is taken for granted that presidents have a *duty* constantly to defend themselves publicly, to promote policy initiatives nationwide, and to inspirit the population. And for many, this presidential 'function' is not one duty among many, but rather the heart of the presidency—its essential task" (original italics).[9] Kennedy may not have been the creator of this paradigm, but without doubt he was one of the foremost subscribers to it. It was his role as an "idealist without illusions," as he described himself, that has impressed itself upon the American people and our conceptions of presidential leadership ever since. We look for our chief executives to do what JFK did. We want our leaders to be, if not quite starry-eyed intellectual visionaries à la Thomas Jefferson, at least possessed of a good concept of where they want to take the country, to have a vision, and actively sell it. Kennedy did just that.

The importance of presenting the journey to the moon as a call-to-arms in which the force of the nation's ideals and the extent of its vigor —always a quality of no little importance to President Kennedy—would be on display is evident from the administration's internal deliberations. In a May 1961 report submitted to him by NASA head James Webb and Secretary of Defense Robert McNamara, the two argued that national prestige was indeed one of the purposes of space exploration. Given the planning, management, and considerable investment of resources necessary, they wrote, "dramatic achievements in space, therefore, symbolize the technological power and organizing capacity of a nation." Space exploration contributed to national glory; the memo continued, "This nation needs to make a positive decision to pursue space projects aimed at enhancing national prestige." The mother lode of prestige would go, the report predicted, to whichever nation successfully sent men to and from the moon. For the United States, this goal became the objective of the Apollo program. As they saw it,

> Our attainments are a major element in the international competition between the Soviet system and our own. The non-military, non-commercial, non-scientific but 'civilian' projects such as lunar and planetary explorations are, in this sense, part of the battle along the fluid front of the cold war. Such undertakings affect our military strength only indirectly if at all, but they have an increasing effect upon our national posture.[10]

There was an urgent need for an American moon program that could garner "great propaganda value" as then-Vice President Lyndon Johnson wrote to Kennedy the month before. National ideals might be important, but other countries would see the space race as synonymous with world leadership and align themselves with the nation that could deliver the most "dramatic accomplishments" in that regard.[11] Little wonder that JFK repeatedly cast space as such a compelling national concern. The administration had to think of how American space efforts would play as an expression of national purpose and thus had to sell its ambitious designs as reflective of traditional American notions of excellence. More would be gained in terms of world opinion, but probably also in terms of domestic support, if space became a noble quest for knowledge and a forum for the United States to demonstrate the resilience of its society, rather than simply another area in which to squabble with the Soviets. With the Kennedy administration only weeks old, a memorandum for a White House conference on space from a congressional committee argued that a more vigorous American approach to space needed to consider the perceptions of the international community. For that reason, the U.S. space program should be structured around civilian, non-Cold War objectives—even as, paradoxically, the purpose in doing so was to beat the Soviets at their own game. Appearance, if not also substance, mattered greatly. "If the space picture which we hold out to the world emphasizes military applications," the memo cautioned, "we may be playing right into the hands of the Soviet Union insofar as public relations and propaganda are concerned. The Soviets have scored many points with other nations because of the 'peaceful' picture which they have painted for their space program. We should not forget this fact."[12]

Kennedy did not forget it. He took this advice to heart, as his rhetoric on space during the rest of his presidency demonstrated. The Kennedy-esque obsession with being competitive and always playing for first place was now applied on a national scale to the American goal of dominating the heavens. Space, "a vital national objective,"[13] as Kennedy defined it, involved far more than bragging rights or scientific breakthroughs. It became a test of American character and of whether the country would continue to lead the world in technology and innovation the way it had in the past. In his 1962 State of the Union message, he compared the nation's space mission to Charles Lindbergh's history-making solo flight across the Atlantic: "Our objective in making this effort, which we hope will place one of our citizens on the moon, is to develop in a new frontier of science, commerce, and cooperation, the position of the United States and the Free World."[14] Traveling to the NASA base at Cape Canaveral that fall, the president declared, "I believe that we are an advancing society, and I believe that we are on the rise...As long as the decision has been made that our great system and others will be judged at least in one degree by how we do in the field of space, we might as well be first."[15] The following day, September 12, 1962, he spoke at Rice University in Houston where his subject was again space exploration. It was, he said, part of the great American tradition of advancement: previous generations had made the United States preeminent in industrial power, inventive capacity, and nuclear technology. The largely unknown world beyond the earth was the next such area of challenge, and enduring peace and security required that Americans take the lead.

One month before the Cuban Missile Crisis, the president deemed space exploration as one of the most consequential initiatives he would oversee as president. He took on the role of idealist-in-chief, while blending in a dash of humor:

> But why, some say, the moon? Why choose this as our goal? And they may well ask why climb the highest mountain. Why, 35 years ago, fly the Atlantic? Why does Rice play Texas? We choose to go to the moon. We choose to go to go to the moon in this decade and do the other things, not because they are easy, but because they are hard, because that goal will serve to organize and measure the best of our energies and skills.[16]

The president cited the British explorer George Mallory who, when asked why he wanted to climb Mount Everest, said, "Because it is there." In concluding his remarks, Kennedy argued, "Well, space is there, and we're going to climb it."[17] And in one of the final times he spoke about space, at the dedication of a new medical facility at Brooks Air Force Base in San Antonio on November 21, 1963, he again framed the space race in the language of a national challenge that had to be accepted: "This Nation has tossed its cap over the wall of space, and we have no choice but to follow it."[18]

Photo 17. President Kennedy, an ardent backer of the American space program, meets with astronaut John Glenn in the Oval Office, February 5, 1962.

Photo courtesy of the John F. Kennedy Presidential Library (Cecil Stoughton); ST-40-1-62

It is hardly surprising that JFK would become forever associated with space and the ultimate triumph of the United States in its quest to reach the moon. He had a vision as to what the country could accomplish in space, and memorably argued for why we *should* commit to such an undertaking. A variety of considerations influenced his demand for a moon program: the effects of invigorating the country, capturing the imagination of people both here and abroad, promoting scientific discovery or simply military enhancement. However we explain the American space effort as defined by the Kennedy administration, it was presidential leadership on a large scale.[19] To be fair, there is reason for skepticism of the president's space agenda. Historian James Kauffman suggested that the decision to go to the moon was very much immersed in political considerations. JFK's dramatic announcement of his moon goal followed the failed Bay of Pigs invasion and the headline-making orbit of Yuri Gagarin; therefore, the immediate objective of the announcement may have been to shift the focus of attention to an American space double-dare and to burnish the president's recently compromised image as a formidable antagonist of the Soviets.[20] And the conviction that the United States should undertake something so ambitious, whether in the service of good old-fashioned American idealism, in pursuit of prestige, or even for the sake of scientific advancement, was not shared by everyone either in the administration or in the scientific community. The Director of the Bureau of the Budget, David Bell, scoffed at the notion that the American image in the eyes of other countries was dependent upon a space program. In a spring 1961 memo to JFK, he thought a better case could be made (and possibly a cheaper one as well) for devoting American resources to solve problems around the world instead of outside of it. "The proposition," Bell stated, "that success in international affairs with these parts of the space program [manned space flight, instead of lower-profile projects in meteorology and communications] is dependent on full-scale participation in...manned space flight competition seems highly questionable."[21] Blunter still was the opinion of Dr. Vannevar Bush, a senior statesman of 20th century American science who had overseen the

Manhattan Project of the World War II years. In a 1963 letter to NASA chief James Webb, Bush did not doubt there were potential benefits of the Apollo program, but disputed that they were sufficient overall to justify the incredible expenditures of money and effort involved. Moreover, he thought the moon initiative inclined too much toward showmanship instead of scientific pursuit. If national prestige was the issue, Bush thought the president's handling of the Cuban Missile Crisis was worth more than a dozen moon landings. Citing the Peace Corps as another such example, he wrote, "Having a large number of devoted Americans working unselfishly in undeveloped countries is far more impressive than mere technical excellence," an odd comment coming from such a renowned scientist. Further, "We can advance our prestige by many means, but [the moon program] is immature in its concept." As far as space exploration as a fount of inspiration was concerned, Dr. Bush, referencing the costs involved, acidly continued, "It inspires youth all right, and it also misleads them as to what is really worthwhile in scientific effort. In fact, it misleads them as to what science is. It is well to inspire a child, and the use of fairy tales is legitimate as this is done...It is wrong to inspire him to have an adventure at his neighbor's expense."[22]

And among the skeptics seemed to be President Kennedy himself. Ironically, he may have given Bush some stiff competition when it came to cynicism as to what the purpose of the space race was. In a cabinet room conversation recorded by JFK's White House taping system on November 21, 1962, just two months after asserting that the country was going to the moon "because it is there," the president pressed James Webb and science adviser Jerome Wiesner to maintain the Apollo moon program as the unquestioned priority at NASA. Webb, as head of the space agency, conceived of the moon program as only one among several important space initiatives. Kennedy felt quite differently, insisting that the moon was "the top priority. I think we ought to have that very clear... this is important for political reasons, international political reasons." "Everything that we do," he said, "ought to really be tied to getting onto the moon ahead of the Russians":

> Otherwise we shouldn't be spending this kind of money because *I'm not that interested in space.* I think it's good. I think we ought to know about it. We're ready to spend reasonable amounts of money, but we're talking about fantastic expenditures which wreck our budget and all these other domestic programs and the *only justification* for it in my opinion is to do it because we hope to beat them and demonstrate that starting behind as we did by a couple of years, by God, we passed them.[23] [italics mine]

Despite the more cynical side of Kennedy's space agenda, I think some positive conclusions can nonetheless be drawn. The popularity the space program enjoyed, both before the United States landed on the moon and since, indicates that JFK did more than simply devise a very expensive way of one-upping the Soviets, or converting his New Frontier campaign slogan into policy. For a nation accustomed to setting and achieving seemingly impossible goals, albeit usually doing so with a mix of idealism and realism, the idea that we could land on the moon and should not settle for second place in space seemed only natural. Kennedy may have acted due to a concern for restoring or augmenting national prestige, but, at least to some extent, it was a perfectly good rationale for a moon endeavor. He decided that, on the issue of space, the United States would lead. The United States would be the best; we would go farther than anyone else—and we did. Given his early hesitation to embrace so ambitious and costly a goal, it may be more accurate to say that he backed into his stirring challenge to the country instead of rushing toward it. It is still a notable example of positive presidential leadership. One aspect that worked in his favor was the always-present Cold War, which seemed to make it easier for an American president to issue national calls to dedication and sacrifice and put the prestige of the nation on the line in pursuit of something. Presidents George H.W. Bush and Bill Clinton were criticized for being unable to define what the nature of American leadership in the world would be with the U.S.-Soviet rivalry gone.[24] To be fair, it could be that anybody occupying the White House in the wake of the Cold War would have been hard-pressed to successfully turn the country's attention to a new grand objective. Many people preferred to savor American victory over communism and focus on domestic concerns, instead of looking for a new Holy Grail to pursue. The point is that Kennedy successfully and eloquently tapped into the nation's desire to think and accomplish on a titanic scale, and in so doing, left his successors with a high bar to reach. It is with good reason, and hardly any surprise, that we have remembered him for his ability to lead by inspiring. Glynn Lunney, who served in the NASA flight director's office during the heyday of the Apollo program, recalled the sense of national purpose, "articulated, of course, at the beginning by John F. Kennedy," that infused the work of NASA and was a key factor as to why it was able to accomplish what it did. "I think we have to be sure," he said, "that we have that kind of component, and not a purely self-serving interest, in our rationales and attempts to justify new space initiatives."[25] It seems no longer sufficient for our chief executives to be mere administrators; Kennedy-esque rhetoric and projections of American power clothed in idealism have become the model to follow, as his space agenda demonstrates.

The conclusion of the space shuttle program marked the twilight of American space exploration, at least for the near future, but for many it has symbolized more. By the time of the final shuttle mission in July 2011, several administrations had proposed programs to develop a successor to the space shuttle. These plans generated meager amounts of interest from both the public and the lawmakers in charge of approving the necessary funding. Little resulted from President Barack Obama's call to inject new vigor into NASA.[26] The final flight of *Atlantis* symbolized, for some, a lowering of American ambitions and the nation's desire to be second to none. If, in the late 1950s and 1960s, space exploration had become synonymous with American excellence, that still held true half a century later. Frank Bruni, writing in the *New York Times* on the eve of the final shuttle liftoff, noted the increasingly prevalent pessimism over the direction in which the country was headed. Bruni lamented the fact that the shuttle *Discovery* was now a historical relic destined for the Smithsonian, no longer an active symbol of American achievement and daring. The three-decade history of shuttle missions, he wrote, was "a preeminent symbol of our belief that there were literally no limits as to where we could go and no boundaries to what we could accomplish...there's no grand mission that represents that kind of storehouse for our confidence and emblem of our can-do spirit that space exploration once did."[27] The stirring visions of space—the grand mission to which JFK committed the nation—appear today more than ever to belong to a different era, an era we remember for its confidence in American capabilities that was personified by a president who could express that confidence so well. History cannot bestow upon John Kennedy a great deal of credit for legislative or policy results, but we are still right to remember him for his ability to inspire and persuade on a national scale, and for his understanding of how important the "vision" component of presidential leadership is.

***

This same sense of optimism that marked Kennedy's time in office was also on display as small groups of predominantly college-age Americans began traveling to nations around the world in the early 1960s to demonstrate their commitment to the service of others. The service-oriented nationalism President Kennedy advocated has endured and been emulated by several of his successors. He inspired the American people with a foreign policy that not only placed greater emphasis on world development concerns, but also provided a means by which the country could address them. Reality, as always, mingled with idealism. JFK was no less committed to a militarily and economically robust United States that was dedicated to containing world communism than were either the post-World War II presidents he followed or preceded. But he used the influence of his office to impress upon—or perhaps, remind—the country of its role as a revolutionary force. The country, he believed, should act as a force for progress in the world. Americans would be rejecting their own history if they were not in the vanguard of international efforts to solve poverty, hunger, and disease in an age of disintegrating colonialism and ascendant nationalism. Kennedy left us with a powerful idea with the Peace Corps: that Americans, including those who were not high-level diplomats, should lead through moral force and the strength of ideas, and not simply with missiles and dollars.

In the years immediately preceding the Kennedy administration, novelists Eugene Burdick and William Lederer diagnosed a highly troubling malady afflicting American foreign policy in their memorable 1958 book *The Ugly American.* They posited that the United States, despite the undeniable superiority of its political and economic systems compared with those of the Soviet Union, was frequently its own worst enemy when working with Third World peoples. This was due to the arrogance, incompetence, and cultural deafness of those who represented the U.S. abroad, whether in official or unofficial capacities. American foreign policy had failed to serve the nation's interests, and a smarter approach would have to utilize our resources more effectively in nations around the world if we were not to suffer a prolonged whittling away of American influence.[28] Such concerns fueled calls for an organization whose purpose would be to provide assistance on a variety of fronts to nations in Latin America, Africa, and Asia through the use of American volunteers. One such proposal for an "International Youth Service" received by the Kennedy campaign in 1960 noted the eagerness of the young to make a positive contribution to the world and the corresponding need for the United States to focus more on peaceful, humanitarian goals in its interactions with other nations.[29] The National Student Association likewise argued in favor of a "Point Four Youth Corps" that would engage in assistance projects of various types. There were, as NSA Vice President for International Affairs James C. Scott pointed out, three different bills in Congress at the time that would create such a corps by establishing a new federal agency. The NSA proposal stated, "The future of...new nations and indirectly, the future of the United States is bound up in the humanism and rapidity of development in these old but now-awakening societies,"[30] and candidate Kennedy likewise made a connection between a youth service organization and American foreign policy. The idea of a national service program did not originate with JFK. Indeed, none of the prospective bills on the matter had come from his Senate desk. Minnesota Senator Hubert Humphrey, Oregon Senator Richard C. Neuberger, and Wisconsin Congressman Henry S. Reuss had been the initial proponents and had introduced bills in Congress for that purpose, before Kennedy made the idea part of his presidential campaign.[31] In late-night remarks to students at the University of Michigan, and later in a speech in San Francisco on November 2, 1960, he cited the "Ugly American" problem the country faced and called for a voluntary "peace corps" made up of young men and women willing to serve a three-year assignment as "ambassadors for peace." The purpose was to create new relationships with other nations that were genuine partnerships, and JFK believed this was as crucial as traditional national defense work. There was, Kennedy said, a marked enthusiasm among young people he had met on the campaign trail, mentioning the Michigan students to whom he had spoken a few weeks previously. Idealism was harnessed not only to the immediate question of the nature of American foreign policy, but to the greater problems of underdevelopment in the Third World and the survival of freedom. In questioning how many in his audience would be willing to temporarily forgo their comfortable American lifestyles and work in another country, he argued, "On your willingness to do that, not merely to serve one or two years in the service, but on your willingness to contribute part of your life to this country, I think will depend the answer whether a free society can compete...I think Americans are willing to contribute. But the effort must be far greater than we have ever made in the past."[32]

Senator Kennedy impressed upon his audiences the necessity of this service-oriented nationalism; President Kennedy wasted little time in setting up what became known as the Peace Corps. Directing his brother-in-law, Sargent Shriver, to report to him on how a Corps would operate, the president received Shriver's recommendation on February 22, 1961 that it be established immediately as a new component of American foreign aid efforts. His memorandum noted there were nearly sixty universities in forty countries already engaged in such work under the International Cooperation Administration, and suggested that several thousand Corps volunteers could be deployed within two years. This widespread interest in development projects presented the United States with a momentous humanitarian opportunity. Challenging Americans in his inaugural address to ask what they were willing to do for their country would not be simply one of many rhetorical flourishes emanating from the Kennedy White House. The new administration set about defining how citizens could act in the service of others, and therefore on behalf of their country, with alacrity—and JFK has been remembered ever since for the way he seized that opportunity. The ideas Shriver delivered to the president were simultaneously visionary, conscious of the problems that would inevitably arise as the federal government set up a new type of program, and remarkable for the rapid, almost slapdash quality which underlay how they would be turned into reality. What he was proposing was "an opportunity to add a new dimension to our approach to the world —an opportunity for the American people to think anew and start afresh in their participation in world development."[33] An additional memo contained Shriver's suggestions for immediate steps: implementation of the Peace Corps through an executive order, appointing a director and an advisory council, a public announcement, pursuit of funding, and a letter to the United Nations. "If you decide to go ahead on these," Kennedy's brother-in-law concluded, "we can be in business Monday morning."[34]

Shriver's communications to the president were dated February 22, 1961, a Wednesday. The Peace Corps was not up and running the following Monday, but the administration was close enough. Kennedy announced at his March 1 press conference that he had earlier that day issued Executive Order 10924 bringing the Corps into existence, to be housed in the State Department, and requested legislation from Congress to make it permanent. Setting a goal of 500 to 1,000 volunteers working by the end of the year, he expressed hope that the new program would be "a source of satisfaction" for the country, and an effort at fostering world peace.[35] Kennedy's Peace Corps had a pronounced effect upon the public, both at the time and ever since. It generated enthusiasm from the American people as well as from foreign countries, as discussed below. A letter to JFK from the office of Harris Wofford, an administration adviser on civil rights and the Peace Corps, advised on May 16 that nearly 8,000 people had already submitted applications. One year later in its first annual report to Congress, the organization reported that during the period of March through June 1961, an estimated 10,000 applications had been received. A strong level of interest continued, with nearly a thousand applications coming in each month through the rest of 1961, and 1962 proving to be a good year for the Corps thus far.[36] National polls showed widespread support for a service organization, with Gallup reporting at the time of Kennedy's inauguration that over 70% of Americans liked the idea, a depth of approval that continued throughout his administration.[37] A Harris Poll in 1963 revealed the Peace Corps to be the third most popular initiative of his presidency, behind "national security" and "Berlin." Application submissions to the Corps continued at a healthy pace that year as well.[38] By that time, it had attracted support not only from young Americans vying to be sent thousands of miles away to live closer to poverty than they ever had before, but also from the lawmakers whose support for a permanent Corps program was necessary. Arizona Senator Barry Goldwater, not one who made a habit of gussying up his opinions in elliptical or congenial rhetoric, praised the Peace Corps, commenting, "I think it is going to be a good instrument...I have been impressed with the quality of the young men and women that have been going into [the Corps]. At first I thought that it would be advance work for a group of beatniks, but this is not so...I'll back it all the way." And although Goldwater's Senate colleague, Richard Russell of Georgia, did not count himself among JFK's strongest allies on a number of issues, the White House must have been gratified to learn, as Shriver reported, that Russell's prior opposition changed to support. Following a visit with American volunteers in Ghana, and coming home impressed with what he had seen and heard, the senator's executive assistant confessed, "We've changed our minds. Keep it up."[39] There was even talk of creating

Peace Corps spinoffs to serve domestic needs. A proposed "Task Force USA" could be set up in a similar manner to the Corps; it would be strictly voluntary, establish a set tenure of service, and be managed with as little bureaucratic weight as possible.[40] A successor organization to the Depression-era Civilian Conservation Corps and an Urban Service Corps were also possibilities. The president's Council on Aging, under the Department of Health, Education, and Welfare discussed setting up a Senior Service Corps to take advantage of the interest and skills of older Americans for volunteer work. Shriver pointed out to JFK that "there are more grandparents in the Peace Corps than there are teenagers."[41]

It would have been a tall order indeed to replace completely the images of the fictional Louis Sears and Joe Bing with that of Homer Atkins of Lederer and Burdick's *The Ugly American* within the brief period of Kennedy's presidency. At the very least, however, the Peace Corps was greeted with a good deal of approval abroad. Early on, it led to heightened expectations in the Third World as to the program's possibilities. "There exists a reservoir of goodwill and hope for you and the new Administration" Wofford reported to JFK after an eight-country tour with Shriver in May 1961.[42] At the same time, "frequent doubts were expressed," as Shriver said, as to whether the United States was really committed to a sustained and cooperative approach to development. The concern was whether the initial enthusiasm would be replaced with American reluctance to trade a lifestyle of comfort and material abundance for an assignment offering little of either. If some domestic observers noted a lingering spirit of national complacency due to that abundance, some foreigners did as well. In other cases, American officials had to contend, at least initially, with a lack of interest in what the Peace Corps could offer. Shriver could report after the trip that, "the Peace Corps is wanted and is welcome in every country we visited. Prime Minister Nehru of India, President Nkrumah of Ghana, and Prime Minister U Nu of Burma want Peace Corps Volunteers and they want them to succeed."[43] The month before, however, American ambassador to India John Kenneth Galbraith relayed to Washington the results of his talks with the Indian government on the Peace Corps. The overall attitude toward it in New Delhi, he said, "may be characterized generally as cautious and only mildly interested."[44]

Predictably, the communist world dismissed the Peace Corps as a publicity stunt with the real American objective being to impose its control over other nations. While some foreign governments were not necessarily opposed to the concept of the Corps, they did question the utility of the volunteers being sent to their countries. Some U.S. diplomatic officials did likewise.[45] In Ghana and Nigeria, officials expressed misgivings about hosting groups of volunteers, many of whom were little more than newly minted college graduates with little or no work experience, certainly not in working thousands of miles from home in a completely different culture.[46] Many of the countries initially approached about the Peace Corps had to be persuaded to participate, and the program's success of which Shriver could boast may have been gained in spite of the unconventional way in which it was born. Peace Corps Director of Public Information Edwin Bayley recalled that much of its initial momentum came because the brother-in-law of President Kennedy was its principal advocate with foreign leaders. Shriver "didn't like that introduction, [but] he had to use it because that's how he got in there. He was royalty to them, a concept which they understood. So we did see the heads of every government every place we visited and got very good treatment and, actually, concessions that otherwise couldn't have been achieved."[47]

Photo 18. JFK meets with Peace Corps volunteers preparing to take their overseas assignments, August 9, 1962.

Photo courtesy of the John F. Kennedy Presidential Library (Rowland Scherman); PX 65-2:2.

Nonetheless, the Peace Corps was acclaimed for the work it did. JFK's brother-in-law traveled to Colombia that fall and sent the president a handwritten letter with his findings on the Corps' progress there. Half a year after Kennedy created the organization, Shriver noted with pride that groups of volunteers were already stationed in thirty towns across the country, engaged in a variety of development projects. Colombian President Alberto Lleras Camargo had requested a 100% increase in the number of Corps volunteers, and Shriver thought plans should be made for expanding the organization's presence elsewhere in South America. The United States was receiving very favorable press coverage in the country, and that included, Shriver pointed out, First Lady Jacqueline Kennedy. According to him, she had become the new "pin-up queen" of Latin America, and many had "dubbed her 'La Reina,' and her picture

appears on many a wall."[48] The accomplishments of the Corps led other
nations to set up their own service organizations. By the spring of 1963,
deputy director Bill Moyers reported to Kennedy that legislation en route
to Capitol Hill providing funding for the Corps through the next fiscal
year would also enable the program to assist other countries in their own
volunteer efforts. Moyers also noted the strong support the Peace Corps
recently received from Princess Beatrix of the Netherlands. During her
April 1963 visit to the U.S., the Princess called the program "a kind of
practical idealism," and met with volunteers destined for Afghanistan; a
"Dutch Peace Corps," the *Jongeren Vrijwilligers Korps*, had been created
the previous month.[49] In the Dominican Republic, Peace Corps workers
came to be known fondly as *los hijos de Kennedy*: "Kennedy's children."
In thousands of small ways, the Corps performed valuable service during
the Kennedy administration, with its effectiveness profoundly measured
more in local community projects and the inter-cultural ties established
than in any permanent, national-level goals achieved by the host nations.
During these years, forty-four nations accepted nearly seven thousand
Peace Corps volunteers, with educational development, agricultural
improvement, health care, and public works being the primary areas
of focus.[50]

While there may have been potential value in the development projects
undertaken and the work experiences and relationships established
with other peoples, JFK and his Corps spokesmen understood that the
greatest value lay in the message—or as American ambassador to Ecuador
Maurice Bernbaum favorably termed it, the "psychological" impact—
the new program conveyed to *both* foreign and domestic audiences.[51]
The administration presented it in loftier terms than as simply a more
benign approach to foreign policy, or even as a means by which young
Americans could put their idealism to good use. The Corps was new—
the phrase "new dimension" of the country's foreign policy was used
repeatedly. Yet, the administration argued that it drew upon a noble
and revolutionary American heritage in which Americans had always
been in the forefront of solving problems and, especially in the wake of

two world wars, fighting for freedom around the globe. At a meeting of
the National Students Association at Yale Law School not long after the
Peace Corps was created, Wofford implored the country to re-engage
with the world and asserted that love of country had to include a concern
with stopping world hunger and disease.[52] At a time when some believed
the aura of revolution belonged to the disciples of Marx, Lenin, and
Mao, Corps leaders charged that the staying power of American ideals
was being tested. "Are we so redundant, so apathetic, so indifferent,"
Shriver, by this time Director of the Peace Corps, asked the Catholic
Interracial Council on June 1, 1961, "that our response to the magnificent
challenge of world revolution is little more than a feeble echo of the past
sacrifices we have made for freedom?"[53] John F. Kennedy came to be
remembered for unlimited potential in a confident era and for demanding
that the country live up to old ideals in a newly invigorated effort. If,
as the fictional President Nixon said at the beginning of this work, the
people looked at the president and saw themselves (or rather, as they
envisioned themselves), Kennedy and his advisers argued that in looking
at the Peace Corps, Americans were actually looking at the story of their
own country. And lest current-day observers dismiss this idea as little
more than hokey salesmanship, the response from the public showed
that the country largely took it seriously and was ready to pursue noble
causes. The idea of the New Frontier included, in terms of the Peace
Corps, newly independent nations trying to develop national economies.
In a speech at the Columbia University School of Business, Wofford
stated, "There is a new generation of Americans waiting to be called to
these new frontiers. 'Go West, young man!' was the call to which earlier
generations of Americans responded. Now the call is: 'Go East, and West,
but especially go South, to the developing lands where pioneering is
needed again."[54] The belief in American exceptionalism was a powerful
conviction, and if Ronald Reagan was later identified with his evocation
of the "shining city on a hill" image, John Kennedy would be remembered
for the idealism that, he asserted, should be one of the nation's primary
exports. Israeli Prime Minister David Ben-Gurion, when asked what he

believed was JFK's greatest contribution to the world, cited the Peace Corps for, if not completely redefining how the United States interacted with the world, nonetheless tilting the nature of that interaction away from preoccupation with the Cold War and toward helping others. It was no minor achievement given the negative emotions soon to be unleashed against the country due to the Vietnam War.[55]

In an article written for *Look* magazine at the one-year anniversary of JFK's assassination, Robert F. Kennedy wrote that his brother "restored to Americans the confidence in our future, the belief that we are destined for greater things...He restored the confidence that people from other countries had in the ideals of our country."[56] I think there is a considerable amount of truth to this. Like the American lunar quest, the importance the Peace Corps assumes in our collective memory of President Kennedy goes beyond the actual results of the program and the nuanced history of the Peace Corps that made it less than entirely successful and Kennedy as less than completely enamored with it.[57] Through the Peace Corps and the Alliance for Progress, Kennedy very effectively promoted a new look for American foreign policy in the 1960s. He could take the pragmatic and idealistic strands behind that policy and leave the American people convinced that the latter strand was the one that most often prevailed.[58] We expect our presidents to do what JFK did in summoning the nation to great causes such as helping other peoples and reminding us of our history. We are, as JFK historian Robert Dallek said, "a country that has consistently been most enamored of its preaching presidents,"[59] and while JFK was not the first president in the "preaching" tradition, he may be the last best example we have of it.

By itself, the way the administration sold the Peace Corps is unremarkable; presidents have often employed high-minded rationales in advocating their agenda. What makes Kennedy unique here, what makes his "practical idealism," so much a part of the way we have remembered him, is not simply that he was so rhetorically masterful in explaining that idealism, but also because it fit so well with the times in which he governed. When he defined service abroad as a type of patriotism—and the language of service-oriented nationalism unites much of the way he and his advisers talked about the Peace Corps[60]—Kennedy was speaking to a citizenry that had prevailed in World War II and then created an astounding degree of national prosperity. Who could say what else the country could accomplish, or rather, could *not* accomplish? Especially for those coming of age in the 1960s who had heard from their parents about the trials of, and ultimate victory over, economic depression and world fascism, the president's declaration that it was now their turn to serve the country would forever associate him with idealistic leadership. Appearing before a meeting of Peace Corps workers on June 14, 1961, he asserted,

> You remember in the Second World War Winston Churchill made one of his speeches, I think at Tripoli, when the 8th Army marched in there, and said they will say [to] you what did you do during the great war, and you will be able to say that I marched with the 8th Army. Well, they may ask you what you have done in the Sixties for your country, and you will be able to say 'I served in the Peace Corps, I served in the United States Government', and I think that people will recognize that you have made your contribution.[61]

Kennedy bought into the concept of the Corps as a new idea built on long-established beliefs, as being closer to the real tradition of American foreign policy than the arms race and political/military alliances of recent years. Corps volunteers would play a prominent role. He continued, "The Peace Corps...gives us an opportunity to emphasize a very different part of our American character, and that which has really been the motivation for American foreign policy, or much of it since Woodrow Wilson, and that is the idealistic sense of purpose which I think motivates us...a real part of our American character."[62] Although we live in a more cynical age, Kennedy's brand of American exceptionalism has remained largely unsullied. As Robert Dallek wrote, "...the Peace Corps became a fixture that Democratic and Republican administrations alike would continue to finance for forty years."[63] Indeed, perhaps the most concrete indication that the Peace Corps vision of service-oriented nationalism has not become a dried-out anachronism of a seemingly more hopeful and innocent long-gone era is the abundant progeny the Corps has produced. Presidents who followed Kennedy tried to institute their own service programs as if to harness for themselves some of the idealism he so effectively embodied. Early in his presidency, Lyndon Johnson created Volunteers in Service to America (VISTA), conceived as a domestic Peace Corps that would make up one part of his larger War on Poverty.[64] George H.W. Bush promoted community service through his Office of National Service. Bill Clinton established his own such program, AmeriCorps, even signing the AmeriCorps legislation with a pen used by President Kennedy when he founded the Peace Corps.[65] More recently, President George W. Bush created the USA Freedom Corps. Announced in his January 2002 State of the Union Address, the USAFC asked Americans to devote two years, or 4,000 hours, during their lifetimes to community service. Bush's challenge was repeatedly compared to that of JFK. The *Philadelphia Inquirer* called the administration's new program "a direct descendant of John F. Kennedy's Peace Corps." The *Los Angeles Times* declared, "Not since John F. Kennedy has a sitting president summoned citizens to the cause of their country. At least, not like this."[66] JFK's summons set the standard for others to follow, and also became a central component of how Americans have remembered those years. One young person recalled the Kennedy years thus: "The whole idea was that you can make a difference. I was sixteen years old and I believed it. I really believed that I was going to be able to change the world."[67] It was surely an outlook shared by many at the time, characterizing the brief period between the complacent 1950s and the disillusionment of the years after JFK's assassination.

***

Popular memory of JFK has influenced what we expect from our chief executives both for better and for worse. President Kennedy, like Joan of Arc in Pierre Nora's examination of popular memory in French history, has been remembered in multiple ways that may or may not conform to the truth. Memory is variable; we do not all remember the late president in the same way, and even when we do share the same overall recollection, that memory can be understood in both positive and negative terms. We remember Kennedy for his ability to connect with people—to inspire, persuade, and establish grand national goals—which has become a model for succeeding presidents. But coexisting with this is a less constructive result of our continuing interest in him: an excessive fascination with the glamorous, fluffy side of his presidency that seems to assume nearly as much importance as any substantive decisions of his administration. Put another way, President Kennedy arguably ranked second to none in his time, and perhaps since then, in his public relations skills. Those skills have influenced not only people's perceptions of him at the time, but also our memory of him in the years since. In remembering him for how he inspired us, we also have remembered him for how he entertained us —for his ability to govern us with images—and this has impacted how we have thought our leaders should interact with us ever since. To be sure, if presidents today devote as much time to image-creating as to policy-crafting, it is not a trend begun by John F. Kennedy. There has been an enduring public interest in the presidency throughout American history, withstanding the fluctuating levels of prestige the office has enjoyed. Kennedy both benefited from the growing importance of image salesmanship, especially due to the rise of television, and accelerated that trend in his 1960 campaign and during his presidency. This turn of events has had implications for how we have thought about politics ever since, because we have reserved a seemingly unshakeable place in our collective memory of Kennedy as a model president.

Many Americans are familiar with the famous debates held in the fall of 1960 between JFK and Republican presidential nominee Richard Nixon, including the interesting public response to their first matchup. Television viewers—those who could see a confident, relaxed, handsome Kennedy against an unshaven, slightly perspiring, and rather shifty-eyed Nixon—thought the former won the contest. Those who tuned in by radio, and thus could only judge the quality of their debate points, thought Nixon did the better job. The importance of the visual and the creation of a celebrity out of a political candidate were components of the Kennedy camp's approach to campaigns—an approach that, at times, was cynical and superficial.[68] An early example of this came in 1946 as Kennedy campaigned for the House of Representatives; referring to the massive amount of money spent in the race, Joseph Kennedy, Sr. declared, "We're going to sell Jack like soap flakes."[69] The importance of money in politics, today and even seventy years ago, hardly requires explaining; one has only to consider the literal bags of cash used to finance Lyndon Johnson's career in the House and Senate around the same period.[70] But it was, to extend slightly Joe Kennedy's metaphor, the packaging of candidate Kennedy, which was so remarkable. What may have been good, even slick, public relations at the time has crystallized into enduring popular memory. The administration's decision, made at press secretary Pierre Salinger's suggestion, to televise presidential press conferences, gave the country a regular dose of Kennedy's humor, command of information, and quick wit. Initial skepticism as to the wisdom or utility of repeatedly putting the president before the American people in so unscripted a setting—journalist James Reston at first called it "the goofiest idea since the hula hoop"—quickly receded as the president's skills as a performer became apparent. Gimmicky the idea may have been, but it was enormously effective in shaping how the public thought of him. An April 1962 Gallup poll reported that nearly three of four adults had had at least some exposure to one of his press conferences. Almost as if the Kennedy press appearances had become a television comedy show all on their own in competition with "The Dick Van Dyke Show," or "The Beverly Hillbillies" of the same period, Gallup queried Americans on what they thought of the president's give-and-take with reporters. Respondents overwhelmingly reacted favorably toward "The 6 O'Clock Comedy Hour," as the president himself reportedly called them. The unscripted nature of the broadcasts, which seemed to heighten the entertainment potential, also earned broad public support.[71] Reporter Hugh Sidey later wrote, "Kennedy's press conferences were dubbed 'the best matinee' in Washington...Always armed with humor, he ruled the stage and exited with his audience wanting more." Jacqueline Kennedy of course gained celebrity status in her own right as a fashion trend-setter and as a paragon of the arts and good taste, on display, for example, in her 1962 televised tour of the White House as it underwent restorations under her direction. She likewise received largely positive reviews for her work, and her impeccable clothes, bouffant coiffure, and aristocratic-sounding voice (different from her husband's Boston accent) all contributed to the perception of the Kennedys as an American version of royalty: highly cultured, yet not pompous, and somehow still able to connect with average citizens.[72] And in an age when many Americans still received much of their news from the print media, the coverage the entire First Family enjoyed in magazines such as *Life* and *Look*—two of the largest circulation publications at the time—was a regular reminder of the glamour, youth, and exuberance that now presided over the nation. Photographs of Kennedy parties and the president's children playing in the Oval Office, represented not simply a record of the day-to-day activities in the White House. They were actual symbols of Kennedy's style of presidential leadership: open, playful, the right blend of formality and nonchalance befitting the most powerful office in the world. Kennedy and his family always seemed interesting.

President Kennedy has not ceased to command interest and adoration from the public, so it should not come as a surprise that the dictum that imitation is the sincerest form of flattery has especially applied to him. In the days and weeks after his death, many were convinced that he deserved a place in American history next to Washington and Lincoln, and polls taken since then have indicated a persistence of that attitude. In a 1975 Gallup poll, slightly more than half the respondents actually listed Kennedy as the greatest American president. Twenty-five years later, another poll showed that Lincoln had replaced JFK for the number one spot; nevertheless, Kennedy tied with George Washington, Ronald Reagan, and Bill Clinton for second place. Kennedy still held second place in a 2001 poll.[73] It would be a stretch to argue that the reason why the public remains practically ready to carve JFK's likeness on Mount

Rushmore is only because of the superficial aspects of his presidency. Still, it is telling that later presidents and would-be presidents have copied him even in the fluff produced for public consumption, as if fluff has become an essential ingredient in winning public affections. Richard Nixon, for example, was captured on film taking walks on the beach at his San Clemente, California home, as well as manning the helm of a boat during a sailing outing, both evocative of Kennedy's famous love of the ocean.[74] Others have tried to emulate his campaign or speaking techniques, or have mentioned him in a way that they hope will give them legitimacy. Former Kennedy press secretary Pierre Salinger ran for the Senate in California in 1964. He attempted to win support by reminding people of his service in the late president's administration, adopting JFK's habit of jabbing the air with a forefinger while delivering a speech, and even acquired a Cape Cod accent when doing so.[75] Ronald Reagan, in his campaign for the California governorship in 1966, mimicked Robert Kennedy in quoting historical or literary figures in the JFK style to give his speeches a more intellectual tint.[76] Some thought Bill Clinton embodied the same attributes that Kennedy had thirty years earlier: youth, a new generation, good looks, the ability to generate enthusiasm from voters through his talent at public speaking and campaigning, and a political outlook that was billed as pragmatic and less ideologically driven. In the midst of the dispute over the results of the 2000 presidential election, Vice President Al Gore and his family engaged in a not-so-inconspicuous Kennedy-esque game of touch football.[77]

Photo 19. President Kennedy's wit and command of information were on display at his televised news conferences, called "The 6 O'Clock Comedy Hour," March 21, 1963.

Photo courtesy of the John F. Kennedy Presidential Library (Abbie Rowe); AR7779-F.

And most recently, Barack Obama's appearance on the national scene generated comparisons with JFK, and this was not only due to the major endorsement he received from Caroline Kennedy and Senator Edward Kennedy. Obama's speaking abilities appeal to younger voters, and his rock-star magnetism led some to observe that no presidential candidate had made such an impact upon the electorate since John Kennedy. The preoccupation with crafting the right appearance for the public—creating the right photo-op or delivering a speech that would not only look good in the next day's newspapers, but also take on historic importance—has arisen in the last half century largely due to Kennedy. He, after all, was very good at influencing how the public thought of him. It has been *because* of his skill in this regard that history's mixed verdict on his presidency has had little effect in diminishing our enthusiasm for him. We have remembered the images he created of himself more than we have his actions. Images, however, cannot and should not substitute for actual achievements, but in the case of the late president, the images often counted for far more than they were worth. Historian Thomas Reeves charged that JFK effectively manipulated people, arguing that the adulation that surrounded him was nothing more than a "mindless worship of celebrity; it was a love affair largely with images."[78]

Richard Nixon, having resigned the presidency in 1974, spent much of the following two decades observing American politics and recalling his own extraordinary political career. Reflecting upon his 1960 debates with Kennedy, the former president argued that politics since then had become simplified, less focused on content and ideas, with a premium placed on showmanship and public relations. Much of this, according to him, was due to the preponderant influence of television.[79] "It is a devastating commentary on the nature of television as a political medium," he lamented in his presidential memoirs, "that what hurt me the most was not the substance of the [debates]...but the disadvantageous contrasts in physical appearance."[80] Aspirants for public office, according to him, now had to focus on being slick if they wanted to win. Engaging the public on anything that really mattered was perhaps secondarily important. His advice to anyone running for Congress, advice that could easily apply to presidential hopefuls as well, was to develop a highly programmed persona and deliver to the voters a campaign message that could play well in commercials and thirty-second clips on the evening news. "Unless [the candidate] learns to be an actor, he will never have a chance to be a legislator," Nixon said.[81] It was a cynical view of campaigning, with the public seemingly uninterested in demanding substantive and relevant discourse on national concerns, and their would-be leaders, therefore, disinclined to provide it. We could attribute the former president's sentiments, in part, to sour grapes. He had, after all, fallen short of the presidency by a fingernail's distance in 1960, perhaps because Kennedy proved far more adept at the game of façade-creating, "soap flake" politics. Nixon may have lost that game, but he proved willing to play it and improve his skills at it nonetheless. While creating a compelling aura of statesmanship and fostering starry-eyed adulation for himself was not quite Richard Nixon's forte, he learned how to do it plausibly enough by the time of his second, successful bid for the White House in 1968. And to be clear, Nixon did not (at least in his memoirs) assign blame for this vapidity in American politics to his old rival; he was too experienced a participant in "the arena," as he termed it, to take such a reductionist view of longer-term political trends. Kennedy's presidency and, just as importantly, his death, coincided with the rise of television as a source not only of entertainment, but of information (and the two often were intermingled), and he skillfully used that medium to an extent few other public figures have. He, like any good politician, understood and capitalized upon trends or developments already under way. To cite a more contemporary example, Bill Clinton effectively utilized the prominence of 24-hour cable news, and especially the growing reach of the Internet in the 1990s, to influence the news and how the public thought of his governance.[82]

But Nixon's observations, insofar as they relate to how we have remembered JFK, still bear much relevance. Kennedy, while he did not invent the politics of the visual, was no bystander, either: he very deliberately defined presidential leadership in terms of performance. He put on a good show for us. The problem we encounter with President Kennedy is that popular memory has been driven mostly by emotions arising from presidential imagery as opposed to concrete examples, or results, of his presidential leadership. Franklin Roosevelt, in the words of historian William E. Leuchtenberg, has left those who have occupied the Oval Office after him "in his shadow," due to his very substantial record of accomplishment. Even Harry Truman and Dwight Eisenhower could cite major policy achievements in both domestic and foreign affairs during their respective eight-year occupancies of the White House. Truman reorganized the nation's defense and armed service agencies into the Department of Defense, signed the National Security Act of 1947 that created the Central Intelligence Agency and the National Security Agency, and promulgated the doctrine of containment of global communism that guided American foreign policy for years to come. Dwight Eisenhower brought the Korean War to an end, solidified and even enlarged the scope of Roosevelt-era social welfare initiatives like Social Security and the minimum wage, and took at least a few halting steps toward arms control with the Soviet Union and cutting the cost and size of the American military establishment.[83] The same, in terms of accomplishment, is not really true with Kennedy. We have remembered him, and he remains so influential, not so much for things he did, but rather because of the graceful and witty manner in which he did them.

I am not suggesting here that the roles of symbolism or acting in the presidency arose solely thanks to President Kennedy. Although different presidents have found greater or lesser success in creating favorable and enduring images of themselves for the public, the "intangibles" of the White House—the leader's ability to lead through image-making and inspiration—have always been present. George Washington himself, knowing that so much of what he did would influence how his successors approached the job of chief executive, and convinced of the importance of creating a sense of reverence, even majesty, among the American people toward their president, gave the new position a blend of regal yet republican splendor. Through the use of weekly levees, the president's birthday as a national holiday, and his stately bearing, Washington understood that how a president presented himself to the public was as much a part of his job as the governing decisions he made.[84]More recently, symbolism has exerted a powerful influence on the way people think and remember their presidents. Garry Wills argued, in his book on Ronald Reagan, *Reagan's America*, that much of the 40th president's appeal derived from his embodiment of a nostalgic, mythical American past that the public found appealing. People responded favorably to a man who appeared to represent a small-town, conservative, values-focused way of life that seemed less and less common by the time he became president. But this mindset, according to Wills, reflected more than just the way the public chose to see Reagan himself. What people believed about the president personally was likewise how we prefer to think about our country in general: that we grow up in loving, stable families where religious, moral, patriotic values are taught and acted out in our lives each day. Reagan acquired the same sort of blank-slate quality that the fictional President Nixon spoke of with respect to JFK in Oliver Stone's film; he takes on all of the attributes we like to ascribe to ourselves collectively, and in so doing, becomes almost a mythological figure.[85] This idea that emotion-laden symbolism can assume a major place in our memory, even becoming central to the way we remember someone, may be more applicable to JFK, a president who served less than three full years in office and therefore left behind many unresolved issues, than it does to Reagan who left office with a longer, deeper record. While I think Wills is correct to point out that Reagan's distinctly "American" story enabled him to form an emotional bond with the public that other politicians of his era who had similar backgrounds could not —Jimmy Carter or Richard Nixon, for example—there are nonetheless shortcomings to his observations.[86]

Why is our memory of JFK potentially a problem? It is not an issue of whether we have remembered John Kennedy "correctly" in the sense of trimming our memory so that it aligns with the historical community's judgments on his administration. The question is what the *continuing effect* upon our ideas about politics that popular memory of the late president has. Our understanding of presidential leadership is, due to our memory of Kennedy, at once compelling and shallow. JFK could, no doubt, appeal to our intellect, but often he was appealing to our emotions as well. And it could be that we place too much importance upon presidential gimmickry and confuse the ability of the president to *market* himself well with the task of *governing* us well. As we judge our presidents and those who want to lead us, with the pleasing images of Kennedy never far from our minds, which of the two do we regard as more important? In his case, it is arguably the former. While some degree of artifice seems to be accepted by the public as part and parcel of one's success in politics, presidential historian Lewis Gould wrote that Kennedy's construction of himself as a celebrity and a statesman went considerably beyond anything that had been done before. If he did not quite install the "culture of celebrity" in the White House, he revived it to the extent that it is still, unfortunately, highly influential in our conception of the presidency and the person who occupies the office.[87] So it is all the more ironic that a man who caused many Americans to see celebrity status as synonymous with statesmanship had his own thoughts on the civic responsibilities of the public in a representative democracy. Kennedy, whose enduring memory has led us to search for another American king with the same glamor and allure, sounded a note of caution similar to Nixon's on the importance that the nature of our political discourse has . This includes what we look for in a leader, the attributes we regard as important in those who wish to lead us, and the issues—grand or mundane—upon which we base our vote. It may really be a double irony, as the future president expressed his concern in his 1955 Pulitzer Prize-winning bestseller *Profiles in Courage*. Ironic, because it was a work that attracted controversy due to charges that Kennedy did not even author it, and that its main purpose was to give him weight as an intellectual prior to his run for higher office[88]—again, the eclipsing of substance by appearance. JFK, in any case, declared the following in the book's conclusion:

> ...democracy means much more than popular government and majority rule, much more than a system of political techniques to flatter or deceive powerful blocs of voters...For, in a democracy, every citizen, regardless of his interest in politics, 'holds office'; every one of us is in a position of responsibility; and, in the final analysis, the kind of government we get depends upon how we fulfill those responsibilities. We, the people, are the boss, and we will get the kind of political leadership, be it good or bad, that we demand and deserve.[89]

The public, Kennedy was saying, must ultimately demand excellence from their elected officials. He has been a "tough act" to follow not simply because of his undeniable charisma, but also because his presidency—and our memory of it—has been balanced so precariously between excellence and effective public relations with a mere gilding of excellence. Popular memory of JFK can, and does, move us to demand from our leaders a willingness to "think big" and lead the country to accomplish great things. However, it also can, and does, serve as a distraction from what really matters in how we are governed. We seem to yearn for another President Kennedy, and upon our memories of him are set expectations not only unrealistic, but to some extent misguided as well. We want a president who can inspire us the way he did, charm us and make us laugh (almost to the point of being an entertainer) the way he did; we want a first lady who is glamorous and cultured the way Jacqueline Kennedy was. Historians on the whole have ranked Kennedy as an average, or slightly above-average, president. From the standpoint of history, there are lessons both positive and negative to be gained in examining his life and his presidency. From the standpoint of memory, the same is no less true. We have remembered him as a great president, and we remain enamored with him, but it is the reasons *why* that make popular memory of JFK, a leader possessed of qualities both substantive and frivolous, very much a mixed blessing upon American politics in the last half century.

In understanding the political impact of that memory, the possibilities
have accompanied the perils.

NOTES

1. Richard Wilson, "What Happened to the Kennedy Program?" *Look* November 17, 1964 (Vol. 28, No. 23), 122.

2. Lewis L. Gould, *The Modern American Presidency* (Lawrence: University Press of Kansas, 2003), 135.

3. Public Papers of the Presidents, American Presidency Project, "Special Message to the Congress on Urgent National Needs: May 25, 1961," available from http://www.presidency.ucsb.edu/ws/index.php?pid=8151 &st=&st1= ; accessed from Internet March 27, 2013.

4. Ibid.

5. Chester J. Pach, Jr. and Elmo Richardson, *The Presidency of Dwight Eisenhower* (Lawrence: University Press of Kansas, 1991), 170-171; 179-180; and "Administrator's Presentation to the President," March 21, 1961, in "National Aeronautics and Space Administration (NASA), 1961: January-March," Presidential Papers, President's Office Files, Evelyn Lincoln, John F. Kennedy Presidential Library, Boston, Massachusetts; accessed online, digital identifier JFKPOF-082-007.

6. On this as on other defense-related issues, candidate Kennedy had criticized Eisenhower for a lack of vision as to what the U.S. should accomplish in space. JFK's campaign preparation materials, in a precursor to how space would be understood once Kennedy and his aides were installed in the White House, noted that there was a definite public relations, or "psychological," side to space exploration, especially considering how space achievements were seen internationally. Gerard J. DeGroot, *Dark Side of the Moon: The Magnificent Madness of the American Lunar Quest* (New York: New York University Press, 2006), 128, 134-136; and "Position Paper on Space Research: Preliminary Paper— August 31, 1960, in "Space," Pre-Presidential Papers, Presidential Campaign Files, 1960, John F. Kennedy Presidential Library, Boston, Massachusetts; accessed online, digital identifier JFKCAMP1960-0993-006.

7. James L. Kauffman, *Selling Outer Space: Kennedy, the Media, and Funding for Project Apollo, 1961-1963* (Tuscaloosa: The University of Alabama Press, 1994), 3.

8. Public Papers of the Presidents, American Presidency Project, "Address to the Nation on Energy: April 18, 1977," available from http://www.

presidency.ucsb.edu/ws/index.php?pid=7369&st=&st1= ; accessed from Internet March 27, 2013.

9. Jeffrey K. Tulis, *The Rhetorical Presidency* (Princeton: Princeton University Press, 1987), 4.

10. "Recommendations for Our National Space Program: Changes, Policies, Goals," James Webb & Robert McNamara, May 8, 1961, in "Johnson, Lyndon B., 1961:January-May" Presidential Papers, President's Office Files, Evelyn Lincoln, John F. Kennedy Presidential Library; accessed online, digital identifier JFKPOF-030-019.

11. Memo to President Kennedy from Vice-President Johnson: "Evaluation of Space Program," April 28, 1961, in "Johnson, Lyndon B., 1961:January-May," John F. Kennedy Presidential Library.

12. "Memorandum for White House Conference, February 13, 1961," from Committee on Science and Astronautics, House of Representatives, in "National Aeronautics and Space Administration (NASA), 1961: January-March," Presidential Papers, President's Office Files, Evelyn Lincoln, John F. Kennedy Presidential Library, Boston, Massachusetts; accessed online, digital identifier JFKPOF-082-007.

13. Public Papers of the Presidents, American Presidency Project, "Executive Order 10976: Suspension of the Eight-Hour Law as to Laborers and Mechanics Employed by the National Aeronautics and Space Administration," November 15, 1961, available from http://www.presidency.ucsb.edu/ws/index.php?pid=58914&st=&st1= ; accessed from Internet March 29, 2013.

14. Public Papers of the Presidents, American Presidency Project, "Annual Message to the Congress on the State of the Union," January 11, 1962, available from http://www.presidency.ucsb.edu/ws/index.php?pid=9082&st=&st1= ; accessed from Internet March 29, 2013.

15. Public Papers of the Presidents, American Presidency Project, "Remarks to the Staff at the NASA Launch Operations Center, Cape Canaveral," September 11, 1962, available from http://www.presidency.ucsb.edu/ws/index.php?pid=8859&st=&st1= ; accessed from Internet March 29, 2013.

16. Public Papers of the Presidents, American Presidency Project, "Address at Rice University in Houston on the Nation's Space Effort," September 12, 1962, available from http://www.presidency.ucsb.edu/ws/index.php?pid=8862&st=&st1= ; accessed from Internet March 29, 2013.

17. Ibid.

18. Public Papers of the Presidents, American Presidency Project, "Remarks in San Antonio at the Dedication of the Aerospace Medical Health Center,"

November 21, 1963, available from http://www.presidency.ucsb.edu/ws/index.php?pid=9534&st=&st1= ; accessed from Internet March 29, 2013.

19. Sunny Tsaio, *"Read You Loud and Clear!" The Study of NASA's Spaceflight Tracking and Data Network* (Washington, D.C.: NASA, 2008), 106, 108.

20. James L. Kauffman, *Selling Outer Space*, 3.

21. "Memorandum for the President: National Aeronautics and Space Administration Budget Problem," from David E. Bell, in "National Aeronautics and Space Administration (NASA), 1961: January-March," John F. Kennedy Presidential Library.

22. Letter to James Webb from Vannevar Bush, April 11, 1963; in "National Aeronautics and Space Administration (NASA), 1963," Presidential Papers, President's Office Files, Evelyn Lincoln, John F. Kennedy Presidential Library, Boston, Massachusetts; accessed online, digital identifier JFKPOF-084-006.

23. JFK's prodding appears to have had an effect, at least in the short term. Wiesner reported to him several weeks later after a trip to the Los Alamos government laboratories that with additional funding made quickly available to NASA, Apollo program milestones could be reached in a shorter period of time. Wiesner predicted that the first attempt at landing on the moon could occur around May 1967, as opposed to October 1967 without the supplemental funding. C-SPAN, "President Kennedy, U.S. Space Program, Cabinet Room, November 21, 1962," available from http://www.youtube.com/watch?v=tilwvlpNSfA ; accessed from Internet March 30, 2013; and "Memorandum for the President: Acceleration of the Manned Lunar Landing Program," from Jerome Wiesner, January 10, 1963, in "Wiesner, Jerome B., 1963," Presidential Papers, President's Office Files, Evelyn Lincoln, John F. Kennedy Presidential Library, Boston, Massachusetts; accessed online, digital identifier JFKPOF-067-017.

24. Michael S. Sherry, "George H.W. Bush:1989-1993"; and Matthew Dickinson, "Bill Clinton: 1993-2001", in Alan Brinkley and Davis Dyer (eds.), *The American Presidency* (Boston: Houghton Mifflin Company, 2004), 490-493, 511-512.

25. Glenn E. Swanson (ed.), *Before This Decade is Out: Personal Reflections on the Apollo Program* (Washington, D.C.: National Aeronautics and Space Administration, 1999), 220.

26. Andy Pasztor, "NASA's Post-Shuttle Space-Exploration Plans Generate Little Excitement," *Wall Street Journal*, July 22, 2011, http://online.wsj.com/article/SB10001424053111903554904576460203278610600.html .

27. Frank Bruni, "In an Earthbound Era, Heaven Has to Wait," *New York Times,* July 7, 2011, A23.

28. William J. Lederer and Eugene Burdick. *The Ugly American* (New York: W.W. Norton & Company, 1958), 271-285.

29. "A Proposal for an International Youth Service," Samuel P. Hays, September 30, 1960, in "Peace Corps" Pre-Presidential Papers, Presidential Campaign Files, 1960, John F. Kennedy Presidential Library; accessed online, digital identifier JFKCAMP 1960-0993-003.

30. "Point Four Youth Corps," James C. Scott, in "Peace Corps: General: Reading file, 16 February 1961 – 28 July 1962, undated" Presidential Papers, White House Staff Files of Harris Wofford, John F. Kennedy Presidential Library, Boston, Massachusetts; accessed online, digital identifier JFKWHSFHW-006-017.

31. "Final Report—The Peace Corps: A Study by the Colorado State University Research Foundation, Fort Collins, Colorado, May 1961," in "Peace Corps: General: Colorado State University Final Report, Ch. 1-6" Presidential Papers, White House Staff Files of Harris Wofford, John F. Kennedy Presidential Library; accessed online, digital identifier JFK-WHSFHW-006-009.

32. Peace Corps, "Remarks of Senator John F. Kennedy," University of Michigan, October 14, 1960, available from http://www.peacecorps.gov/about/history/speech/ ; accessed from Internet May 20, 2013.

33. "Report to the President on the Peace Corps," Sargent Shriver, February 22, 1961, in "Peace Corps: Shriver report and recommendations, February 1961" Presidential Papers, President's Office Files, Evelyn Lincoln, John F. Kennedy Presidential Library; accessed online, digital identifier JFKPOF-085-014.

34. Peace Corps Director of Public Information Edwin Bayley recalled years later that there had not been much initial planning in how the program would operate. They often found themselves improvising when they met with foreign leaders, who were accustomed to more traditional types of foreign aid, as to what the Corps would actually do in their countries. The nebulous quality of the Corps idea, plus the fact that it was JFK's brother-in-law making the sales pitch, produced enough initial commitments from those leaders to begin deploying volunteers. "The 'Eisenhower Page,'" Sargent Shriver, February 22, 1961, in "Peace Corps: Shriver report and recommendations, February 1961" John F. Kennedy Presidential Library; and Transcript. Edwin R. Bayley Oral History Inter-

view #2, 12/19/1968, by Larry J. Hackman. John F. Kennedy Oral History Collection, John F. Kennedy Presidential Library, Boston, Massachusetts.

35. "President John F. Kennedy's News Conference #5," March 1, 1961, in "1 March 1961" Presidential Papers, President's Office Files, Evelyn Lincoln, John F. Kennedy Presidential Library; accessed online, digital identifier JFKPOF-054-007; and Public Papers of the Presidents, American Presidency Project, "Executive Order 10924—Establishment and Administration of the Peace Corps in the Department of State: March 1, 1961," available from http://www.presidency.ucsb.edu/ws/index.php?pid=58862&st=&st1= ; accessed from Internet May 5, 2013.

36. "Letter to President Kennedy from Deirdre Henderson," May 16, 1961, in "Peace Corps, 1961: January-June" Presidential Papers, President's Office Files, Evelyn Lincoln, John F. Kennedy Presidential Library; accessed online, digital identifier JFKPOF-085-015; and "Peace Corps: 1st Annual Report to Congress for the Fiscal Year Ended June 30, 1962," in "Peace Corps: First annual report, July 1962" Presidential Papers, President's Office Files, Evelyn Lincoln, John F. Kennedy Presidential Library; accessed online, digital identifier JFKPOF-086-003.

37. "Final Report—The Peace Corps: A Study by the Colorado State University Research Foundation, Fort Collins, Colorado, May 1961," in "Peace Corps: General: Colorado State University Final Report, Ch. 1-6" Presidential Papers, White House Staff Files of Harris Wofford, John F. Kennedy Presidential Library.

38. "Memorandum for the President: Weekly Summary of Peace Corps Activities" October 29, 1963, in "31 October 1963: Background Materials" Presidential Papers, President's Office Files, Evelyn Lincoln, John F. Kennedy Presidential Library; accessed online, digital identifier JFKPOF-061-006; and Robert Dallek, *An Unfinished Life*, 339; and James N. Giglio, *The Presidency of John F. Kennedy*, 158.

39. "From the Director," February 15, 1962, and "Memorandum for the President," from Robert Sargent Shriver, Jr., February 12, 1962, in "Peace Corps, 1962: January-March" Presidential Papers, President's Office Files, Evelyn Lincoln, John F. Kennedy Presidential Library; accessed online, digital identifier JFKPOF-085-018.

40. Under the proposal, the program would be equivalent to (though not a replacement for) peacetime military service. As Shriver wrote to Attorney General Kennedy, in a memo that also went to JFK, "The main thrust of the program would be to encourage a period of voluntary service by young men and women at the completion of their schooling. In this

respect, peacetime service would take the same place in the cycle of a person's life as military service traditionally has...We are not proposing to interfere with existing arrangements for the recruitment of military manpower through Selective Service." "Task Force USA—An Alternative Proposal," from Robert Sargent Shriver, Jr., to Attorney General Robert Kennedy, in "Peace Corps, 1962: July-December" Presidential Papers, President's Office Files, Evelyn Lincoln, John F. Kennedy Presidential Library; accessed online, digital identifier JFKPOF-086-002.

41. Ibid.; and "Memorandum for the President" from Robert Sargent Shriver, Jr., June 8, 1962, and "U.S. Department of Health, Education, and Welfare News Release," June 5, 1962, from "Peace Corps, 1962: April-June" Presidential Papers, President's Office Files, Evelyn Lincoln, John F. Kennedy Presidential Library; accessed online, digital identifier JFKPOF-086-001.

42. "Memorandum for the President," May 25, 1961, in "Peace Corps, 1961: January-June" Presidential Papers, President's Office Files, Evelyn Lincoln.

43. "Statement of Robert Sargent Shriver, Jr., Director of the Peace Corps, in Chicago, Illinois, May 17, 1961," in "Peace Corps, 1961: January-June," John F. Kennedy Presidential Library.

44. "Memorandum to Mr. Shriver from John K. Galbraith—Discussions with the Indian Government Regarding the Peace Corps," April 29, 1961, in "Peace Corps: Countries: India, April 1961: 18-29" Presidential Papers, White House Staff Files of Harris Wofford, John F. Kennedy Presidential Library; accessed online, digital identifier JFKWHSFHW-006-022.

45. For example, Ambassador Leland Barrows, representing the United States in Cameroon, regarded the Corps as primarily a public relations effort whose target audience was strictly domestic. Burrows commented years later, "I always felt that the Peace Corps, particularly under Shriver, was operated much more with the American public in mind than with the needs of the countries we were helping." Transcript. Leland J. Barrows Oral History Interview, 02/04/1971, by William W. Moss. John F. Kennedy Oral History Collection, John F. Kennedy Presidential Library.

46. Robert Dallek, *An Unfinished Life*, 339; and Transcript. Edwin R. Bayley Oral History Interview #1, 10/10/1968, by Larry J. Hackman. John F. Kennedy Oral History Collection, John F. Kennedy Presidential Library.

47. Transcript. Edwin R. Bayley Oral History Interview #2, John F. Kennedy Oral History Collection.

48. "Letter to President Kennedy from Sargent Shriver," October 27, 1961, in "Peace Corps, 1961: January-June" Presidential Papers, President's Office Files, Evelyn Lincoln.

49. "Memorandum for the President—Weekly Summary of Peace Corps Activities," from Bill Moyers, April 23, 1963, in "24 April 1963: Background materials" Presidential Papers, President's Office Files, Evelyn Lincoln, John F. Kennedy Presidential Library; accessed online, digital identifier JFKPOF-059-008.

50. James N. Giglio, *The Presidency of John F. Kennedy*, 157-158; and Gary May, "Passing the Torch and Lighting Fires: The Peace Corps," in Thomas G. Paterson (ed.), *Kennedy's Quest for Victory*, 288; and "The Peace Corps: JFK's Bold Legacy," *Look* June 14, 1966 (Vol. 30, No. 12), 38.

51. Transcript. Maurice M. Bernbaum Oral History Interview #1, 06/09/1983, by Sheldon Stern. John F. Kennedy Oral History Collection, John F. Kennedy Presidential Library.

52. "The President's Remarks to Advisory Council Peace Corps," from Office of the White House Press Secretary, May 22, 1961, in "Peace Corps, 1961: January-June," and "Report to the President on the Peace Corps," Sargent Shriver, February 22, 1961, in "Peace Corps: Shriver report and recommendations, February 1961," and "Excerpts from Some Talks on the Peace Corps—Talk to the Annual Spring Assembly, New England Region, National Students Association, Meeting at Yale Law School," March 11, 1961, in "Wofford speeches: Excerpts from Talks on the Peace Corps, 11 March 1961" Presidential Papers, White House Staff Files of Harris Wofford, John F. Kennedy Presidential Library; accessed online, digital identifier JFKWHSFHW-014-023.

53. "Text of Remarks by Robert Sargent Shriver, Jr., at the Dinner of the Catholic Interracial Council at the Conrad Hilton Hotel, Chicago, Illinois," June 1, 1961, in "Shriver, R. Sargent: Speech at Catholic Interracial Council, 1 June 1961" Presidential Papers, White House Staff Files of Harris Wofford, John F. Kennedy Presidential Library; accessed online, digital identifier JFKWHSFHW-014-017.

54. "Talk to Annual Dinner of the Alumni Association, Columbia University School of Business, January 31, 1962, by Harris Wofford, Jr.," in "Wofford speeches: Annual dinner, Alumni Association, Columbia University School of Business, 31 January 1952" Presidential Papers, White House Staff Files of Harris Wofford, John F. Kennedy Presidential Library; accessed online, digital identifier JFKWHSFHW-014-027.

55. Transcript. David Ben-Gurion Oral History Interview #1, 07/16/1965, by E.A. Bayne. John F. Kennedy Oral History Collection, John F. Kennedy Presidential Library; and Herbert S. Parmet, *JFK*, 354.

56. T. George Harris, "Eight Views of JFK: The Competent American," *Look* November 17, 1964 (Vol. 28, No. 23), 61.

57. For a further explanation, as well as an in-depth look at how the Peace Corps worked in practice—the good and the bad—see Gary May's essay in the Thomas Paterson anthology on Kennedy's foreign policy. Gary May, "Passing the Torch and Lighting Fires: The Peace Corps," in Thomas G. Paterson (ed.), *Kennedy's Quest for Victory*, 284-316; and James N. Giglio, *The Presidency of John F. Kennedy*, 156-157.

58. The Alliance for Progress was the administration's grand project for spurring economic growth, democracy, and improvements in health and education throughout Latin America. Unveiled in March 1961, its humanitarian rationale coexisted with the need to fight communism by replacing Fidel Castro's Cuba with the United States as the hemisphere's true revolutionary force. "A policy of social idealism," as Arthur Schlesinger, Jr. commented, "was the only true realism for the United States." Lawrence Freedman, *Kennedy's Wars: Berlin, Cuba, Laos, and Vietnam* (Oxford: Oxford University Press, 2000), 124; and Robert Dallek, *An Unfinished Life*, 340.

59. Robert Dallek, *Hail to the Chief*, 1.

60. I have cited a couple of examples in this regard, but I will point out one more. Sargent Shriver, in testimony before the House Foreign Affairs Committee in August 1961, in which he requested that Congress establish the Peace Corps on a permanent basis, noted that the same "reservoir of eagerness" displayed by Americans in previous challenges such as the two world wars was needed again in the Third World. Just as the call to national service had previously meant a willingness to combat fascism abroad, the patriotic obligation by the early 1960s was the effort to meet the needs of peoples around the world. This, Shriver argued, represented the "highest dedication" of Corps volunteers to the service of their nation and to the people for whom they served. "Statement of Robert Sargent Shriver, Jr. Before the Foreign Affairs Committee of the House of Representatives, August 11, 1961," in "Shriver, R. Sargent: Statement before Foreign Affairs Committee, 11 August 1961" Presidential Papers, White House Staff Files of Harris Wofford, John F. Kennedy Presidential Library; accessed online, digital identifier JFKWHSFHW-014-020.

61. "Remarks of the President at Peace Corps meeting in Chamber of Commerce Auditorium, Washington, D.C." June 14, 1961," in "Peace Corps, 1962: April-June," John F. Kennedy Presidential Library.

62. Ibid.

63. Robert Dallek, *An Unfinished Life*, 340.

64. Robert Dallek, *Flawed Giant*, 1979.

65. John Robert Greene, *The Presidency of George Bush* (Lawrence: University Press of Kansas, 2000), 149-150; and Bill Clinton, *My Life* (New York: Alfred A. Knopf, 2004), 547.

66. David E. Rosenbaum, "The State of the Union: Spending Plans; A Vision of an America Devoted to Volunteer Duties," *New York Times*, January 30, 2002; and William Neikirk, "More National Service Urged," *Chicago Tribune*, January 30, 2002; and John Balzar, "Volunteerism: A Way to Grind the Callouses Off Our Hearts," *Los Angeles Times*, February 13, 2002; and "Citizens Urged to Serve Their Country as Volunteers," *Milwaukee Journal Sentinel*, January 30, 2002; and Ron Hutcheson, "Bush Moves to Establish his New Volunteer Program," *Philadelphia Inquirer*, January 31, 2002.

67. Terry H. Anderson, *The Sixties* (New York: Pearson Longman, 2004), 25; and Godfrey Hodson, *America in Our Time*, 5-12.

68. Lewis L. Gould, *The Modern American Presidency*, 135-136.

69. Evan Thomas, *Robert F. Kennedy*, 48.

70. See, for example, John Connally's recollections of this during his time as a campaign aide during LBJ's 1948 bid for the Senate in the second volume of Robert Caro's multi-volume biography of Johnson. Robert A. Caro, *The Years of Lyndon Johnson: Means of Ascent* (New York: Alfred A. Knopf, 1990), 274-275, 277.

71. Sally Bedell Smith, *Grace and Power*, 121-122; and Robert Dallek, *An Unfinished Life*, 335-336.

72. Goodman, Jon, et al., *The Kennedy Mystique: Creating Camelot* (Washington, D.C.: National Geographic, 2006), 66; and Sally Bedell Smith, *Grace and Power*, 255-257.

73. Historians in general have not been nearly so generous, rating Kennedy as average or just above average—but nowhere near "great." "Above average" was the consensus of two surveys of scholars in 1982 and 2000, although one study among historians in 1988 opined that JFK had been "the most overrated figure in American history." Robert Dallek, *An Unfinished Life*, 699-700.

74. Nixon, however, had a harder time mastering the blend of elegance and casualness that Kennedy could pull off. Recalling the beach photo op, presidential photographer Ollie Atkins later wrote, "[Nixon] was wearing what he considered casual clothes: shoes and socks, long trousers, and a light-blue sport shirt under a Camp David jacket—a dark blue windbreaker jacket with a big presidential seal on the front. He looked like the chairman of the board out for a walk in between acquisitions. For the record, that's about as casual as Richard M. Nixon ever got." Ollie Atkins, *The White House Years: Triumph and Tragedy* (Chicago: Playboy Press, 1977), 45, 111; and Melvin Small, *The Presidency of Richard Nixon* (Lawrence: University Press of Kansas, 1999), photo section.

75. Salinger was successful in winning the Senate seat vacated by the retirement and subsequent death of Senator Clair Engle. His Senate career was a brief five months, as he failed to win a full term in November 1964. Salinger's candidacy engendered skepticism about his qualifications. His service as JFK's press secretary led many to believe that the only basis for his run was the former president. As the *Washington Post* reported, if he received the Democratic nomination for the Senate seat, "It will be because of his association with Mr. Kennedy." Julius Duscha, "Salinger Makes JFK Image His Basis of Hopes," *Washington Post,* May 23, 1964, A2; and Paul R. Henggeler, *In His Steps,* 100.

76. Lou Cannon, *Governor Reagan: His Rise to Power* (New York: PublicAffairs, 2003), 138.

77. Ron Goldwyn, "Bush Forces Counter Gore Recount," *Philadelphia Enquirer,* November 11, 2000, http://articles.philly.com/2000-11-11/news/25611563_1_florida-point-man-al-gore-gore-forces .

78. Thomas C. Reeves, *A Question of Character,* 414-415, 420.

79. Richard Nixon, *In the Arena: A Memoir of Victory, Defeat, and Renewal* (New York: Simon & Schuster, 1990), 198.

80. Richard Nixon, *RN: The Memoirs of Richard Nixon* (New York: Simon & Schuster, 1990), 219.

81. Richard Nixon, *In the Arena,* 202.

82. Matthew Dickinson, "Bill Clinton: 1993-2001," in Alan Brinkley and Davis Dyer (eds.), *The American Presidency,* 527.

83. Lewis L. Gould, *The Modern American Presidency,* 108-109, 120; and David L. Stebenne, "Dwight D. Eisenhower: 1953-1961," in Alan Brinkley and Davis Dyer (eds.), *The American Presidency* (Boston: Houghton Mifflin Company, 2004), 388, 391, 395.

84. Joseph J. Ellis, *His Excellency: George Washington* (New York: Vintage, 2005), 192-194.

85. Garry Wills, *Reagan's America: Innocents at Home* (New York: Penguin, 2000), 445-448, 458-460.

86. Americans during Reagan's presidency may not have bought into this glorified picture as much as Wills argues they did. Wills points out that the President could count young people among his many supporters, but they would have had a harder time identifying with Reagan's old-fashioned, small-town values; what, then, motivated them to support him? And is the enduring popularity he commanded solely due to the mythmaking he engaged in, or could it also stem from real accomplishments? Or, taking a more negative view, was that mythmaking regarded by the public as more important than administration blunders such as Iran-Contra? The public, at least during Reagan's presidency, may have had a better sense of reality—be it positive or negative—than Wills thinks.

87. Lewis Gould, *The Modern American Presidency*, xiii, 135-136.

88. James N. Giglio, *The Presidency of John F. Kennedy*, 11-12.

89. John F. Kennedy, *Profiles in Courage*, 264-265.

CONCLUSION

> A famous death will always corrupt some people. The memory of
> our important men is inevitably stained by the banality of their
> admirers. We know of course that thousands and perhaps millions
> will be made off this death; the In Memoriam industry, so versatile,
> inventive and fast, has already moved in...We have seen it with
> all other valuable deaths.
>
> —M. Edelson, writing in the *National Review*, following the
> assassination of Robert F. Kennedy, June 1968[1]

It has been suggested that the crucial reason why John Kennedy is so
revered, that what ultimately secured him a sacred place in American
history, was his shocking and untimely death, rather than what he
accomplished during his life. Historian Michael Kazin, writing in an
anthology on the American presidency, begins the essay about him by
saying, "John F. Kennedy was more important dead than alive. Of no other
president in the twentieth century could that blunt judgment be made."[2]
And consider famed reporter Edward R. Murrow's comment, "I have had
great difficulty in trying to reach some judgment regarding that young
man's relation to his time...there remains for me a considerable element
of mystery...I always knew where his mind was, but I was not always sure
where his heart was."[3] The caprices of history, those events and people
beyond the control of the person being remembered, may ultimately
mean more than the decisions that person made or the intentions he or
she had, even if what they did or tried to do, arguably, was worthy of
being remembered positively. It is, to be sure, an unsettling idea when
talking about memory. It suggests how contingent and artificial popular

memory can be if any difference of events, minor or significant, could have resulted in an entirely different way of remembering. What if Abraham Lincoln had not been assassinated and had to cope with the herculean challenges of Reconstruction? What if his efforts to politically restore the former Confederate states had drowned in the same acrimony with Congress as those experienced by his successor? Lincoln's standing in our collective memory, while it may have remained high nonetheless, would have been tempered considerably; we might see him as both a great *and* a failed president. What if there had been no World War II, or at least no event leading to direct American involvement, and Franklin Roosevelt had left office in 1941 after two terms? Would he then be remembered as a great president, or as much less than that—as a leader whose efforts undoubtedly mitigated the problems of the Great Depression but did not really solve them? Would we remember FDR as essentially a more effective and charismatic Herbert Hoover? In the case of John Kennedy, what if he had not been killed and had to face the domestic and foreign difficulties that plagued LBJ? In the case of Vietnam, Johnson did not undertake any major policy shifts (publicly, at least) that would have imperiled his election to a full term. But, by early 1965, he faced a fateful divergence of choice: commit the United States far more deeply to the struggle or begin a withdrawal of American personnel. Had President Kennedy been reelected, which seems probable, he would have likely found himself facing the same problem as he prepared to begin his second term. We would be judging him and remembering him based on the choice he made and on his record of eight years as president, not on three years as president and fifty years of "might-have-beens."

Still, there is opportunity in examining popular memory. While JFK's assassination resulted in an abbreviated presidency, many have attached to him whatever qualities or accomplishments they believe he could have realized had he lived. Kennedy as a *symbol* has become very powerful. Because memory can be so nebulous, seemingly possessing its own agency while also reacting to those who harness it, we can see what it creates under different circumstances and when applied to different purposes.

This study has focused on popular memory of President Kennedy in a political context: how local and national leaders used it and realized how successful and counterproductive memory could be, how that memory was shaped both then and later, and how popular memory should be understood on its own terms—apart from how we rank Kennedy as a historical figure. As one could expect, the tendency to make JFK the protagonist of our greatest hopes for the country and the world has presented a problem for historians. Whether Americans' high regard for his presidency results from the belief that he was a great president, lingering sadness over his death, or our preference to remember the past as a happier time than the present, the fact remains that public opinion of President Kennedy has moved in the opposite direction from the consensus of the historical community. The American people have largely ignored historians' admonishments that our high opinion of him has failed to reflect the very flawed aspects of JFK as a human being and as a leader. Kennedy's cavalier attitude towards women, for example, has been written about extensively. His womanizing, as Garry Wills noted, was so compulsive and blatant that he needlessly put himself at risk, and it led him and his aides to lie and cover up repeatedly in order to avoid what could have been a politically debilitating scandal.[4] Nor should Kennedy's numerous affairs be understood as simply a personal weakness. Thomas Reeves argued that the president's actions were highly unbecoming to the great office he held. By placing himself at risk, he was violating the trust that the American people had conferred upon him; John Kennedy, a highly skilled shaper of his image, effectively manipulated many people. And while recognizing the late president's undoubted intelligence and ability to inspire, as well as his capability to achieve great things, Reeves contended that his central failing was a disturbing absence of moral scruples. This defect, in turn, affected him in so many personal and political ways: his need to lie and cover up his dalliances, his reputed connections with organized crime, his involvement in unsuccessful assassination plots against Fidel Castro, his involvement in a successful one against South Vietnamese President

Diem, and his rather oblivious attitude toward the problems faced by black Americans.[5] Herbert Parmet even went so far as to suggest that JFK had essentially played the American people for fools and must bear some responsibility for the national problems he had failed to resolve or even address adequately. The potential for greatness was certainly there —but all too often, it remained only potential.[6]

Former Kennedy advisors, even decades later, still maintained that the greatness attributed to their boss was well deserved. Former JFK speechwriter and advisor Ted Sorensen has remained loyal to their standard litany of the late president's achievements: saving the world from nuclear war during the Cuban Missile Crisis, improving the lives of black Americans (or, as he said, "turning this country's direction on its treatment of black citizens completely around"), space exploration, and creation of the Peace Corps.[7] "Without demeaning any of the great men who have held the presidency in this century," Sorensen has argued, "I do not see how John Kennedy could be ranked below any one of them."[8] Years later, JFK's disciples continue to see the Kennedy administration, and the end of it, as a point of departure for the nation. As Richard Goodwin mournfully wrote, "Indeed, 'my' sixties never happened. The decade contained a promise, an augury of possibilities, an eruption of confident energy. It was smothered and betrayed by a needless tragedy of such immense consequences that, even now, the prospects for a restorative return remain in doubt."[9] Twenty years after Kennedy's death, Arthur Schlesinger, Jr. insisted that the images and memories of him as a noble figure were not contrived, but real: "Did he fool us? I think not. The public man was no different from the private man."[10] The American people, to a great extent, still subscribe to this version of the Kennedy presidency. Many of us have either heard or read about the grimier aspects of JFK as a person and as a national leader, but it has not made much difference in how we remember him.[11] Faced with a choice of either seeing him as human and his presidency as less than we had previously thought it was, or remembering him as heroic and the years the United States was under his leadership as a glorious period of unlimited promise, we repeatedly choose the latter.

These clashing forces—Kennedy's legacy as president versus popular memory—are present today even in the primary (or, at least, the earliest) scholarship through which younger generations learn about John Kennedy: American history textbooks. The appraisals of his administration that students receive are far from hagiography, but there is still a sense that the seeming glamour and optimism he represented matters, and continues to be remembered, just as much as Kennedy's legacy. Textbooks often perform the same dual task of not only explaining what JFK did and what happened during his presidency, but also describing popular memory of him. They play a major role in constructing the "prosthetic memory" of which Alison Landsberg spoke. Most high school and college students who do not intend on studying history receive their most concentrated exposure to Kennedy and his era through this medium. Historian Eric Foner wrote in one such text, "John F. Kennedy served as president for less than three years and, in domestic affairs, had few tangible accomplishments. But his administration is widely viewed *today* as a moment of youthful glamour, soaring hopes, and dynamic leadership at home and abroad" (italics mine).[12] A realistic assessment of his successes and missteps as president, Foner notes, plus the information we now have on his personal failings, have really not changed how Americans continue to remember him. The conceptions of JFK we still hold somehow remain valid despite the awareness that not every moment of the Kennedy White House was one of glory. This seems to be a fair characterization of how other recent classroom surveys present the issue. One textbook actually uses the "Camelot" metaphor to describe the Kennedy presidency, noting the influence of the president's style and intellectual veneer. The authors take stock of his leadership shortcomings, such as the Bay of Pigs failure and his hesitation to support civil rights earlier in his presidency, but still conclude that, "Kennedy had given hope to people who had none."[13] Students who read *America Past & Present* are told that JFK governed largely as a conventional, hard-line cold warrior who initiated an American military buildup; increased our role in Vietnam; won a rather mixed, "bittersweet" victory over the Soviet Union in the Cuban Missile Crisis; and displayed a "pattern of belated reaction" in addressing the civil rights struggle. Yet, the authors argue, with perhaps a bit of overreach, the late president remained "a symbol of hope and promise for a whole generation."[14]

This is not to suggest that sources like these are, on the whole, inaccurate in how they treat Kennedy. Rather, they highlight the difficulty in studying him: we *judge* his presidency one way, but we tend to *remember* it in another. The student cannot help but be intrigued that a man who served so briefly, and who, in the area of policy achievements, did not leave much behind, is still presented as such a galvanizing force in 20th century American history. Part of the reason for this was, of course, JFK's sudden death, and the resulting conviction that greater things were in store for the country had he not been killed. In *The American Promise*, the authors describe the early 1960s as a period of "style and promise," filled with a new feeling of inspiration and empowerment among young people, although this was mitigated by the president's "unremarkable" list of legislative successes. The authors conclude the segment on the Kennedy years by citing *New York Times* reporter James Reston: "What was killed was not only the president but the promise...He never reached his meridian: We saw him only as a rising sun."[15] What these sources collectively convey to students is that popular memory of JFK was, and continues to be, defined by ideas of what he represented (youth, public service, the arts, inspiration, etc.), what he intended to do, and the manner in which he governed—as much as it is influenced by what he actually achieved.[16]

My hope is that this book contributes at least a little to our under-standing of JFK, although I do point out that other authors have made important contributions to the study of President Kennedy as related to popular memory. In *JFK For a New Generation*, Conover Hunt chronicled the assassination, aftermath, and impact of the event on recent American history and popular culture for, as the title of her work indicates, those who came of age in the 1990s. In her book *Covering the Body: The Kennedy Assassination, the Media, and the Shaping of Collective Memory*, Barbie Zelizer examined the crucial role of the media by telling the story of how the media both reported the assassination and influenced the way the public remembered it.

What I have tried to do in adding to this small but important body of literature is to offer a discussion primarily of the *political* angle of JFK and popular memory because he has remained influential in our political system [17] (as well as, I think, because it is interesting as a strictly historical topic). John Kennedy has ongoing importance. In his rise to prominence as a presidential candidate, Barack Obama has been the most recent American politician to benefit from the comparison with the late president, but he was hardly the first. Memory of JFK has appeared repeatedly in American elections during the last forty years. Candidates have tried to mimic him stylistically, as we have already seen, and to tie themselves ideologically to him by claiming to be a liberal in the Kennedy tradition. Some of Robert F. Kennedy's supporters had invested so much emotionally in seeing a Kennedy elected president that they briefly entertained the idea of putting his younger brother Edward on the 1968 Democratic ticket in the vice-presidential slot. If elder brother Robert had been considered the natural successor to John, Edward became the successor to Robert and, as the new leader of the family, the guardian of the Kennedy legacy (in this case, of *two* glorified siblings). By placing him on the ticket in 1968 with Hubert Humphrey, Kennedy supporters "would not feel Robert Kennedy died in vain," in the words of one RFK campaign worker.[18] The 1969 Chappaquiddick incident inflicted considerable damage on Ted Kennedy's career, especially his presidential prospects. Nonetheless, Kennedy challenged incumbent President Jimmy Carter for the 1980 Democratic nomination. Carter prevailed, but perhaps the most memorable moment of Senator Kennedy's presidential quest came during his convention speech, giving the audience flickers of the traditional Kennedy eloquence.[19]

Other Democrats in the past thirty years have also striven to follow JFK's lead by perpetuating the idea of him as a committed liberal, with themselves carrying his standard. Kennedy historian James Giglio referred to Democrats Paul Tsongas, Michael Dukakis, Al Gore, and Gary Hart (and we can add to this list Bill Clinton) as "Democratic neoliberals." These so-called children of Kennedy committed themselves to a liberal agenda —presumably an agenda JFK would have approved—while trying to avoid accusations of favoring big-government programs á la Lyndon Johnson and the Great Society.[20] In 1992, this renewed enthusiasm for liberal policies culminated in the nomination and election of "New Democrat" Bill Clinton. The photograph of Clinton as a teenager shaking hands with JFK at the White House appeared frequently during the 1992 campaign. Kennedy-oriented symbolism appeared at Clinton's inauguration, as he paid his respects at the late president's gravesite with Kennedy family members the day before being sworn in, and his inaugural address contained some elements and themes reminiscent of JFK. Barack Obama's support from Caroline Kennedy, Senator Ted Kennedy, Ethel Kennedy (widow of RFK), and JFK speechwriter Theodore Sorensen, as well as the parallels between his career and President Kennedy's led to some favorable comparisons between the two in the 2008 election season. Obama, like JFK, marketed himself as representing a break from the past, a new kind of candidate. Obama was also the author of best-selling books that increased his notoriety, and the Illinois senator attracted support from journalists and some public policy experts the same way Kennedy had.[21]

The fact, however, that President Kennedy is still revered by many Americans does not mean that politicians trying to compare themselves with him will always be successful. Casting oneself as his ideological successor, or even as being comparable with him in one way or another, may or may not work. Perhaps the most obvious, and amusing, example of this came during the 1988 presidential election in the vice presidential debate between Dan Quayle and Lloyd Bentsen. Quayle, running with George H.W. Bush, faced skepticism that he was too young for the second most important position in the country. During the debate, Quayle argued that his experience more than compensated for his youth and compared his record with that of JFK: "I have far more experience than many others that sought the office of vice-president in this country. I have as much experience in the Congress as Jack Kennedy did when he sought the presidency." Bentsen, thinking that a favorable comparison between Quayle and John Kennedy was an insult to the latter, quickly responded, "Senator, I served with Jack Kennedy. I knew Jack Kennedy. Jack Kennedy was a friend of mine. Senator, you are no Jack Kennedy."[22] Presidents Clinton and Obama, their respective similarities to Kennedy notwithstanding, did not always succeed in their efforts to be compared with him. While both were praised for their charisma and public speaking abilities, their White House rhetoric was largely unmemorable; their speeches often were discussions (sometimes lengthy) of policy details or proposals instead of the imagery and persuasive prose commonly found in JFK's addresses.[23] And in one of the few stumbles committed by the 2008 Obama campaign, Senator Obama claimed that his father had been able to study in the United States thanks to travel funding arranged by then-Senator Kennedy. That led eventually to the marriage of Obama, Sr. and Ann Dunham; Senator Obama argued that he owed his "very existence" to the beneficence of JFK. This turned out not to be true. Obama's father had arrived in the U.S. as part of a study group the year before Kennedy's donation enabled another group of African students to come.[24]

In concluding this work, some explanation is appropriate on how popular memory is written about, or more specifically, the challenges involved in doing so. The foremost challenge is the simple fact that memory is intangible. One is trying to draw boundaries around something that is formless, and because of that, it can be difficult to see it as an entity with power or definite meaning. This effort contrasts with, for example, researching JFK and American relations with West Germany during his presidency. There, the objectives, motivations, background discussions and reactions from the principal players are more likely to be thoroughly

documented. Because a great deal of evidence upon which to base a study
of such a topic exists, a subject like this takes on a more definite character.
But the hazy quality of memory presents a problem for the author writing
about it decades after the events in question because that haziness stems
from what we often do *not* see in the primary sources. It is not always
clear what motivates people to act in a certain way, and we do not always
record the exact reasons behind *why* we do what we do. During the course
of my research, I was pleased but also sometimes surprised when people
very clearly cited the public's memory of President Kennedy in bare
political terms, although I think this proved to be the exception overall. I
did occasionally encounter this clarity, but even in the realm of internal
White House conversations it could be rare. Memoirs and President
Johnson's taping system yielded several examples of the realization of
how important the public's emotions for Kennedy were from a political
standpoint. Speaking with Florida Senator Smathers, Johnson explicitly
made the connection between his predecessor, the enactment of his tax
cut, and the political viability of the Democratic Party (and, needless
to say, of himself) in the 1964 elections. Dr. Martin Luther King, Jr.
observed in another phone call that honoring the memory of JFK *had* to
assume a primarily political dimension through the passage of his civil
rights legislation. Arthur Schlesinger, Jr. bitterly recorded a variation of
this in his diary: LBJ was trying to coast along on JFK's agenda while
simultaneously attempting to "erase" his memory. And Johnson aide
Marvin Watson, if the story he related in his memoirs is credible, bluntly
told DNC chairman Bailey that the memory of Kennedy—as essentially a
political commodity—rightfully belonged to his constitutional successor,
to be used for his own benefit. Obvious references to that memory, or the
recognition that invoking it carried political benefits, were fairly few in
number, and more often the presence or importance of memory needed
to be teased out of the primary sources.

But doing this presented another potential pitfall: the temptation to
read too much into references to the late president wherever they were
found. Finding those references repeatedly, in a variety of places among

numerous people, can uncover the practical uses of popular memory at work, but overanalyzing some brief mention of JFK in a speech or newspaper article may, or will, assign it an importance it was never intended to have. The power of popular memory can be seen by reading between the lines where it is not talked about directly, but it remains true that sometimes a cigar can turn out to be simply a cigar. And especially when the issue is President Kennedy's death, we can understand how those tasked with carrying on in his name would have needed to be tasteful—if nothing else, circumspect—in how they attached themselves to his memory. For anybody who lived through it, this was a highly traumatic and emotional event, and we cannot overlook the fact that many Americans regarded it as the time as a *personal* tragedy. Anyone who sought to invoke the "martyred" president had to do so carefully and a bit elliptically. We really cannot expect, in looking at the records from the first few weeks of the Johnson presidency, or at how Robert Kennedy's aides remembered his hesitant steps toward deciding on a presidential bid, that they would have talked openly about memory of JFK in terms of its political efficacy. The idea that the slain president, with only Washington and Lincoln as his supposed equals in American history, was being used for political gain would have been seen as crass and opportunistic—characteristics that indeed were assigned to LBJ and RFK. And yet, at the risk of being crass, if the memory of Kennedy was not to become simply a topic for historians to ponder, what other purpose could it have been used for? We may regard it as inevitable or natural that the nation would have paid tribute to Kennedy in any number of ways, but there was a complex and even contradictory response from the three cases discussed in this work, and also perhaps among the public, as to how it should be done. In each case, the protagonists recognized that memory of Kennedy mattered. Yet, there was hesitation over being too overt in trying to benefit from it, but also a willingness to use that memory without going *too* far with it, and finally, a conviction that it could and *should* be used for something lest he be forgotten. All of these impulses merged as Dallas city leaders, Lyndon Johnson, Robert Kennedy, and the public tried to understand what JFK meant in death, and what they could accomplish in response. Many must have realized that even the deepest and most sincere reverence for the late president would still need some practical application if he were to mean anything, as if squeezing the juice out of his memory was the best way to preserve the fruit.

Eric Foner's study of American freedom is another example of how an abstract idea can in fact be examined as a concrete, even energetic, entity. Freedom has always been a powerful concept throughout American history. It has been invoked to explain why we became our own nation, to justify our actions abroad (especially in the twentieth century) and sometimes at home, and to define what makes the United States unique in the world. But Foner argues that freedom has been a *changing* concept during the past two centuries: different groups in different eras have disagreed and sometimes clashed over what exactly freedom means in political, social, and economic terms, and for whom. Far from being simply an unchanging, lofty idea to which Americans have always professed fidelity as a part of our national identity, freedom instead has had particular meanings and has been used for specific objectives. During the Great Depression, for example, many people came to understand freedom in economic terms, with Franklin Roosevelt and others arguing that strictly political freedom had little real value unless citizens were also endowed with at least a reasonable standard of living. The New Deal, moreover, was sold not simply as a series of necessary measures to confront widespread economic strife. More broadly, the legislation enacted during the 1930s signified that the federal government was the ultimate guarantor of freedom, not only with respect to safeguarding national sovereignty, or the ability of citizens to participate in their government, but now including the ability to feed one's family and to at least a minimal amount of economic security in old age.[25] Writing about how the idea of freedom is important not simply as an abstract force in the background of our history, but because of its ability to mean different things to different people in different eras, and because of the very definite consequences of this, Foner observes thus:

> Freedom embodies not a single idea but a complex of values...A morally charged idea, freedom has been used to convey and claim legitimacy for all kinds of grievances and hopes, fears about the present and visions of the future...As groups from the abolitionists to modern-day conservatives have realized, to 'capture' a word like freedom is to acquire a formidable position of strength in political conflicts.[26]

The same is true when we think about popular memory and President Kennedy. Foner took an idea that appears abstract because we all supposedly believe in it and acknowledge it as an enduring force in our history. But examined up close, freedom had provoked far more disagreement over its meaning—and therefore, its uses, and therefore, who is to benefit from it. Memory takes on a similar dynamic and raises similar questions. We say that we remember JFK, that we memorialize him, or that we pay tribute to him. But what do we actually mean? What specifically are we choosing to remember? To what extent are our predominant memories of him distorted or incomplete? Does it even matter whether what we have remembered aligns with the truth? Does popular memory, at least insofar as Kennedy is concerned, ever become fairly settled in terms of what we remember, or is it subject to continual reassessment, or even irrelevance, as time goes on and more of the nation's collective memory is "prosthetic"? Freedom, in other words, is an enduring American concept and there will probably continue to be differing opinions as to its definition and scope, but will memory of JFK have any importance for us fifty or one hundred years from now?

All of this brings us back to the idea of Pierre Nora's *lieu de mémoire*. While it was not my intention to use his "site of memory" idea as a sort of theoretical framework—to use President Kennedy and popular memory to prove or disprove Nora—his anthology on memory and French history provides a similar comparison with the subject matter herein. The idea behind Nora's *lieu de mémoire* is that we commonly recognize certain historical events or people as important due to the change that occurred because of them, but we do not all remember a particular event or person the same way. In one such example, Joan of Arc has been remembered through several centuries by the French people in multiple ways, depending on which group is invoking her and what their purposes are. Memory is not objective. Although a discussion of Nora's analysis is beyond the scope of this work, suffice it to say that Nora differentiates memory from history in part because history is supposedly grounded in the dispassionate study of past events. It is a "representation of the past."[27] Memory, strangely enough, is more about the *present* than we may think. Emotion and perception are very much a part of what and how we remember, and memory can exist on different levels. Nora defines one as "memory as an individual duty," resulting in people who are not historians rebuilding the past through such activities as genealogical studies of their families, or to preserve the activities of the present by documenting important events from their lives. Yet, memory can also be a means of identifying with a group, even if the group is an entire country.[28] The great French heroine has had ongoing usefulness as different groups of the nation simultaneously pay tribute to her while trying to benefit from her historical glow. Joan has even been invoked in recent decades as a symbol of European unity, thus seeming to give her seal of approval to the increasing political and economic fusion of France with the rest of Western Europe. The use of Joan of Arc for more self-serving purposes—winning elections—led Michel Winock to comment in the Nora anthology, "For some, Joan's sword symbolized not patriotic unity...but partisan combat."[29]

Admittedly, it is a cynical conception of memory that we commemorate a revered historical figure not for its own sake or because he or she represents the history and triumphs of a nation, but for particular reasons that may not command much reverence. This view suggests that we do not always have the purest or most honest of motives in how and why we remember. But it also points out how, over the course of several decades or even centuries, the same symbol can unite while still instigating dispute as to what that symbol means and who "owns" it. Such has certainly been true in how Americans have remembered John F. Kennedy. His memory has been colored and shaped to emphasize whatever aspect of him proved useful at the time. What we remember, in other words, is oftentimes more influenced by what we *want* and *choose* to believe, instead of what is actually true. Dallas remembered JFK for his belief in tolerance, brotherhood, and dedication to grand ideals because that is how the city could overcome the hatred directed toward it in the weeks and months after the assassination. The belief that he was the embodiment of such grand attributes should be taken with skepticism, but that hardly mattered. We have seen likewise with Lyndon Johnson. He encouraged the American people to believe that his predecessor was a civil rights president, and to memorialize him as such through one of the most important civil rights laws of our history—even though Kennedy's record on the issue reveals a hesitant and late commitment to the cause. And Robert Kennedy remembered his brother as unwilling to involve the country in Vietnam any more than he already had, for fear that greater American participation would have led to disaster. This, of course, is little more than speculation. JFK's contradictory course of action on Vietnam has confounded us over the years.[30]

So memory, paradoxically, is not always about remembering what actually happened or what reality is. The question of why popular memory has taken a different direction from the historiography on JFK is because memory simply does not depend solely on facts. And because so much of what we remember about Kennedy is what he *said* or what we think he *intended* to do, more than what he actually did, we can credit him for solving any problem, and for making the world the more hopeful place it surely would have been had he lived. As one writer on JFK observed, "The alchemy's magic might have been reversed—gold returned to base metal—had Kennedy remained in office. But in death, Kennedy never fell short of his goals...He continued to represent a glowing future, *one that could never be* [original italics]. His death didn't mean the end of his power, but its fulfillment."[31] The ambiguity that is permanently a part of John Kennedy has somehow nonetheless produced a certainty in how we have remembered him.

The way we remember or commemorate an event or historical figure says as much (or possibly more) about our agenda and interests as it does about the actual thing being remembered. In the case of JFK, we have remembered only the positive aspects of his life and presidency, and magnified them considerably. Building him up to the extent that we do enables us to remember his time in office as a period of indisputable national greatness and innocence—meaning that we can remember ourselves the same way. As Garry Wills wrote, "The Kennedys rightly dazzled America. We thought it was our own light being reflected back on us. The charismatic claims looked natural to a charismatic country."[32] So devastatingly succinct is Anthony Hopkins' remark in *Nixon*: "When they look at you, they see what they want to be." A character's line crafted by a film writer reveals one of the main components of popular memory: our own preferences and needs in how we commemorate. The *real* John F. Kennedy, like the *real* Joan of Arc, isn't necessarily what is remembered; it may not even matter. Memory, at least in the case of JFK, is not about depicting the reality of him, however great or mundane it may be. Instead, it is about constructing a set of images and attributes we assign to Kennedy that reflect what we want to remember, emphasizing those aspects of his life that serve our purposes. The fact that we prevent the seedier side of John Kennedy from negatively influencing popular memory only highlights, like the case of Joan of Arc in the Nora anthology, the ease with which we can direct memory to where we want it to go.

Memory of John Kennedy becomes whatever we want it to become, and the fact that he has meant different things to different people is proof enough of Nora's assertion that we can all remember the same person or event "without feeling any unanimity" about it.[33] And as long as we still find value in identifying ourselves or our cause with JFK—as long as we can still use our 35th president to legitimize what we do and promote ourselves by remembering him—popular memory of him will remain as powerful as Dallas city leaders, Lyndon Johnson, and Robert Kennedy all discovered it to be.

NOTES

1. M. Edelson, "The Week: Robert F. Kennedy, RIP," *National Review* July 2, 1968 (Vol. 20, No. 26), 644.
2. Michael Kazin, "John F. Kennedy: 1961-1963," in Alan Brinkley and Davis Dyer (eds.), *The American Presidency* (Boston: Houghton Mifflin Company, 2004), 397.
3. W.J. Rorabaugh, *Kennedy and the Promise of the Sixties*, 227.
4. Garry Wills, *The Kennedy Imprisonment: A Meditation on Power* (Boston: Little, Brown and Company, 1981), 28-29.
5. Thomas C. Reeves, *A Question of Character*, 406-407, 414-415.
6. Herbert S. Parmet, *JFK*, 353-355.
7. "JFK: The Inside Story," *Parade* May 4, 2008, 23.
8. Gretchen Rubin, *Forty Ways to Look at JFK* (New York: Ballantine Books, 2005), 285.
9. Richard N. Goodwin, *Remembering America*, 8.
10. Thomas C. Reeves, *A Question of Character*, 421.
11. Gretchen Rubin, *Forty Ways to Look at JFK*, 119-120.
12. Eric Foner, *Give Me Liberty! An American History: Volume 2—From 1865* (New York: W.W. Norton & Company, 2008), 973. (2nd ed.)
13. Mark C. Carnes and John A. Garraty, *American Destiny: Narrative of a Nation, Volume 2—Since 1865* (New York: Pearson Longman, 2006), 827, 834. (2nd ed.)
14. Robert A. Divine, T.H. Breen, et al., *America Past & Present, Volume 2, Special Texas Edition—Since 1865* (New York: Pearson Custom Publishing, 2005), 859-866, 869. (7th ed.)
15. James L. Roark, Michael P. Johnson, et al., *The American Promise: A History of the United States, Volume II—From 1865* (Boston: Bedford/St. Martin's, 2002), 1023-1027. (2nd ed.)
16. See also John M. Murrin, Paul E. Johnson, et al., *Liberty, Equality, Power: A History of the American People, Volume II—Since 1863* (Belmont, CA: Wadsworth/Thompson Learning, 2005), 895-900 (4th ed.); and Thomas A. Bailey, David M. Kennedy, et al., *The American Pageant: A History of the Republic* (Boston: Houghton Mifflin Company, 1998), 937-945. (11th ed.)
17. John Hellman, *The Kennedy Obsession*, 146.
18. "Will Edward Kennedy Now Move Up?" *U.S. News & World Report* June 24, 1968 (Vol. 64, No. 26), 40.

19. Peter Collier & David Horowitz, *The Kennedys: An American Drama* (New York: Warner Books, 1984), 547-564.

20. James N. Giglio, *The Presidency of John F. Kennedy*, 282.

21. Larry Sabato, *The Kennedy Half Century: The Presidency, Assassination, and Lasting Legacy of John F. Kennedy* (New York: Bloomsbury, 2013), 370-371, 378, 396-399.

22. Paul F. Boller, Jr., *Presidential Campaigns* (New York: Oxford University Press, 1996), 385.

23. Larry Sabato, *The Kennedy Half Century*, 378, 396-399; and Matthew Dickinson, "Bill Clinton, in Alan Brinkley and Davis Dyer (eds.), *The American Presidency*, 527.

24. Larry Sabato, *The Kennedy Half Century*, 397-398; and Michael Dobbs, "Obama Overstates Kennedys' Role in Helping His Father," *Washington Post*, March 30, 2008.

25. Eric Foner, *The Story of American Freedom* (New York: W.W. Norton & Company, 1998), 196-197, 204-205.

26. Ibid., xv-xvi.

27. Pierre Nora, "General Introduction," *Realms of Memory*, 3.

28. Ibid., 10-11.

29. Michel Winock, "Joan of Arc,"*Realms of Memory*, 469.

30. That is to say, JFK moved in both directions regarding Vietnam during his presidency; for this reason, his ultimate intent remains one of the principal areas of debate among historians. He opposed deploying American combat troops to South Vietnam, yet deepened our commitment by greatly increasing the number of military advisers. At different times in his career, he both accepted and questioned the "domino theory." Indeed, his intended remarks at the Trade Mart in Dallas reiterated the importance of continued involvement in some form. Citing several nations that were beneficiaries of American foreign aid, including South Vietnam, the President was to have said, "No one of these countries possesses on its own the resources to maintain the forces which our own Chiefs of Staff think needed in the common interest. Reducing our efforts to train, equip, and assist their armies can only encourage Communist penetration and require in time the increased overseas deployment of American combat forces." Historian Lawrence Freedman argued that it is difficult to say whether JFK would have acted differently from LBJ on Vietnam. Kennedy likely would have made a more genuine effort to find an exit strategy, but "Kennedy, like Johnson, would have faced a growing mismatch between his commitment to South Vietnam and the means

available to sustain this commitment." Kennedy biographer Robert Dallek postulated that, especially after the Diem coup in early November 1963, JFK was increasingly disinclined to continue expanding the American presence. Dallek cited Kennedy's comment to an aide that a full-scale review of American options in Vietnam would be undertaken in early 1964. In appraising the President's possible choices, historians Lawrence Bassett and Stephen Pelz argued that what truly was a contradictory administration record left him in a difficult place. "Though some of his defenders have claimed he would have withdrawn...after his re-election in 1964, they underestimate the degree to which Kennedy had committed himself and the country to supporting a non-Communist Vietnam. Kennedy would have had to admit the failure of his major counter-insurgency effort." Bassett and Pelz continue, "More likely than withdrawal was a continued search for the right combination of means and men to win the war...Kennedy would probably have ruled out sending in United States Army infantry divisions, but short of that limit, he would probably have continued to make a major effort to succeed." In the end, there remains ample ground to argue for either withdrawal/negotiation, or escalation/continued American commitment, had JFK not been killed. Public Papers of the Presidents/American Presidency Project, "John F. Kennedy: Prepared Remarks for Delivery at the Trade Mart in Dallas, November 22, 1963," available from http://www.presidency.ucsb.edu/ws/index.php?pid=9539&st=&st1=#axzz1N0GuGfRh; accessed from Internet May 21, 2014; and Lawrence Freedman, *Kennedy's Wars*, 400, 413; and Robert Dallek, *An Unfinished Life*, 684-686; and Lawrence J. Bassett and Stephen E. Pelz, "The Failed Search for Victory," in Thomas G. Paterson (ed.), *Kennedy's Quest for Victory*, 226, 252.

31. Gretchen Rubin, *Forty Ways to Look at JFK*, 294.
32. Garry Wills, *The Kennedy Imprisonment*, 275.
33. Pierre Nora, "General Introduction," *Realms of Memory*, 7.

BIBLIOGRAPHY

UNPUBLISHED PRIMARY SOURCES

Bridwell Library

    Collection on Levi Olan

    Subject Files, William A. Holmes

DeGolyer Special Collections Library

    Earle Cabell papers

    J. Erik Jonsson papers

    Stanley Marcus papers

Department of Justice

    Speeches of Attorney General Robert F. Kennedy (online)

John F. Kennedy Presidential Library

    David F. Powers Personal papers

    JFK Library permanent exhibit, explanatory materials, library website and online interactive exhibits

    Pre-Presidential Papers

    Presidential Campaign Files, 1960

    Presidential Papers

    President's Office Files, Evelyn Lincoln

    White House Staff Files

Harris Wofford

John F. Kennedy Oral History collection

Edwin R. Bayley

David Ben-Gurion

Maurice M. Bernbaum

Leland J. Barrows

Robert F. Kennedy Oral History collection

Joseph W. Alsop

John J. Burns

C. Douglas Dillon

William O. Douglas

Rowland Evans, Jr.

Robert F. Kennedy Senate papers

Robert P. Fitzgerald Personal papers

Selected Speeches of JFK (online speech texts)

Tom Putnam (Director) email exchange

Lyndon B. Johnson Presidential Library

Legislative Background and Domestic Crises File

Office Files of White House Aides

Richard N. Goodwin

Mike Manatos

Fred Panzer

Ben Wattenberg

Henry H. Wilson, Jr.

Lee White

Reports on Enrolled Legislation

Selected Speeches and Messages of LBJ (online speech texts)

Byron Skelton papers

Statements of LBJ

White House Central Files

Oral History collection

Stewart Alsop

George Reedy

Peace Corps

Remarks of Senator John F. Kennedy, October 14, 1960 (online)

Sixth Floor Museum at Dealey Plaza

"John F. Kennedy and the Memory of a Nation," Main Exhibit and explanatory materials

Oral History collection

Jerry Bartos

Bronson Havard

Rev. William A. Holmes

Lee Jackson

J. Erik Jonsson

Dr. Glenn Linden

Robert Staples & Barbara Charles

Wes Wise

Visitor Memory Books (digitized)

PUBLISHED PRIMARY SOURCES

Atkins, Ollie. *The White House Years: Triumph and Tragedy.* Chicago: Playboy Press, 1977.

Beschloss, Michael R. (ed.). *Jacqueline Kennedy: Historic Conversations on Life with John F. Kennedy.* New York: Hyperion, 2011.

Beschloss, Michael R. (ed.). *Taking Charge: The Johnson White House Tapes, 1963-1964.* New York: Simon & Schuster, 1997.

Califano, Jr., Joseph A. *The Triumph and Tragedy of Lyndon Johnson: The White House Years.* College Station: Texas A&M University Press, 2000.

Carney, Francis M. and H. Frank Way, Jr. (eds.). *Politics 1964.* Belmont, California: Wadsworth Publishing Company, Inc., 1964.

Clinton, Bill. *My Life.* New York: Alfred A. Knopf, 2004.

Fitzpatrick, Ellen. *Letters to Jackie: Condolences from a Grieving Nation.* New York: Ecco, 2010.

Germany, Kent B. and Robert David Johnson (eds.). *The Presidential Recordings of Lyndon B. Johnson: The Kennedy Assassination and the Transfer of Power, November 1963-January 1964*, Volume Three. New York: W.W. Norton and Company, 2005.

Goodwin, Richard N. *Remembering America: A Voice from the Sixties.* Boston: Little, Brown and Company, 1988.

Guthman, Edwin O. and C. Richard Allen (eds.). *RFK: Collected Speeches.* New York: Viking Penguin, 1993.

Guthman, Edwin O. and Jeffrey Schulman (eds.). *Robert Kennedy in His Own Words: The Unpublished Recollections of the Kennedy Years.* New York: Bantam Press, 1988.

Holland, Max (ed.). *The Presidential Recordings of Lyndon B. Johnson: The Kennedy Assassination and the Transfer of Power, November 1963-January 1964*, Volume One. New York: W.W. Norton & Company, 2005.

Johnson, Lady Bird. *A White House Diary*. Austin: University of Texas Press, 2007.

Johnson, Lyndon B. *The Vantage Point: Perspectives on the Presidency, 1963-1969*. New York: Holt, Rinehart and Winston, 1971.

Kennedy, Edward M. *True Compass: A Memoir*. New York: Twelve, 2009.

Kennedy, John F. *Profiles in Courage*, Memorial Edition. New York: Harper & Row, 1964.

Kennedy, Robert F. *Thirteen Days: A Memoir of the Cuban Missile Crisis*. New York: W.W. Norton & Company, Inc., 1968.

Kennedy, Robert F. *To Seek a Newer World*. New York: Bantam Books, 1968.

Lincoln, Evelyn. *Kennedy and Johnson*. New York: Holt, Rinehart and Winston, 1968.

Nixon, Richard. *In the Arena: A Memoir of Victory, Defeat, and Renewal*. New York: Simon & Schuster, 1990.

Nixon, Richard. *RN: The Memoirs of Richard Nixon*. New York: Simon & Schuster, 1990.

O'Donnell, Helen. *A Common Good: The Friendship of Robert F. Kennedy and Kenneth P. O'Donnell*. New York: William Morrow and Company, Inc., 1998.

Plouffe, David. *The Audacity to Win: The Inside Story of Barack Obama's Historic Victory*. New York: Viking, 2009.

Public Papers of the Presidents: Carter, Jimmy

Public Papers of the Presidents: Kennedy, John F.

Public Papers of the Presidents: Johnson, Lyndon B.

Salinger, Pierre and Sander Vanocur (eds.). *A Tribute to John F. Kennedy*. New York: Dell Publishing Co., 1964.

Schlesinger, Jr., Arthur. *Journals: 1952-2000.* New York: The Penguin Press, 2007.

Sorensen, Ted. *Counselor: A Life at the Edge of History.* New York: Harper-Collins, 2008.

Sorensen, Ted. *The Kennedy Legacy: A Peaceful Revolution for the Seventies.* New York: The Macmillan Company, 1969.

Strober, Gerald S. and Deborah H. *"Let Us Begin Anew:" An Oral History of the Kennedy Presidency.* New York: HarperCollins Publishers, 1993.

Watson, W. Martin and Sherwin Markman. *Chief of Staff: Lyndon Johnson and His Presidency.* New York: Thomas Dunne Books-St. Martin's Press, 2004.

Newspapers and Periodicals

The American Archivist

American Historical Review

Chicago Tribune

Christianity in Crisis

Congressional Record

Dallas Morning News

Dallas Times Herald

Fortune 500

Government Information Quarterly

Houston Post

In the Capital

Legacies

Life

Look

Los Angeles Times

Milwaukee Journal Sentinel

The Nation

National Geographic

National Review

New Republic

New York Times

Newsweek

Parade

Philadelphia Inquirer

Time

U.S. News & World Report

Vanity Fair

Wall Street Journal

Washington Post

SECONDARY SOURCES

Abbot, Arlinda. *Dealey Plaza: The Front Door of Dallas.* Dallas: The Sixth Floor Museum, 2003.

Anderson, Terry H. *The Sixties.* New York: Pearson Longman, 2004.

Andrew III, John A. *Lyndon B. Johnson and the Great Society.* Chicago: Ivan R. Dee, 1998.

Bailey, Thomas A., David M. Kennedy, et al. *The American Pageant: A History of the Republic.* Boston: Houghton Mifflin Company, 1998.

Baker, Leonard. *The Johnson Eclipse: A President's Vice Presidency.* New York: The Macmillan Company, 1966.

Bass, Warren. *Support Any Friend: Kennedy's Middle East and the Making of the U.S.-Israel Alliance.* New York: Oxford University Press, 2003.

Bassett, Lawrence J. and Stephen E. Pelz, "The Failed Search for Victory: Vietnam and the Politics of War," in Thomas G. Paterson (ed.),

Kennedy's Quest for Victory: American Foreign Policy, 1961-1963. New York: Oxford University Press, 1989.

Ballinger, Lacie. *The Rededication of the John Fitzgerald Kennedy Memorial: June 24, 2000.* Dallas: The Sixth Floor Museum, 2000.

Beaver, Frank. *Oliver Stone: Wakeup America.* New York: Twayne Publishers, 1994.

Beschloss, Michael R. *The Crisis Years: Kennedy and Khrushchev, 1960-1963.* New York: HarperCollins, 1991.

Bishop, Jim. *The Day Kennedy Was Shot.* New York: Gramercy Books, 1968.

Blow, Steve, and Sam Attlesey. "The Tenor of the Times: Far right-wingers and Democratic discords set the stage for Kennedy's visit," in Steve Blow, et al., *November 22: The Day Remembered as Reported by The Dallas Morning News.* Dallas: Taylor Publishing Company, 1990.

Boller, Jr., Paul F. *Presidential Campaigns.* New York: Oxford University Press, 1996.

Boller, Jr., Paul F. *Presidential Wives: An Anecdotal History.* New York: Oxford University Press, 1998.

Bryant, Nick. *The Bystander: John F. Kennedy and the Struggle for Black Equality.* New York: Basic Books, 2006.

Bugliosi, Vincent. *Reclaiming History: The Assassination of President John F. Kennedy.* New York: W.W. Norton & Company, 2007.

Bzdek, Vincent. *The Kennedy Legacy: Jack, Bobby and Ted and a Family Dream Fulfilled.* New York: Palgrave Macmillan, 2009.

Cannell, Michael. *I.M. Pei: Mandarin of Modernism.* New York: Carol Southern Books, 1995.

Cannon, Lou. *Governor Reagan: His Rise to Power.* New York: PublicAffairs, 2003.

Carnes, Mark C., and John A. Garraty. *American Destiny: Narrative of a Nation, Volume 2—Since 1865.* New York: Pearson Longman, 2006 (2nd ed.).

Caro, Robert A. *The Years of Lyndon Johnson: Means of Ascent.* New York: Alfred A. Knopf, 1990.

Caro, Robert A. *The Years of Lyndon Johnson: The Passage of Power.* New York: Alfred A. Knopf, 2012.

Caroli, Betty Boyd. *First Ladies: From Martha Washington to Michelle Obama.* New York: Oxford University Press, 2010.

Catton, Bruce. "Introduction," in *Four Days: The Historical Record of the Death of President Kennedy compiled by United Press International and American Heritage Magazine.* New York: American Heritage Publishing Co., Inc., 1964.

Collier, Peter and David Horowitz. *The Kennedys: An American Drama.* New York: Warner Books, 1984.

Dallek, Robert. *Flawed Giant: Lyndon Johnson and His Times, 1961-1973.* New York: Oxford University Press, 1998.

Dallek, Robert. *Hail to the Chief: The Making and Unmaking of American Presidents.* Oxford: Oxford University Press, 1996.

Dallek, Robert. *An Unfinished Life: John F. Kennedy, 1917-1963.* Boston: Little, Brown and Company, 2003.

DeGroot, Gerard J. *Dark Side of the Moon: The Magnificent Madness of the American Lunar Quest.* New York: New York University Press, 2006.

Dickinson, Matthew. "Bill Clinton: 1993-2001," in Alan Brinkley and Davis Dyer (eds.), *The American Presidency.* Boston: Houghton Mifflin Company, 2004.

Divine, Robert A., T.H. Breen, et al. *America Past and Present, Volume 2, Special Texas Edition—Since 1865.* New York: Pearson Custom Publishing, 2005 (7th ed.).

Donald, David Herbert. *Lincoln.* New York: Simon & Schuster, 1995.

Donaldson, Gary. *Liberalism's Last Hurrah: The Presidential Campaign of 1964.* Armonk, New York: M.E. Sharpe, 2003.

Ellis, Joseph J. *His Excellency: George Washington.* New York: Vintage, 2005.

Evans, Rowland and Robert Novak. *Lyndon B. Johnson: The Exercise of Power*. New York: The New American Library, Inc., 1966.

Eppridge, Bill. *A Time It Was: Bobby Kennedy in the Sixties*. New York: Harry N. Abrams, Inc., 2008.

Fairbanks, Robert. *For the City as a Whole: Planning, Politics, and the Public Interest in Dallas, Texas, 1900-1965*. Columbus: Ohio State University Press, 1998.

Flournoy, Craig. "Dallas on Trial: Accusations and Self-Doubts Torment the City," in Steve Blow, et al., *November 22: The Day Remembered as Reported by the Dallas Morning News*. Dallas: Taylor Publishing Company, 1990.

Foner, Eric. *Give Me Liberty! An American History, Volume 2—From 1865*. New York: W.W. Norton & Company, 2008 (2nd ed.).

Foner, Eric. *The Story of American Freedom*. New York: W.W. Norton & Company, 1998.

Freedman, Lawrence. *JFK's Wars: Berlin, Cuba, Laos, and Vietnam*. Oxford: Oxford University Press, 2000.

Giglio, James N. *The Presidency of John F. Kennedy*. Lawrence: University of Kansas Press, 1991.

Goodman, Jon, et al. *The Kennedy Mystique: Creating Camelot*. Washington, D.C.: National Geographic, 2006.

Goodwin, Doris Kearns. *Lyndon Johnson and the American Dream*. New York: Harper & Row, 1976.

Gould, Lewis L. *The Modern American Presidency*. Lawrence: University Press of Kansas, 2003.

Graff, Harvey. *Dallas Myth: The Making and Unmaking of an American City*. Minneapolis: University of Minnesota Press, 2008.

Greene, John Robert. *The Presidency of George Bush*. Lawrence: University Press of Kansas, 2000.

Halberstam, David. *The Best and the Brightest*. New York: Ballantine Books, 1969.

Halberstam, David. *The Unfinished Odyssey of Robert Kennedy.* New York: Ramdom House, 1968.

Heath, Jim F. *Decade of Disillusionment: The Kennedy-Johnson Years.* Bloomington: Indiana University Press, 1975.

Hellman, John. *The Kennedy Obsession: The American Myth of JFK.* New York: Columbia University Press, 1997.

Henggeler, Paul R. *In His Steps: Lyndon Johnson and the Kennedy Mystique.* Chicago: Ivan R. Dee, 1991.

Herring, George C. *America's Longest War: The United States and Vietnam, 1950-1975.* New York: McGraw-Hill, Inc., 1996.

Hersh, Seymour M. *The Dark Side of Camelot.* Boston: Little, Brown and Company, 1997.

Hilty, James W. *Robert Kennedy: Brother Protector.* Philadelphia: Temple University Press, 1997.

Hodgson, Godfrey. *America in Our Time: From World War II to Nixon —What Happened and Why.* Princeton: Princeton University Press, 2005.

Hufbauer, Benjamin. *Presidential Temples: How Memorials and Libraries Shape Public Memory.* Lawrence: University Press of Kansas, 2005.

Huffaker, Bob. "Epicenter of Grief," in Bob Huffaker, et al. *When the News Went Live: Dallas 1963.* Lanham: Taylor Trade Publishing, 2004.

Hunt, Conover. *JFK For a New Generation.* Dallas: The Sixth Floor Museum and Southern Methodist University, 1996.

Isserman, Maurice, and Michael Kazin. *America Divided: The Civil War of the 1960s.* New York: Oxford University Press, 2000.

Johnson, Robert David. *All the Way with LBJ: The 1964 Presidential Election Campaign.* Cambridge: Cambridge University Press, 2009.

Jones, Howard. *Death of a Generation: How the Assassinations of Diem and JFK Prolonged the Vietnam War.* New York: Oxford University Press, 2003.

Kagan, Norman. *The Cinema of Oliver Stone.* New York: Continuum, 2000.

Kaiser, Charles. *1968 in America: Music, Politics, Chaos, Counterculture, and the Shaping of a Generation.* New York: Grove Press, 1988.

Kaiser, David. *The Road to Dallas: The Assassination of John F. Kennedy.* Cambridge: The Belknap Press, 2008.

Kane, Joseph Nathan Kane. *Presidential Fact Book.* New York: Random House, Inc., 1998.

Kauffman, James L. *Selling Outer Space: Kennedy, the Media, and Funding for Project Apollo.* Tuscaloosa: The University of Alabama Press, 1994.

Kazin, Michael. "John F. Kennedy: 1961-1963," in Alan Brinkley and Davis Dyer (eds.), *The American Presidency.* Boston: Houghton Mifflin Company, 2004.

Knight, Peter. *The Kennedy Assassination.* Jackson: University Press of Mississippi, 2007.

Kritzman, Lawrence D. "In Remembrance of Things French," in Pierre Nora, ed. *Realms of Memory: Rethinking the French Past* (Vol. I). Translated by Arthur Goldhammer. New York: Columbia University Press, 1996.

Kurtz, Michael L. *The Kennedy Assassination Debates: Lone Gunman versus Conspiracy.* Lawrence: University of Kansas Press, 2006.

Landsberg, Alison. *Prosthetic Memory: The Transformation of American Remembrance in the Age of Mass Culture.* New York: Columbia University Press, 2004.

Lane, Mark. *Rush to Judgment.* New York; Holt, Rinehart & Winston, 1966.

Lederer, William J. and Eugene Burdick. *The Ugly American.* New York: W.W. Norton & Company, 1958.

Leslie, Warren. *Dallas Public and Private: Aspects of an American City.* New York: Grossman Publishers, 1964.

Leuchtenberg, William E. *In the Shadow of FDR: From Harry Truman to George W. Bush.* Ithaca: Cornell University Press, 2001.

Livingstone, Harrison Edward, and Robert J. Groden. *High Treason: The Assassination of JFK and the Case for Conspiracy.* New York: Carroll & Graf Publishers, 1998.

McKnight, Gerald D. *Breach of Trust: How the Warren Commission Failed the Nation and Why.* Lawrence: University of Kansas Press, 2005.

McPherson, James M. (ed.). *To the Best of My Ability: The American Presidents.* New York: Dorling Kindersley, 2000.

Maraniss, David. *When Pride Still Mattered: A Life of Vince Lombardi.* New York: Touchstone, 1999.

Marrs, Jim. *Crossfire: The Plot that Killed Kennedy.* New York: Carroll & Graf Publishers, Inc., 1989.

May, Gary. "Passing the Torth and Lighting Fires: The Peace Corps," in Thomas G. Paterson (ed.), *Kennedy's Quest for Victory: American Foreign Policy, 1961-1963.* New York: Oxford University Press, 1989.

Mercer, Bill. "Gunman, Mob, and Mourners," in Bob Huffaker, et al. *When the News Went Live: Dallas 1963.* Lanham: Taylor Trade Publishing, 2004.

Milkis, Sidney, and Michael Nelson. *The American Presidency: Origins and Development, 1776-2002.* Washington, D.C.: CQ Press, 2003.

Minutaglio, Bill, and Steven L. Davis. *Dallas 1963.* New York: Twelve, 2013.

Murrin, John M., Paul E. Johnson, et al. *Liberty, Equality, Power: A History of the American People, Volume II—Since 1863.* Belmont, CA: Wadsworth/Thompson Learning, 2005 (4th ed.).

Newfield, Jack. *Robert Kennedy: A Memoir.* New York: E.P. Dutton & Co., Inc., 1969.

Nora, Pierre. "General Introduction: Between Memory and History," in Pierre Nora (ed.), *Realms of Memory: Rethinking the French Past* (Vol. I). Translated by Arthur Goldhammer. New York: Columbia University Press, 1996.

O'Brien, Michael. *John F. Kennedy: A Biography.* New York: St. Martin's Griffin, 2006.

Pach, Jr., Chester J., and Elmo Richardson. *The Presidency of Dwight Eisenhower*. Lawrence: University Press of Kansas, 1991.

Palermo, Joseph A. *In His Own Right: The Political Odyssey of Senator Robert F. Kennedy*. New York: Columbia University Press, 2001.

Palermo, Joseph A. *Robert F. Kennedy and the Death of American Idealism*. New York: Pearson Longman, 2008.

Parmet, Herbert S. *JFK: The Presidency of John F. Kennedy*. New York: Penguin Books, 1984.

Paterson, Thomas G. "Fixation with Cuba: The Bay of Pigs, Missile Crisis, and Covert War Against Castro," in Thomas G. Paterson (ed.), *Kennedy's Quest for Victory: American Foreign Policy, 1961-1963*. New York: Oxford University Press, 1989.

Paterson, Thomas G. "John F. Kennedy's Quest for Victory and Global Crisis," in Thomas G. Paterson (ed.), *Kennedy's Quest for Victory: American Foreign Policy, 1961-1963*. New York: Oxford University Press, 1989.

Patterson, James. *Grand Expectations: The United States, 1945-1974*. New York: Oxford University Press, 1996.

Payne, Darwin. *Big D: Triumphs and Troubles of an American Supercity in the 20th Century*. Dallas: Three Forks Press, 1994.

Perry, Barbara A. *Jacqueline Kennedy: First Lady of the New Frontier*. Lawrence: University Press of Kansas, 2004.

Posner, Gerald. *Case Closed: Lee Harvey Oswald and the Assassination of JFK*. New York: Anchor Books, 1993.

Quigg, H.D. "Town in Torment," in Bruce Catton (ed.), *Four Days: The Historical Record of the Death of President Kennedy compiled by United Press International and American Heritage Magazine*. New York: American Heritage Publishing Co., Inc., 1964.

Rabe, Stephen G. *Eisenhower and Latin America: The Politics of Anti-Communism*. Chapel Hill: The University of North Carolina Press, 1988.

Rabe, Stephen G. *The Most Dangerous Area in the World: John F. Kennedy Confronts Communist Revolution in Latin America.* Chapel Hill: The University of North Carolina Press, 1999.

Reeves, Richard. *Portrait of Camelot: A Thousand Days in the Kennedy White House.* New York: Abrams, 2010.

Reeves, Thomas C. *A Question of Character: A Life of John F. Kennedy.* New York: The Free Press, 1991.

Roark, James L., Michael P. Johnson, et al. *The American Promise: A History of the United States, Volume II—From 1865.* Boston: Bedford/St. Martin's, 2002 (2nd ed.).

Rising, George. *Clean for Gene: Eugene McCarthy's 1968 Presidential Campaign.* Westport, Connecticut: Praeger, 1997.

Rorabaugh, W.J. *Kennedy and the Promise of the Sixties.* Cambridge: Cambridge University Press, 2002.

Rubin, Gretchen. *Forty Ways to Look at JFK.* New York: Ballantine Books, 2005.

Sabato, Larry. *The Kennedy Half Century: The Presidency, Assassination, and Lasting Legacy of John F. Kennedy.* New York: Bloomsburg, 2013.

Sandbrook, Dominic. *Eugene McCarthy: The Rise and Fall of Postwar American Liberalism.* New York: Alfred A. Knopf, 2004.

Schlesinger, Jr., Arthur. *Robert F. Kennedy and His Times.* Boston: Houghton Mifflin Company, 1978.

Schlesinger, Jr., Arthur. *A Thousand Days: John F. Kennedy in the White House.* Boston: Houghton Mifflin Company, 1965.

Schoen, Douglas E. (ed.). *On the Campaign Trail: The Long Road of Presidential Politics, 1860-2004.* New York: ReganBooks, 2004.

Schulman, Bruce J. *Lyndon B. Johnson and American Liberalism: A Brief Biography with Documents.* Boston: Bedford/St. Martin's, 1995.

Scott, Peter Dale. *Deep Politics and the Death of JFK.* Berkeley: University of California Press, 1993.

Sherry, Michael S. "George H.W. Bush: 1989-1993," in Alan Brinkley and Davis Dyer (eds.), *The American Presidency*. Boston: Houghton Mifflin Company, 2004.

Shesol, Jeff. *Mutual Contempt: Lyndon Johnson, Robert Kennedy, and the Feud that Defined a Decade*. New York: W.W. Norton & Company, 1997.

Small, Melvin. *The Presidency of Richard Nixon*. Lawrence: University Press of Kansas, 1999.

Smith, Michael. *Say Goodbye to America: The Sensational and Untold Story Behind the Assassination of John F. Kennedy*. Edinburgh: Mainstream Publishing, 2001.

Smith, Sally Bedell. *Grace and Power: The Private World of the Kennedy White House*. New York: Random House, 2004.

Sorensen, Theodore C. *Kennedy*. New York: Harper & Row, 1965.

Stebenne, David L. "Dwight D. Eisenhower: 1953-1961," in Alan Brinkley and Davis Dyer (eds.), *The American Presidency*. Boston: Houghton Mifflin Company, 2004.

Steel, Ronald. *In Love with Night: The American Romance with Robert Kennedy*. New York: Touchstone, 2000.

Summers, Anthony. *Conspiracy*. New York: Paragon House, 1989.

Swanson, Glenn E. (ed.) . *Before This Decade is Out: Personal Reflections on the Space Program*. Washington, D.C.: National Aeronautics and Space Administration, 1999.

Thomas, Evan. *Robert Kennedy: His Life*. New York: Simon & Schuster, 2000.

Thompson, Robert Smith. *The Missiles of October: The Declassified Story of John F. Kennedy and the Cuban Missile Crisis*. New York: Simon & Schuster, 1992.

Toplin, Robert B. (ed.). *Oliver Stone's USA: Film, History, and Controversy*. Lawrence: University Press of Kansas, 2000.

Tsiao, Sunny. *"Read You Loud and Clear!" The Story of NASA's Spaceflight Tracking and Data Network*. Washington, D.C.: NASA, 2008.

Tulis, Jeffrey K. *The Rhetorical Presidency*. Princeton: Princeton University Press, 1987.

Welch, Frank D. *Philip Johnson & Texas*. Austin: University of Texas Press, 2000.

Witcover, Jules. *Party of the People: A History of the Democrats*. New York: Random House, 2003.

White, Theodore H. *The Making of the President 1964*. New York: Atheneum Publishers, 1964.

Wicker, Tom. *JFK and LBJ: The Influence of Personality upon Politics*. New York: Penguin, 1968.

Wills, Garry. *Reagan's America: Innocents at Home*. New York: Penguin, 2000.

Wills, Garry. *The Kennedy Imprisonment: A Meditation on Power*. Boston: Little, Brown and Company, 1981.

Winock, Michael. "Joan of Arc," in Pierre Nora (ed.), *Realms of Memory: Rethinking the French Past* (Vol. II). Translated by Arthur Goldhammer. New York: Columbia University Press, 1996.

Wiseman, Carter. *I.M. Pei: A Profile in American Architecture*. New York: Harry N. Abrams, Inc., 1990.

Woods, Randall. *LBJ: Architect of American Ambition*. New York: Free Press, 2006.

Zelizer, Barbie. *Covering the Body: The Kennedy Assassination, the Media, and the Shaping of Collective Memory*. Chicago: The University of Chicago Press, 1992.

AUDIOVISUAL SOURCES

Bobby. Written and Directed by Emilio Estevez. The Weinstein Company Home Entertainment. 2007. DVD.

Dangerous World: The Kennedy Years. Produced by ABC. 1997. Videocassette.

JFK. Produced by Oliver Stone, Barbara Kopple, and Danny Schechter. Warner Home Video. 2003 (original edition 1991). DVD-Video, Special Edition Director's Cut.

LBJ: The American Experience. Produced by PBS. 1997. Videocassette.

Nixon. Produced by Oliver Stone, Stephen J. Rivele, and Christopher Wilkinson. Walt Disney Video. 1995. Videocassette.

Oliver Stone Remarks at the National Press Club, January 15, 1992. C-SPAN: http://www.youtube.com/watch?v=Pjy6dUlF3Lk .

Oliver Stone Testimony before the House Government Operations Subcommittee, January 1992. C-SPAN: http://www.youtube.com/watch?v=mq7hDywWOZI .

"President Kennedy, U.S. Space Program, Cabinet Room, November 21, 1962. C-SPAN: http://www.youtube.com/watch?v=tilwvlpNSfA .

"Robert F. Kennedy, 1964 Democratic Convention," *The Greatest Speeches of All Time*. CD. Rolling Bay, Washington, 1996.

Thirteen Days. Directed by Roger Donaldson. New Line Home Video. 2001. DVD.

Index